The Most Powerful People in the World

The City-Changing Power of Called Believers

Robert Linthicum

Urban Loft Publishers | Skyforest, CA

The Most Powerful People in the World
The City-Changing Power of Called Believers

Urban Loft Publishers
P.O. Box 6
Skyforest, CA 92385
www.urbanloftpublishers.com

Senior Editors: Kendi Howells Douglas & Stephen Burris
Track Editor: Jared Looney
Copy Editor: Tammie Weatherly
Graphics: Elisabeth Clevenger Arnold

ISBN-13: 978-0-692-87308-3

Grateful acknowledgement is given for use of the following:

The governing body of First Presbyterian Church of Pomona, CA, its "Session," both approves the material contained within Chapter 1 of this book and grants permission for its use within this book, approval also has been given by Lisa and Derek Engdahl, Bree and Tom Hsieh, and Coco and Joe George of their personal accounts contained within this material.

The Session of LaVerne Heights Presbyterian Church of LaVerne, CA both approves the material contained within and grants permission for the use of material referring to this church found in Chapters 12 and 13.

Rev. Julie Roberts-Fronk, pastor of First Christian Church of Pomona, CA, grants permission for the use of the paragraph written in Chapter 15 regarding First Christian Church.

The Office of the General Assembly of The Presbyterian Church (USA) grants permission for the use of the excerpt from 6.011 and 6.012 of "The Westminster Confession of Faith," as contained in *The Book of Confessions,* published by the Office of the General Assembly of the Presbyterian Church (USA).

InterVarsity Press grants permission for designated material to be used from Robert Linthicum's book, *Transforming Power,* published by InterVarsity Press in 2003, used by permission of InterVarsity Press, P.O. Box 1400, Downers Grove, IL, 60515, USA, www.ivpress.com.

Wipf and Stock Press grants permission for designated material to be used from Robert Linthicum's book, *Building A People of Power*, published by Wipf and Stock Publishers in 2015, www.wipfandstock.com.

Zondervan Publishing House grants permission for designated material to be used from Robert Linthicum's book, *City of God, City of Satan,* published by Zondervan in 1991, used by permission of Zondervan/HarperCollins Christian Publications, www.zondervan.com.

Then there came a voice to Elijah the prophet that said,
"What are you doing here, Elijah?"
Elijah answered, "I have been very zealous for the Lord, the God of Hosts;
For the Israelites have forsaken your covenant, thrown down your altars,
And killed your prophets with the sword.
I alone am left, and they are seeking my life to take it away."

I Kings 19:13b-14

Series Preface

Urban Mission in the 21st Century is a series of monographs that addresses key issues facing those involved in urban ministry whether it be in the slums, squatter communities, *favelas*, or in immigrant neighborhoods. It is our goal to bring fresh ideas, a theological basis, and best practices in urban mission as we reflect on our changing urban world. The contributors to this series bring a wide-range of ideas, experiences, education, international perspectives, and insight into the study of the growing field of urban ministry. These contributions fall into four very general areas: 1—the biblical and theological basis for urban ministry; 2—best practices currently in use and anticipated in the future by urban scholar/activists who are living working and studying in the context of cities; 3—personal experiences and observations based on urban ministry as it is currently being practiced; and 4—a forward view toward where we are headed in the decades ahead in the expanding and developing field of urban mission. This series is intended for educators, graduate students, theologians, pastors, and serious students of urban ministry.

More than anything, these contributions are creative attempts to help Christians strategically and creatively think about how we can better reach our world that is now more urban than rural. We do not see theology and practice as separate and distinct. Rather, we see sound practice growing out of a healthy vibrant theology that seeks to understand God's world as it truly is as we move further into the twenty-first century. Contributors interact with the best scholarly literature available at the time of writing while making application to specific contexts in which they live and work.

Each book in the series is intended to be a thought-provoking work that represents the author's experience and perspective on urban ministry in a particular context. The editors have chosen those who bring this rich diversity of perspectives to this series. It is our hope and prayer that each book in this series will challenge, enrich, provoke, and cause the reader to dig deeper into subjects that bring the reader to a deeper understanding of our urban world and the ministry the church is called to perform in that new world.

Dr. Kendi Howells Douglas and Stephen Burris,
Urban Mission in the 21st Century Series Co-Editors

Table of Contents

Introduction

When the death threat came, I quaked in my boots!

I was pastoring a midsize inner-city church in Chicago, Edgewater Presbyterian Church. My family and I lived in and I ministered to the most ethnically diverse poor city neighborhood in America's second largest city. Both Edgewater Church and I were deeply committed to the creation and building of a neighborhood community organization, the Organization of the North East (ONE). We had become intensely involved through ONE in fighting crime, prostitution, the pornographic industry, and the red-lining of housing in that community of 120,000. We had just been successful in closing down a major pornographic outlet and greatly increasing a police presence in the Edgewater Uptown community. ONE had seriously injured the local crime mob. But now they had decided to strike back!

They struck back by spreading on the local informal "grapevine" of the neighborhood that they were going to exhibit their power. And they would do that by "taking out" one of the most visible community's leaders. They even had the temerity to announce the leader they would execute. It was to be me!

I was scared! I might be a Christian. And I might be committed to the doing of justice in our urban neighborhood! But I was also scared–plenty scared–because I knew that this gang would be true to its word!

The ONE leadership met to decide what to do. And we determined together that we would not allow ourselves to be intimidated by this threat. In fact, we decided to ignore the threat, as if it were not even necessary to give it any notice at all! But that did not stop my fear.

For the next year, every Sunday I stepped into my pulpit, every time I walked the streets of my community, every time I climbed into my car and turned the ignition key–I didn't know whether that action would be my last! The mob never acted upon their threat[1]–but I didn't know that until much later!

Meanwhile I chided myself because I obviously lacked the faith of a Bonhoeffer,[2] the determination of a Latimer,[3] or the death-facing serenity of a Polycarp.[4] Why was I so intimidated by this death threat? To find solace in this crisis, I turned to the journal I had kept since seminary days.

Years earlier, when I was in seminary, I had been introduced to the idea of keeping a journal. The professor had suggested that, if we were to actually go into ministry, it would be wise for each of us to maintain a daily journal that would record, not only our significant engagements of the day, but also what we were learning from our daily biblical reflection, prayer life, and our interactions with people. That had sounded like a really great idea to me so, whenever I reflected on scripture for my personal spiritual formation (as opposed to studying it to prepare for a sermon or lesson), I wrote what I was discovering in my journal. And for my first few years in ministry, I had been very diligent in maintaining that journal. And that was why I felt such a great shock.

I opened my journal and read the immediately previous entry! I was stunned to see that this entry had been written ***four years earlier***! It had been more than four years since I had last allowed scripture to speak to me either about my personal walk with God or my ministry. And if I hadn't let scripture lead me for four years, that meant I hadn't personally prayed or been alone with God or even nurtured my own spirituality with a community of people! Rather, I had only been a professional Christian–a pastor! That was when I realized that the reason I felt so intimidated at

---

[1] Actually, we discovered later that the gang concluded that our organizing of the leadership of that community was so well distributed that, no matter how many people they might kill, there would always be more leaders to take their place. So they decided that the community wasn't worth fighting over, and moved to another Chicago neighborhood.

[2] Dietrich Bonhoeffer (1906–1945) was executed by the Nazi government because of his involvement in a plot to assassinate Adolf Hitler.

[3] Bishop Hugh Latimer was burned at the stake in Oxford, England in 1555 as part of effort to make Reformed Christianity the religion of England, and saying to his companion, Ridley, "(With our deaths), we shall light such a fire throughout all England that it will never go out!"

[4] Polycarp was bishop of Smyrna and was burned at the stake in 155 AD for refusing to deny Christ with the words, "Eighty and six years have I served him; how then can I blaspheme my king who saved me?" *Martyrium Polycarpi*, IX.

this death threat was because *I was spiritually bankrupt,* and thus not able to deal with such a threat! So what should I do?

The first thing I did, obviously, was to restore my daily devotional reading of scripture, praying, and journaling. But that was hardly enough. I needed to face this spiritual void in my life. But how to accomplish that?

As I reflected on it, I realized that my most productive spiritual time previously had been when I was attending a Christian college. So I decided to go back to school once again, and work on my doctorate. I didn't want to leave my ministry at Edgewater Church. But I was able to discover a non-residential program offered by San Francisco Theological Seminary, and entered into it. For the next five years, I worked on my doctorate while continuing my ministry in that Chicago neighborhood.

Four years after the death threat, I was visited by a Pastor Nominating Committee of a large Presbyterian church in a wealthy enclave in the Detroit (MI) metropolis. They invited me to become the senior pastor of that church. I was rather confused because all my ministry had been in small to midsize inner-city churches. How could I be an effective pastor of a large, wealthy city church? Then they explained their rationale. That church and its neighborhood was contiguous to what had become the poorest urban census tract in the United States, Census Tract 5130.[5] And these church leaders realized that there was no future for this church unless it bridged the gap between that next-door poor neighborhood and that church. Consequently, they had decided that they needed for their senior pastor a person who had the organizing skills and track record to lead that congregation through this transition. And in their opinion, that was me!

I couldn't resist such a challenge. So soon my family and I moved to the Grosse Pointe community of Detroit and I became the senior pastor of the Grosse Pointe Woods Presbyterian Church.

It seemed like a good fit. And I began to enjoy pastoring the Woods Church. But within about six months of my beginning there, I began to realize that I was in trouble. I had learned well in my former churches how to organize the congregation in addressing the substantive needs of the neighborhood around that church. But I didn't

---

5 Statistics provided by the U.S. Census Bureau for 1970, the standard used being the ranking of census tracts upon an index of housing value, based on the typical sales price of single family homes and the monthly rent of other units.

have the foggiest idea how to deal with the spiritual and relational (particularly family-related) needs of my church members. I had done more one-on-one counseling of church members in my first six months of ministry at the Woods Church than I had done in the entire thirteen years of ministry in my three previous churches. But I felt I wasn't being of any real help to any of them. If what you wanted was for me to help you organize your neighborhood to reduce street crime–no problem! But keeping a warring husband and wife together? I had no idea how to proceed. So I realized I badly needed direction from people who were ***both*** experienced in spiritual formation and yet also clearly committed to and living into urban ministry among the poor. But where would I find that combination in 1976?

It was at this moment of self-discovery that I began paging through a Christian magazine, and saw an announcement of a workshop being held by the Church of the Saviour in Washington, DC, at their Maryland retreat center, Wellspring, in April, 1976. From the 1960s through the 1990s, the Church of the Saviour[6] had a profound impact upon its contemporary urban scene and, for that matter, upon Christianity itself. I knew of it, and had a high respect for its highly intentional lifestyle which manifested itself in significant mission engagement in inner-city Washington, DC. So here were people both as committed to working for urban justice for the poor as well as experienced in spiritual development far beyond my experience. Consequently, I decided to attend that announced workshop. Little did I realize that, in going to that event, my life and my ministry would never be the same!

I arrived at Wellspring, apprehensive and rather uneasy about what might transpire. Our first evening began well–visiting together and discovering that those attending were clergy and laity from a number of urban churches throughout the USA. We had a good dinner together, did some singing and a little sharing together. And then my heart sank to my shoes! The retreat leader explained the importance of silence as a spiritual discipline that would bring us into deeper alignment with God. And then,

---

[6] Begun in 1946, COS was a highly intentional ecumenical congregation, focusing upon both personal and corporate spiritual formation (what they called "the journey inward") and concrete, deeply engaged, hands-on mission ("the journey outward"), seeing both in tandem with each other in order to build a truly effective community of believers capable of significantly impacting its city and the world. It is now divided into a number of small faith communities, carrying on its disciplines of biblical study, personal spiritual formation, group life, tithing, and engagement with fellow members in concrete mission in the world. See the bibliography for books on COS.

horrors of horrors, she announced that we would be in silence until 3:00 p.m. the next day!!! How was I ever going to survive that long without speaking?

Well, that's what we did. We moved into that silence at 8:00 p.m. that evening, and remained in it until 3:00 the next afternoon, with our first spoken words after the silence being our worship of God. The question we were asked to work with during that silence was, "What does it mean for me to be childlike?" And that silence and the answer to that question became the most profound good news to me. This is what I wrote in my journal regarding that time of silence:

"I walked down to the farmhouse and the lake while vainly trying to recall when I was last a child. A collie came running off the porch of the farmhouse and began accompanying me up the hill back to the Wellspring retreat center. Suddenly, the image flashed before me of taking a walk along the Wissahickon Creek[7] in Philadelphia with the collie of the owner of the house where my mother had her apartment. We reached the top of the hill here at Wellspring and I sat down on a bench enjoying the panorama. The collie came and, wrapping himself around my legs, lay down in front of me. The image came to me of sitting on the top of a large rock outcropping–the highest point of the Wissahickon–and surveying the vista of the valley and the river below. That collie also wrapped himself around my legs and lay down in front of me. We were all alone–just him and me–with the hot sun beating down on us, warming us through as I listened to the chirping of birds, the droning of insects and drinking in the vast green sea of tree-tops below us. I was 12 years old, home from the orphanage[8] for the summer. It was the last time I would be a child. For ahead of me lay my decision to become a Christian (which would be my first step into adulthood), rheumatic fever, and the first sensing of a call into urban ministry.

So what does it mean to be childlike? It means the joy of being solitary–to sit alone on a rock with your dog on a hot summer day, a whole panorama before you. It means centering down, enjoying being alone, not speaking, receiving the quiet, expectantly waiting for God. So as I reflect on that nearly forgotten boy sitting on that

---

[7] A forest preserve along a tributary of the Schuylkill River.

[8] My father died when I was six, and my mother, no longer able to care for me, made me a ward of the State of Pennsylvania which then, in turn, placed me in a Philadelphia orphanage until I graduated from college; we were allowed to go home for Christmas, Easter, and a two-week summer vacation.

outcropping with his dog, I realize I will be a truly spiritual person able to carry on a truly life-transforming and community-building ministry in my church and city only if I make time to escape from the never-ending responsibilities and regularly, systematically center upon being alone with God."[9]

The next day, our workshop members took a field trip into the Adams-Morgan neighborhood of Washington where much of the work of the Church of the Saviour among the poor took place. There we visited several of their missions: Release (an ex-convict support effort), Jubilee Housing (a housing corporation for the poor), the Potter's House (a coffee house where community residents were encouraged to hang out), the Potter's House Bookstore, and learning of the unique structure for mission and spiritual formation that had been developed by COS–its "mission groups."

The church carried on its mission to the world, we discovered, through "mission groups." But what is a mission group? "A mission group is a small group of people (five to twelve), conscious of the action of the Holy Spirit in their lives, enabling them to hear the call of God through Christ, to belong in love to one another, and to offer the gift of their corporate life for the world's healing and unity."[10] The mission group was the instrument used by COS to enable each person's journey inward and journey outward to come together within the context of a community of fellow-believers, as focused upon a particular human need toward which each mission group member felt called. In other words, the mission group became the practical, concrete structure by which the church lived out its commitment to both spiritual formation and the priesthood of all believers. It was the structure by which the church both reached within and out to the world!

Our time on that excursion then ended with us going over to the COS center (not a church building, but rather a house) to meet with its founding and still-current pastor, N. Gordon Cosby. What he shared in our meeting there drew the entire experience together for me. He suggested that any intentional, serious Christian needs to follow six disciplines if he/she wants to discern and live into God's call upon his/her life:

---

[9] "Journal of Robert Linthicum,"April 11, 1976.

[10] N. Gordon Cosby, *Handbook for Mission Groups* (Waco, TX: Word Books, 1976), 54.

1. "Commit yourself to the development of your inner life in Jesus Christ;
2. Follow the contemplative disciples (daily prayer, Bible study, a time of silence, journaling);
3. Get removed from your church weekly and gain transcendence over it, so that you can contemplate it;
4. Regularly place yourself under the discipline of receiving "truth-telling" from significant others (spiritual direction);
5. God's new call will come to you out of the above and it will always come through the world's pain and as a strong sense of over-extension;
6. As you issue the new call to mission in your congregation, be willing to fail and to fail repeatedly. You must incarnate the death and rising again of Christ in yourself by believing in new life coming out of your failures."[11]

As you can well imagine, by this time my mind was busy thinking how I could apply all these new insights to my ministry at the Woods Church. But at our closing session the next day, one of the leaders said something that spoke deep truth to me. She quoted these words from the great Jewish mystic, Martin Buber.

"When a man grows aware of a new way in which to serve God, he should carry it around with him secretly, and without uttering it, for nine months, as though he were pregnant with it, and let others know of it only at the end of that time, as though it were a birth."[12]

I took that workshop leader's advice, and said little about that workshop when I returned to Detroit. Rather, I focused on Cosby's recommendation that I foster my contemplative disciplines, arranged for a spiritual director from COS who met with me monthly by letter or in person regarding my spiritual formation, took time to foster relationships with my family (one of my spiritual disciplines was to take my wife on a date once each week), and continued my ministry at the Woods Church.

---

[11] Linthicum, *Journal,* Wednesday, April 12, 1976.

[12] Martin Buber, *Ten Rungs: Hasidic Sayings* (New York: Schocken Books, 1947), 84, 74.

Over the next nine years (the remainder of my time at the Woods Church), the impact of that COS workshop was manifested both in the spiritual formation and the urban mission of that church. We shaped the spiritual renewal of the church around our worship and study as a congregation. Worship, of course, was focused on our weekly Sunday gatherings. But it also included the conducting of five congregational retreats a year, all of which focused on spiritual formation. And we trained a number of people in the art of spiritual direction, making such direction available to many of our members who requested it. Our study as a congregation was centered around our weekly "Geneva Academy" (named after the school of Christian living that was the predecessor of the University of Geneva in Switzerland and John Calvin's primary instrument for the teaching and the spread of the Reformed faith). Each Wednesday night, about a quarter of our church members would gather at the church for dinner together, worship, and then study. The adult education of our Geneva Academy was built around a core curriculum, with additional elective courses offered from time to time. It took three years to complete the core curriculum, with one year surveying the Old Testament, the second year the New Testament, and the third focusing on church history and the church in contemporary society.[13] Around 40% of the congregation eventually completed the core curriculum. Of course, we also offered adult classes on Sunday mornings (as well as children's Sunday School and youth classes).

Our church members particularly embraced the discipline of mission groups, finding them a significant vehicle for carrying out our urban ministry in the Grosse Pointe, to census tract 5130 and throughout Detroit. The times of worship, support of each other, and study were crucial parts of each group's life together. Gospel faith was shared with the constituency we were seeking to reach through the work and witness of each mission group. And the work of some of those mission groups provided social services and care to the larger community, such as a weekday preschool, two simultaneous free senior lunch programs every weekday (one held at the Woods Church and the other in census tract 5130), and the UPLIFT youth ministry in 5130 which built leadership in children and youth. But other mission groups focused on

---

[13] The Old and New Testament portions of the core curriculum were published by the Institute of Church Renewal as the "People's Bible Study" between 1980 and 1982. It consisted of curricula, two textbooks (*The People Who Met God* [an Old Testament survey]) and *The People Who Turned the World Upside Down* [New Testament survey]), and was marketed throughout the USA and Canada. Both curricula were eventually taught in over 900 churches.

addressing substantive and even systemic issues. Thus, Woods Church mission groups were primary in creating People in Faith United (PIFU), a broad-based community organization of the six churches in 5130, six Grosse Pointe churches and five community groups; this organization combined the efforts of our seventeen institutions and the residents of 5130 to work on common justice goals for that community. The PIFU Housing Corporation built or renovated over 100 homes in 5130, making them available to local residents whose sweat equity was their down payment. Crossroads Jobs provided emergency aid, referral services and job placement. PIFU (including the Woods Church's dedicated mission groups) was responsible for getting the city of Detroit to rebuild the infrastructure of 5130 (including streets, sewer, electrical and gas lines, and building a vest-pocket park), successfully negotiated with the Detroit school system to create a new high school in 5130, and convinced one of the "Big Three" automobile companies to build a new truck factory which employed and trained more than 70% of 5130's job-seekers. About 250 Woods Church members (25% of the congregation) participated in the life and work of these mission groups.

And what of my continuing relationship with Church of the Saviour? I remained in the spiritual direction program of COS for the next nine years, and attended at least two workshops or retreats a year held by Wellspring, COS or its "Ministry of Money." My investment in COS reached its apex in a month-long "reverse pilgrimage" my teen-age son and I took with both members of that congregation and other wealthy Christians. We traveled to and worked hands-on among the urban poor in Hong Kong; Bangkok, Thailand; and in Calcutta, India. Our work in Calcutta was with the Missionaries of Charity, the religious order led by Mother Teresa. She met with all of us several times, but also took time for individual meetings with us. When she met with me, she asked me, "Do you love Jesus in the distressing disguise of Asia's urban poor?" Until that trip, I had never even thought about Asia's urban poor. But with those words, I heard the beginnings of a new call to the empowering of urban poor throughout the world (rather than just in the USA) which culminated three years later in my leaving of the pastorate and assuming the leadership of World Vision's ministry to the urban poor in Asia, Africa, and Latin America (but that's another story).

As a result of the threat upon my life made while my Chicago church and I worked for social justice revealed to me my personal spiritual bankruptcy. That bankruptcy wasn't significantly addressed for several years until I discovered the

Wellspring ministry of Washington's Church of the Saviour. Exposure to COS's life and ministry helped me to see church as God intended it to be, built around the doctrine of call. As a result of this exposure, it was not only my personal spiritual bankruptcy that was addressed. It was also a discovery of the absolute importance of building any church (whether urban or rural) around the understanding of and acting out of the doctrine of call. Whether called "vocation" (as in the Roman Catholic, Orthodox, and Reformed traditions) or "the priesthood of all believers" (as in much of Protestantism), it is the recognition that Christianity is not a spectator sport! Not just clergy or religious, but lay people also are called to be ministers of Jesus Christ. Every single Christian is a minister. And to speak of someone who is a Christian but not a minister is a contradiction of terms! To be a Christian is to be a minister.

This book is part of the series, "Urban Ministry in the 21st Century." It is the conviction of this series and this book that an urban church can't have a transforming impact upon its city for Christ and His Kingdom unless that church is practicing the priesthood of all believers. All believers–and not just the ordained clergy–must see themselves as called by God in particular ways to work for that city's transformation. Consequently, joining a community of like-minded Christians for mutual support, spiritual formation, and a common mission of seeking the "shalom" of that city is central to that calling. When you have a church so focused upon its calling and seeing every one of its members called by God to be integral to the accomplishing of that mission, then you have a church that has the capacity, ability, and willingness to change that city! Examining how a church can gain and then act upon that kind of clarity, and how each of its members can also clearly perceive and act out their respective callings is the purpose of this book! Here is how we will seek to accomplish that objective:

The Most Powerful People in the World is divided into three distinct parts. The first part, "The Most Powerful People in the World," introduces the reader to the biblical concept of call. After presenting an example of one called city church in Chapter 1, we will look at the three most essential ingredients in God's call to us. Those are "the caller," "the called," and "the call." One begins the exploration of "call" by starting with the One who calls us into such service. In Chapters 2 and 3, we will examine the continuing cycle of scripture describing how God acts to create, choose, and call God's people to serve God in specific ways. In Chapter 4, we will then examine "the called" by looking at one of the most pivotal statements in scripture describing the call of all of God's people (each with his or her unique gifts) to serve God and work for the transformation of a pagan city.

Finally, in the next three chapters, we will look at the nature of the call itself. In Chapter 5, we will reflect upon the common task to which all of God's urban people have been called and then the specific manifestations of that common task in our individual lives and work. This will include, in Chapter 6, an examination of the apostolic crowd with whom Jesus trusted in the carrying out of his mission ("Profiles of Vocation") and then, in Chapter 7, the careful examination of one life and ministry–that of Moses–as a virtual template of the journey of discovering and living into one's call ("Principles of Vocation").

The second section, "Your Call: Discovered and Lived," deals with the all-important question, "How can I discover God's call for me?" We will explore this topic with four dimensions of discernment. In Chapter 8, "Nurturing My Deep Gladness," we will discover how to name and nurture the deep gladness of one's life ("the way in is out"). The next chapter, "Discovering My Deep Hunger," will explore how to identify and then claim the pain of the world that most impacts you ("the way out is in"). Chapter 10, "Building My Life in Community," will recognize the importance of the Body of Christ in the identifying of your personal call and sustaining you in it ("the way to self is through others"). And Chapter 11, "Calling Forth My Gifts," will explore how you can better understand your call by understanding your strongest personal gifts ("the way to others is through self"). All of these chapters will include concrete, specific actions and exercises you can do to help you better discern your call.

The final portion of this book is "Your Church's Call: Organized for Action." In these final four chapters, we will focus upon the local church as discovering its own unique call as a community and institution, and living out that call through the calls of its members. Thus, in Chapter 12, we will provide a concrete strategy for enabling your church to discern its unique call. In "Little Groups that Can Transform Your City" (Ch. 13), we will examine the strategy for developing and implementing mission and ministry groups. In Chapter 14, "Reshaping the Systems," we will investigate how the church can move beyond providing social services, advocacy, and community development to working for substantive change in the values and intentions of the political, economic, and values-sustaining systems of your city. Then, in the final chapter of the book, "Living Out Vocation," we will draw together the insights from this book, giving practical suggestions on how to get started in energizing yourself and your congregation to become profoundly city-changing by enabling its people to discover and then work together to reach and transform your city for Christ and His Kingdom!

Life-changing and institution-changing insights do not come from a single person's imagination or experience. They come from experience placed upon experience, learning upon learning. It is accumulative, with a host of people–each with his/her unique insights and perspectives—contributing to the emerging new vision! Consequently, I clearly recognize that I do not stand alone in articulating the biblical concept of vocation or call. Twenty-one centuries of Christians doing theology and a previous 2,000 years of biblical history all have gone into understanding both the unique call of God's people and of each person. The biblical and historical contributors I will note throughout this book.

But there are also specific people who have been my contemporaries who have contributed to my self-understanding and action, as well. And I want to specifically thank them now. The first are dear people from the Church of the Saviour in Washington, DC: its former pastor N. Gordon Cosby and his wife Mary, Don and Gloria McClanen (Don having been director of COS' Ministry of Money and Gloria a part of the Wellspring mission group), my spiritual director Carol Fitch, Wellspring's Mur Carrington and the author, Elizabeth O'Connor. The second group would be the people of the churches I have been privileged to serve who were eager to discover and live into their own call: First Presbyterian Church of Pomona (CA), Grosse Pointe Woods Presbyterian Church (Detroit, MI), and LaVerne Heights Presbyterian Church (LaVerne, CA). Finally, there have been my "companions on the way"–people and groups over the past 40 years who explored with me, taught me, learned from me, and joined me in seeking God's call to our respective cities; I am grateful for you all.

And now, on to addressing God's challenge to us, "What Are You Doing Here, Christian?"

PART I

The Most Powerful People In The World

Chapter 1

The Little Church That Could

"What are you doing here, Christian?" This question, first asked by God of Elijah the prophet, stands before anyone called by God into the city. What does God want us Christians to be and to do in the city? The most powerful present city-changing response to that question about which I know was given by the believers in the little church that could!

First Presbyterian Church of Pomona, CA, is only a shadow of its former self—less than a hundred members, when once it was over 2,000. But its present influence upon its neighborhood, its city, and upon southern California far exceeds what it was at its numerical height. This is the story of how a small church is significantly changing its city and region for Christ and His Kingdom! And that is because it sees itself as a called church made up of called people!

First Presbyterian Church of Pomona came into being soon after the birth of the city of Pomona in 1888. The city and church grew up together, and then aged into different entities than either they began or intended to become. It all happened in this way:

The Early First Church

A New Church for a New City

In 1871, federal legislation was passed that gave to the Southern Pacific Railroad exclusive rights to provide freight and passenger service to southern

California.[14] Once that decision was made, the Southern Pacific had to decide whether it would run its main track to Los Angeles or to San Diego (the two major towns on the southern California coast). The Los Angeles county supervisors wanted to be sure that Los Angeles would get that contract, so they paid to the Southern Pacific a subsidy of $600,000 plus the promise of a fully paid new depot at the center point between the eastern entrance city of San Bernardino and its proposed western terminus—Los Angeles.[15] That depot would offer three advantages to the railroad: (a) abundant water to fill the boiler of a nearly-depleted engine; (b) a fruitful valley for the creation of a town where passengers arriving from the east could settle and invest their wealth in the building of the economy of the region; and (c) an abundance of fruit to be carried by the trains back to eastern markets. The location of that depot continues to be used daily today. It is the Pomona station near Garey and First Street.

Smelling money in the air, several entrepreneurs descended upon this potential and still unnamed city even before the Southern Pacific track could be laid and the depot built. Between them they founded what would become the primary development agency of Pomona.

Even before that Southern Pacific depot was finished, this development consortium had gone to work to guarantee that the unnamed city growing around the depot would be the dominant and wealthy city of the valley. Because the wealth of this valley would obviously lie in its steadily expanding fruit orchards, these "town fathers" decided to call both the depot and the town growing around it, "Pomona." They chose the name Pomona, because Pomona was the mythical Roman goddess of fruit, orchards, and vines.

---

[14] Much of the statistical material on both church and city used in this chapter is taken from the paper, "Report of the Mission Discernment of First Presbyterian Church of Pomona, CA, 2009–2010" (Pomona, CA: First Presbyterian Church, July 4, 2010), and is based both upon original research from the historical archives of the Pomona Public Library; the U.S. Census Bureau; the Pomona Unified School District; Claritas; the Federal Bureau of Investigation; the Neighborhood Knowledge California group of the University of California in Los Angeles; Research Services Division of the Presbyterian Church (USA); and several research websites. Used by permission of the Session of First Presbyterian Church of Pomona, CA.

[15] The problem with trains reaching southern California was that it is separated from the rest of the continental US by a north-south mountain range. Therefore, the train tracks coming from Denver, St. Louis, or Chicago would have to run through the only mountain divide level enough to accommodate train access to southern California. At that divide, the town of San Bernardino had been built.

One of the developers divided the city into an eight-block square, each block containing eight lots and making up what is now the parish area of First Presbyterian Church. The land upon which the Southern Pacific track was already laid, he named "First Street." The primary business section would be built immediately south of the train depot on Second, Third, and Fourth Streets. Just south of the railroad depot would be the area where Pomona's biggest and most impressive retail stores would be placed. The largest lots and best housing would be built north of the railroad tracks and more moderate housing south of the business district.

Once the land had been plotted, the consortium began advertising heavily in eastern cities to get would-be buyers to go west and seek their fortune in this fruitful valley. To feed the potential boom, the Southern Pacific offered tickets at unbelievably low rates: $40 from New York City and $32 from Chicago. People began pouring in.

Pomona boomed overnight, going from 300 residents in 1886 to over 3,000 in 1887. Over $300,000 in construction was initiated in 1887, averaging 50 new homes every month. The value of the lots skyrocketed, from an average of $65 in 1876 to over $10,000 by 1887. The future of Pomona now seemed guaranteed. It was during this rapid growth that a Protestant church was birthed—First Presbyterian Church, followed soon after by an Episcopal and then a Baptist church.

It was during this time that the Rev. Charles F. Loop, founding pastor of the Episcopal Church in Pomona, made a trip with his family to Florence, Italy. While visiting the Uffizi Gallery in Florence, he happened upon a statue of the goddess Pomona. Taken with its beauty, he arranged for a duplicate to be carved from snow-white marble by the Italian artist, Antonio Frilli, shipped it back to the United States, and presented it to the City Council in 1889. That statue has been the primary icon of the city ever since. In fact, that original statue can still be viewed today in the foyer of the Pomona Public Library.

First Presbyterian Church grew almost from its inception so that, by the early 1900s, it constructed its second sanctuary in the most prestigious area of Pomona. By the 1930s, First Church[16] had grown into a "mega-church" with more than a thousand children in its Sunday church school, a packed sanctuary every Sunday, and the church

---

[16] For the remainder of this chapter, First Presbyterian Church will be primarily referred to as "First Church."

pastored by one of the most prestigious clergymen of the Presbyterian denomination—Dr. Louis Evans.

First Church continued as a primarily white, middle and upper class, wealthy and large church for the next twenty years. The model of ministry under which the church operated in its "heyday" was that of the "Tall Steeple Church." Its own congregation saw it as big (large membership, high attendance, central to the life of the city), white and wealthy, politically connected, formal in its worship, and with a highly educated membership. These demographic factors suggested that its place in the forefront of the history of Pomona seemed secure!

The "Tall Steeple" model of church successfully continued for First Church as long as the community surrounding it remained primarily white and well-to-do. But immediately after the end of the Second World War, the community began to shift significantly, becoming increasingly an Hispanic and working-class community. Homes were either razed for stores or were converted into apartments, and the people living in the community became increasingly poor. The result was that First Church's congregation began to move out of Pomona, and people transferred membership to churches in their new communities. The membership of First Church began to seriously erode.

Fighting for Survival

What was going wrong? It was simply that the way of doing ministry which the church had embraced for nearly 80 years was proving inadequate in a changing community and times. The church seemed unable to adapt. It was not that they didn't try in the 1980s; it was that what they tried didn't work.

First, the people of First Church expended considerable energy in doing church the only way they knew how to do church. But they increasingly failed at this effort as membership continued to erode and giving dropped. Faced with steady membership erosion, the leadership hunkered down and conducted ministry as they always had—but harder. They expected different results. But, instead, they experienced only continued failure.

Second, they decided to break the pattern with an alternate plan in the mid-1980s. They attempted a church plant in the rapidly growing area of Pomona named Phillips Ranch. Their intention was to sell the old church plant and move the First

Presbyterian congregation out to Phillips Ranch as soon as there was a sufficiently established branch of the church there to receive them. However, this effort also failed.

Then came the final straw! In 1985, the sanctuary burned to the ground and the entire church complex—except for its education building—was destroyed by the flames. It seemed all was lost. What, now, could they do?

It was then, in 1985, that I first entered the picture (full disclosure: I eventually became the interim pastor of First Church from 2009 through early 2012). In the Presbyterian denomination, it is the regional body—the presbytery—that holds the church's property, installs and dismisses the pastors, and monitors the life of each local congregation (I'm sure you've always wanted to know how the Presbyterian denomination operates). The presbytery is kind of like a corporate bishop. Pomona Presbyterian belongs to the Presbytery of San Gabriel, as did I (as an ordained Presbyterian minister—even though I was working for a non-Presbyterian ministry at the time). The presbytery asked me to work with the church in the light of the crisis they were facing as a congregation and help them gain a new vision of what they could become. I accepted the assignment, and began meeting with the church's leadership to help them find a way out of their dilemma.

I failed miserably. I found not only a church devastated by their loss and hopelessly confused as to what to do; I also found a church unwilling to do more than just "keep on keeping on." As everything I suggested or tried failed. I became as discouraged as they were. So I concluded my work with them, and then prepared my report to presbytery. I suggested in the report that I saw no viable alternative available to the church, and therefore recommended that First Church be closed.

But God had other plans. Happily, the presbytery never got around to following my advice, and so First Church limped along for another decade, unsure of what to do but still surviving. And then God went to work!

A New Church for an Old City

God Moves In Mysterious Ways

In the 1990s, two realities occurred that helped First Church effectively address its changing situation. The first was pastors that were sensitive to the movement of the Holy Spirit and could discern, join, and support that movement. The first such pastor was the Rev. Santos Ramos, who guided the church through the turbulent time of change that the church had to face. He was to be the first of continuing strong pastoral leadership, now being carried out by the Rev. Adam Donner through his gentle style, his strengthening of the church's theological capacity, and his expectant willingness to take any step of faith that will strengthen his church's capacity to "work for the welfare of the city."

The second was laity who could also sense the Spirit's movement, and joined it. This movement began in a most inauspicious way when some leaders in the InterVarsity Christian Fellowship (IVCF)[17] chapter at the nearby Claremont Colleges[18] decided to offer a summer project in Pomona for their undergraduate students where the students could live in Pomona's inner city and minister to children and youth there. First Church expressed its receptivity to having the students live at the church and work in the poor and largely Hispanic neighborhood surrounding the church.

That summer internship, in turn, led to a number of Claremont Colleges students feeling increasingly called by God to First Church and its neighborhood. But those students went far beyond talk; they acted out this call by moving into Pomona after they graduated, living in community at the church, seeking to carry out ministry in the neighborhoods surrounding the church, and becoming active members of First Church. That, in turn, led to two more pilgrimages of students and young adults in the mid- and late-1990s, both from other colleges and from the incarnational mission organization, Servant Partners. Thus, First Church began to undergo profound change as it moved toward becoming increasingly an intimate mission community. What were those changes?

---

[17] InterVarsity Christian Fellowship (IVCF) is "an inter-denominational, evangelical Christian campus ministry, working with students and faculty on college and university campuses." Retrieved from https://en.wikipedia.org/wiki/InterVarsity_Christian_Fellowship). It is the oldest and largest such Christian organization for college and graduate students in Great Britain (1877), Canada (1928), and the United States (1938). It currently has 985 chapters on 649 college campuses in the USA, many of which are specialized. IVCF focuses its campus chapters on the building of community, inductive Bible study, and both international and local missions Retrieved from https://intervarsity.org/.

[18] The Claremont Colleges is a consortium of undergraduate and graduate specialty schools in the city of Claremont, which is immediately northeast of the city of Pomona. Its undergraduate schools consist of Claremont McKenna College, Harvey Mudd College, Pitzer College, Pomona College, and Scripps College. Its graduate schools consist of Claremont Graduate University, Claremont University Consortium, Lincoln University/Claremont School of Theology, the Keck Graduate Institute, and the Peter Drucker Graduate School of Economics. There are several IVCF chapters functioning within the Claremont Colleges.

- The former college students and Servant Partners mission workers became deeply involved in the church as a result of feeling a call to urban mission and the desire to live out their faith through the church in a poor community;
- The church was refreshingly hospitable to the student ministry and the growing young adult congregation. The people of First Church actively invited them in, were willing to invest money in their work, and integrated them into the life and work of this church;
- These former students began work with neighborhood kids and with families, addressed community concerns and over the years moved beyond solely providing social services to increasingly addressing the systemic issues that caused the people to be poor and hurting;
- A new worshipping community was built that integrated contemporary culture (music, informality, teachings rather than classical sermons) and yet honored and celebrated the great traditions of worship and music of the historic church;
- First Church then articulated its mission as being "to engage, equip and empower families to follow Jesus and together participate in public life for the spiritual health and restoration of Pomona."[19]

It is important to understand the intentionality with which these former IVCF students approached both life and ministry in the city of Pomona. Close to 100 young adults have thus far moved to Pomona to participate in this incarnational style of ministry. Some have done this for a few years, but far more have been at it for a decade or even more than 20 years.

All those who have been part of this pilgrimage have committed themselves to the practices of both shared incarnational ministry and of spiritual disciplines. The primary standard has been a commitment to move to and live in the poor urban community surrounding First Church. For some, that has meant property rental, but for most it has meant financial and personal investment in that community by purchasing their home there. So they are "putting their money where their mouths are." Other standards have included faithful participation in the life of First Church

---

19 "Report of the Mission Discernment of First Presbyterian Church of Pomona, CA," 12.

beyond Sunday worship, the building of a supportive community of believers, building their neighborhood into a genuine caring community, working intentionally in the public life of Pomona, and being committed to one's spiritual formation.

The spiritual disciplines that each of those committing to incarnational ministry are expected to practice are: daily times of personal prayer and biblical reflection; weekly attendance and participation in the Sabbath worship of First Church; participation in a "house church" twice a month which includes inductive Bible study, prayer, and fellowship; the giving of a minimum of a tithe to First Church and to community ministries; and working for the movement of the city of Pomona toward a growing microcosm of the city of God. In other words, for everyone who has embraced incarnational ministry in Pomona, there is the strong sense of the call of God into that life and witness.

What, then, is the impact upon a church of having a large number of young adults joining the church and moving into that city out of a sense of call to lay ministry? What happens when a congregation enthusiastically receives them with open arms? The result is a small inner-city congregation that is 124 years old and yet isn't what you would expect a 124-year-old aging inner-city church to be.

Thus, whereas the typical inner-city congregation has an average of 52% being 60 years of age or older, this congregation has 78% of its members between 30 and 59 years of age. Rather than only 55% being involved in the church beyond worship three or more hours per month, 82% of the congregation is so engaged. Rather than only 60% living within four miles of the church, 85% do. Rather than 98% of the congregation joining the church because they like the sermons, people, or experience, 88% have joined the church because they feel called by God there (irrespective of the quality of the sermons, the friendliness of the people, or the overall experience).[20] Finally, besides attending worship each Sunday, about 85% of the congregation gathers in designated groups twice a month to engage in Bible study. But this is not the Bible study of one person giving a lecture to others who patiently listen. The Bible study conducted by this congregation is in the inductive style, with each phrase and sentence reflected and journaled upon and applied by each person present at that study; thus, it

---

[20] Statistics on the "Typical Presbyterian Church" provided by Research Services, The Presbyterian Church (USA). Comparative statistics on Pomona Presbyterian Church were gathered from the congregation on January 10, 2010.

is a study that truly forms people spiritually. So it is that both the interior life of the church and its mission outreach testifies to the fact that those young adults are there because they believe God called them there. And they will stay there, doing the work to which God has called them, until God calls them away to another ministry.

Let's look at the stories of just a few of these people. As we consider the stories of three different couples who have invested in the work in Pomona through community organizing and non-profit efforts, it is important to realize that their work would never have happened without the 30 to 50 other people who stuck it out, living in community, assuming servant tasks in an old church they never expected to take (like counting the offering, or doing sound for the services, or hosting new groups of interns coming through for lunches, or maintaining a three-story 100-year old building).

Lay People Called to the City

Lisa and Derek Engdahl have been a most formative couple in God's shaping of First Church into what it is today. Lisa was born into the Adamovich family in Minneapolis, MN, and grew up both there and in Edina (a suburb of that city). Her mother was a German immigrant, and her father's parents emigrated from Yugoslavia to a Northern Minnesota mining community. Both of them grew up in poverty but were committed to the pursuit of "the American dream." Her father worked primarily for one employer during his entire work life—a hospital—but he rose from his initial job there as an orderly to eventually become administrator of the hospital and vice president of its corporation. Their family attended church regularly and sought to live out Jesus's teaching by including people without family in their family. Lisa made the decision to follow Christ while she was in junior high school when her brother shared the Gospel with her after having a transformational encounter with Christ. When approaching graduation from high school, Lisa decided to attend Occidental College in Los Angeles, and thus left the ice of Minneapolis for the warmth of southern California—and she has stayed here ever since.

Occidental was a rich experience for Lisa, especially because she became involved in the local chapter of InterVarsity. IVCF's primary emphases on the building of community, inductive Bible study, and both international and local missions all had particular impact upon Lisa.

Lisa had always wanted to become a doctor. Consequently, she had completed all her pre-medical studies and internships. But in her senior year at "Oxy," she felt particularly called to join the staff of IVCF. The call came as a surprise, but she felt great joy in the direction God was leading her. Thus, after graduation, she began working at specific IVCF campus chapters in southern California. Serving IVCF for 15 years, Lisa eventually became director for IVCF's Greater Los Angeles region, which included Los Angeles, Riverside, San Bernardino, and Orange County campuses. Increasingly, however, she felt called to ministry among the urban poor and began to integrate this calling with her campus work, bringing students with her to volunteer at homeless shelters and tutoring programs for urban youth.

Unlike Lisa, Derek Engdahl grew up as a southern California "home-boy." He was born in Los Angeles, moved with his family to the LA suburb of Diamond Bar when he was five, and grew up in the area in which he still lives today—the Pomona Valley of Los Angeles County. Derek's father pastored the Presbyterian church there that Derek and his family attended.

Like Lisa, Derek enrolled at Occidental College, but they only met briefly. He discovered that out of the 1600 students at Oxy, 160 were involved in IVCF's in-depth Bible study. So he also got involved in that study and thus became engaged in the work of IVCF. During the summer between his junior and senior years at Oxy, Derek worked among the poor in the nearby city of Pasadena, and there began dealing with the implications of receiving Jesus as Lord. After he graduated from Oxy, he was asked by the Oxy IVCF leaders to "stick around" for a year, and that led him into becoming staff there. Then fate stepped in.

Both Lisa and Derek "happened" to get assigned (God moves in mysterious ways) to staff IVCF's work at the Claremont Colleges (see above). One thing led to another—and in due time, they discovered each other, fell in love, and got married. But, both individually and together, they were also a part of a growing transformation at the Claremont Colleges of students and IVCF staff focused on deepening their relationships with Jesus and each other, with the goal of making their lives count for more than simply making money or securing their place in history.

Much of this kind of reflection was done at retreats held by the Claremont IVCF chapters off-campus at nearby churches. One of the facilities regularly used was First Presbyterian Church of Pomona. Attending those retreats, students began to take notice of their surroundings—an aging and struggling church in a poor and marginalized inner-city neighborhood.

Derek, Lisa, and a few students began attending worship at First Church. Then they decided to do a summer urban project. The church was delighted to have them undertake that project. They housed the students on the second floor of their large community building; in fact, the church even remodeled a kitchen on that floor for their use. Derek and Lisa led that summer project, including significant reflection-time on both the students experiences and biblical interaction. Both they and a number of the students increasingly discerned that they were being called to city ministry—not as clergy in a church, but as laity making their homes there.

So the move began, as both students and graduating students moved into the inner city of Pomona, worked with families in the neighborhood surrounding the church, and gradually entered into the life of First Church. Thus, on both the part of the students and of the church members, there was an openness to follow the strange and uncharted paths into which God was leading them.

This openness of spirit was demonstrated to Derek by one 90-year-old church member who began attending the contemporary worship each Sunday (primarily attended by the students and IVCF staff) rather than the traditional worship (primarily attended by the "old-timers"). When Derek said to that 90-year-old how remarkable it was that someone of his generation would so enjoy contemporary worship music, this old member responded, "Actually, I hate this kind of worship. But if this is what it takes to draw the young adults, then I'm all for it and will support it fully." It was that kind of openness and commitment that gave Derek great hope for the future of First Presbyterian Church.

Derek moved into an apartment in Pomona in 1998 when he joined the ministry of Servant Partners. When Derek and Lisa married in 1999, she joined Derek in Pomona and also became a part of that organization. They sought to be Christ's presence to their neighbors and to know God more deeply. A few years later they bought a home in their community, after receiving the gift of a down payment from their friends in IVCF.

Servant Partners, the ministry that both Derek and Lisa had joined, "sends, equips, and trains those who want to share their lives with the urban poor and see urban slums transformed."[21] It carries on this ministry through the strategies of church-planting, community organizing, and leadership training. This ministry currently has 14 teams working in 10 countries. Derek is now the co-general director and field director of Servant Partners, while Lisa is the other co-general director, as well as director of leadership development.

As Lisa reflects upon her own sense of her call, she sees it as being a slowly changing call. Initially, it was simply to follow Jesus wholeheartedly as a collegian, and then as Inter Varsity staff, sharing the Gospel with students. It has now matured to include a call to her husband and child. But it has also been a steadily evolving call into the recognition that she increasingly experiences God most deeply through ministering among the poor. God began to lay foundations for her call to ministry among the urban poor through the stories of her parents, for whom poverty was not an abstract concept but a personal reality. It is Isaiah 61 that particularly articulates for her that mission: the healing of people to be restored to the fullness that God has for them within the midst of rebuilding the city. By marrying Derek, moving to Pomona, and joining Servant Partners, she recognizes that her call is a call to the urban poor—both personally in Pomona, and through Servant Partners to the urban poor throughout the world.

Likewise, Derek's call has been a steadily maturing call. He sees scripture as calling all God's people to care for the poor amongst us, and obedience to that Word has been formative to him—"fully in or not at all" as he puts it. But it has been a specific call to him, to be lived out through Servant Partners and First Church. And it has also been clear to Derek that his call should be lived out not as an ordained minister, but as a lay person. That is an intentional choice. The important point of Derek's call, however, is that choosing to be in Christian mission as a lay person does not have to mean a dearth of theological astuteness; anyone who has read Derek's

---

[21] "Servant Partners was created to be a work that combined God's call to proclaim the good news to every nation, and God's call to love and serve the poor." Today, it has 14 teams (usually consisting of three to eight staff) "planting churches, training leaders, and organizing communities" in Asia, the Middle East, Africa, Latin America, and North America. It also conducts a two-year internship program, a short-term internship, and a publishing venture. Retrieved from www.Servant Partners.org.

book, *The Great Chasm,*[22] recognizes that he speaks from significant theological depth. Being a lay person doesn't mean you have to be theologically dumb.

Tom and Bree Hsieh (pronounced "Shay") came to Pomona from opposite ends of the world. Bree hails from North Dakota, and Tom has traveled the furthest to Pomona; he hails from Taipei, Taiwan.

Bree Devones was born in Washington state, but moved with her family to Rapid City, South Dakota, where she went to elementary school, and then to West Fargo, North Dakota, for her teenage years. For her tertiary education, Bree chose Grinnell College in Iowa. Her life to that point had been one of living in a middle-class Roman Catholic family; God was simply a part of her everyday life. But her time at Grinnell opened up a much more dynamic path of faith. She began attending the InterVarsity chapter meetings, and in a Bible study in her freshman year was struck by Peter's response to Jesus's call, so that Peter "immediately left his nets and followed him" (Mark 1:18). She acted out that call by beginning to follow Jesus in the campus context, and then by taking an urban ministry trip with her IVCF chapter, where she felt a strong call to the urban poor. In her senior year, Bree traveled to Los Angeles to visit the work of Servant Partners. Moved deeply both by their acted-out ministry to LA's urban poor and their practice of life in community, she completed her college education and then joined Servant Partner's two-year internship in South Los Angeles.

Tom was born in Taipei to a Chinese family that was Christian; his grandfather was an ordained minister. Because of significant tensions between Taiwan and the Chinese Communist government on the mainland (which desired to reclaim control of Taiwan), Tom's grandfather encouraged his children to migrate to America. Tom's uncle, Stephen immigrated to the United States first, and took a pastorate in Ida Grove, Iowa. He sponsored Tom's family to come to the United States, and they made their first home in America in the small town of Ida Grove. But while Tom was a small boy, the family then moved to southern California, near Los Angeles. It was in the LA suburbs of Sepulveda, West Covina, and South Pasadena that Tom grew into adulthood.

---

[22] Derek Engdahl, The Great Chasm: How to Stop Our Wealth from Separating Us from the Poor and God (Pomona, CA: Servant Partners Press, 2015).

As a youth, Tom was active in a Taiwanese Presbyterian Church in the nearby town of Alhambra. He was a leader in their youth group, even organizing church retreats. He received Christ as his own Savior while in junior high, but it was not until his college years that he became serious about his relationship with Christ. As a student at Harvey Mudd College in Claremont, California, he joined the local IVCF chapter and became a disciple of Jesus Christ.

As a Harvey Mudd student, Tom was introduced to First Presbyterian Church through a Servant Partners conference that was held there. He took little note of the church, but was quite interested in the mission and work of Servant Partners to work for the spiritual and physical liberation of the urban poor. So, after graduating from Harvey Mudd, he attended the Servant Partners two-week orientation at First Church, and then entered into a two-year internship in Pomona. He moved into one of the poorest sections of Pomona to live among the people there and to build relationships with them. When Derek Engdahl, Tom's former IVCF staff leader at Harvey Mudd College, began the development of an intentional community within First Presbyterian Church, Tom joined that effort.

Though Tom and Bree were both in Servant Partners, they were unaware of each other until they both attended an organization-sponsored "Prayer for the Nations" event, and "happened" to sit next to each other. They enjoyed visiting with each other, but went their separate ways. Then, to their surprise, a month later they met again at a birthday party—and it was at that party that they really took note of each other and began to build a relationship. That relationship resulted in marriage in 2001, a shared commitment to the urban poor, elder leadership at First Church, a home near the church, and two marvelous children!

Examining both Tom and Bree's life story thus far provides a significant example of how God's call to each of us deepens and broadens over time, if we are giving ourselves in obedience both to Him and that call. Both of them believe that their initial calls was to the poor, then to the poor of the city, then a specific call to Pomona, and then to First Church of Pomona, as it ministered to the urban poor around it. Those respective calls then became a call to each other, symbolized by their marriage in 2001. But marriage did not end their respective calls. It was simply that after their wedding, their continuing personal calls were also wedded together into common calls of commitment to the urban poor, acted out through their individual calls.

For Bree, her call increasingly became a call to creativity, first through creative problem solving, which is very useful in urban-poor ministry, and then to the creative arts, which can transform areas of spiritual, emotional, and physical poverty in profound ways. After simply learning how to invest herself in the people who lived around her in their urban poor neighborhood, she began developing as a leader and joined the staff at First Church as their ministry coordinator. Her vision broadened, however, to the urban poor of the world, so she returned to Servant Partners, working alongside others to develop that organization and equip people for this broader international incarnational ministry. While working with Servant Partners, she was called to the role of mother, raising a family, and buying a home just a few blocks from First Church. Now, Bree is journeying with Jesus through writing and painting as well as continued work with Servant Partners and investment in many individuals and organizations within the city of Pomona.

For Tom, his call increasingly was lived out in the world of business. Like Bree, Tom concentrated upon ministry in their immediate neighborhood to their apartment. Thus, Tom was the first to arrive on the scene when a man was shot and died in front of their apartment (Bree made Tom promise not to run outside every time there was gunfire until after the shooting had stopped!). Bree and he "took in a teenage girl whose mother was killed in a car accident and whose father was in jail. They also took in an entire family of five who were struggling to be free of past gang connections and needed help until they could find stable housing and employment."[23]

But Tom's call soon moved beyond that Pomona neighborhood to all of Pomona, the Inland Valley, and even Los Angeles. Thus, he was pivotal in the formation of Pomona Hope, a Christian community development corporation based at First Church that works with the poor families in southeast Pomona, to tutor students and develop their leadership capacities, to develop technological and arts skills, and even to care for a community garden together. Tom has played an ongoing role in the broad-based organizing effort of the Industrial Areas Foundation (IAF) and its local affiliate, Inland Communities Organizing Network (ICON) in dealing with systemic crime and safety, environmental, educational, political, and economic concerns in the

[23] Engdahl, *Chasm*, 196.

Pomona area and throughout the 4,000,000 population Inland Empire of southern California.

The most important part of Tom's call, however, was his call to be a Christian influence in the world of business. While completing his initial commitments to Servant Partners, Tom became involved in the early development of EarthLink. As EarthLink grew from a struggling small operation to a major communications technology giant, Tom grew along with it where he played senior executive roles. This meant that his income kept growing at a remarkable rate, so that he and Bree were faced with a major problem. Since they felt called to the urban poor in Pomona and since Tom also felt called to being a Christian conscience in the business world, what should they do about the significantly increasing income with which Tom was being rewarded for his contributions to Earthlink? Simply put, Tom found himself making more than $200,000 a year in a community where the average American family lived on only $40,000. What, then, should they do?

What Bree and Tom decided was that they, too, would live like an average family on $40,000 a year, and then give away the rest. And that is what they did. Tom and Bree learned the joy of "hilarious giving" (the literal meaning of the Greek word *"hilaros,"* often translated as "cheerful" in II Cor. 9:7's statement, "God loves a cheerful giver"). That money went to support the mission outreach to Pomona and the world done both by First Church and Servant Partners, and it also went to mission causes around the world. But it also went for "hilarious" purposes as well, like the time that Tom took the entire First Church congregation to Disneyland. As Derek Engdahl tells it in his book, *The Great Chasm,* "Tom would show up to meetings and fancy dinners in his beaten-up Geo. Once, he pulled up to a five-star hotel for a meeting and handed his keys to the valets, who looked at his car and started laughing. He joined them."[24]

EarthLink eventually moved its corporate headquarters to Atlanta in 2006 and offered Tom the option to pursue continued opportunity with them in Atlanta. But Tom did not yet feel called away from his ministry and life in Pomona. And so he took his leave of EarthLink in early 2007. What would he now do? Tom continued to feel called into ministry in the world of business and felt called to anchor that business in Pomona itself. So in early 2007, after being unemployed during the birth of his

---

[24]Engdahl, *Chasm*, 196.

daughter Kadence and for the first three months of her life, he started up his own business, SplinterRock—a communications consulting company.

His business has been successful so that he can continue to engage in "hilarious giving." But he has also discovered that this business has enabled him to be more deeply engaged in the city of Pomona and the Inland Valleys, working for justice for the urban poor. SplinterRock, as his own business, gives him a flexibility that working for someone else cannot give. And his status as a successful businessman has allowed him to become a leader in the civic and business worlds of the Inland Valleys. This has included cooperating with the work of ICON in demanding justice for the poor and, consequently, taking unpopular positions on business issues that impact Pomona's poor. Such positions could have led to alienation from the business community. But, instead, it has led to a grudging respect for Tom in the eyes of the "movers and shakers" of Pomona, so that a new work can be done to build Pomona into a more accurate reflection of city as God intends city to be.

The strength of Tom and Bree's call to the urban poor and the powerful of Pomona is captured in something I heard Tom share with the First Church congregation several years ago. "God called us to this city and to this church," he declared, "and we will stay here seeking to live into that call until God releases us from that call." It's not, in the final analysis, about us. It's all about God and how God chooses to do God's work in the city!

Joe and Coco George. Coco is a Japanese-American who was born and raised in the USA. Her real name is Yumiko Sasaki George, but when she was a little girl, her three-year-old brother couldn't pronounce "Yumiko" so, picking up on the "ko" sound in her name, began calling her "Coco." The name stuck, and she has been known as "Coco" ever since.

Coco was born in Tucson, AZ, but moved with her family to Claremont, CA, when three years old. So she grew up in a fairly well-to-do and academic community (Claremont is known as "the city of trees and PhDs"). Coco and her family went to First Baptist Church in Pomona, where she decided to follow Jesus at the age of 12 and was baptized there. After she finished high school, she enrolled as a pre-med student in Pomona College in Claremont.

Joe was born in Phoenix, AZ, and lived his first 18 years there. He grew up in a nominal Christian home. But in high school, Joe became friends with a youth who had a radical conversion experience and was quite vocal about it. The friend was so persuasive in sharing with Joe about his conversion that Joe became a Christian also. He took eagerly to following Jesus, including reading through the entire Bible as well as everything he could find written by C. S. Lewis. The two friends were part of a para-church high school group related to Campus Crusade —and it was that group that was "church" to them. But the two friends never attended an actual church. Therefore, the first church Joe ever attended was years later when Coco and he began attending First Presbyterian Church of Pomona.

Since his older brother went to Pomona College, he commended it to Joe who then decided to attend it. Thus, Joe moved to southern California, and has lived there ever since.

Soon after arriving at Pomona College, Joe met Lisa Engdahl, who invited him to attend the IVCF chapter at the college. He did that, and found that chapter not only a welcoming place but eventually a spiritual home.

The IVCF chapter was studying Jesus's parable of the sheep and goats (Matt. 25:31– 46), its question, "When did I minister to you, Lord?" and the Lord's answer, "Just as you did it to one of the least of these . . . , you did it to me!" The entire fellowship was challenged with "our neighbor is different than we elite college students; our neighbor is the poor in Pomona; how do we relate?" Joe decided that he had to be doing more than simply going to college. So he became a part of a group that developed an after-school program for children of the poor. It was housed at First Presbyterian Church of Pomona. This early program would become the forerunner of what would eventually become Pomona Hope—the community development corporation created by First Church that now conducts a comprehensive work within Pomona (see below). But Joe also discovered that he loved working with and teaching children so that eventually teaching became a career for him. He began attending the first "real" church he had ever known—First Church of Pomona.

Coco remained on the fringe of the Pomona College IVCF until fully committing to the group her junior year. But she and Joe first met at an IVCF annual event, "Campus by the Sea" (IVCF owns a rustic campus on Catalina Island, 20 miles offshore Los Angeles, which hosts major training events [kind of a spiritual "boot camp"] called "Campus by the Sea"). They began a relationship together, dating for five years, then engaged for one, before getting married in 1998.

Coco joined Joe in tutoring and working with the children in the Pomona after-school program at First Church. When she graduated from Pomona College in

1993, she spent a summer in Jackson, Mississippi, volunteering in the evangelical ministry to the urban poor, "Voice of Calvary." There, she and two Korean American women worked in tutoring and mentoring relationships with African American children living there; it was an unusual and very creative mixing of cultural traditions.

While Coco was doing a summer ministry in Jackson, Joe traveled to Manila, Philippines, to live and minister in an urban slum there. That experience was transforming for Joe, who saw people living on the margins of life in great poverty but with an openness and receptivity to God that he had not seen elsewhere. More than ever, it convinced him that he belonged in Pomona. Coco had a similar experience when she volunteered in a town hospital 100 miles southeast of Calcutta, India. Both Joe's and Coco's experiences ministering among the Two-Thirds World poor convinced them that God's call to them was to likewise minister with the urban poor, but to do so in Pomona—which was God's city for them!

Coco had entered Pomona College intent on becoming a medical doctor (and thus entered their pre-med program). But as she approached graduation, she found her life moving in other directions. She was, of course, dating Joe. Tutoring neighborhood children in Pomona had awakened in her a real love both for the poor and for Pomona itself, which she found more "real" than the rarified atmosphere of Claremont in which she had grown to adulthood. She realized that a medical career would not be right for her. A friend suggested she look at the field of physical therapy. Once she graduated from Pomona College, she began working on her master's degree in that field at Western University of the Health Sciences (which, coincidentally, has its campus just a few blocks from First Presbyterian of Pomona).

Joe graduated from Pomona College in 1994, and then volunteered with IVCF for a year at the Claremont colleges. But he moved to Pomona in 1995 and began substitute teaching, discovering that he really loved it. He went to graduate school for one year, then began teaching in a middle school in nearby Covina while continuing to live and be in ministry in Pomona. Joe has remained at that Covina school since 1996.

Coco, meanwhile, graduated from Western University and became a physical therapist at Pomona Valley Hospital, the large regional hospital in the heart of Pomona. There she has worked for the past 13 years.

It is intriguing to talk with both Coco and Joe to see how God moved in both of their lives to bring them together, to bring them to Pomona, and to call them to both work together and separately for Christ's kingdom in the city of Pomona and through

First Church. Joe's call began with the discovery that Christ is real and that the kingdom of God is a personal and social reality worth working for. The initial challenge that came to him was to live life with meaning in Christ or to live with no ultimate meaning—and he chose meaning. In college, he simply wanted people to experience Christ and to embrace the kingdom of God, but he had no objectives, strategy, or structure to accomplish that. His summer in Manila and his volunteer work in the establishment of the after-school children's program, and his discovery of First Church as a dynamic environment to grow the gospel in the city called forth his commitment to Pomona's urban poor and his loyalty to a concretized body of Christ—First Church. He entered that work, in Joe's words, with "super naïve assumptions," but over time he both learned to temper expectations and to allow his commitment to city and church to both grow and to be acted out in intriguing ways. That commitment has been lived out by buying a home in Pomona; joining with Coco in intentionally sending their two girls to the local public school; being willing to accept leadership roles at First Church; and investing time, effort, and work in the continuing development of Pomona Hope.

Growing up in a Christian family and in church as a continuing presence in her life, Coco had to go through the personalizing of her Christian faith. That happened at Pomona College and in her involvement in IVCF, which enabled that learned faith to be transformed into her own dynamic faith. That faith took on practical service dimensions when she responded to the eagerness and delight of children at the First Church after-school program, and then in Christian service not only among them but also in Mississippi and in India. Her faith became grounded when she found and also helped to build a vital community of faith at First Church. It began being lived out in a new way when she began building a life together with Joe and then their children by becoming wife and mother. Buying a home in Pomona required a concrete level of commitment to a specific neighborhood, including participation in the social, political, and economic life of their neighborhood, particularly including leadership in her children's local school Parent-Teachers Association.

Now, what are the next risky steps of faith to which the Georges are being called? What are the present cutting edges to the living out of their calls to Pomona's urban poor? For Joe, it is increasing commitment to Pomona Hope. He is now the chairperson of their Board of Directors, working to deepen its transforming impact upon the Pomona neighborhood around First Church. Thus, he plays a strategic role in building its academic enrichment; its life skills and personal development efforts; its performing arts classes in music, dance, and drama; and the development of its community garden. Coco finds herself moving into the mentoring of people—a new role for her. This began with her mentoring over the summer months new interns that come to First Church and to Pomona Hope from across the United States, seeking to explore life and ministry in the city. That call from God is now extending to long-term, long-range mentoring of young Christians seeking to discover and to live into God's call to them for their lives. So, for both Coco and for Joe, growth in their Christian formation has also meant the continuing extension of their call to ministry among the urban poor.

Joe and Coco's calling can be best captured in their simple effort to extend neighborhood hospitality. That is best lived out through the way they use their house. Their home includes an enormous backyard, which includes fruit trellises, a vegetable garden, a considerable lawn and play area, and all shaded with ancient trees. The Georges regularly host neighborhood gatherings there. Perhaps their most popular gatherings are their Summer Movie Festival on Friday nights when they invite their neighbors, coworkers, and First Church members to their backyard for refreshments to watch a classic old movie on a large screen. This hospitality captures their conviction that being called to the city must extend beyond fostering church, sharing the faith, providing social services, and working for justice; it must include as well the building of a sense of neighborhood community, of people simply gathering together, sharing and eating together, and simply "hanging out" together. For all of this is necessary for building the shalom community in the city!

But Not Just People Are Called

But God's call is not simply to individuals or couples within a church. God's call is to the specific church itself. Each call to each specific church is different than God's call to another church.

First Presbyterian Church is, in many ways, a traditional Protestant congregation. It holds Sunday morning worship, conducts a Sunday school for children, has an active youth program, is active in higher councils of the denomination, and builds its decision-making around an elected governing board called a "Session." But in other ways, it is a unique inner-city congregation.

As we have earlier demonstrated, a sizeable majority of the congregation sees itself as called by God to intentional urban ministry in the inner city of Pomona and have acted out that conviction by moving into the community, buying homes there, and entering into the life and fabric of that community. This is why the church is essentially made up of young and early middle-age families rather than an older population. First Church has sought to live out that engagement through its presence; prayer and worship; proclamation; and its practice of social services and ministries of compassion. But the church has also chosen to act out its engagement of the city of Pomona by two primary mission thrusts.

The first thrust is broad-based organizing. It is a member of ICON[25] a southern California "Inland Empire"[26] organizing effort of the IAF.[27] As a member institution, First Church has been deeply involved in fighting for the reduction of crime, the protection of the rights of immigrants (including undocumented workers and their families), educational reform, and workforce development. In addressing these community issues, First Church has been in the forefront in getting 5,000 streetlights installed to combat crime, closed a major drug distribution center just one block from the church, got a bond measure passed so that the public school system would do major repairs to school buildings, and got the Pomona public adult education

[25] ICON (Inland Communities Organizing Network) is an organization of organizations (churches, synagogues, unions, schools, non-profits, etc.), with the primary mission to build the power of the people in public life. ICON organizes Inland Empire institutions to successfully address issues of common concern and to develop the assets of families, neighborhoods, and local institutions. ICON focuses on identifying, developing, and training the people of its member institutions to work together to engage for justice in public life. ICON is an affiliate of the IAF (see below). Retrieved from www.icon-iaf.org.

[26] The Inland Empire is a region in southern California, directly east of the Los Angeles metropolitan area and comprising the western portion of Riverside and San Bernardino Counties. It has a population of over four million people in a 40–square-mile area, making it the thirteenth most populous metropolitan area in the USA. Its name comes from the fact that it lies 60 miles inland from Los Angeles and the Pacific Ocean. In the eighteenth through mid-twentieth centuries, its primary economy was cattle ranching and citrus groves, but today it is warehousing (it's the largest warehousing area in the world outside Hong Kong); shipping; and residential, industrial, and commercial development. It has the lowest per capita income in the Greater Los Angeles Metropolitan Area and the highest immigrant percentage.

[27] The Industrial Area Foundation (IAF) is an organizing network that provides training, resources, and the preparation, supervision, and accreditation of professional organizers. It was founded by Saul Alinsky in 1942 to coordinate his organizing work in major US cities. It works today in 78 cities throughout the US, Canada, and Europe. Its national initiatives include the building of affordable housing, organizing parents to be involved in the decision-making and schooling of their children's schools, job creation, training, and placement.

and job training program restored when it was shut down because of budget constraints.

An example of how First Church and ICON worked together for the good of the people of Pomona is the work of its "Don't Trash Pomona" campaign.

Members of First Church discovered that there was a multi-million dollar corporation that was seeking to build a regional waste transfer station not far from the church that would serve 11 cities and unincorporated Los Angeles County. Further, they discovered that the project would be in the church's neighborhood—one of the poorest and most polluted neighborhoods in the city. Further yet, the station would be within a one-mile radius of nine schools. In addition, they learned that it would add 610 large diesel truck trips per day through their neighborhood which would exceed air quality standards by over three times the maximum threshold set for public health and add the risk of cancer.

Recognizing this was a larger issue than the church itself could address, it worked with ICON and its other member institutions to organize to stop the trash station. ICON led a campaign for nearly two years, in which it organized its member institutions, and formed alliances with local residents, businesses, and other community groups. Over 1,000 letters of opposition were sent to the Pomona Planning Department and added to the Environmental Impact Report. Hundreds of residents and business owners attended three public hearings to oppose the project, and numerous newspaper articles, neighborhood walks, and presentations by ICON made the public aware of the realities of this project. The Pomona Planning Commission voted to deny the project. After being voted down by the Pomona Planning Commission, the company appealed the decision about the project to the Pomona City Council. An additional 6,000 letters of opposition were sent to the Pomona City Council. But a head count of the intentions of Council members suggested that ICON and First Church could lose the vote.

Therefore, ICON leaders met together to discuss what course of action to take. Consulting with one another, local business leaders, and other residents who had taken leadership in the campaign, ICON brought a set of demands to the developer of this project. Thus, ICON negotiated an agreement with the developer and the city which modified and mitigated some of the most negative consequences of the proposal.

Although ultimately approved by the council, the waste transfer station plan included these demands negotiated by ICON, which then became requirements for the developer to continue to meet in order for the building and then operation of the station to be permitted. Those requirements were:

- The trash tonnage processed by the facility was reduced by one-third.
- Trash collection would be from the City of Pomona only, not the other 10 cities.
- The company's trucks had to be converted to CNG alternative fuel.
- No commercial diesel trucks were allowed to use the facility.
- A diesel refueling station was removed from the project, thus reducing truck traffic by another 12%.
- The company agreed to fund and is paying the city of Pomona $100,000 per year for a full-time code enforcer to work to improve code compliance in Pomona's highly polluted industrial zone.
- Pomona residents were guaranteed job placement priority and training at the facility.

A community watchdog group, "Clean and Green," was created, with ICON playing a major role in its formation and continuance. The practical results of these restrictions meant total truck trips were reduced by over 40%, the damaging health impacts of diesel particulate matter was minimized, children were safer in their trips to and from school, and the risk of cancer from this waste project was eliminated.[28]

The second thrust has been the church's creation and continuance of Pomona Hope (www.pomonahope.org). Pomona Hope is a separate 501(c)(3) corporation created by First Presbyterian Church in order to manage its services to Pomona and particularly the church's immediate neighborhood. Pomona Hope seeks to strengthen Pomona's youth, families, and its neighborhood by creating a safe environment for kids and by providing educational opportunities and programmatic support to the residents. Its current major effort is in the operation of its After-School program, its Center Street Community Garden, and its summertime Summer Enrichment Program. These efforts offer to all children and families in the

[28] www.icon-iaf.org

neighborhood surrounding the church the opportunity for one-on-one tutoring; help with their studies; recreational programs; and arts, music, and drama.

The testimony of one mother is particularly moving. She wrote,

> We have been involved with After School with Pomona Hope for the last two years. Our commitment to the program is so strong that, after planning to move to a different city, we changed our minds and decided to stay in Pomona so that our kids could continue to attend the After School Program. Luis, our fourth grader, especially didn't want us to leave Pomona, because Pomona Hope Kids meant that much to him. Also, we have stayed committed to the program because we see that our kids are doing very well in school . . . Jessica, our second grader, is now reading at the fourth grade level. When she began attending the program last year, she could barely read.
>
> If Pomona Hope didn't exist, our children would have a more difficult time doing their homework because sometimes my husband and I don't understand it and can't help them. . . . What Pomona Hope is doing for kids is really needed.[29]

As mentioned earlier, the mission of First Presbyterian Church of Pomona is "to engage, equip, and empower families to follow Jesus and together participate in public life for the spiritual health and restoration of Pomona."[30] Whether such families are neighborhood/city families or church member families, the church's objective is to see them "follow Jesus" and to "together participate in public life." Thus, the church seeks to share with families that do not know Jesus the message of the fullness of life in Christ and in Christ's community (whether that means their alignment with First Church or with some other church). It also means that the church both works with these families and undertakes strategic action in the public arena of Pomona, the Pomona Valley, the Inland Empire, the state of California, and the nation. This means using the structures that are at its disposal, particularly Pomona Hope and the ICON organizing effort. It means addressing together the issues that the people, so organized, identify as their most urgent or important issues, whether that be

---

[29] Retrieved from www.pomonahope.org.

[30] "Report of the Mission Discernment of First Presbyterian Church of Pomona, CA," 27.

education, employment, health care, environmental health, crime and safety, mortgage foreclosure, or immigration issues.

The elements for such engagement in public life and in the strengthening of families are strategies that "engage, equip, and empower families." "***Engagement***" is "hands-on" direct involvement of the members of the congregation in service of its neighbors in Christ's name, and in working side-by-side with the people of the community in addressing both common issues and issues unique to that community. "***Equipping***" is to build the *capacity* and *ability* of people or groups to act. "*Capacity-building*" is understood as the facility or power to produce, perform, or deploy; thus, in the case of employment, one has the tools and the knowledge to perform a particular job. "*Ability*" is to have the skills to perform that job. The work of "***empowerment***" is to build within people and families (especially those who have been repeatedly exploited) the will to act on their own and their neighbor's behalf. To do so, they must have both capacity and ability as well as willingness to be successful. To build such capacity and ability, and to motivate the willingness of the people is a part of the mission of this church. In all these strategies, First Church built its work around the principle: "Never do for others what they can do for themselves."

The structure this church uses to carry out its mission is "mission groups." In 2010, the church made the bold decision to close down all its committees. In their stead, they created what they called "mission groups," which they felt was the most conducive structure to implement their statement of mission to "engage, equip, and empower" both its families and the families in its neighborhood to "participate together in public life for the spiritual health and restoration of Pomona."

But what is a "mission group"? The church defined a mission group as "a small group of church members and friends who feel called to gather together for a period of time both to undertake a common mission and to build a strong life in Christ together."[31] People joined these groups, not because they were asked to serve (and felt guilty in not accepting), but because they felt called by God to that mission. The group then provided for them an opportunity to work with other equally focused people to plan and carry out that mission, while also supporting each other in their respective and shared spiritual journeys together. The people of the church initially created six

---

[31] "Report of the Mission Discernment of First Presbyterian Church of Pomona, CA," 34.

mission groups: Children's Outreach and Ministry; The Center Street Community Garden; the ICON Core Team; the Pomona Hope Mission Group; Youth Outreach; and Ministry and Worship, and most of the church members joined at least one of these groups. The mission groups then became the backbone of the congregation in the implementing of the mission of the church.

Finally, the ultimate task of First Church's mission is to work for "the spiritual health and restoration of Pomona." This is the carrying out of the vision of Pomona as it should be—a city genuinely living in *shalom*. The elements of such a *shalom* was suggested to First Church by the author of Isaiah 65:20-25:

- Health care for all, contributing to longevity and ending infant mortality *("No more shall there be an infant that lives but a few days, or an old person who does not live out a lifetime; for one who dies at a hundred years will be considered a youth, and one who falls short of a hundred will be considered accursed." Isaiah 65:20)*;
- Decent, secure, and affordable housing for everyone *("They shall build houses and inhabit them; they shall not build and another inhabit;" 65:21a, 22a)*;
- Jobs that provide adequate income and bring meaning to people's lives *("They shall plant vineyards and eat their fruit; they shall not plant and another eat;" 65:21b, 22b)*;
- No great disparities in income, wealth, position, or status *("They shall not build and another inhabit; they shall not plant and another eat; my chosen shall long enjoy the work of their hands. They shall not labor in vain, or bear children for calamity;" 65:22–23)*;
- Neighborhoods that are stable and safe *("The wolf and the lamb shall feed together, the lion shall eat straw like the ox . . . They shall not hurt or destroy on all my holy mountain." 65:25)*;
- People living in a loving relationship with God, thus living out the confession, "Man's chief end is to glorify God and to enjoy God forever"[32]

---

[32] "The Westminster Shorter Catechism," answer to question 1, *The Book of Confessions* (Louisville, KY: The Office of the General Assembly, The Presbyterian Church [USA], 1999), 175.

("Before they call I will answer; while they are yet speaking I will hear." 65:24);

- People living at peace with one another *("They shall not hurt or destroy on all my holy mountain." 65:25).*

The central belief around which all Christians have traditionally gathered is the doctrine of the sovereignty and providence of God. That is First Church's starting point and ending point. God is sovereign over all of life and consequently nothing occurs that is outside his will. Affirmation of the sovereignty of God has led First Church's members toward two inevitable conclusions:

First, since God is Lord, no human being can be your lord and master; therefore, any government, any business, or even any church built upon domination, greed or tyranny is wrong—and must be corrected.

Second, since God is Lord, and the Church is God's people, it is the Church that must be engaged in the shaping of the morality, ethics, and the social fabric of all of human society—its politics, economics, education, and social services as well as its spirituality. That is the mission to which First Presbyterian Church of Pomona has committed itself.

On Sunday, July 4, 2010, First Church decided to formally make a commitment to one another as the Body of Christ by conducting together a covenanting ceremony. It was part of that Sunday's worship. They built that service on the covenant renewal ceremony held by Israel immediately before its entrance into the Promised Land (Deut 29:2–33:29). Binding themselves and each other together in this covenant, the members and friends of First Presbyterian Church of Pomona declared in unison together:

> We are a fellowship that exists because of God's sovereignty, initiative, and love. Therefore, we aim to live in the humble reality that we have all fallen, rebelled against God, and deserve death, but Christ alone is our atonement; we have been redeemed by the blood of the Lamb, who gave his life as a ransom for many.
>
> Therefore, we covenant together to share the good news of the Kingdom with others and work and pray for God's will to be done on earth as it is in heaven. We will work and pray for His shalom in our lives and in our world as we submit in obedience to

> His commands: to love God and our neighbor, and to preach good news to the poor. Since we believe that God is Lord, and the Church is God's people, we covenant to be engaged in the shaping of the morality, ethics, and the social fabric of Pomona. It is to this mission we, the people of Pomona Presbyterian Church, commit ourselves before God and each other.[33]

Conclusion

What does this exploration of the life and ministry of First Presbyterian Church of Pomona teach us about the city-changing power of called Christians? It teaches us three things:

First, individual churches need specific calls. D. L. Moody, the famed evangelist of the nineteenth century, was asked by a Chicago newspaper what would be his definition of a great urban preacher. He responded, "The greatest urban preacher is the pastor who climbs into his pulpit each Sunday with the Bible in one hand and the newspaper in the other." In other words, Moody saw authentic urban ministry as being both grounded in solid biblical theology ("the Bible in one hand") and the ability to make that theology relevant to a specific context ("the newspaper in the other"). We think of the Church—the Body of Christ—as a called-out people. And believing that is simply good, sound theology. But it is crucial that any given church needs to see itself as being a called church. And that call needs to be a specifically articulated call. What Pomona Presbyterian Church illustrates to us is the power of a church that very specifically understands its call as a congregation, can clearly articulate it, has developed a structure to implement that call, and can live out that call through the lives of its members engaged intentionally in the political, economic, educational, social, and spiritual arenas of that city.

Second, called churches can only be made up of called people. It is likely impossible, no matter how clearly a church might understand its unique call by God to its city and neighborhood, to carry out that call without a highly intentional, incarnational, mission-focused, and spiritually formed congregation. It must be made up of Christians who have been willing to be open to hearing God's call to them (no

33 "Report of the Mission Discernment of First Presbyterian Church of Pomona, CA," 49–50.

matter how uncomfortable); have made the hard spiritual, social, economic, and political decisions that they have needed to make; and now "keep on keeping on" living out that call in the situation into which God has placed them.

Third, intentional churches can grow from ordinary churches if there are both clearly called leaders and a congregation willing to change. Most often, Christians who take the doctrine of call seriously believe that one must create a new congregation in order to experience a truly called church made up of called Christians. This is simply not true. Churches can change! If God can convert individuals, God is certainly capable of converting institutions as well—even ecclesiastical institutions. Thus, First Church saw itself from its very origins as a "tall steeple church," a large, middle- and upper-class wealthy church, well-placed and influential within the power structure of the city of Pomona. For many decades, this was indeed the case. But "time and chance happen to us all," and as its neighborhood economically deteriorated and ethnically changed, the church still continued to operate under this perception of itself. But then an alternative commended itself to First Church—students and young adults called by the gospel to the city on behalf of the poor who were willing to literally "put their money where their mouths were." The church took its chances and cast its lot with those students. A new church was birthed out of this old church; thus, the old church lived on as the church that God would call to that poor community in Pomona, CA!

So the lesson of First Church is that God calls churches to a specific ministry in a specific community, fills that congregation with Christians who themselves are called to be change-agents for God in that community, and thus can transform the life of an old church to become the church as God intended in that city.

So this is the story of one church. But how do we put such transformation into action? Well, first we must begin with clarity about the biblical doctrine of call. This we will now explore by reflecting together on the biblical understanding of the Caller, the called, and the call itself.

Chapter 2

God as Creator-Caller

If we are going to think together about the calls of lay people in living out the faith in everyday life, the place to begin that reflection is with the Bible. What does scripture have to say about our call to be "Christ-ones" in the city into which God has placed us?

In order to look carefully at the biblical witness, we must consider three distinct and yet related concepts. That is, we cannot reflect upon the Judeo-Christian doctrine of vocation or call without exploring the Bible upon: (a) the divine Caller; (b) a called people; and (c) the biblical insights on call itself. We must look at the biblical witness of God as the one who creates, chooses, and calls us; the people and communities called by God; and the nature of call itself.

In order to undertake this quest together, we will examine in this chapter the subject of God the Creator Caller. In the next chapter, we will continue our examination of God as the Caller by exploring the work of both choosing and calling Israel, the Church, and us as individuals. In the following chapter, we will then look at who are the people and the types of people called by God. And then, in the three chapters that follow Chapter 4, we will examine carefully the actual teaching of scripture about call itself (it will take us three chapters to cover the concept).

So, without further ado, let's begin where all reflection on call should begin—with the Person and Work of the Caller Him/Herself!

Who Is God?

> There is but one only living and true God, who is infinite in being and perfection, a most pure spirit, invisible, without body, parts, or passions, immutable, immense, eternal, incomprehensible,

> almighty; most wise, most holy, most free, most absolute, working all things according to the counsel of his own immutable and most righteous will, for his own glory; most loving, gracious, merciful, long-suffering, abundant in goodness and truth. . . . God hath all life, glory, goodness, blessedness, in and of himself; and is alone in and unto himself all-sufficient, not standing in need of any creatures which he hath made, nor deriving any glory from them, but only manifesting his own glory in, by, unto, and upon them; he is the alone fountain of all being, of whom, through whom, and to whom, are all things; and hath most sovereign dominion over them, to do by them, for them, or upon them, whatsoever himself pleaseth.[34]

How do you describe God? The above statement was the effort of the working group created by the English Parliament to describe God, contained within their 1647 document, "The Westminster Confession of Faith." What is intriguing about the Westminster Confession's definition of God from the perspective of this book's subject, however, is that it defines God by restating the classic attributes of God used in any formal systematic theology. God is typed as being eternal, omnipresent, omniscient, omnipotent, immense, immutable—all of these being concepts that are the opposite of who we understand ourselves to be as humans. But rather than use these technical words, the Westminster Confession uses descriptive words. Thus, "omnipotent" becomes "almighty," "omniscient" becomes "most wise," "omnipresent" becomes "immense," etc. But whether the technical theological term is used or a descriptive word understandable to the theologically untrained, the significance of the definition of God used in the Westminster Confession is that God is essentially seen as what we humans are not—the opposite of us.

This, of course, is the classical way of describing God. But although it has long been thus used, it neglects one particular attribute of God which is a dominant characteristic that appears throughout the entirety of both the Old and New Testaments. That dominant characteristic is that God is seen as the One Who Calls

---

[34] "The Westminster Confession of Faith," *Book of Confessions* (Louisville, KY: The Presbyterian Church [USA], 2016). Portions of 6.011 and 6:012, 151–152. Used by permission.

Forth—the one who called a universe and world into existence; who calls nations and peoples, cities and churches; who calls each individual person to become what God intends that human to be. The God of the Bible is the Calling God. And the entire biblical doctrine and practice of the call of laity and clergy originates from this starting point—the understanding and appreciation of God as the Calling God.

In the scriptures, the Calling God is defined in three ways. First, our God is the Creating God. Second, he is the Choosing God. And third, she is the Calling God. Let's now look at the first attributes.

God as the Creating God

God is presented in scripture, not as the distant and inaccessible God in far-off Mount Olympus, but rather a God who is down in the very muck and scum of the earth, creating new life. The very name that Israel gave to itself—"Yisrael" (or even better, "yisra-El," "El" being the generic name of God in Hebrew) says as much about God as it does about the people of Israel. The name literally means "God-wrestlers"—those who (as symbolized by Judah in Gen. 32:22–32) wrestle with God. That's the kind of God the God of the Bible is—one who wrestles with people and nations—and perhaps even with creation. He's the God who "mixes it up"! And he mixes it up, creating wholeness out of chaos, in five venues: in the creation of the physical abode, in the creation of humanity, of Israel, the Church, and of us as individuals. Let's look at the biblical emphasis.

God the Creator of Heaven and Earth

We begin our exploration of God the Caller with an exploration of the biblical understanding of God as creator.

God as creator is found throughout the warp-and-woof of the Bible. There are, in reality, 224 direct references to God in Scripture as the creator or maker of the world or life within that world. But there are hundreds of additional oblique references to God as creating life for a distinct purpose and with a distinct calling (more on this later).

The first such image of God as the Creating God is as creator of the universe and of the world, both as a single act and as a continuing act. Let's sample just a few of these many images that move through the warp-and-woof of scripture.

Genesis 1:1–2:3 begins salvation history. "In the beginning when God created the heavens and the earth, the earth was a formless void and darkness covered the face of the deep, while a wind from God swept over the face of the water. Then God said, "Let there be light," and there was light. And God saw that the light was good."[35]

In the first creation story (Genesis 1), God creates the world in six days and rests on the seventh, thereby establishing a day of Sabbath rest and the entire concept of the sabbatical after having brought order out of chaos. This first chapter of Genesis concludes in the second chapter by stating, "Thus the heavens and the earth were finished, and all their multitude. And on the seventh day God finished the work that he had done, and he rested on the seventh day from all the work that he had done. So God blessed the seventh day and hallowed it, because on it God rested from all the work that he had done in creation" (2:1–3).

When scripture deals with the creative work of God, it stresses that God created the universe *ex nihilo* (out of nothing) (cf. John 1:3; Heb. 11:3; II Peter 3:5). But in the first verses of Genesis 1, the emphasis falls on God's progressive ordering of the world, not out of nothing, but out of formlessness, chaos, and emptiness.

The first verse of the Bible can be translated "In the beginning, God created the heavens and the earth" (KJV, RSV). But it can also be translated with equal legitimacy, "In the beginning *when* God created the heavens and the earth" (NRSV, NJPS). Whatever way the translator wishes to translate this verse, it is describing creation as a "soup" of chaos and darkness with no form, purpose or order to it. The six-day work of creation, undertaken by God described in Genesis 1, then, is that of God bringing order and restraint out of chaos (Psalm 104:59). Creation is thus understood as ordering, as imposing a design on formlessness and chaos.

This scripture then goes on to describe God as hovering or brooding over this chaos, like an immense eagle covering the chaos with its outstretched wings and, step-by-step, making this chaos into a habitation for human beings (1:2). Each act of creation occurs in six steps, each step following exactly the same pattern, as follows:

- Creation occurs through the word: "God said"

---

[35] *The New Revised Standard Version Bible* (New York: Division of Christian Education of the National Council of the Churches of Christ in the United States of America, 1989). Used by permission. The NRSV is the translation of the Bible used throughout this book, unless otherwise noted.

• A command is used from God:	"Let there be . . ."
• What was commanded happens:	"And it was so."
• An evaluation occurs:	"It was good."
• A chronology is stated:	"The first day."

This scripture records the creation that occurs on the first day. The primordial "soup" of chaos is lightless and landless. It is unordered and unfilled. God thus speaks to it, "Let there be light." Light is created and that light separates itself from the brooding darkness. "And God saw that the light was good." "And there was evening and there was morning, the first day." This is then followed by additional spoken acts of creation: separation of the earth from the universe, the separation of land from sea, the birthing of life upon the earth, the appearance of sun and moon from the mist previously covering the earth, the creation of the animal world and then, finally, the creation of humanity. But for what purpose was this magnificent act of creation done?

"In the beginning was the Word, and the Word was with God, and the Word was God," St. John declares (John 1:1). The Word was God. It is the word of God that speaks the universe, the earth, and all its creatures into being. But what is particularly unique about the creation story is that it concentrates not upon the process but the ***Actor***. God spoke the creative instruction ("Let there be light"). And *then* it happened! The text doesn't tell us how it happened. It simply states that it happened. The point is that the author of the creation story tells us that God spoke the word—God ordered the creation—and it was so. And because it was so, it was deemed "good." Creation didn't occur by happenstance but by the acted-out Word of God. The universe, the solar system, the earth, all life upon the earth is all God-breathed. "The spirit of God moved upon the face of the waters" (1:2). "And God saw that was good."

Essentially, what the first chapter of Genesis presents to the reader is the reality that the work of God is the work of creating order out of chaos, habitation out of formlessness. God is at work ordering a new world so that all creation will praise Him and will share in the world God created as God intended it to be—humanity living in relationship with God and each other, acting justly in public life and perceiving all wealth as a gift continuously being given by the creative God to guarantee that there are no poor. It is the beginning of the process by which God acts through creating, choosing, and calling both all humanity and each person to join with God in shaping the world into the world that God intends for all peoples. Thus, from its very origins, the biblical message is one of God always at work creating the world and shaping humanity to work for God's kingdom by living out God's choice and call of them for the good of the world. That is the "theophany" or "manifestation" that God would bring upon this world that he chose, with his word, to create.

But God as creator doesn't end with the "Big Bang"! God is not the president at the new season's opening major league baseball game, throwing out the first ball and then retiring to his oval office. God is always in the process of creating and re-creating the world, life upon that world, and especially those made in his image—human beings.

Psalm 107:33–43 states it well. This psalm demonstrates the *chesedh* love of God toward those who love him, particularly when they are in trouble. It begins, "O, give thanks to the Lord, for he is good for his steadfast love (*chesedh*) endures forever. Let the redeemed of the Lord say so, those he redeemed from trouble and gathered in from the lands, from the east and from the west, from the north and south" (107:1–3).

The Psalmist then demonstrates this steadfast and gracious love of God for his people by giving four examples. The scripture portion on which we are presently reflecting deals with Israel's arrival at the Promised Land and therefore their departure from the wilderness, their crossing of the Jordan River into Palestine, and their resulting abode there. "(Yahweh) turns rivers into a desert, springs of water into thirsty ground, a fruitful land into a salty waste, because of the wickedness of its inhabitants. He turns a desert into pools of water, a parched land into springs of water. And there he lets the hungry live, and they establish a town to live in. They sow fields, and plant vineyards, and get a fruitful yield" (vv. 33–37).

The author envisions a Canaan where, "because of the wickedness of its inhabitants," both the land is sick and the people evil. This is changed by the new presence of Israel who come from the desert through the miraculous crossing of the Jordan River, and then turn Palestine into "pools of water" and "springs of water." The result is the creating of an oasis of plenty and a people who "sow fields and plant vineyards and get a fruitful yield." What is significant here is the writer's assumption that God continues active in creation—with or without the help of humanity. In this particular instance, it is the Israelites coming into the Promised Land from a wilderness experience who nurture from the earth abundance and growth. Thus, they are called, not only to inhabit a promised land but also to nurture it. But that abundance is still a gift from God, continually turning "a desert into pools of water, a parched land into springs of water" (107:35).

The Psalmist thus ends this hymn with the instruction, "Let those who are wise give heed to these things, and consider the steadfast love (*chesedh*) of the Lord" (vs. 43).

Romans 8:18–25 is even more grandiose in its vision of continuing creation. Paul states, "I consider that the sufferings of this present time are not worth comparing with the glory about to be revealed to us. For the creation waits with eager longing for the revealing of the children of God; for the creation was subjected to futility, not of its own will but by the will of the one who subjected it, in hope that the creation itself will be set free from its bondage to decay and will obtain the freedom of the glory of the children of God. We know that the whole creation has been groaning in labor pains until now; and not only the creation, but we ourselves, who have the first fruits of the Spirit, groan inwardly while we wait for adoption, the redemption of our bodies. For in hope we were saved. Now hope that is seen is not hope. For who hopes for what is seen. But if we hope for what we do not see, we wait for it with patience" (8:18–25).

Here, Paul's vision exceeds all boundaries. He asserts that the entire created order is in bondage to decay. It is, in other words, "running down" (the second law of thermodynamics). Therefore, Paul asserts, it is subject to decadence and to sin. But such collapse is not inevitable. God, the creator of the cosmos, is still at work in the cosmos. And he is at work in the cosmos through Jesus Christ. "Creation will be set free from its bondage to decay and will obtain the freedom of the glory of the children of God" (Romans 8:21). The created order will be saved. It will someday be set free from its own entropy and decay. And when it is set free from its seemingly inevitable running down, it will experience the same "freedom" and "glory" as do "the children of God."

It is, Paul suggests, as if creation is in the process of childbirth, "groaning in labor pains" to bring forth that which none of us has the capability to understand. But it will be a new creation, a new universe, and a new cosmos, as God would have it be. And the only way we can begin to glimpse this magnificent work of redemption and liberation that God is doing through Christ with the entire created order is to examine that work in the light of the work God is doing in us—for our redemption witnesses to us of "the first fruits of the Spirit." As God has done a miracle in our lives, so God will do a miracle in all of creation.

Paul presents in Romans 8 a remarkably comprehensive understanding of salvation. The Godhead, he states, is involved in creation and redemption at cosmic, societal, and personal levels—and one does not comprehend the fullness of the work of Christ unless one embraces the reality that salvation is meant by God for the entire created order (the universe and the earth) as well as for society and the individual.

Salvation, Paul teaches in this passage, is a process, not a product. Do not confuse conversion with salvation, the apostle suggests. Conversion may be a momentary decision when we determine to follow Christ and to work for his shalom kingdom. It may be for many a most dramatic decision. But the work of salvation in each of us is a lifetime work (we have been saved, we are being saved, we will be saved). The work of salvation to bring society to the place that they truly embrace shalom may take a millennium or two (or maybe even three). The work of salvation to transform the universe into God's intentions for it when he created it may take billions or even trillions of years. For it does not come easily. It is like the work of childbirth, the pain of labor that must have its time and must continue until the birth of the new has come. The work of salvation goes on—a process of transformation that cannot be rushed, but also cannot be stopped. So God is in the creation business—not only making humanity in God's image but also the world and the cosmos itself. And humanity has been created, chosen, and called to play a strategic role in enabling that work of creation to happen. This is the grace-filled intentions of God the Creator.

God the Creator of Human Society

But God is not only the creator of the universe, the world, and of human beings. More particularly, God is the creator of human-kind; that is, he is creator not only of them but of their societies as well. All *homo sapiens* are created by God for a purpose. A part of that purpose is lived out through the kind of society these humans create for themselves. In other words, God's work of creation in human society is lived out through the work of creation these humans undertake together. Again, there are many scriptures that speak to this truth, but let us consider at least these two passages.

Colossians 1:15–28 begins in earnest Paul's argument intended for the Colossian church. That church had, without understanding its consequences, adopted the teaching that, in order for them to be good Christians, they needed to embrace the worship of spirits, angelic beings, and the "elemental spirits of the world" (2:8, 20). This had, in turn, caused them to disengage from public life as a church into an introspective and privatized faith. Paul sought to provide a corrective to this false teaching and practice by presenting a biblical understanding of power. He begins that examination of power by starting with Jesus Christ. By arguing Christ's power, Paul hopes to demonstrate to the Colossians that they need to live out Christ's power by working for the transformation of Colossae into a likeness of the kingdom of God. So he begins his argument by getting them to consider how Jesus exercised power.

Paul wrote:

> (Jesus) is the image of the invisible God, the firstborn of all creation; for in him all things in heaven and on earth were created, things visible and invisible, whether thrones or dominions or rulers or powers—all things have been created through him and for him. He himself is before all things, and in him all things hold together. He is the head of the body, the church; he is the beginning, the firstborn from the dead, so that he might come to have first place in everything. For in him all the fullness of God was pleased to dwell, and through him God was pleased to reconcile to himself all things, whether on earth or in heaven, by making peace through the blood of his cross (1:15–20).

On the face of it, this passage seems to be a theological statement about the importance of Jesus Christ. But in reality, it is a very political statement.[36] What Paul is arguing is the supremacy of Jesus Christ. The Greek word particularly used by Paul in this passage to refer to Jesus is *arche* or "the one who holds the primary position of authority." *Arche* can be used for a human leader (e.g., ruler of the synagogue, magistrate, judge, chief priest, governor), but it can also be used to describe someone who holds the key position in an organization (like a court, a city council, a business, a church), or even the "spirituality" of the one holding pivotal authority in such an organization.

Jesus, Paul states in Colossians 1:15–20, is the *arche* of reality, the very first principle or essence of life (in the words of the Nicene Creed, "God from God, Light

---

[36] The most thorough study of Paul's theology of the "principalities and powers" in the New Testament, as well as the political understanding of the contemporary Roman and Israelite worlds, has been made by Walter Wink, *Naming the Powers* (Minneapolis: Fortress, 1984); *Unmasking the Powers* (Minneapolis: Fortress, 1986); and *Engaging the Powers* (Minneapolis: Fortress, 1992). His argument on the politicality of the "principalities and powers" was so cogently argued and so overwhelmingly documented that few biblical scholars of today question it.

from Light, true God from true God, begotten, not made"). As the *arche*, Paul is teaching here, Jesus is the creator of all things. And his creative work has included "all things in heaven and on earth, things visible and invisible, whether thrones or dominions or rulers or powers."

That formula of "thrones, dominions, rulers, and powers" is political language. Since Jesus is the *arche* and has created all things on earth, he has therefore created all earthly "thrones" (the seat of a government), "dominions" (the territory of a government), "rulers" (the individuals who run each government), and "powers" (the vehicles of a government by which it enforces its will, like laws of the state and the military). Thus, Paul is developing the argument that Jesus is the creator of the Roman Empire and the Israelite nation. Both governments (and any other government) are accountable to him, and he has determined their task of working for justice and mercy as an integral part of molding life into God's intentions for it. Therefore, Jesus is the true Caesar, is head over the state, and is working "to reconcile to himself all things, whether on earth (political entities) or in heaven (angelic/demonic extensions of earthly entities), by making peace through the blood of his cross."

Christ's death, Paul therefore teaches, is the act by God that will bring about a reconciliation of all governments and states into one holy kingdom of God—the *shalom* community. And the work of the church is to be engaged in public life as Christ's reconciling body, seeking by its intervention to bring about the conversion of the Caesars of this world to Christ (Col. 1:24–29; 2:8–15; Eph. 1:15–22; 2:11–22; 3:7–13).

But how is the church to go about exercising the power that Jesus has invested in it as the *arche* of all political, economic, and religious systems of the world and of the world itself? The church (including the church in Colossae) is to exercise Christ's power by being a suffering servant, not by imitating the powers of control and domination of the world.

The next portion of this scripture (Col. 1:21–28) begins with Paul's reminder to the Colossian Christians that they were, at one time, "estranged and hostile in mind, doing evil deeds." But Jesus demonstrated his power toward them by both dying for them and calling them to die to the standards of Rome. Thus, they embraced the standards of Christ and his Kingdom. Through his redemptive work on the cross, Jesus has made us "holy and blameless and irreproachable" before God. Such transforming work as we know that Christ has done in us is an indication of the power he has at his disposal to work for the transformation of Israel, Rome, and the entire political, economic, and spiritual order of the world. That is why you Colossians who have been so redeemed need to keep "your eyes on the prize"—"securely established and steadfast in the faith, without shifting from the hope promised by the gospel."

But how do we set free that power to impact and transform the world politically, socially, economically, and spiritually? We set free that power by imitating how Jesus used such power. We become a servant of Christ to the world—even when that entails suffering. Paul is the prime example of such service.

"I became its (the church's) servant according to God's commission that was given to me for you, to make the word of God fully known, the mystery that has been hidden throughout the ages and generations but has now been revealed to his saints" (vv. 25–26). God wanted to transform the Gentile world as well as the Jewish one, the Roman Empire as well as the Jewish Temple, pagan economics as well as the economics of the Mosaic Law. God has done that transformational work through Jesus Christ. But now it becomes our task, as the followers of Jesus, to "warn everyone and teach everyone in all wisdom, so that we may present everyone mature in Christ." And we do that, not by imitating pagan and Jewish political, economic, and religious structures in their lust to dominate, oppress, and control but by imitating Jesus in being a suffering servant in our engagement of the world and its systems. Therefore, Paul argues, imitate me as I act as a suffering servant, for that is the role you must play as well.

The political message throughout the book of Colossians is not only that politics and religion *do* mix. They *must* mix if society is ever to experience itself as the *shalom* community. The indicator that the political arena of a society is following God's intentions for it is that it is acting justly and mercifully. The church, as a mediating institution in society, is to be about the task of seeking to pressure its society's political institutions to be truly just in their management of public life while being particularly compassionate toward those who could become powerless. In this way, the church contributes toward bringing each throne, dominion, ruler, and power under the lordship of Christ and fulfilling that role that God intends it to fill.

Isaiah 65:17–25 is remarkable because it is one of the clearest statements in scripture about God's specific societal intentions for the human order. Whereas the Colossian statement above presented a conceptual understanding of how the church is to be engaged in public life as the acting out of its calling of God the Creator, the Isaiah passage presents a very vivid and specific statement of what God would create ***through our engagement in society*** for any given city or society.

What did God create human society to be? Isaiah begins, "For I am about to create new heavens and a new earth; the former things shall not be remembered or come or mind" (Isa 65:17). The prophet tells us that God's intentions for society, when fully enacted, will radically alter the present reality of existence, so that it will be as if we are in "new heavens and a new earth." This is a motif throughout the second part of Isaiah (42:9; 43:18; 51:6). In much of that book, it is a promise for Israel (42:9; 43:18), but in this portion the prophet takes a radical step, and envisions this "new heavens and a new earth" for all humanity. This, of course, is the passage that is used in Rev. 21:1 to introduce its vision of the "New Jerusalem."

What does God's society look like? Isaiah declares, "Be glad and rejoice forever in what I am creating; for I am about to create Jerusalem as a joy, and its people as a delight. I will rejoice in Jerusalem, and delight in my people; no more shall the sound of weeping be heard in it, or the cry of distress" (vv. 18–19).[37]

We do not often think of our society as the City of Joy. But that is what God wants it to be. God wants to ***delight over the world*** and wants God's people to find joy in it as well. The church is called to be a cheerleader to the city. It is also called to name all that is evil and dark about our society, and particularly to confront society's systems and structures when they act in exploitive and oppressive ways. But in order to be truly effective in the world, the church cannot allow itself to be overwhelmed by its evil. It must take delight in its city, in the people surrounding the church, and in each other in the community of faith. There is much to love in every city.

> No more shall there be in it an infant that lives but a few days, or an old person who does not live out a lifetime; for one who dies at a hundred years will be considered a youth, and one who falls short of a hundred will be considered accursed. For like the days of a tree shall the days of my people be (vv. 20, 22b).

---

[37] As shared in the first chapter of this book, this Isaianic vision of society as God created it to be was used by First Presbyterian Church in Pomona, CA, in helping them determine what should be their ministry priorities within the city of Pomona and the Inland Empire region of southern California.

The city is to be a place of ***health and longevity***, and the church has the responsibility to work for that longevity and health care of its inhabitants. To live in the kind of health conditions that foster infant mortality, deprive people of adequate health care, or take adult life prematurely is unacceptable. The work of the church must include advocacy for adequate health care for all society's inhabitants. That means not only dealing with direct health care but with the very conditions of a city or society that produce ill health. That means a concern with the issue of stress. It also means a commitment to ***environmental issues***. Health care means more than adequate medical care for all; it also means dealing with the variegated stress of the city and with the city's environmental degradation. The Bible indicates that such concern needs to be part of the work of the church in society.

"They shall build houses and inhabit them. They shall not build and another inhabit" (vv. 21a, 22a).

Isaiah instructs God's people to be concerned about how people live in their society. Housing, he says, is a right for all people, irrespective of their wealth or poverty. That means ***adequate housing for all***, so that everyone has a home and no one is forced to live on the street. It means just housing, housing fairly distributed to everyone, whether one is powerful or a "nobody," whether one is rich or poor. Isaiah states it magnificently: "They (the common people) shall not build and another (the wealthy) inhabit (the homes)." And finally, it means safe housing. The church is to work for safe and well-built housing so that there are no tenements, no slums, no cardboard and tin shacks.

"They shall plant vineyards and eat their fruit. They shall not plant and another eat. My chosen shall long enjoy the work of their hands. They shall not labor in vain" (vv. 21b-23a).

A dominant theme throughout both Old and New Testaments (e.g., Deut. 15:4–12; Acts 4:32–37) is ***the equitable distribution of wealth***. "Give me neither poverty nor riches," goes a Jewish proverb, "grant me only my share of bread to eat, for fear that surrounded by plenty, I should fall away and say 'Yahweh—who is Yahweh,' or else, in destitution, take to stealing and thus profane the name of my God" (Prov. 30:8–9). One should neither be too rich nor too poor, the author of Proverbs states; it is enough to have only my fair share of wealth—and no more!

Scripture stresses the importance of building an adequate economic base under an entire people—not for a few to hoard wealth while others go hungry.

Scripture passages like Jer. 22:3–5 and Eph. 6:9 indicate how both Old Testament Jews and New Testament Christians were seeking to deal with economics justly and equitably. Although many of these particular economic recommendations are irrelevant to us today, their operating premise can be instructive as we seek to build an urban economics for the twenty-first century. Isaiah calls us to bend our godly efforts to the development of a secure, balanced economy that enables each person to work and to make a valuable contribution to the furtherance of the well being of the city, while eliminating all poverty.

"They shall be offspring blessed by the Lord—and their descendants as well. Before they call I will answer, while they are yet speaking I will hear" (vv. 23b-24).

Perhaps that which most separates a biblical vision of the kingdom of God from the utopias of dreamers such as John Stuart Mill, Adam Smith, or Karl Marx occurs precisely at this point. Each such visionary builds his utopia on the premise that such an ideal world is achievable. Each utopia is built on the premise that humanity is essentially good and if the formula devised by the visionary is followed, then society will reach that utopia.

Scripture is different. It operates on the premise that although humanity is made in the image of God, that image is implacably scarred by the existence of sin (thus humanity is redeemable only by the action of God). Human beings will therefore corrupt every good plan humanity devises. Only God can make society work as God redeems us and then creates in us a new community. The difference therefore between the utopias of visionaries and the kingdom of God is that the first is centered on the perfectibility of humanity and the latter is centered on the graciousness of God. Relationship with God is the center of the transformed biblical city.

Isaiah brings out this insight most clearly in this passage on the idealized Jerusalem. In the city as God intends city to be, God will be in such close relationship with his people that "before they call I will answer; while they are yet speaking, I will hear." ***Relationship between God and God's people*** will be so intimate that God will respond to their longing for him even before they have placed that longing into words. The description is almost one of a lover responding to his beloved at the moment before she reaches for his reassurance, or of a mother anticipating the needs of her baby even before the baby begins to cry. This is the intimacy God covets between Yahweh and the people of the city. And it is the task of the church to cultivate that intimacy between the people of its society and God.

Isaiah completes his vision with the words, "The wolf and the lamb shall feed together; the lion shall eat straw like the ox; but the serpent—its food shall be dust! They shall not hurt or destroy on all my holy mountain" (vs. 25).

The chief end of human existence in Isaiah 65 is **"shalom.**" God's intentions for society end with that which proves whether this city is indeed the city of God—whether or not its populace lives in shalom. It is the responsibility of the church to work for this shalom wherever that church may be placed. This is perhaps most dramatically stated by Jeremiah the prophet as he instructs the Jewish exiles living in the hated city of Babylon, "Work for the shalom of the city to which I have sent you; pray to Yahweh on its behalf, since on its shalom your shalom depends" (Jer. 29:7, my translation). The most appropriate worship of God is the service of humanity. A primary responsibility of the church is to seek the reconciliation and shalom of all humanity.

Isaiah 65 provides for us one of the clearest and most concrete statements in scripture of what the biblical writers and leaders mean when they speak of the New Jerusalem or Zion or the shalom community or the kingdom of God. A society of adequate health care; the end to infant mortality; healthy longevity; elimination of stress and of environmental pollution; adequate and fairly distributed housing for all; jobs for everyone at levels of skill that cause people to find fulfillment; economic development; legal systems that are just; relationship of all society's people with God; and an entire society living at peace with one another encapsulates God's intentions for the world. This is what the Old Testament prophets longed for. This is what Jesus gave his life for (see, for example, Luke 4:16–21). And this is what the church, empowered by Christ's resurrection, is called to work for. This is the shalom community!

The vision of human society summarized here is the world as it should be—human society as created and still intended by God. That vision is given many names in scripture. But it is best known by the title coined by Jesus of Nazareth—"the kingdom of God." That kingdom is to be the focus of our life and vision as Christians. That kingdom is what we are to be working toward. And that vision is what we pray for every time we pray the "Lord's Prayer." The realizing of the kingdom of God—human society as God intends—is what the mission both of Israel and of the Church should be the focus of our life, witness, and mission.

God the Creator of Israel

An essential scriptural perspective throughout the warp-and-woof of the Old Testament is that God is not only the creator of the physical universe and human society, but God is also the creator of a particular people—the nation of Israel. Although there are many scriptures to sound this theme (e.g., Gen. 17:1–22; Isa. 41:20; 65:18; Jer. 31:31–33; I Pet 4:19), perhaps the most beautiful is Isaiah, 43:1–7.

But now thus says the Lord,
He who created you, O Jacob,
He who formed you, O Israel:
"Do not fear, for I have redeemed you;
I have called you by name, you are mine.
When you pass through the waters, I will be with you;
And through the rivers, they shall not overwhelm you;
When you walk through fire you shall not be burned,
And the flame shall not consume you.
For I am the Lord your God, the Holy One of Israel, your Savior.

I give Egypt as your ransom, Ethiopia and Serba in exchange for you.
Because you are precious in my sight, and honored, and I love you,
I give people in return for you, nations in exchange for your life.
Do not fear, for I am with you;
I will bring your offspring from the east,
And from the west I will gather you;
I will say to the north, 'Give them up,'
and to the south, 'Do not withhold';
Bring my sons from far away and my daughters from the end of the earth—
Everyone who is called by my name,
Whom I created for my glory,
whom I formed and made."

"He who created you, O Jacob, he who formed you, O Israel." "Israel, whom I created for my glory, whom I formed and made." Isaiah 43:1–7 is a poem of hope in which God says to a defeated, exiled people, "Do not fear, for you are mine" (43:1b). This is the primary message of what must be one of the most beautiful and deeply moving poems in scripture, written to the Jewish people held in exile in a foreign nation.

The author of this passage uses some key words or phrases in this promise—key statements to which we must pay attention. First, he states to that still captive Israel, "Do not fear." Those words make up the primary phrase that moves like a refrain through Isaiah 40- 55. It is a reminder to Israel that, although their present reality of exile seems bleak indeed, God is on the move and will bring about both their liberation from Babylon and their restoration to their beloved Promised Land.

Second, the author specifically has God say, "I have redeemed you." The word "redeemed" is used infrequently elsewhere in the Old Testament in reference to God (only in Job 19:25; Pss. 19:14; 78:35; and Jer. 50:34). But it is used a total of ten times in Isaiah 40-66. It is therefore obviously an important concept to the author of Isaiah.

When we Christians hear the word "redemption," we automatically think of the act of sacrifice by Jesus on the cross that brought about our salvation. But that is only an adaptation of the word. "Redeem" actually means "to buy back" or "to repossess," and it is primarily an economic term. It means to free one from a legal or financial obligation by a transaction or agreement that takes place. Because of its economic roots, therefore, it is rarely used of God's actions (see the above paragraph), but is often used of a person—such as the "kinsman redeemer" in the book of Ruth (where it is used 20 times in that context).

Thus, for Isaiah to have God say, "I have redeemed you" is to have God declare, "I have bought you back." The Israelites have suffered in their exile and captivity, but God has acted to set them free through Persia, so that God has "bought them back" and has now "repossessed" them. Consequently, they have once again become God's "property" and belong to Him. And what He chooses to do with his property is to banish all their fear and to return them to the Promised Land!

Third, the writer has God declare, "I have called you by name; you are mine." When we hear the phrase, "I have called you by name," we interpret that to mean that God takes note of or recognizes us and thus gives credibility to us. That is what we assume the author is saying God has done to Israel. But that is a modern reading of that phrase; it is not what that phrase meant in fifth century BCE Israel.

The phrase, "I have called you by name" is used frequently in Isaiah 40-55 (40:26; 43:1; 44:5; 45:3–4; 48:1). It is a technical term used for indicating the establishment of sovereignty over a person. For a king to "call you by name" means that the king has selected you from his court to bring you under both his protection and his authority. For a superior (in this case, God) to call someone by name means that the one who names the other is declaring sovereignty over that one so named. The person named now comes under that sovereign's protection but is also under his authority and is therefore accountable to the overlord. That this is the sense of that phrase is confirmed by the parallel construction of Israelite poetry (in which the same truth is said twice but with different words) by following the phrase, "I have called you by name" with the phrase, "You are mine." In other words, you, Israel, now belong to God!

Thus, in this simple statement, "Do not fear, for I have redeemed you; I have called you by name; you are mine," God is promising a great deal to Israel. God is telling them not to live in fear because God has brought Israel back and repossessed them, making them his property. He has established his sovereignty over them so that they now live under his protection and authority. So, now that God "owns" them and has reclaimed them as his sovereign subjects, there is no reason why they should fear the power of Babylon, Persia, or any other nation or god.

But a message of "do not fear" impacts the hearer of that message in direct proportion to whom it is giving that instruction. If one does not have the power to protect the person who is being told, "do not fear," then that promise is hollow. If, on the other hand, it is an extremely powerful person making that promise, the promise can be received with great trust, hope, and conviction. Who is it, then, who instructs captive Israel not to fear?

The promise begins, "But now thus says Yahweh; he who created you, O Jacob, he who formed you, O Israel, 'Do not fear'" (vs. 1a). This is no mere mortal speaking this assurance to Israel—whether peasant, priest, or king. This is Yahweh Himself making this promise. And who is Yahweh? He is the creator of the world and of the universe. He is the one who creates human society, both in fact and in vision ("the kingdom of God"). And He is the One who has shaped Israel and brought it into being. It is God who brings each and every one of God's people into existence. This, consequently, is One who can deliver, and therefore can be trusted.

After the prophet presents God's promise to Israel, "Do not fear, for I have redeemed you; I have called you by name; you are mine," the writer continues through verse 7 presenting the evidence for why Israel should not fear the new thing God is doing to bring about their redemption, their liberation from slavery, and their restoration to their Promised Land.

Not only is Yahweh God the creator of the universe, the world, human society, and of Israel, the author of Isaiah declares; he is also the deliverer of Israel in the Exodus. "When you pass through the waters, I will be with you; and through the rivers, they shall not overwhelm you. When you walk through fire you shall not be burned, and the flame shall not consume you. For I am the Lord your God, the Holy One of Israel, your Savior" (43:2–3a).

Consider what Isaiah is stating here. "I am the Lord your God" is a direct quotation from the most formative document coming from the Exodus—the Ten Commandments (Exodus 20:2). "When you pass through the waters" is a reference to Israel's crossing of the Red Sea, as they were miraculously delivered by Yahweh from almost certain annihilation by Pharaoh's army. "When you walk through fire you shall not be burned" refers to the means by which God delivered Israel from Pharaoh's wrath, the cloud of fire that swept down in front of the charging Egyptian army and held them at bay until all the Israelites had made good their escape. "When you pass through the rivers, they shall not overwhelm you" is a reference to Yahweh's division of the Jordan River so that the Israelites might cross on dry ground into the Canaan that would become their inheritance.

In other words, what God is saying to Israel through this poem is that Yahweh is not only the creator of the world. He is also the One who creates history and who led Israel out of that slavery inflicted by the most powerful nation in the world. If God could both create them and shape history to bring about their liberation, can they not trust him now to liberate, redeem and "call them by name"?

Thus, God concludes in this poem, "Do not fear, for I am with you; I will bring your offspring from the east, and from the west I will gather you; I will say to the north, 'Give them up.' and to the south, 'Do not withhold'; bring my sons from far away and my daughters from the end of the earth—everyone who is called by my name, whom I created for my glory, whom I formed and made" (vv. 5–7).

God is giving a great assurance to Israel here. He is saying, "I am presently on the move to liberate you and to return you to Israel. And those whom I liberate will not only be those who have been exiles in Babylonia ("the east"), but also Israelites who might have been enslaved by any regime anywhere ("Egypt, Ethiopia, Seba"—vs. 3b; the "west, north, and south"—vv. 5–6). God will bring about a new creation—the third creation following the creation of the earth and the creation of an old Israel from Egyptian slavery. This will be a third creation—God's new creation of God's people. He will achieve this new creation by ingathering all of God's people from around the world, who will be liberated from oppression, exploitation, and domination, who will be purchased back and redeemed by God and who will return to God's new Jerusalem to begin the building of the world as God intended it to be!

God the Creator of the Church

But God is not only the creator of the universe, the world as it should be ("the kingdom of God"), and of Israel. God is also the creator of the New Israel—the Church! One passage that sounds this theme exceedingly well is John 15:1–27.

John 15:1–8 speaks of God's work of creating the church by using what is one of the best-known metaphors in the Bible. Jesus declares to his disciples, "I am the true vine, and my Father is the vine grower. He removes every branch in me that bears no fruit. Every branch that bears fruit he prunes to make it bear more fruit. You have already been cleansed by the word that I have spoken to you. Abide in me as I abide in you. Just as the branch cannot bear fruit by itself unless it abides in the vine, neither can you unless you abide in me. I am the vine, you are the branches. Those who abide in me and I in them bear much fruit, because apart from me you can do nothing" (15:1–5).

Jesus makes three primary points in this sharing with the disciples. First, he states that it is he who is the vine, while they are its branches (15:4–5). Second, the work of the branches is to "bear much fruit" (15:2, 8). Third, the branch remains fruitful through its dependence upon and its abiding in the vine (15:4–7). What does Jesus mean by these three assertions?

This is the final "I Am" statement appearing in the Gospel of John, "I am the vine." But what does he mean by "vine"? In order to be able to unpack this extremely pivotal statement by Jesus to his disciples, we must first answer the question, "What did the metaphor of vine mean to the Jewish people of Jesus's day?" And that requires us to ask, "How was the metaphor of "vine" used in the Old Testament?"

The image of the vine is used over 200 times in the Old Testament. It was a crucial image for a nomadic people, because it was an indication of the intentional transition of that people from being nomads who followed their flocks to being a settled people, becoming "rooted" in a single place. This was because the first thing "settlers" would do would be to plant vineyards (which then required them to "stay put" in order to tend those vines). And that vineyard would, with care, likely continue to grow and supply that people with sustenance for hundreds of years. The presence of the vineyard would very literally "root" these nomads in a single place, and thus would enable them to settle down, build villages and even cities, and thus build a civilization for themselves. They might continue to raise herds of sheep or goats and follow those flocks as they foraged for food, but they would now have a place where they were anchored, to which they would always return.

It is intriguing that when the metaphor of vine is used throughout the Hebrew Bible, it is always used of Israel itself. The essential message communicated by the prophets using this image to describe Israel was that Israel was a failed vineyard. Thus, in Isaiah 5:1–7, Israel is likened to a formerly productive vineyard planted and tended by Yahweh. Such loving care should have meant that this vineyard would bring forth choice grapes. But, instead, it has brought forth only wild grapes and will therefore be dug up and disposed of by Yahweh.

Likewise, Jeremiah 2:21 states that Israel, planted by God as God's vineyard, has become degenerate. Ezekiel 19:10-14 laments a great vineyard ("Mother Israel") that is "plucked up" and "cast down," and thus destroyed. And Hosea 10:1 depicts Israel as an empty vine that brings forth fruit that only benefits itself and not God nor the world. In each case, Israel is "the vine" of God which demonstrates that it has become an unproductive vine, and is thus rejected by God.

For Jesus to declare, "I am the true vine, and my Father is the vine-grower" (15:1) was both most shocking and totally unexpected. In so declaring himself the "true vine," Jesus makes the first of three primary points. First, he declares that he—and not Israel—is the true vine, that his followers are only branches of the vine, and that God is the vine-grower (15:1–5).

At the time Jesus made this statement, this was an exceedingly shocking statement. By doing so, Jesus has done three things. First, he has put himself in the place of Israel, in essence stating that *he* is the chosen person much as Israel is the chosen people. Second, he has stated that he is the "true" vine, as opposed to Israel as the "false" vine." By using the word "true," Jesus recalls the Jeremiah 2:21 passage, in which the prophet states that although God chose Israel as the "true" vine, their faithlessness has required that "trueness" to be passed on to another. Now, Jesus states that it is he who has inherited that true and faithful role that Israel was to play. Finally,

Jesus states that "my Father is the vine grower." What makes the true vine true is the presence of the vine grower who creates, cares, and tends it. Therefore, the vine remains true only if it is centered in "abiding" in God.

Thus, in this metaphor, the church is not the true vine. It is simply the branches, the offshoots of the true stock, the vine. The branches of a grape vine might cover several acres of land and be highly productive. But what gives those branches the power to bear fruit is the vine stock's rootedness in the ground. Thus, the branches are peripheral to the stock, and may be from time to time cut off (in fact, will be cut off as part of the pruning necessary to create the most productive vine). But it is the stock of the vine that is important and must be maintained, and it is the vine grower's job to so maintain it. Thus, what Jesus is saying here is that it is he and not his disciples who is the new, true, and faithful Israel. He is the vine!

Second, the work of the branches is to "bear much fruit" (15:2, 8). The very existence of all those who follow Jesus is justified only by whether they "bear much fruit." But what is actually meant by "bearing fruit"?

Well, what did "to bear fruit" mean in Jesus's day? And once again, we can't answer that question without referring to the Hebrew Bible.

To "bear fruit" was a common Old Testament term to speak of a community's faithfulness or obedience to God. Thus, Psalm 1:3 tells us that those who take delight in the Law and are faithful in obedience to it are those who are "like trees planted by streams of water which bear their fruit in its season." Conversely, the vineyard so carefully tended by God yielded "only wild grapes" (Isaiah 5:2b); it was not faithful to God's call (5:7) to it. Likewise, God says of Israel in Jer 2:21, "I planted you as a choice vine from the purest stock. How then did you turn degenerate and become a wild vine?" The vine had obviously not been obedient to God's law and had proven faithless to the covenant.

"To bear fruit," therefore, meant to the Jew of Jesus's day that one was living out in his or her own life the covenant made between Israel and Yahweh to do justice, to love each other with forgiving love, and to walk humbly with God (see Micah 6:8). One's "fruit" or actions were proof positive that one was being faithful to the shalom vision for one's society that manifested itself in justice, equitable distribution of wealth, and oneness with God.

Thus, "bearing fruit" is being faithful to the covenant made between God and God's people—that is, the practice of the shalom community. Jesus is saying that those who say they are following him but act with greed, oppression, avarice, seeking to control humanity, or the ignoring of the plight of the poor, are acting in a way that is a direct contradiction to God's intentions for humanity. In the case of such people, we must inevitably conclude that they are not and have never been a part of that shalom community. Therefore, their being "gathered, thrown into the fire, and burned" is the inevitable consequence of their unwillingness to embrace Christ and His Kingdom.

On the other hand, if they are seeking to be faithful and obedient to Christ in their actions and in their lives, such action is the inevitable manifestation that they have made such a faith commitment. In their situation, therefore, God will "prune" them in order to increase their faithfulness, because no human being is fully committed to God's kingdom. Thus God, in his grace and mercy, allows us to experience hard times, misfortune, or rebuke in order to deepen our commitment to him.

Perceiving "bearing much fruit" as faithfulness to Jesus's shalom community makes the most sense when one considers the primary theme of the Gospel of John. That theme is that Jesus has come to Israel as the countercultural Christ who is building an alternative community to that of the Jewish political, economic, and religious leaders who have embraced the values of greed, oppressive power, and religious control while espousing the Mosaic values of justice, equity, and relationality. Therefore, living out in one's life and actions a relational and just faith is proof positive that the disciple "bears much fruit." The follower of Jesus is called to be faithful and obedient as the sign that he or she does, indeed, belong to Jesus's alternative community.

Third, the branch remains faithful through its dependence upon and its abiding in the vine (15:4–7). A recurring sub-theme running through this scripture is the necessity of the Christian and the Christian community to "abide" in Jesus in order to sustain that Christian's faithfulness to the God who created them.

This is a logical extension of the vine analogy. The vine stock (i.e., Jesus) is rooted in the nourishment and empowerment that the vine grower (God) gives to it through his tending, watering., and fertilizing the soil. Thus, the vine stock is alive and useful to God as long as it "abides" (that is, receives its nourishment and life) in God.

Likewise, the branches remain alive, healthy, and bear fruit to the degree that they remain connected to the vine. Those branches receive their nourishment from the vine stock. Thus, to the degree that they "abide" in the vine (as the vine "abides" in

God) will they remain faithful, obedient, and consequently useful to both the vine and to the vine-grower?

What Jesus was essentially saying to his community of faith is that they will remain vital in their faith and love and obedience to Jesus's intentions for the world only as they remain in an intimate relationship with him. They must "abide" or "remain" in him. The word "abide" communicates permanence and steadfastness about it—a "keeping on keeping on." The very choice of this word by Jesus expresses his commitment to build an alternative community to humanity's typical society of unilateral power, greed, and alienation. Jesus desires to create not only a community centered in relationship with God, just and equitable, but also a community that lasts forever—that "abides."

The Christian community must be built upon embrace, Jesus is developing here—a continuing dynamic relationship with God through relationship with Jesus, and a vital, caring relationship with one another. As God embraced us by creating us as a community as well as individuals (see below), so we are called into an embrace of one another and, indeed, the whole world. Only being a godly, loving presence with each other and a life of mutuality provides the foundation by which the Christian community can both be God's continuingly alternative community to the world and God's means for building that world. "The vine imagery symbolizes how the life of the Christian community is shaped by love and intertwined with the abiding presence of God and Jesus."[38]

God the Creator of Each of Us

But God is not only creator of the Church and Israel as his people. God is also the creator of every one of us as the unique individuals we are. God's creation, choice, and call of us is most touchingly presented in Hebrews 11:29– 12:2.

Throughout the eleventh chapter of the book of Hebrews, the author presents a metaphor of a great race run by Old Testament heroes of faith. Beginning with the words, "Now faith is the assurance of things hoped for, the conviction of things not seen" (Heb. 11:1), the author of Hebrews grounds that definition of faith by reminding us of God's creation of the universe and God's creation and call of Abel, Enoch, Noah,

---

[38] G. O'Day, "The Gospel According to John," *The New Interpreter's Study Bible.* (Nashville, TN: Abingdon Press, 2003), 1939.

Abraham and Sarah, and Moses. Then, beginning with Hebrews 11:29, this author continues his recital of God's creation and call of God's people with the escaping Israelite slaves taking the step of faith into the Red Sea, not knowing what would happen but nevertheless obedient to the instructions of Moses. It was their faith, as well, that brought down the walls of Jericho during the conquest of Canaan. And the author commends a Gentile, a woman and even a prostitute, Rahab, "because she had received the spies in peace."

Having rehearsed Israel's worthies from Abel through Abraham and Moses to Rahab, the author of Hebrews then summarizes what would otherwise be much too long of a list. "And what more should I say? For time would fail me to tell of Gideon, Barak, Samson, Jephthah, of David and Samuel and the prophets—who through faith conquered kingdoms, administered justice, quenched raging fire, escaped the edge of the sword, won strength out of weakness, became mighty in war, put foreign armies to flight" (11:32–34). He speaks of the faithful action of many, some mentioned by name and others not so—but the point is that he presents those of faith as being the faithful ones who may have known triumphs but also knew defeat, persecution, rejection, and torment. Yet in the midst of their difficulties, they went on believing in God's promises and keeping their "eyes on the prize." They were, in the words of this author, those "of whom the world was not worthy."

The author of Hebrews then concludes this chapter with the powerful words, "Yet all these, though they were commended for their faith, did not receive what was promised, since God had provided something better so that they would not, apart from us, be made perfect" (11:39–40).

With these words, the author of Hebrews connects the Israelite heroes with the Christians of his day. These models of faith sensed the powerful ways in which God was at work to create society into the world as God intended. But none of them lived to see it actually accomplished. There was something more, as if all creation waited on tiptoe for the coming of Jesus and his kingdom. But that "something more" was coming, in God's timing, to the earth and would embrace these ancient worthies in the faith in that coming, as well as those who have seen and met Jesus, and who are now alive (at the time of the writing of this epistle). "They would not, apart from us, be made perfect," the author writes. And, in a profound sense, "we would not, apart from them, be made perfect" either—for we are all of one body, one people of faith. So it is, the author is telling us, that all of God's people will be brought together into one magnificent creation when God's kingdom comes as Jesus intends it to come.

Then this magnificent passage reaches its shining apex at the beginning of the twelfth chapter. "Therefore, since we are surrounded by so great a cloud of witnesses, let us also lay aside every weight and the sin that clings so closely, and let us run with perseverance the race that is set before us, looking to Jesus, the pioneer and perfecter of our faith, who for the sake of the joy that was set before him endured the cross, disregarding its shame, and has taken his seat at the right hand of God" (12:1–2).

The image conjured by the author of Hebrews is a dramatic one. In the metaphor of a race, he presents both life and the corporate struggle of God's people to realize the kingdom of God. But it is not just any sort of race. It is a marathon. Those running that race have been running from city to city, over hill and dale, through thickets, fording streams, up steep hills, mile after mile after mile, hour after hour. Finally, the Christians running this race reach their city destination, running through its streets toward the stadium. Suddenly, they burst into the stadium, and as they do the crowd rises to its feet, cheering them on. That crowd is made up of all those Old Testament worthies who had once run the race themselves. But now they watch the young Christians running it in their stead. And they stand to their feet and cheer them on. Emboldened by those cheers, these Christian marathoners cast aside the weight of their own exhaustion, their screaming muscles, their aching calves, the discomfort of lungs feeling like they will burst, and they run with all their spent might toward the prize at the end of the stadium. They feel exhausted, they are in deepest pain, they feel like they will almost certainly collapse.

And then they see him—they see him standing at the finish line, waiting for them to arrive. It is Jesus, "the pioneer and perfecter of their faith"—the one who himself ran this marathon of life and ran it to certain death, to the cross, to the shame of that execution. Yet, he ran it with joy, with hope, with conviction, and with an overwhelming love for all those on the track, all those in the field, all those in the stands who had themselves been faithful or were now being people of faith, so that they can join Jesus at taking "his seat at the right hand of the throne of God," the seat of the winner of this race.

For in the race of faith, in the race of faithfulness, there is not a single winner. There is Jesus. There is Abel and Enoch and Noah; Abraham and Sarah and Isaac; Jacob and Esau and Joseph; Moses and the escaped Israelite slaves and Rahab; Gideon and Barak and Samson and Jephthah David and Samuel and the prophets. But there are still others, not recorded by the author of Hebrews. There is Peter and Mary Magdalene, Paul, John, Mary and Martha. There is Origen and Athanasius, Augustine and Bernard of Clairvaux, Abelard and Heloise, Anselm and Aquinas, Wycliffe and Hus, Luther and Calvin, Wesley and Wilberforce, Harriet Beecher Stowe and Theodore Weld, Mother Teresa and Teresa of Avila, Charles Finney and Martin Luther King Jr. All have been winners in this race that does not end until God's Kingdom comes.

And now—now it is our turn. We join the race. We run the marathon. We have entered the stadium, buoyed by the cheers of centuries and centuries of the faithful. And now we see Jesus at the finish line. And he is standing there, arms open wide for us all—all of us who are running. So we run toward him, "the pioneer and perfecter of our faith." And we will all be winners of that race of life!

The point of this passage is that God—the great Creator God—created not just galaxies and universes and worlds, not just humanity and human society, not only his people Israel and his people the church—this same God created you and me. God created us as individuals, choosing us to be his own, giving us a purpose and calling for our lives, and endowing us with the gifts and the community to carry out that mission. We are created—and chosen and called—to run! And so we run. We run toward Jesus. We run to faithfully carry out God's call to us to join God in the work of creating the city and the world as it should be. And when our race in life is over, and we have won the prize that is placed on our heads by Jesus, we then climb into the stands of that magnificent stadium, there to cheer on all the others who keep on pouring through the gates into that stadium, as they run the race in which we also ran. And this is what the Christ life is all about.

Chapter 3

God as the One Who Chooses and Calls

Who is it that asks, "What are you doing here in this city, Christian?" It is the God who not only creates, but who has also chosen and called you.

The God Who Chooses

The Bible-wide characteristic of God as the One who chooses is expressed in scripture through God's choosing of Israel and the Church to be God's people, and of each of us. We will now examine all three of those ways God chooses us.

There are 132 references in scripture to God choosing people, nations, and communities. God has created to use these chosen ones in specific ways. Let us examine the chosen peoples of Israel and the Church, and then examine a few specific individuals.

Israel

"How odd of God
To choose the Jews."

Thus wrote the British journalist William Norman Ewer, to which Leo Rosten replied,

"But not so odd
As those who choose
A Jewish God
Yet spurn the Jews!"[39]

---

[39] "William Norman Ewer," Retrieved from Wikipedia, https://en.wikipedia.org/w/index.php?title=William_Norman_Ewer&oklid=67797356.

Now, where did a people get the idea that they are the "Chosen People"? And where did others get the idea they could embrace a Jewish God but spurn the Jews? Where did the Jews ever get the idea that they are God's chosen people anyway?

Well, they got it from God! And they got it from way back at the very origins of the Bible itself. One of the oldest parts of the Bible is Exodus 19:1–24:8, and is called "The Book of the Covenant."[40] Here is the story of the creation of that book around which the book of Exodus would eventually be built.

The Book of the Covenant. After the final defeat of Pharaoh and of Egypt at the Reed Sea, the emancipated slaves of Israel knew that their next major order of business was to meet with the God who had rescued them from certain annihilation. Moses had earlier said to Pharaoh, "Let my people go that they may worship me in the wilderness" (5:1). The Israelites now broke camp, left the shore of the Reed Sea and followed Moses out into the desert toward Mount Sinai. There, they were to worship God and learn from Yahweh what they were next to do. So they now set forth to Mount Sinai.

Three months later, they arrived at the famed mountain. Their journey of three months had not been smooth, for there had been discord, conflict, and even rebellion on the way. But now the former slaves had arrived at the sacred mountain where Moses had first met God at the burning bush. The people stood before the mountain, awed not only at its great height but at the clouds that belched forth from it, the roar and the fire that symbolized God's presence there. Moses climbed the mountain to meet with God, while the people stood in fear and trembling below.

As God had met with Moses earlier on that mountain, so Yahweh met once again with Moses. There, God issued a call to Israel. And that day, God made as binding a covenant with Israel as he had previously made with Abraham, Isaac, and Jacob. Throughout its subsequent history, Israel would look back to that event at Mount Sinai as the formative event of its nation. In the covenant begun there, Israel found itself as a faith community, a people who could not understand themselves apart

---

[40] "The Book of the Covenant" is specifically named as such in Exod. 24:7. It is presented in commentary on Exod. 19–24 in the *Cambridge Annotated Study Bible* (Cambridge, UK: Cambridge University Press, 1993), 62–67; *The Jerusalem Bible* (Garden City, NY: Doubleday, 1966), 100–104; *New Interpreter's Study Bible* (Nashville, TN: Abingdon Press, 2003), 113–114; "Excursus: Covenant," *Oxford Annotated Bible* (Oxford, UK: Oxford University Press, 1962), 91–99.

from the covenant to which they were committed. Here is the story of the creation of that "Book of the Covenant" as Israel told it.

The Book of the Covenant begins with God's choosing of Israel. In his initial encounter with Israel at Mount Sinai, God declared, "You have seen what I did to the Egyptians, and how I bore you on eagles' wings and brought you to myself" (Exod. 19:4). This was the first of an uncounted number of times in the Old Testament in which God reminded Israel of what he had done for them. The reason was plain: God's covenant with Israel was built upon God's deliverance and liberation (salvation) of them. Because God had freed them from Egyptian tyranny and had provided for them as they traveled the desert, he now expected Israel to center their national and individual life in Yahweh through loving him and obeying him.

After reminding Israel of what he had done, Yahweh issued his call to the nation. "Now therefore, if you obey my voice and keep my covenant, you shall be my treasured possession out of all the peoples. Indeed, the whole earth is mine, but you shall be for me a priestly kingdom and a holy nation" (19:5–6a).

God selected one nation, Israel. Two important insights are presented here in the Exodus 19 account of God's choice of Israel to be God's people. First, God selected one nation, the nation of Israel, to be his representatives before the world. This choice was an arbitrary act of God's grace, for Israel had done nothing to deserve selection. In fact, if anything, Israel's actions ought to have dissuaded God. But such actions had not so dissuaded God. God had chosen them. And God had chosen them precisely because they were the poorest and weakest nation at that time on the face of the earth. He chose "what is weak in the world to shame the strong; God chose what is low and despised in the world, things that are not, to reduce to nothing things that are, so that no one might boast in the presence of God" (I Cor. 1:27b-29).

In reviewing the covenant made between God and Israel, the author of Deuteronomy said it best when he wrote, "It was not because you were more numerous than any other people that Yahweh set his heart on you and chose you—for you were the fewest of all peoples. It was because Yahweh loved you and kept the oath that he swore to your ancestors, that Yahweh has brought you out with a mighty hand, and redeemed you from the house of slavery, from the hand of Pharaoh king of Egypt" (Deut. 7:7–8).

Israel called to be priests. Second, God had selected and called Israel to be a "kingdom of priests and a holy nation." They had been chosen in order to center both their national life and their individual lives in the love of Yahweh and the love of their individual and corporate neighbors. But how were they to live out that love of God and humanity? They were to live that out by becoming a "kingdom of priests and a holy nation."

What did that mean—to be called to be a "kingdom of priests and a holy nation"? What it meant was that Yahweh had called Israel to a specific responsibility, a definite "job"—that of being priests. Whether they were conducting business with each other or trading with the nations, whether they were adjudicating quarrels within families or working for national justice for the poor among them, whether they were dealing with children ostracized by other children or whether they were dealing with the immigrant from another country who was living among them, they were to act as priests. By designating all Israel as a holy nation of priests, Yahweh had revealed the essence of his choice of them. That choice involved both special privilege and heavy responsibility. Being called to a national priesthood meant that they had been selected as the intermediary between God and humankind; that was the "special privilege." But it bore "heavy responsibility" as well, for the fate of the world rested on their obedience of leading the world (through their service of God and humankind) back to God!

When Moses descended from Mount Sinai for the first time, he brought to the people of Israel this announcement from God that they were chosen. What would the people now do? The author of Exodus tells us, "The people all answered as one: 'Everything that Yahweh has spoken we will do.' When Moses had told the words of the people to Yahweh, Yahweh said to Moses, 'Go to the people and consecrate them today and tomorrow.'" (19:8, 9b-10b). So Moses consecrated the people, and God made the covenant with them to become a nation of priests and a holy nation (19:16–25). It was in the light of this call to the people from God and their consequent acceptance of that call that God then gave to Moses the Ten Commandments. It was the responsibility of the Ten Commandments (a portion of the Book of the Covenant—Exod. 20:1–17) to summarize how being "a kingdom of priests and a holy nation" was to be lived out.

The Ten Commandments was meant to be a model for the new lifestyle under which the Israelites were to live, the way they were to live out being "a nation of priests." As the newly rescued ("saved") people of God, the Israelites were to build a new national and personal life, symbolized in their covenant with God. The Ten Commandments were a listing of those ten elements at work in any society which tend to destroy that society. If the Israelites were to murder, commit adultery, or covet, if they were to make Yahweh and his love secondary in their daily lives, their society would crumble. If, on the other hand, the Israelites obeyed God and treated other persons as the Ten Commandments outlined, they would be well on their way to becoming a kingdom of Yahweh's priests in the world. By following this treaty in both national and personal life, the Israelites would become a little "garden of Eden" in the midst of the wickedness and injustice of the rest of the world. As others saw how Israel lived in obedience to the one, true God and their service of humankind, they would also turn to Yahweh—and the world would become what God had created it to be!

In essence, the decisions made by Israel at Mount Sinai set Israel on a course from which they could later never fully extricate themselves. At Mount Sinai, Israel made the decision to build a nation, not on the ways of Pharaoh but on the ways of Yahweh. No matter how individual leaders of Israel or even the nation as a whole sought to re-embrace the ways of Pharaoh in their lust to be "like all the other nations of the world," they could not—for the corporate memory and the constant pressure of prophets reminded them of the unique directions in which that nation had decided to move. In responding to God's choice of them as a nation of priests, Israel had decided on a profoundly different direction for building a nation.

The action of the Israelites in embracing the Ten Commandments released upon the world a new social imagination that would never again be able to be blocked out. Through the Law that was created over the years and centuries following that meeting at Mount Sinai, that new social imagination now had the liturgics to constantly keep re-stimulating that imagination in every new Israelite generation (its worship) and the political and economic structure and systems that were designed to treat all its people justly, share wealth, and bear a common commitment to the elimination of poverty anywhere in its nation. And most profoundly of all, it moved beyond ideals to the creation of actual legislative vehicles to guarantee that the world as God would want it to be would continue. Those legislative vehicles included Sabbatical Years that freed slaves, forgave debts and revived land (Deut. 15:1–11); Jubilees that redistributed wealth (Lev. 25:8–55); kings who read and abided by Torah (Deut. 17:14–20); judges who refused to be bribed (Deut. 16:18–20; 17:8–13); cities of refuge to limit violence and guarantee fair trials (Deut. 19:1–10); no interest to be charged on loans (Deut. 23:19–20); and immediate payment of wages to avoid exploitive use of that money by employers (Deut. 24:14–15) (to name a few).

Thus, at Mount Sinai, Israel covenanted with Yahweh to reject for its future the politics of unilateral power and oppression, the economics of greed and exploitation, and a religion of domination that typified the reign of every Pharaoh. Rather, through the Ten Commandments, Israel embraced a society as God created it to be—a world of political justice for all people no matter who they might be, economic equity for all, the elimination of poverty throughout that society, the care and even celebration of their environment, and the centering of all of that nation's life in a God who loves and makes covenant with God's people. And that is the importance of the Book of the Covenant—and of God's choosing of Israel to be "a kingdom of priests and a holy nation"!

The Church

"You did not choose me, but I chose you. And I appointed you to go and bear fruit, fruit that will last" (John 15:16a).

But Israel was not God's only chosen people. In due time, God also chose the Church! Thus, Paul—who was both the church's earliest apostle to the Gentiles and a former Pharisee and rabbinical expert in the Jewish Law—wrote in Ephesians 1:3–14 one incredibly long sentence—256 words long! In this unbelievably long sentence, Paul tells us what God has done for us. He tells us:

- God "*blessed* us in Christ with every spiritual blessing" (1:3)
- He "*chose* us before the foundation of the world" (1:4)
- He "*adopted* (us) as his children through Jesus Christ" (1:5)
- He "*redeemed*" and "*forgave*" us through Christ's redemptive work (1:7–8)
- He has "*made known to us* the mystery of *his will*" (i.e., what we are called to do as God's people) (1:9)
- He has "*marked (us) with* the seal of *his Holy Spirit*" (1:13).

Thus, Paul is telling us that everyone of us as Christians and all of us as the Body of Christ have been blessed, chosen, adopted, redeemed, forgiven, have come to know God's will, and are marked with the Holy Spirit. All of this God has given to us through the sacrificial death and resurrection of Jesus Christ. But precisely what does Paul mean by these words? Let's look at each of them.

First, God has "blessed us in Christ with every spiritual blessing" (1:3). The Greek language has two words that are translated by our one English word "bless." The word Paul chose, *eulogeo,* means "to speak well of." But the way Paul chooses to use *eulogeo* throughout his letters all have to do with suffering or with sacrifice. The common concept of blessing or of "speaking well of" another is the thought that there is cost involved when we are a blessing to others. Thus, it cost God to "bless us in Christ with every spiritual blessing," and that cost will be revealed in the suffering and death of God's own son. That is what it means for us to be "blessed" by God.

"Chosen" is the next word used to describe what God has done for us. God has "chosen us before the foundation of the world" (1:4). The word "chosen" is another word rarely used by Paul[41]—in fact, it is used by him in only one other scripture, I Cor. 1:26–29—but there, its use is magnificent.

"Consider your own call, brothers and sisters," Paul writes in I Cor. 1:26–29. "Not many of you were wise by human standards, not many were powerful, not many were of noble birth. But God chose what is foolish in the world to shame the wise; God chose what is weak in the world to shame the strong; God chose what is low and despised in the world, things that are not, to reduce to nothing things that are, so that no one might boast in the presence of God."

God doesn't pursue the "brightest and the best," Paul says. He goes after ordinary people—folk who may not be politically powerful, who may not have great wealth, who may be seen as foolish, weak, and of the lowest possible castes. But God chooses these people to glorify God in the world by the ways they choose to live and act with integrity. God selects "ordinary" people so that God might adopt, redeem, forgive, and then use them. In this way, God makes clear that, when those people faithfully use power and money and leverage wisely to bring about change, it isn't because they are so clever, but because God is working in and through them.

Paul writes, "(God) chose us in Christ before the foundation of the world to be holy and blameless before him in love" (1:4). The apostle is stating that God chooses people for a relationship with Himself. It is not so much that we choose God as it is that God chooses us! And God chooses us, not because there is anything particularly lovable or desirous about us (we are all miserable sinners), but because of Christ's sacrificial work for us. That choice of us is "before the foundation of the world," and we are chosen so that we can be "holy (that is, set apart and dedicated) and blameless

---

[41] It should be noted that although Paul rarely used the word "chosen," he presented the concept of God's choice of us as an integral part of his theology (cf. Rom. 8:29–33; 9:6–26; 11:5–28; 16:13; Col. 3:12; I Thess. 1:4; II Thess. 2:13; Titus 1:1).

before him in love." That is, one is chosen, not because she is chosen, but because God has intentions for her that will be acted out in and through her life.

"Adopted" is the third work God has done for us Christians. Adoption is a term used a great deal by Paul. For example, in Rom 9:4–5, he speaks of the Jews and writes, "To them belong the adoption, the glory, the covenants, the giving of the law, the worship, and the promises; to them belong the patriarchs, and from them, according to the flesh, comes the Messiah, who is over all."

But Paul also develops the idea that Gentile Christians are also adopted by God. Writing to Roman Christians, he states, "you did not receive a spirit of slavery to fall back into fear, but you have received a spirit of adoption" (8:15). And to the Gentile Christians of Galatia, he writes, "When the fullness of time had come, God sent his Son, born of a woman, born under the law, . . . so that we might receive adoption as children" (Gal. 4:4–5b).

Paul faced a dilemma in his theology of grace. That dilemma was caused by the belief of the Jewish people—including Jewish Christians—that Israel had been chosen by God and therefore were the natural children of God. But if you believed that, then *ipso facto,* Gentiles were not and could not become children of God. Paul solved that conundrum by positing his doctrine of adoption. That is, although one must grant that Gentiles are not "natural" children of God, yet it must also be maintained that because of Christ's sacrifice for them, they are "adopted" by God into God's family. They are not natural children, but they are "adopted" children, and therefore receive all the privileges and rights of being as much a part of God's household as are God's natural children—the Jews.

In Ephesians 1:5, therefore, Paul writes, "(God) destined us for adoption as his children through Jesus Christ, according to the good pleasure of his will." In other words, he is saying that Christians are children of God—whether they are formerly pagan Gentiles, Gentiles who converted to Judaism, or are Jews. All Christians are children of God, because God has acted to adopt us into his family. We didn't become part of God's family because we were born to God. We are part of God's family because God chose to choose us and to adopt us into his family. And this God did, not because we are such "beautiful babies," but because of Christ's sacrificial death for us.

"Redeemed" and "forgiven" us. Paul writes, "In him, we have redemption through his blood, the forgiveness of our trespasses, according to the riches of his grace that he lavished on us" (1:7–8). Both redemption and forgiveness are necessary for us to be freed from the bondage of sin, and our salvation hasn't occurred until both Christ has died to redeem us and God has chosen to forgive us. That is why Paul includes both in this single statement of what God has done for us. Thus, he is telling us that we who are Christians—whether Jew or Gentile—are already chosen by God from "before the foundation of the world," we have been redeemed and forgiven, and thus our adoption into the household of God has been made complete by that transformation that God has wrought within us through Jesus Christ.

"God has made known to us the mystery of his will." Paul writes, "according to his good pleasure that he set forth in Christ, as a plan for the fullness of time" (1:9–10a). What Paul is stating here is that God has a marvelous plan for both the Body of Christ and each individual within it. Thus, God has a marvelous plan for your life, which he activated by blessing, choosing, adopting, redeeming, and forgiving you.

"Marked with the seal of the Holy Spirit." Finally, Paul concludes his list of what God has done for us by declaring, "You were marked with the seal of the promised Holy Spirit; this is the pledge of our inheritance toward redemption as God's own people, to the praise of his glory" (1:13b-14). As a newly confessed Christian, it would be appropriate for you to be baptized. That baptism was the "seal," the guarantee, the secure stamp or sign upon your life that you had; indeed, been blessed, chosen, adopted, redeemed, forgiven, and called by God to live into his plan for your life. And so baptized, the early Christians believed, the "promised Holy Spirit" would fall upon you as he fell upon Jesus at his baptism. Thus, by participating in the act of baptism and believing in the descent of the Spirit upon the initiate, the entire Christian community would acknowledge God's work that had been done and was continuing to be done in you, and would welcome you into its community with arms of love.

But now comes the truly important question to Paul. Why has God done this work in each of us and in all of us as Christians? Why has God blessed, chosen, adopted, redeemed, forgiven, called, baptized, and filled us with God's Spirit? This introduction to the book of Ephesians now reaches its apex of intention. God has done this great work within each of us and all of us, Paul writes, so that we, as God's adopted family, might participate in God's "plan for the fullness of time, to gather up all things in him, things in heaven and things on earth" (1:10), so that we "might live for the praise of his glory" (1:12b).

But what does Paul mean by his reference to "(God's) plan for the fullness of time, to gather up all things in him, things in heaven and things on earth"? It is his code for the political, economic, and religious institutions of earth—and especially of Rome—and their matching "principalities and powers" in the heavens (cf. Col. 1:15–16).

Since Paul means here the systems of the government, of the marketplace, and of religion, he is stating that the church is to be active in participating on the side of God in challenging the systems here on earth, even as the angels wage comparable war in the heavens. What Paul is declaring is that ***the church is to be involved in public life as its essential mission!***

Involvement in public life is what the church is to primarily and essentially be about. Paul is not suggesting that our involvement in public life is optional or tangential to the purpose, work and life of the church. It is the essential job of the church! That is why we exist. And that is why we are blessed, called, chosen, adopted, redeemed, forgiven, and granted the power of the Holy Spirit—so that we can be the kind of people God caused us to be in working for the transformation of our world's political, economic, and religious systems into systems more like those of heaven—the just, equitable, and relational community of shalom that God created us all to be. To settle for anything less as our essential mission is for us to be disobedient and unfaithful to God's choosing of us.

But not just Paul wrote about the church as being God's new chosen people. So did Peter, in a truly magnificent statement: "You are a chosen race, a royal priesthood, a holy nation, God's own people, in order that you may proclaim the mighty acts of him who called you out of darkness into his marvelous light" (I Peter 2:9).

It was my privilege to pastor a "tall-steeple" church in Chicago for seven years. That pastorate was most formative in my embrace of the strategies of community organizing as we sought to cope with a community in crisis and close to collapse. And that experience shaped the future direction of my ministry and of my life.

Edgewater Presbyterian Church had, at one time, been a church of significant stature in Chicago. Founded soon after the Civil War, by the 1920s it had grown into a congregation of over 1,500, occupying a magnificent Italian Renaissance building. It was known as "the silk-stocking church" of Chicago because it was in the middle of the most fashionable district of Chicago next to Lake Michigan and had a wealthy congregation, including eight millionaires.

But by the time I was called to become its senior pastor, the church and its neighborhood had fallen onto hard times. The congregation was only one-third its former membership. All its millionaires and most of its wealthy had long since departed. A faithful core of white, middle-class members commuted in to the church from the suburbs to which they had fled. But at least half of the congregation I inherited still lived in the neighborhood but also reflected the changes that had occurred to that neighborhood. They were now African, African-American, Asian, Hispanic, Native-American, and Appalachian whites, and most were poor. The mansions that had once surrounded the church had mostly disappeared and had been replaced by four- to six-story cheaply constructed apartment buildings with full families crowding into one, two, or three rooms. Our neighborhood had become the primary terminus for mentally ill patients that had been dismissed from Illinois's public mental hospitals that had been closed to save costs.

I was proud of how Edgewater Church chose to respond to its neighborhood. That church's ministries included a day-care center for the mentally ill; a clothing distribution center and care center; professional counseling and ombudsmen services for people looking for jobs or wrestling with problems too great for them to manage; and even a coffee house where people could gather out of Chicago's cold, have a cup of coffee, and talk with church members who would listen. It was because of the destitution of the neighborhood that our church and the other churches formed a community organization—the Organization of the North East (ONE)—that continues to this day, an organization that enabled the people and institutions to confront the political and economic powers of Chicago to protect the interests of the people and to defend the poor.

But perhaps the ministry of Edgewater Church about which I was most proud was a liturgy that somehow worked its way into our Sunday worship. As our congregation gathered for worship, I would look out on a bag lady sitting next to a dowager, a mentally ill person in his own world sitting near a business man, a young upwardly mobile adult sitting next to a worn-out and grizzled African-American elder, and I would think "This is what the kingdom of God really is like." Then I would step into the pulpit, and I would begin ***every Sunday morning worship*** with the same question, "Who are we who gather here?" Every Sunday the congregation would spring to life as they answered in the strongest voice imaginable, "We are a chosen race, a royal priesthood, a holy nation, God's own people, that we may declare the wonderful deeds of him who called us out of darkness into his marvelous light" (I Pet. 2:9, RSV). And for one brief shining moment, that motley crew of the rejected of the earth became God's own people, standing tall, singing bold, and proclaiming who, in reality, they truly were!

This scripture from I Peter has two distinct emphases to it. The first emphasis is Peter's witness to what the Church is called by God to be. He uses specific terms to refer to the church. We are "a chosen race," "a royal priesthood," "a holy nation," "God's own people," "you who have received mercy."

Each term is significant, and has been carefully chosen by the author. First, we Christians are "a chosen race." Peter is referring directly to Exod. 19:4–5. "You have seen what I did to the Egyptians, and how I bore you on eagles' wings and brought you to myself. Now therefore, if you obey my voice and keep my covenant, you shall be my treasured possession out of all the peoples." It is not so much that we choose God as God chooses us. And in this passage, Peter is reminding this "motley crew" of Christian peasants that they have been chosen by God—called out from the priorities and standards of the world and called in to this new community of people at one with God and each other.

Second, we are "a royal priesthood." This continues the reference to Exod. 19. Verse 6 states, "But you, Israel, shall be for me a priestly kingdom and a holy nation." What Israel was once called to be, now the Church is called to be. We, too, are "a royal priesthood," those who have access to God to offer God our worship, our work, and ourselves.

Third, we are "a holy nation." In Exodus 19:6, God directly refers to Israel as "a holy nation." But this is a theme throughout scripture, perhaps most beautifully expressed in Deut 7:6, "For you are a people holy to the Lord your God; the Lord your God has chosen you out of all the peoples on earth to be his people, his treasured possession." To be "holy" means to be "set apart," to be chosen and dedicated to a particular use.

Fourth, Peter calls the church "God's own people." This is better translated "a people for God's own possession." We are those whom God covets, whom God wants to possess. This expresses almost the sense of God's addiction to us and to a relationship with us. God yearns after us and wants us as God's own. This, again, is a theme throughout the Hebrew Bible (cf. Deut. 7:6; Isa. 43:21; Mal. 3:17). That this is the most important indicator of God's love for us is manifested in the fact that Peter cannot help but return to that designation a total of three times. First, he calls us "God's own people." Second, he reiterates, "Once you were not a people, but now you are God's people." Third, to strengthen what he has just proclaimed, he writes, "Once you had not received mercy, but now you have received mercy."

What is significant about these four titles that Peter gives to the Church is that they are all Old Testament titles. What Peter has done has been to apply to the Church the Hebrew Bible's terms for Israel. By doing this, Peter extends the work of Yahweh in the Old Testament to the Christians of the New Testament. He includes the Church in the people of God in order to assert that God's chosen consist of those who were called out by God in the Old Covenant under Moses and in the New Covenant under Jesus. We are all one people, a holy nation of both Old Testament worthies and New Testament Christians and their progeny elected by Yahweh (see Heb. 11:1– 12:2)!

But for what have we been elected? The second emphasis of this passage is what the Church is called by God to do. Peter continues, "in order that you may proclaim the mighty acts of him who called you out of darkness into his marvelous light" (2:9b). Being chosen by God is not so much privilege as it is responsibility. You have been saved to serve. You are "a chosen race, a royal priesthood, a holy nation, God's own people" so that you will act upon that chosenness, and "proclaim the mighty acts of him who called you out of darkness into his marvelous light." The sign that you are chosen is that you want to serve your new Master by reaching out in both compassion and passion to the world. The Church is not the church unless it is a Servant Church, a church on behalf of others, a church that both longs and works hard to bring this world "out of darkness into God's marvelous light."

The Church is mission. And being in mission is to most profoundly be the Church. It is to such single-mindedness in working for the transformation of the world into God's kingdom of shalom that we are called to be "a chosen race, a royal priesthood, a holy nation, God's own people."

Strategic Individual Chosen People

God not only chooses a nation and a people. The God who is The Caller also chooses individuals. Perhaps the place for us to begin is with God's choosing of the founder of the Jewish people and the foundation of the Christian Church.

Abraham. When we think of Abraham, we think of him being called by a god whom he did not know and did not worship to leave his home, his extended family, and his livelihood in a city in Mesopotamia to follow that unknown god to the mysterious region of Canaan which he did not know and had never visited before. But that is not the key story of Abraham's journey with God. The truly pivotal story is the rather strange event presented in Gen. 15:1–18.

This scripture seems a strange passage. It tells of Abraham (then called "Abram"; only later is his name changed by God to Abraham) and God quarreling over the patriarch's inability to sire a son and thus pass on his lineage. God commands Abram to "bring a heifer three years old, a female goat three years old, a ram three years old, a turtledove, and a young pigeon" (15:9), to cut them apart lengthwise, and then to lay on the ground each pair of the two halves opposite one another with a path between them. The text then tells us that, when the sun had gone down, "a smoking fire pot and a flaming torch passed between these pieces" (15:17b) and God promised to Abram that he would indeed give him a son. Through that son, the entire land of Palestine would be given to Abram's descendants.

This story sounds strange to our twenty-first-century ears, for it is describing a cultic practice we neither understand nor appreciate. What was going on here? And what does it have to do with God's fulfillment of God's promise of a son for Abram?

This incident is the next logical step begun with God's call to Abram to leave his city of Haran and follow God to Canaan. In that initial call, God promised Abram that he would be the father of a great nation through whom God would bless all humankind. That nation would be God's means by which all people would find shalom, joy, and ultimate meaning in life—"all the families of the earth shall be blessed" (Gen. 12:3) because of Abram.

So, according to the Genesis narrative, Abram did as God commanded and migrated to Canaan, establishing himself in God's land. But Abram still had no child, and without a child to be his heir, God's promise to bless all the peoples of the earth through Abram's descendants would be an impossibility. Genesis 15 tells the second story about Abram's commitment to God. It is the story of the covenant made between God and Abram that indicated he was the chosen of God, and that chosenness would be demonstrated through the birth of a son.

In the ancient Near East, the covenant was the primary means by which agreements were made. Written contracts were not normally used. We know about the nature of this covenant making through the Mari tablets that explain the covenanting process in detail. It is those tablets that make sense out of this otherwise mystifying story.

When two participants would come to binding agreement upon a matter, they would verbally make the agreement to each other. Then, those making the agreement would slay a bird or an animal, divide it in two, and lay the two pieces as mirror images upon the ground but with a pathway between them. Then those making the agreement would walk between the halved animals while repeating the agreement before witnesses. In essence, the covenant maker, by walking through the halved animal or bird, was declaring "may you do the same to me and cut me in half if I break this covenant with you."

If, on the other hand, one of the parties to the covenant was not making any commitment, he merely observed. But those making the covenant would walk between the halved animals. Thus, the covenant was binding only upon those who walked through the halved animals—so binding, in fact, that if one party to the covenant broke the agreement, the other would have the legal right to kill him!

In the dramatic story told in Genesis 15, God made a covenant with Abram to create an entire nation through him. Then God made that covenant specific by promising this nearly 100-year-old man would physically sire a son through his 100-year old wife!

The Bible tells us that Abram "believed the Lord, and the Lord reckoned it to him as righteousness" (Gen. 15:6). But God wanted to confirm his promise to Abram; he wished to make a binding covenant with this wanderer. Therefore, God instructed Abram to slay several animals and birds, cut them in half and lay their divided bodies over against each other, creating a pathway between them. Then God, in the symbolic form of a fire pot and torch, passed between the halved animals, repeating his promise to Abram.

It is particularly notable that it is ***God*** who passes through the halved animals, repeating the covenant. It is ***not Abram***. Abram sits and observes. In other words, it is God who makes the covenant with Abram, not Abram with God. God is the actor. Abram is the recipient. It is God who is taking all the risk—not Abram. God had bound himself securely to his promise—that Abram would have a son who would become the forebear of an entire nation through which all the world would be blessed. If God did not fulfill his promise, Abram would have the prerogative to "kill" him (that is to reject him as God). But God asked nothing of Abram. There was no response that would cause Abram to break covenant, no reason for God to "kill" him. And Abram chose to "believe the Lord." As a sign of this commitment by God to Abram, God changes his name to Abraham (17:5), from "exalted ancestor" to "ancestor of a multitude"!

This is the first clearly evident presentation and demonstration of the concept of grace in the scriptures. And it is a clear indication of God's choosing of Abraham to become the "ancestor of a multitude," the founder of the Jewish people and of the nation of Israel.

Jesus and John the Baptizer. Because we affirm Jesus as the Second Person of the Trinity, God the Son, we don't often think of Jesus as being "chosen" by God. But he was. And this was a significant theme throughout the gospel records. A good example is Luke 1:68–79, the prayer of thanksgiving spoken by the priest Zechariah upon the birth of his son, John (the Baptizer).

In this prayer, Zechariah differentiates between the birth of "my messenger" and "the messenger of the covenant"—two very distinct people. Zechariah's emphasis upon "my messenger" refers to his newborn son, John, and is in the final four verses of the prayer (vv. 76–79). The "messenger of the covenant," on the other hand, is Jesus of Nazareth (not yet born, and therefore not yet named—see Luke 2:21) and is the focus of verses 68–75.

Although one would think that Zechariah would start with his son (John the Baptizer), instead he begins with Jesus, the "messenger of the covenant." The coming of John was for the purpose of announcing God's coming action through Jesus, and therefore it is Jesus who is the center of Zechariah's prophecy, not his son. It was not about John!

Zechariah's Song has become one of the standard liturgies of the church, called "*The Benedictus*" (because it begins, "Blessed be the Lord God of Israel"). The hymn is set in a psalm mode which, by its very nature, blesses and glorifies God. It is a commentary of the extraordinary events that have taken place over those few months—the announcement that God is on the move in the miraculous conceptions that have occurred in both Elizabeth and Mary, the birth of Zechariah's son who is destined to be a great prophet of God and forerunner (and foreteller) of the coming of God's "messenger of the covenant," and the weaving of both John's story and Jesus's story into one tapestry of redemption.

God's action, Zechariah proclaims, is "to raise up a mighty savior for us in the house of his servant David" (vs. 69). That was the principle objective of God's amazing action over the previous months. John is simply a key player in the acting of God's will, but he is not that savior. The coming of that person who would liberate God's people around the world was prophesied by God's prophets over hundreds of years (vs. 70). The salvation that person will accomplish is comprehensive in its scope. It would be for humanity's "redemption" (vs. 68). But it would also be so that "we would be saved from our enemies and from the hand of all who hate us" (vs. 71). It would "show mercy" upon us but would also return God's people to "(Abraham's) holy covenant (with God)" (vs. 72), so that Israel, "being rescued from the hands of (its) enemies" will be able to live as a nation "in holiness and righteousness before (God) all our days" (vs. 75). This savior, this king, Zechariah proclaims, has been chosen by God from the very beginnings of time to bring salvation and liberation, not only to individual Israelites, but also to Israel and to all humanity.

And what is John's role in all this? "And you, child, will be called the prophet of the Most High, for you will go before the Lord (i.e., Jesus) to prepare his ways, to give knowledge of salvation to his people through the forgiveness of their sins" (vv. 76–77). Whereas Jesus is the Son of God Most High (vv. 32, 35), John is to be the Prophet of God Most High. His task is a single task: "'to prepare the way for Jesus" (vs. 76b). And John is to "prepare the way for Jesus" through two actions. First, he is to announce the coming of Jesus, to center the focus on "the messenger of the covenant" and not on "my messenger" and, therefore, to create a sense of eager anticipation among God's people. Second, he is to prepare people to be open and ready to receive the message, ministry, and call to them by Jesus by the act of "the forgiveness of their sins" (vs. 77b).

The ritual of water baptism was to be the means John would use to enable God's people to become reflective of their own greed, lust for power, and compulsion to dominate and control so that they would repent of such sin and thus become most receptive to the work that Jesus was to accomplish as "the messenger of the covenant." If the people were indeed open and receptive enough, Jesus would then be able to "give light to those who sit in darkness and in the shadow of death and to guide their feet into the way of shalom" (vs. 79). For that "shalom community," awaiting those willing to be so guided, would be a nation and a people committed to the building of their life together as a community of justice, equitable distribution of wealth, the elimination of poverty, and lives lived knitted together in God—the very definition of the Hebrew word, "shalom"!

What is particularly intriguing about the *Benedictus* is the inclusion of a number of people in God's choosing of them for specific purposes. Clearly, this psalm is centered upon God's choosing of Jesus to be "the messenger of the covenant" to give knowledge of salvation to his people by the forgiveness of their sins." But it is also about God's choosing of John the Baptizer to be "the messenger" who is to be "the prophet of the Most High" who will "go before the Lord to prepare his way."

What is even more intriguing is that it includes, by inference, other people to carry out God's choosing of Jesus and John. Thus, God has chosen the teenage Mary to be the mother of Jesus, Elizabeth and Zechariah to be the elderly parents of John, and Zechariah to be the one who will announce to the Jewish world what God has done through the birth of these two boys. Thus, it is not only the Son of God who is chosen. God also chooses the one who announces his coming, a teenage girl and her carpenter fiancé, a minor Jewish priest and his elderly wife. It takes a host of people to bring about the fulfilling of God's vision for the world.

God as the Calling God

We conclude our exploration of God the Caller by looking directly at God as the God who calls us into his service. As we do so, we may discover that the God who created us not only chose every one of us to follow him but called us to live out that choice in the very priorities and commitments of our lives.

There are 137 direct references in scripture to God calling a people (nation), a church, and individuals to specific service in God's Kingdom.

Israel

An emphasis throughout the Old Testament is that Israel is not only a *chosen* people, but also a *called* people. They are called to be on a mission—to create a society as God intends it to be, to live out that society before the eyes of the world, and in light of that lived-out witness, to become the example to other nations of what their societies can be like if they, too, embrace Yahweh as their God. This is nowhere so clearly and poetically stated than in Isaiah 55:1–11.

Isaiah 55:1–11 is a celebration of the covenant that exists between Yahweh and Israel. It is likened to an abundant and magnificent banquet hosted by God and given to Israel as God's gift to them and in which they can fully partake.

"Ho, everyone who thirsts, come to the waters; and you that have no money, come, buy and eat! Come, buy wine and milk without money and without price. Why do you spend your money for that which is not bread, and your labor for that which does not satisfy? Listen carefully to me, and eat what is good, and delight yourselves in rich food. Incline your ear, and come to me; listen, so that you may live. I will make with you an everlasting covenant, my steadfast, sure love for David" (55:1–3).

This is a statement of full, unadulterated grace. The banquet of the covenant is a free gift from God to Israel. It requires no money to purchase its food and drink. It demands no labor or action from the Israelites. It is God's free gift to Israel. They are simply to receive it and delight in God's abundant giving to them. All that Israel needs to do is to respond to God's covenantal love for them. They are to embrace it, to accept that they are already accepted, to believe that they are already loved by God—loved enough for him to make "an everlasting covenant" with them!

The text continues. "See, I made him a witness to the peoples, a leader and commander for the peoples. See, you shall call nations that you do not know, and nations that do not know you shall run to you, because of the Lord your God, the Holy One of Israel, for he has glorified you" (55:4–5).

God had made an "everlasting covenant" with David that continues down the centuries with Israel. This emphasis on the Davidic covenant is found throughout the warp-and-woof of Hebrew scripture. What makes this statement particularly noteworthy, however, is that the author extends that covenant to the world—the next logical step in the living out of God's covenant with Israel.

"See, you shall call nations that you do not know, and nations that do not know you shall run to you." That is, God's people are called by God to reach out to and impact the entire world—both the peoples of the world and the nations (that is, the corporate entities of the peoples) of the world. God's grace, originally reserved for Israel, will be brought by Israel (and, later the Church) to all the world. God's people are found far beyond Israel itself, for God is at work to transform all humanity and the societies created by humanity everywhere throughout the world.

This Old Testament lesson then continues with well-known words. "Seek the Lord while he may be found, call upon him while he is near; let the wicked forsake their way, and the unrighteous their thoughts; let them return to the Lord, that he may have mercy on them, and to our God, for he will abundantly pardon. For my thoughts are not your thoughts, nor are your ways my ways, says the Lord. For as the heavens are higher than the earth, so are my ways higher than your ways and my thoughts than your thoughts" (55:6–9).

God's grace, once offered exclusively to Israel, is now offered to the peoples and institutions of the whole world. These people and political, economic, and religious systems—whoever they are and wherever they may be—can become the world as God intended it to be, the community of shalom. All the peoples and systems of the world can live out of a framework of justice, equitable distribution of wealth, the elimination of poverty, and personal and corporate relationship with God and each other. God's grace is for all.

All it requires to access that grace on the part of people and of the institutions of society is for those people and systems to "seek the Lord," to "call upon God," to "forsake their (former) ways and thoughts," to "return to the Lord." If they so choose to act, then Yahweh will "have mercy on them" and will "abundantly pardon" them. And it is Israel (and later, the Church) that is called by God to extend that offer of grace through their presence, prayers, practice, proclamation, and their powerful work for the transformation of whatever society in which they find themselves.

Why is God a god of grace, acting with such compassion to all the world? "My thoughts are not your thoughts, nor are your ways my ways, says the Lord. For as the heavens are higher than the earth, so are my ways higher than your ways and my thoughts than your thoughts" (vv. 8–9). God's whole embrace of grace as the underlying premise of God's very being in relationship to humanity exceeds and even defies all human imagination (cf. 64:4; Rom. 11:33; I Cor. 2:9; Eph. 3:20). Grace permeates the very being of God. We cannot conceive of any human being or any entity so grace-centered and grace-dominated. But this is who Yahweh is. And this is what our God yearns for each human and all human society to discover and embrace for themselves.

And how do we know that this promise of God is true? "For as the rain and the snow come down from heaven, and do not return there until they have watered the earth, making it bring forth and sprout, giving seed to the sower and bread to the eater, so shall my word be that goes out from my mouth; it shall not return to me empty" (vv. 10-11).

The Church

But not only is Israel a people called by God to serve God in the world. So, too, is the Church. This is perhaps most magnificently stated by Paul the Apostle in Paul's "Great Commission," given in Romans 8:26–39.

To put this powerful passage into context, we must review the entirety of Romans 8. In Romans 8:1–11, Paul had declared that it is through Jesus Christ that God had fulfilled the obligations of all people and the systems they have constructed to order their life together. All the demands that our systems make upon us, all the demands that the specter of death and corruptibleness of our own personalities make upon us, have been met and satisfied in Christ. In his death, Christ has met all the conditions of the law, all the conditions of the systems. He faced the worst of death for us, he plumbed the depths of human depravity—both individual and collective depravity. In that humiliating act, Christ took upon himself all that personal, corporate, and systemic evil could ever do. By taking such evil upon himself, Christ has liberated us—and all human institutions—from evil's complex grasp.

In Romans 8:12–17, Paul seeks to explain the unique relationship between God and those who are the chosen of God by using the Roman metaphor of adoption. God has acted through Jesus Christ to adopt us into God's family. Because we have been chosen and adopted by God into God's family, we are full heirs to all the benefits of such legal association with God. We are heirs to the tradition of a politics of justice, an economics of equity and elimination of poverty, a religion of family relationship with God and all our brothers and sisters of that family. Further, we are "joint-heirs" with Jesus or, in other words, on equal footing with Jesus in our shared inheritance. Jesus may be the natural son and we adopted children, but we are no less children of our adopting father-God than is Jesus. So, no matter how we might feel about ourselves at any given time, the real issue before us is not whether we are chosen and accepted by God. We are! That's what the gospel is all about. The only issue we face is whether we can accept that we are accepted.

In Romans 8:18–25, Paul moves into what is probably the most profound insight in Romans 8. Salvation doesn't just have to do with us as individuals, Paul asserts. Nor does it have to do solely with the redemption of our political, economic, and religious systems. It has to do with God's transformation of the entire cosmos (8:18–25). Although the universe is in danger of always "running down" (the second law of thermodynamics) and is consequently subject to decay and sin, its collapse is not inevitable. God is at work in the cosmos through Jesus Christ for its own salvation. It is to experience, in Christ, the same "freedom" and "glory" as do "the children of God."

What Paul has done in Romans 8 has been to argue a threefold salvation. Jesus has died in order to bring about the redemption of individuals (e.g., Rom. 8:12–17), the salvation of the corporate structures of society (e.g., 8:1–11) and then, finally, the redemption of the entire universe from entropy and decay (e.g., 8:18–25). Thus, Paul understood salvation as being, at one and the same time, individual, corporate, and cosmic; of being personal, social, and systemic. For to Paul, Christ had come to save the entire created order and all that is in it. That was the kind of God Paul embraced. And that is the kind of God he asks us to embrace, as well.

Now, in Romans 8:26–39, Paul concludes this remarkable chapter on the comprehensive nature of God's salvation of life.

First, he returns to his theme of adoption first presented in 8:12–17 to summarize his doctrine of election. Sometimes, Paul reminds us, we don't *feel* very called or adopted by God! The world tumbles in upon us. Problems and conflicts and issues arise in our lives. The political, economic, or values systems around us treat us harshly because we don't conform as Christians to their expectations. Sometimes those systems act unjustly and even oppressively toward us; sometimes we feel taken advantage of and even exploited. And sometimes we simply feel beaten down by the opposition because of our "long obedience in the same direction."[42]

It is at such times that we can very much feel like giving in, of simply accepting defeat, or of wanting to hide away and let life pass us by. But it is precisely at that time and sensing our depression that God's Spirit goes to work on our behalf. The Holy Spirit both buoys up our beaten-down spirit and even prays for us before the throne of grace. And through the Spirit's intercession, God strengthens us and renews our determination so that we might continue that "long obedience in the same direction." It is the very intervention of the Holy Spirit on our behalf when life becomes darkest for us that is the true indicator that we are, indeed, called and adopted by God to be God's children.

---

[42] First introduced in the book, *Beyond Good and Evil* by Friedrich Nietzsche, this phrase was popularized by Eugene H. Peterson in his book, *A Long Obedience in the Same Direction: Discipleship in an Instant Society* (Downers Grove, IL: InterVarsity Press, 1980).

Having asserted the work of the Spirit in the lives of these Roman Christians, Paul then reminds them of what it means to be called and chosen by God. He does so by reciting to them the process by which they are transformed from people of the "flesh" to people of the "Spirit," from people who once rejected God to people who are now embraced by and embrace God. That order that Paul declares here is that each of us are "foreknown" by God, then "predestined," then "called," then "justified," and then "glorified" (vv. 29–30).

What Paul is reminding the Roman Christians here is that God set God's heart on them long before they were even aware of God ("foreknew"), God chose them to be people who would be "conformed to the image of his Son" ("predestined"), God then called them to God's self, so wooing them to God's self that God proved irresistible to them ("called"), God redeemed them through Christ ("justified"), and has continued to work within them and through them to more closely become "Christ-ones" in and to the Roman world ("glorified"). And this God did within a "large family" (literally, "with many brothers [and sisters]"), so that this profound change in and to us is not done in isolation but to an entire community who is being wooed to God and is then being used by God to change the world around them.

Can you imagine what good news this was to people who were feeling overwhelmed, dominated, and even crushed by Rome? What is intriguing about this statement is that Paul is not trying so much to make a theological statement (even though it is a most profound theological statement) as he is seeking to be pastoral. He is taking notice of the hard demands and the power of the opposition that faces the Christians in Rome as they seek to be faithful to Christ in the very heart of the Evil Empire. So he is seeking to buoy up these Roman Christians in the midst of their struggle—not by speaking spiritual superficialities to them, but by using theology to minister to these over-extended Christians! Thus, theology really shouldn't be done in the ivory towers of academia as much as it should be done out in the streets and alleys of the city, where what might appear to be intellectually offensive shows itself to be powerfully therapeutic as Christians struggle to live out the gospel while under the attack of the principalities and powers of this world.

That is exactly what Paul deals with in his closing statement of Romans 8. And that closing statement has provided inspiration and hope to millions of Christians over thousands of years, as they have sought to faithfully live out the gospel in the midst of systems of oppression, exploitation, and domination.

> What then are we to say about these things (such persecution and oppression of us Christians)? If God is for us, who (of consequence could possibly be) against us? He who did not withhold his own Son, but gave him up for all of us, will he not with him also give us everything else? Who will bring any charge against God's elect? It is God who justifies. Who is to condemn? It is Christ Jesus, who died, yes, who was raised, who is at the right hand of God, who indeed intercedes for us. Who will separate us from the love of Christ? Will hardship, or distress, or persecution, or famine, or nakedness, or peril, or sword? As it is written, "For your sake we are being killed all day long; we are accounted as sheep to be slaughtered."
>
> No, in all these things we are more than conquerors through him who loved us. For I am convinced that neither death, nor life, nor angels, nor rulers, nor things present, nor things to come, nor powers, nor height, nor depth, nor anything else in all creation, will be able to separate us from the love of God in Christ Jesus our Lord (8:31–39).

This is a virtual crescendo of praise, meant to sweep up the reader in worship and adoration. But it is also an exceedingly profound statement that we need to examine carefully. For in a few sentences, it captures the very essence and the very power of the Gospel of Jesus Christ!

Paul begins this closing statement by reminding the Roman Christians, "You face overwhelming, unilateral power when you face the resistance of individuals to the Gospel, of the political domination by Roman law and military might, of the economic power of the empire and the religious sway of Jewish, Greek, and Roman priests. You face even greater power when you confront the spiritual and demonic darkness that lies behind these systems and provides them their authority and potency. Who are we Christians who come up against such power? Why, we are those who have been foreknown, predestined, called, justified, and glorified by God! We have the greatest power of all—God—on our side. And if God is for us, who or what of any consequence could possibly mount a winning campaign against us?"

Romans 8 ends with a profound statement of power. It is declaring that we, as God's resurrection people, are unstoppable—not because we are so personally powerful, but because we serve a God of power who works in and through us.

Paul develops his argument by posing a number of questions (vv. 33–35). "Who will bring criminal charges against God's elect and possibly have his accusation succeed?" "Who is the judge who is going to condemn us in a court of law?" "Who can separate us from the love of Christ by throwing us in jail?" "Can anything that the systems throw at us—hardship, distress, persecution, famine, nakedness, peril, sword (all of these are punishments of the Roman legal system)—stop us?"

It is obvious when one looks at these questions that Paul has in mind the Roman legal system. He is saying that neither prosecutor nor judge nor jailer nor even executioner can intimidate those who belong to Christ. Each question is answered, in their order, "God decides what is good or evil, not the prosecutor. It is Jesus Christ who condemns—not the judge. It is God who protects those who belong to Christ, no matter what the jailer or the executioner or any lackey of the state might try to do to them."

In other words, what Paul is stating here poetically is that, in the final analysis, nothing that a political, economic, or religious system or that individuals might do to a Christian or to the church can possibly stop God's actions to transform the world. There is no opposition big enough to beat God!

But Paul is not through yet. He continues, "In all these things we are more than conquerors through him who loved us. For I am convinced that neither death nor life, nor angels, nor rulers, neither things present nor things to come, nor powers, nor height, nor depth, nor anything else in all creation, will be able to separate us from the love of God in Christ Jesus our Lord" (8:37–39).

Paul creates four parallel constructs here. He states, first, that neither death nor life can separate us from God; what "the powers" may do to our bodies will not stop the work we have started for Christ and his kingdom. Second, neither angels nor rulers can stop us, "angels" referring in this context to those spiritual forces in the universe that are demonic while "rulers" refers to those who head the Roman and Jewish political, economic, and religious establishments. Third, neither "things present" nor "things to come" (or better translated "neither what happens today nor what may happen tomorrow")—thus, not even time can stop us. Fourth, neither "powers nor height nor depth" can stop the Christian effort; "powers" is referring to the cosmic evil powers (Satan and his minions), while "height nor depth" is an astrological term. Many ancient peoples believed that their destiny was preordained by the stars. "Height" (*hupsoma*) was a technical astronomical term for a star at its zenith and consequently of greatest influence upon humanity, while "depth" (*hathos*) was a star on the horizon, waiting to rise and to gain control over a person.

Thus, what Paul is saying, although it appears to be most poetic, is in reality an extremely profound statement. He is saying, "Whether you live or whether they kill you; whether you are persecuted by the political, economic, and religious powers of our society or by demonic powers; whether you are influenced most by your past, your present, or the fear of the future; whether you face cosmic evil powers or some other abusive force which doesn't occur to Paul at this time (i.e., "nor anything else in all creation")—nothing, absolutely nothing can separate you Roman Christians from the love of God that comes to you in Christ Jesus your Lord!"

Thus, in these magnificent words, Paul sums up his entire argument given in Romans 7– 8. Sin is comprehensive. It is individual; it is social; it is economic; it is political; it is religious; it is cosmic. It is personal; it is corporate; it is universal. "But where sin abounds, grace does much more abound"! For God has provided for the salvation of individuals, of their systems and society, and even of the cosmos. And for you who are chosen, called, adopted, redeemed, and transformed by Christ, you cannot be beaten back by sin in any form. You may be accused before the law. You may be found guilty by the state. You may be condemned to prison or even to execution. You may face hardship, distress, persecution, famine, nakedness, peril, or sword. But you can never be defeated. And you cannot be defeated because you are on God's side, and God is going to win. God has the final power. So, even if they take away your life, they still can't win—for you will wake up in the arms of Jesus! With such a way of looking at both their life and mission, there was now no way for the enemies of Christianity to defeat the Christian effort to transform the Roman (or any other) empire into "the kingdom of our Lord and of his Christ"!

This is a scripture about the power of God as expressed through the Christian gospel. God's resurrection people are unstoppable—not because we ourselves are so powerful, but because God is. We are called as God's people to work for the kingdom of God. And when we are so centered on Christ and working for his kingdom, then nothing can stop us (8:35), not even the systems of the world nor the Evil One (8:38). Rather, we are more than conquerors (8:37) who cannot be separated from the love of God in Christ Jesus our Lord (8:39). Only as we commit ourselves to work for God's kingdom, keeping before ourselves the vision of the world as God intended it to be, can we have a significant impact upon the world as it is. And it is only in being absorbed by such work do we discover why it is that God chose, called, adopted, redeemed, justified, and glorified us as his own!

This is Paul's "Great Commission"—that life-centering objective to which we've been called. This is the great privilege we have been given as we seek to follow our resurrected Lord and Savior, Jesus Christ, into his world to seek its transformation into his kingdom by using the relational power he has placed at our disposal.

Individuals

But it is not simply Israel or the Church—communities of faith—that are called by God. It is all of us as individuals. Each one of us has been created and chosen for a purpose. And God calls us to that work that he has for us—whether it is a single work at a single point of time, or whether it is a lifetime vocation. Let's look at two examples in scripture.

Gideon was a judge and warlord of Israel during the period of the judges who destroyed the power of the rival Midianite nation and gave Israel forty years of ensuing peace. But what was most significant about Gideon in regard to our present study was his call from God to assume leadership of Israel's army and to destroy the Midianites.

At the time of God's call to Gideon, he was a young man, a farmhand working for his father. While resting from his labors in the heat of the sun, Gideon meets God under an oak tree in Ophrah. God says to Gideon, "Go in this might of yours and deliver Israel from the hand of Midian; I hereby commission you" (Judges 6:14b). Gideon demurs, offering not-very-convincing rationale for not assuming the responsibility. The patient God replies, "But I will be with you, and you shall strike down the Midianites, every one of them" (vs. 16).

Gideon still is uncertain, asking for proof. So God gives him proof that he is meeting with God and not just a stranger. God commands Gideon to prepare a meal for him (which Gideon ought to have offered to do as a necessary element of mideastern hospitality—but he didn't). Then, when Gideon brings the meal to him, the Lord touches the food with his staff and it immediately bursts into flames and is consumed.

But Gideon is still truly unconvinced. Pretending to be convinced, Gideon cautiously destroys an altar to the god Ba'al (he does it at night, so that no one could see him do it) and when he receives the inevitable negative reaction by Midian, he calls in the Israelite troops. But he is still afraid to follow God's command and attack

Midian. So God meets with Gideon once again, and Gideon places his challenge before God. "I am going to lay a fleece of wool on the threshing floor; if there is dew on the fleece alone, and it is dry on all the ground, then I shall know that you will deliver Israel by my hand, as you have said" (vs. 37). The next morning, that is what Gideon finds; God has been faithful to the challenge.

But that's still not enough to convince Gideon. He meets again with God and says, "Let me, please, make trial with the fleece just once more; let it be dry only on the fleece, and on all the ground let there be dew" (vs. 39b). The next day, that is exactly what happens. Gideon bows to the inevitable, accepts God's call, and proceeds to go into battle against the Midianites, destroying their capability of mounting an attack again.

The story of Gideon ends badly. He is successful in conquering the foes of Israel and guides the tribes into forty years of peace. But he also builds significant wealth and power for himself, and finally ends creating an idol and requiring worship of it by the people of Israel. Thus he leads Israel back into apostasy.

But the point of the story of Gideon for our purposes is the demonstration of the amazing patience of God with us. Gideon resisted God's call to him. Consequently, he needed repeated and significant indications from God that this call was genuine, and that he needed to accept it. He finally did accept it—probably because he saw no viable alternative. And both he and the nation prospered because of his obedience to that call. But Gideon also used that call to build his own position, power, wealth, and influence in Israel. So he is as much a sign to us of the misuse of call for one's own benefit, thus being a warning to us as we seek to be faithful to God in God's call to us in our city.

Timothy. In II Tim. 1:1–14, Paul the Apostle begins to reflect upon the faith journey of Timothy, a disciple of Paul's. Paul writes, "I am reminded of your sincere faith, a faith that lived first in your grandmother Lois and your mother Eunice and now, I am sure, lives in you" (1:5). Paul has seen faith in Christ passed from grandparent to parent to son. But now Timothy has come to the place in his faith journey when he is about to take on the call of a church to be its pastor. Thus, Paul urges Timothy to live out that faith he has learned from others in his own faithful actions within the church and in public life. "Rekindle the gift of God that is within you," he urges Timothy, "for God did not give us a spirit of cowardice, but rather a spirit of power and of love and of self-discipline" (vv. 6, 7).

How is faith in Christ to be lived out in faithful action? In the ministry to which Timothy is being called, what should faithful action look like? Paul states that he expects of Timothy "power," "love," and "self-discipline." He does not expect "cowardice." And Paul adds, "Do not be ashamed, then, of the testimony about our Lord . . . but join with me in suffering for the gospel, relying on the power of God . . . carry out God's purpose and grace" (vv. 8–9). He expects Timothy not to be embarrassed at the gospel, to be willing to suffer, and to carry out God's purpose in his ministry.

Paul then moves on to reflect on his own faith and its faithful living out in the public arenas of both church and state. "For this gospel I was appointed a herald and an apostle and a teacher, and for this reason I suffer as I do. But I am not ashamed, for I know the one in whom I have put my trust, and I am sure that he is able to guard until that day what I have entrusted to him" (vv. 11–12).

Paul has invested his life and all his service in the belief that Jesus is Lord and Christ, and is sufficient for Paul's salvation. God's redemptive grace "was given to us in Christ Jesus before the ages began, but it has now been revealed through the appearing of our Savior Christ Jesus, who abolished death and brought life and immortality to light through the gospel" (vv. 9–10). And he has lived out that embrace of belief by becoming a bold herald of the gospel, an apostle and a teacher of the Christian faith, drawing people to Christ, founding churches and getting those churches engaged in public life. "For this reason I suffer as I do"—often the consequence of living such a convictional life. Thus, Paul is implying, Timothy ought to imitate Paul. Timothy can know that Paul's faith in Christ is authentic because of the concrete ways that faith has been lived out in Paul's actions.

But now, Timothy has come to the place where he is ready to leave the protective wings of Paul as his mentor and teacher—as well as to leave Lois and Eunice—and embrace "a holy calling, not according to our works but according to God's own purpose and grace, given to us in Christ Jesus before the ages began" (vs. 9). The call now goes beyond Paul's, Lois's, and Eunice's expectations, for it is God's call to Timothy. And Timothy is ready to accept that call.

So Paul wishes for Timothy. "Hold to the standard of sound teaching that you have heard from me, in the faith and love that are in Christ Jesus. Guard the good treasure entrusted to you, with the help of the Holy Spirit living in us" (vv. 13–14). Paul has invested much in the spiritual formation and leadership development of Timothy, as have both Lois and Eunice. And now he is asking Timothy to wisely use that investment in acting out his faith.

There is a very intriguing word that Paul uses in his instructions to Timothy that gives us insight into Paul's perspective of his relationship with Timothy. The word "standard" (vs. 13) in Greek has the sense of a model or a preliminary draft or design about it; it was used a great deal in the discipline of architecture to suggest a preliminary drawing or actual construction that tests out the architectural worthiness of a structure before it is built of permanent materials and can no longer be changed. Thus, what Paul is saying to Timothy is, "When you were being mentored by me and learning from me (as well as from your grandmother and mother before I came along) how to live and act as a Christian and as a church leader in today's Roman world, you constructed for yourself a model of what it means to do ministry. Well, now it's time to move from model to reality. Take all that you learned from those years Lois, Eunice, and I invested in you, and carry out that model in your ministry as you go forth into the real world with all of its trials and temptations. "Guard the good treasure entrusted to you," and use it wisely so that the church is strongly built, people come to know Christ, and the church impacts the society around it bringing that society closer to God's intentions for it. Do this, "with the help of the Holy Spirit living in (you)." Thus, Timothy, you are now called to faithfully live out and practice the faith invested in you by us and which you so eagerly embraced for yourself. That is our call to you for ministry."

So how well did Timothy do in the living out of his call? We don't know, because he is not further mentioned in the Bible. But, according to Eusebius, he eventually became the first bishop of the city of Ephesus, and there is substantive evidence that he was martyred there on Jan. 22, 97 AD because of his opposition to the licentious festivities surrounding the cult of Diana (an Ephesian goddess). So, if this tradition is right, then Timothy was most faithful in carrying out his calling from God.

Gideon and Timothy were two people called to specialized ministries. They are not alone in scripture. Rather scripture is full of the calls of all sorts of people to all kinds of ministry. We will examine in the next chapter a far more comprehensive panoply of both the number of people and the diversity of ministries to which not only clergy but primarily laity have been called. And many of those calls were to life and work as God's people in the city.

Conclusion

The focus of this book is on the reclaiming of the reality that lay-people are called as much by God as are clergy to the city. Laity are called as much as clergy to "live and move and have their being" in their city, to join in the building of life together in a community of faith, and there to work for the transformation of that city and their neighborhood into an approximation of the kingdom of God. So God's question, "What are you doing here, Christian?" is not a question solely to urban pastors. It is a question to all of us who are in the city because we believe God has called us there!

But to truly explore the city-changing power of called Christians, we must first examine the biblical doctrine of vocation ("call"). That requires us to examine three primary aspects of the biblical doctrine of call. First, we must examine that characteristic of God that is most ignored in much of theology—God as the One who creates, chooses, and calls us—which we have done in this and the previous chapters. Second, we must explore biblical teaching on those who are called to a specific vocation—such as urban lay ministry; we will do that in the next chapter. And, finally, we need to look hard at the nature of call itself; that will take us three chapters (Chapters 5 through 7) to explore.

In this and the previous chapters, we have examined God as the One who calls us. We have discovered an enormous amount of scripture that focuses upon God as Caller. And we have explored God as Caller by examining three separate but definitely related aspects of call—God as Creator, as the One Who Chooses, and God as Caller. The conclusion that I believe can be drawn from this exploration is the central role of God as Caller within nature, society, history; God's people as expressed through Israel and the Church; and in each one of our lives. God has a marvelous plan for the world—and we have the distinct privilege of being called to be an integral part of making that plan happen.

So we have explored God as Caller. Let us now begin the exploration of ourselves—we who are called by God to be a crucial part of God's city- and world-changing power. On to the next chapter!

Chapter 4

The Called

All that Christian laypeople want is what most clergy take for granted: the sure and certain call of God upon their lives.

The world today declares us all as insignificant, unimportant, and purposeless. It teaches us that we exist to be a spending (and sometimes earning) unit—a unit which keeps the economy going. Vocation declares the opposite. It says that we are created in the image of God, are redeemed by divine intervention, are chosen, and called to make a profound difference by serving Christ in a particular way in the world. That's why people flock to congregations that center their congregation in a personal experience with Christ which is lived out in their lay ministry in the city; those people want their lives to count for something besides "getting and spending."

A Lay Bible

One begins to capture the depth of the concept of vocation which moves throughout the Bible when one takes a look at the occupations of those most used by God in the Bible. We tend to think of the Bible being made up of "religious" people—people obedient to and carrying out the will of God in their lives. Indeed they were—but what comes as a shock is to realize that most of the spiritual leaders in both the Old and New Testaments were laypeople—not clergy!

In the Old Testament era, the professional religionists in Israel were the priests—both the Levitical priesthood and the Aaronic priesthood. The primary responsibility of the priests was to maintain the liturgy and rites of the temple and of Israelite worship, as laid down in the last four Books of Moses (Exodus, Leviticus, Numbers, Deuteronomy) and later works evolving from those books.

In the New Testament, there were three groups of religious leaders. The priests were the most powerful, and continued the tradition of their ancestors by maintaining the liturgy and rites of the magnificent temple built by Herod the Great in Jerusalem. They were organized under a "high priest" who moderated the "Sanhedrin," a body of seventy senior priests who made final adjudication on all religious, legal, and economic matters in Israel under the authority of Rome.

The Pharisees were the largest body of religious leaders in the New Testament. Pharisees were teachers of the law and therefore were the spiritual leaders of the synagogues—dispersed gatherings of Jews in every city and town who met on each Sabbath for the worship of God and the study of the Hebrew scriptures (the synagogue later became the model Christians used to create local churches throughout the Roman empire).

The Sadducees made up the third body of religious leaders during the period of the New Testament. Jesus refers to them as "scribes" and "lawyers," as well as "Sadducees." (Incidentally, do not confuse the New Testament use of the word "lawyer" with our use of that term to denote an "attorney at law"; ours is primarily a secular profession providing defense or prosecution of those who are on trial, whereas the lawyer of biblical times was a religious office interpreting the Mosaic law.) The primary responsibility of the Sadducees was as interpreters of the Law of Moses, for they were experts in that Law. They tended to hold an extremely conservative view of the Law, refusing to believe in anything (e.g., angels, heaven, the resurrection) not explicitly taught in Exodus, Leviticus, Numbers, or Deuteronomy.

When you list the most important people in the Bible, however, it is obvious that a vast majority of them were in occupations we would consider secular today. Abraham was a wealthy bedouin. Moses was a prince of Egypt and, in later life, a shepherd. Joshua was a military leader. Rahab was a prostitute. Samuel was a judge. Ruth was a farmer, wife, and mother. Saul, David and Samuel were all kings—as were Ahab, Hezekiah, and Josiah. Elijah was a settler, and Elisha was a farmer. Daniel was the mayor of Babylon. Nehemiah was the cupbearer to the Persian emperor and governor of Jerusalem. Esther was a queen of the Persian Empire. Joseph was a carpenter, and Mary was a wife and mother. Jesus was a carpenter, as was James his brother, following in the path of their father, Joseph. Peter was a fisherman, as was his brother Andrew. Mary and Martha were home-makers, but Mary Magdalene was likely a manager of a considerable estate and Joanna a part of King Herod Antipas's court.

Matthew was a tax-collector, Luke was a doctor, Paul was a tentmaker (but was in training to become a Pharisee), and John was also a fisherman.

Paul's understanding of his call is particular instructive. In I Cor. 9:16–27, he wrote, "I do not boast of preaching the gospel, since it is a duty which has been laid on me; I should be punished if I did not preach it! If I had chosen this work myself, I might have been paid for it, but as I have not, it is a responsibility which has been put into my hands" (9:16–17, New Jerusalem Bible).

What is intriguing about this statement are the assumptions of Paul that clearly underlie it. His occupation was that of a tentmaker; his vocation was a preacher of the gospel—for which he was not to be paid! This was not a job to him; it was a calling—perhaps even a calling he didn't particularly want to do. Rather, it was a duty, a responsibility laid upon him by God. He had not chosen to be a preacher, church-planter, missioner, and apostle; it had chosen him! He had been given this responsibility by God—and he was not going to be disobedient to this heavenly call (Acts 26:19).

Therefore, Paul concluded that each of us is called to run a particular race for Christ and His Kingdom; each of us is called to fight a particular fight (9:24, 26). We must "keep our eye on the prize," and the only legitimate prize for us who call ourselves Christians, Paul would suggest, is to be working for the coming of the Kingdom of God within the kingdoms of this world (including, for Paul, Rome).

But how do we "keep our eyes on the prize"? What does it take to win the race in which each of us is involved (vs. 24b)? To be effective in the ministry to which each of us is called requires us to hone our capacity, our ability, and our willingness to win that race—and that, in turn, requires training (vv. 25–27).

We have to be willing to build our capacity—to learn how to be in the right place at the right time and to take advantage of the opportunities that offer themselves to us. It means gaining real clarity on the mission toward which we are called and, consequently, to what we are ***not*** called. It means that we have to hone our skills in confronting and negotiating with the leaders of the systems of the world. But above all, it means being willing to get engaged even when it causes us extreme anxiety. We are only as effective for Christ and His Kingdom as we prepare and train ourselves and risk being engaged in public life.

Therefore, following Paul's lead, "I do not run aimlessly, nor do I box as though beating the air; but I punish my body and enslave it, so that after proclaiming to others I myself should not be disqualified" (9:26–27). In other words, when working for the Kingdom of God, no less than in working out in sports, "where there is no pain; there is no gain!"

The people who most dominated Old Testament history and were the most long-lasting in their influence were the prophets. It was Israel's prophets, and not its priests, who shaped the spiritual and political landscape of Israel. It was the prophet's interpretation of the Law; their insistence upon the king, priest, and people acting in justice; and their definition of true religion as "doing justice, loving mercy, and walking humbly with God" (Micah 6:8) which shaped Jewish self-understanding (even up to today) and set the stage for the coming of Jesus and of Christianity.

It is intriguing, therefore, to note how few of the prophets were themselves professional religionists. In reality, of the 21 major or writing prophets in the Old Testament, the occupation of five was in the political arena, six were professional prophets, two were farmers, one was a shepherd, one was a labor leader and artisan, five were unknown—and only two (Ezekiel and Zechariah) were priests![43] For example, the four great prophets of the "golden age" of prophecy—the eighth century BCE—included a prince (Isaiah), a farmer (Hosea), a shepherd (Amos), and a small town

[43] The occupations of the Old Testament writing and major prophets were as follows:

Prophet	Occupation
Moses	Prince, military leader, shepherd
Samuel	Judge (adjudicator of the Law)
Nathan	Court functionary
Elijah	Settler, prophet
Elisha	Farmer
Isaiah	Prince and politician
Jeremiah	Prophet
Ezekiel	Priest
Daniel	Statesman, mayor of Babylon
Hosea	Farmer
Joel	Prophet
Amos	Shepherd
Obadiah	Unknown
Jonah	Unknown
Micah	Small town artisan and labor leader
Nahum	Unknown
Habakkuk	Unknown
Zephaniah	Prince and politician
Haggai	Prophet
Zechariah	Priest
Malachi	Unknown

artisan and labor leader (Micah). It was people like these who were the outstanding spiritual leaders of Israel.

The same pattern holds true in the New Testament. Jesus was a carpenter. Although he was called "rabbi," that was a sign of respect being paid to him as an obviously wise teacher. But in reality, he had neither been ordained to the priesthood nor officially approved as a rabbi. He chose an itinerant lifestyle and ministry, and depended upon the generosity of strangers for his sustenance, but his work was that of a carpenter. The same can be said of his followers—the twelve disciples, the seven women that followed Jesus, and others who became Christians after Jesus's death and resurrection. Only one leader of the early church—Paul—was a truly approved and recognized religious leader. And he was eventually rejected by the Jewish religious aristocracy that had earlier ordained him.

The undeniable conclusion that must be drawn from biblical history is that God used laypeople as a primary instrument of mission, and to a much greater extent than clergy. It was not only ordained priests or clergy in whom God primarily invested the building of his people or whom he trusted with his Kingdom, but those who were fishermen, shepherds, statesmen, artisans, physicians, business people, military leaders, and carpenters.

Surprisingly, there are 155 distinct occupations named in the Bible, and the primary people called to serve God were from most of those occupations. Some left those occupations to serve God (e.g., Peter); some used their occupation as an economic base for carrying out their larger call (e.g., Paul). But most directly lived out their mission call from God through their occupation (e.g., David).

The indisputable fact is that God primarily worked through laypeople in the Bible and not religious leaders. He worked through them by enabling each of them to discover God's call to them to serve him in the world. That we have concentrated spiritual leadership of the people of God in the hands of the officially ordained is a travesty of biblical faith which saw relationship with God lived out in the marketplaces and homes and institutions of the world—and is a clue why today's church is in the trouble it is in.

Some Specific People of Vocation

Thus far, in this chapter, we have briefly examined the broad sweep of God's dependence upon laypeople faithfully responding to God's call, as God's means for bringing transformation into life. Let us now look more closely at some specific individuals—some well known and others who were quiet in their witness—as they discovered and acted upon God's call to them.

Epaphroditus

If we had to name a strategic person from scripture, the likelihood would be small that the person selected would be Epaphroditus. We know next to nothing about him except what can be deduced from Paul's brief mention of him in his letter to the Church in Philippi. Paul, likely writing to the Philippian church from his jail in Rome, makes mention of Epaphroditus.

> I think it necessary to send to you Epaphroditus—my brother and co-worker and fellow soldier, your messenger and minister to my need; for he has been longing for all of you, and has been distressed because you heard that he was ill. He was indeed so ill that he nearly died. But God had mercy on him, and not only on him but on me also, so that I would not have one sorrow after another. I am the more eager to send him, therefore, in order that you may rejoice at seeing him again, and that I may be less anxious. Welcome him then in the Lord with all joy, and honor such people, because he came close to death for the work of Christ, risking his life to make up for those services that you could not give me (Phil. 2:25–30).

Then, Paul mentions him one more time in this letter: "You Philippians indeed know that in the early days of the gospel, when I left Macedonia, no church shared with me in the matter of giving and receiving, except you alone. For even when I was in Thessalonica, you sent me help for my needs more than once. . . I have been paid in full and have more than enough; I am fully satisfied, now that I have received from Epaphroditus the gifts you sent, a fragrant offering, a sacrifice acceptable and pleasing to God" (4:15–18).

Beyond these few words about him, we know nothing about Epaphroditus. He does not appear elsewhere in the Bible nor in any historical records of the day nor even in church tradition. We don't know who he was, what his status was in the church in Philippi, nor his work nor life. There is no evidence to suggest that he was a clergyperson of the church, but rather an ordinary layperson. All that we know of Epaphroditus, we must conclude from these brief statements by Paul. We know, for example, that he lived in Philippi and was an active part of the church there. We know that he bore a substantive gift to Paul while the apostle was imprisoned in Rome—and since it was likely a money gift, this tells us that the church saw him as being both scrupulously honest and faithful to the performance of a task. We know from Paul's response to the gift that it was significant encouragement to the apostle, both for what it was and for the esteem it represented in which the church held Paul; this esteem and encouragement was likely borne by Epaphroditus to Paul, as well as the gift itself. We know that Epaphroditus became seriously ill in Rome to such an extent that Paul was afraid he would die. But he had recovered sufficiently to be ready to return and was apparently anxious to return. And so Paul sent him on his way, bearing the letter to that church that has now become the biblical book of Philippians. And that is all we know about Epaphroditus.

But we know something else about Epaphroditus as well. We know from what Paul wrote that Epaphroditus did not perceive himself simply as a package and message carrier; he was no postman. He had come to Rome to minister to Paul, and to do so in the stead of and on behalf of the Philippian church. And the package and message were only a part of that larger mission.

Thus, Epaphroditus felt called by God to this mission. What was significant about this call was that it was a short-term call. Who knows what the larger calling of his life was? But for the moment, his calling was to care for and encourage Paul. And that is exactly what Epaphroditus did. Therefore, he is an excellent model to us of call—illustrating that one's call need not be for a lifetime or of a monumental nature so that the world can stand amazed. One's call can be for only a short season and may only minister to one person—but it is every bit as important and every bit as strategic to Christ and his kingdom—for it is accomplishing what God wants accomplished in that time and place for the people for whom it is intended. That is the power of the call of Epaphroditus.

Hosea

The faithful living out of Hosea's call is one of the saddest and most tragic stories occurring in scripture. It is therefore a message to us that faithfulness to one's call does not necessarily mean happiness, success, nor even a sense of fulfillment in executing that call.

Hosea 1:2–10 is one of the most dramatic prophecies in the Old Testament. This prophecy is not in words only but is acted out. Such acting out was a popular form of prophecy, in which the prophet engages in symbolic actions to dramatize his words; it is, in essence, "putting his money where his mouth is." Isaiah did this by giving his children symbolic names (Isaiah 7:3, 14; 8:3, 8); Jeremiah wore a yoke to symbolize Judah's coming submission to Babylon (Jer. 27–28); and Ezekiel tells of his grief at his wife's death to share with Judah God's grief in destroying Jerusalem (Ezek. 24:15–27). But nobody's action prophecy was as dramatic and as personally life-impacting as was Hosea's.

Hosea was a prophet in the northern kingdom of Israel during the reign of Jeroboam II (793–753 BCE). From the text, we know that he was a farmer by trade. But he was also a lay prophet.

In Hosea 1:1, the prophet names four kings of Judah whose combined reigns filled the period Hosea prophesied to Israel. This may imply that Hosea's prophecies were so disturbing to King Jeroboam of Israel and made the prophet so rejected in that nation that he had to escape to the southern kingdom of Judah, living his final years in that kingdom. Hosea was a contemporary of the prophets Isaiah and Micah in Judah.

The acted out prophecy of Hosea is found in Hosea 1:2–10. God instructs Hosea to take a whore as his wife. He chooses Gomer, daughter of Diblaim. Outside of her father, nothing is known about Gomer except that she is "a wife of whoredom." She might have been a cult prostitute who had sexual intercourse with men as an acting out of the escapades of the Canaanite gods Ba'al and Astarte (Ashera) whose frequent sexual unions guaranteed the fertility of the lands. On the other hand, she may have been simply a harlot. But whichever she was, God instructs Hosea to select a prostitute to be his wife because "Israel commits great whoredom by forsaking Yahweh."

God then instructs Hosea to have children by Gomer. He does so, and names the first "Jezreel," the second "Lo-ruhamah" and the third "Lo-ammi."

The names of Hosea's children are significant. "Jezreel" was the name of a most beautiful and fertile valley where Gideon won a great victory for the Lord. It is also the name of that valley's chief city where the Israelite general Jehu assassinated King Joram, Joram's mother Queen Jezebel, and all the kin of the house of Omri and Ahab who had ruled the northern kingdom for 27 years. Jehu had then become the new king of Israel, founding a dynasty that would reign for 98 years, of which Jeroboam II would be its next-to-last king (his son, Zechariah would reign for only six months). By naming his son Jezreel, Hosea is reminding Israel of its magnificent beginnings as God brought the Hebrews into the Promised Land and this fertile valley and under the judges, defeated their enemies. But God is also reminding them of the bloodshed, destroying of dynasties, and violence that was begotten by violence. As Omri had overthrown the previous Israelite monarchy, Ahab had sought to convert Israel from loyalty to Yahweh to that of Ba'al and the Jehu dynasty had been birthed in the bloodshed that had destroyed the Omri dynasty, so "the house of Jehu" would be ended by the violent death of its final king, Zechariah. What goes around comes around as violence begets violence.

The second child of Hosea and his first daughter was named "Lo-ruhamah." That name means "no mercy" (literally, "she has not received mercy"). By naming his daughter in this way, Hosea was proclaiming to King Jeroboam and to Israel that the northern kingdom was now outside the mercy of God, for God had withdrawn his mercy in the light of Israel's unfaithfulness to the "marriage covenant" between Himself and them. Intriguingly, Hosea is careful to point out, "But I will have pity on the house of Judah (the southern kingdom) and I will save them by the Lord their God; I will not save them by bow, or by sword, or by war, or by horses, or by horsemen" (1:7). The northern kingdom of Israel will be destroyed by Assyria, but God would rescue Judah from Assyria, and would do so not by military power or strategy but by God's direct intervention. And this, of course, is exactly what happened (II Kings 17:5–23; 18:13- 19:37).

The third child of Hosea was named "Lo-ammi." This is the most powerful name. Lo-ammi means, in Hebrew, "Not My People." This is a direct reversal of the traditional formula used in Israel to describe its relationship with God, "I shall be God to you, and you shall be my people" (Exod. 6:6–7; Lev. 26:12; Deut. 26:17–19). Now, Hosea declares through the name of his third child, "You are not my people and I am not your God"! Israel has been divorced from God! God has cancelled the covenant between God and Israel because of Israel's "lust" after other gods, other nations (treaties with Assyria that eventually rob them of their independence), and political and economic systems that reward the powerful with wealth and control while oppressing, exploiting, and dominating the people. God can take their harlotry no longer, and now separates himself from the northern kingdom forever. Their demise at the hands of Assyria is now only a matter of time.

But the prophecy doesn't end there. Hosea concludes this horrible message with these words: "Yet the number of the people of Israel shall be like the sand of the sea, which can be neither measured nor numbered; and in the place where it was said to them, "You are not my people," it shall be said to them "Children of the living God." The people of Judah and the people of Israel shall be gathered together, and they shall appoint for themselves one head; and they shall take possession of the land, for great shall be the day of Jezreel" (1:10-11).

The prophecy has come full circle, as has Israel's life—from out of Jezreel back to Jezreel. Israel must receive the most bitter of punishments for their great sin extending over 200 years as a nation—the sin of religious harlotry, political oppression, and economic exploitation. But there is dawn after the darkness. Yahweh will act to reunify Israel and Judah under one Messianic king. They shall take possession of the land once again, and the Davidic nation of Israel will live as God intended them to live, becoming a blessing to the world!

The tragedy of Hosea is that God called him to marry a prostitute, have three children by her, and use both the actions of marriage to Gomer and the names of the three children to call Israel to accountability for their religious, political, and economic sin, and the destruction it will inevitably bring upon them. The prophet was obedient to this call from God. There is no indication in the text that the result of Hosea's obedient action ever worked for the good of Hosea, Gomer, or the three children. This prophecy certainly destroys in our minds any naïve belief that "everything will work out just fine." It sometimes doesn't, and being obedient to God's call is no guarantee that everything will be fine. Life is not always fair—even to those who are obedient to God's call to them.

Esther

Esther 7:1–10 and 9:20-22 contain the central scenes of the story of Esther, the Jewish queen of the Persian Empire, who was called by God to rescue Israel from almost certain annihilation.

The story of Esther begins not with this Jewish woman but with her predecessor on Persia's throne, Vashti. Overwhelmed with the beauty of his wife, the Persian emperor Ahasuerus (Xerxes) orders Vashti to appear naked before his courtiers at a banquet, so that all can be impressed by her beauty. Offended by his demand, Vashti refuses and is therefore banished from the royal court. The king divorces Vashti and then begins a search for her replacement. He finds a woman of equal beauty in Esther, a Jewish virgin presented to the king by Mordecai (her adopted father, a strategic player in the emperor's court and a Jew). The king marries her and has her crowned as Persia's new queen (Esther 1– 2).

Later, Mordecai uncovers a plot against King Ahasuerus, reports it to Queen Esther who reports it to the king, who then stifles the plot (2:19–23). This action on Mordecai's part plays a strategic role in the later actions of the king and his court.

Another courtier, Haman, is seeking to build his personal power and influence in the court. He sees Mordecai as his chief rival and both more favored and trusted than himself because of Mordecai's uncovering of the plot against the king. How can Haman eliminate his rival? Recognizing that Mordecai was personally impervious because of his favor with King Ahasuerus, Haman devises a plot to exploit Mordecai's national origin as the means to eliminate him (3:1–6).

Haman tells the king that the Jewish people "do not keep the king's laws" and are, by their very existence, a threat to the monarchy and the peace of the empire. Therefore, he proposes that on a particular day (the thirteenth day of the month of Adar), all Jews would be hunted out, killed, and their property confiscated by the state. Ahasuerus agrees, unaware that both Mordecai and his queen are Jews (Haman is very aware that Mordecai was a Jew—that's why he hatched the plot, but there is no indication in the book of Esther that he realized that Esther was a Jew, also). The king gives the order for the purging of the Jews (3:7–15).

Mordecai soon gets word of the king's order, considers his options, and realizes that the only person who has the capacity to influence Ahasuerus in this matter is Queen Esther. He goes to her and pleads his case, pointing out to her that her status as queen will not protect her from the king's command (4:1–14). He then ends his plea with the words for which the book of Esther has become so well known: "Who knows? Perhaps you have come to royal dignity for just such a time as this" (4:14b)?

These words form the basic message of the Old Testament book of Esther. "Perhaps you have come to royal dignity for just such a time as this"! It was not that

God wished to honor Esther by making her the queen of the Persian Empire; it was instead for her to assume the great responsibility of saving her people from the annihilation God knew would otherwise come upon the Jewish people. This moment was the moment of Esther's call from God. How would she respond to this call?

Esther responds to God's call by commanding Mordecai to organize the Jews to hold a fast on her behalf as she pleads the Jews' case to the emperor. She then concludes, "After that (the fast), I will go to the king, though it is against the law; and if I perish, I perish" (4:16b). But why would this action cause Esther to perish? Why would she fear speaking to her husband? It is because such a request of the king, if it offended him, could cause her death![44]

Esther devises a scheme that she thinks will keep her from being executed but would enable her to present her case before Ahasuerus that will make him more responsive to her request. She plans a banquet for him and invites Haman to the banquet. She then gets the king's permission for the banquet (much less risky than making a direct request of him to change the law). Esther holds the banquet for the two men and gets the king to agree to another banquet for the three of them. Haman, overwhelmed with such an indication of his unique and high status in the empire, becomes overconfident. He thus begins plotting Mordecai's death during the Jewish purge by having a gallows built upon which Mordecai can be publicly hung (5:1–14).

Haman's plot is temporarily compromised by the king's decision to honor Mordecai for his uncovering of the plot against the king (6:1–13). Mordecai is thus honored and that honoring grates terribly on Haman, but he bides his time. And his time finally comes.

Esther holds the second banquet for Ahasuerus and Haman. And it is at that second banquet, with the guards down of both the king and Haman, that Esther launches her use of the power at her disposal (that is, her status in the kingdom and the unique relationship she has with the king as his wife, lover, and queen) to protect the Jews.

---

[44] In going to the king and requesting him to change the law, Esther is not doing a light thing. It was against Persian law for anyone to enter the presence of or speak to the king—not even his wife! To do so was to court death. Further, an edict made by the Persian emperor was considered inviolate and could not be rescinded (it could be modified). Therefore, in approaching and speaking to the king on this matter without being bidden by the king to do so and to ask him to change the law, Esther was placing herself in danger of being killed on the spot!

Ahasuerus, overwhelmed with the beauty and generosity of his queen, magnanimously declares to her, "What is your petition, Queen Esther? It shall be granted you—even to the half of my kingdom" (7:2). Esther's response is a plea. "If I have won your favor, O king, and if it pleases the king, let my life be given me—that is my petition—and the lives of my people —that is my request. For we have been sold, I and my people, to be destroyed, to be killed, and to be annihilated." (7:3–4). Of course, the response of the king was, essentially, "What are you talking about?" And Esther spills out the entire plot of Haman.

The king "rose from the feast in wrath," and went out into the garden to compose himself. He realizes how Haman had played him for the fool, and what an injustice the king has committed against the Jews by his unthinking declaration made upon Haman's report. Meanwhile, Haman is stunned at the news that the queen is a Jew and would therefore come under the same edict that would eliminate Mordecai and the Jews. He sees not only his plot but also his entire career and even his life unraveling before his eyes. He throws himself at the queen's feet (she is lying semi-reclined in the dining fashion of the day) to beg her forgiveness and to attempt to salvage his plans. But the king returns, uses Haman's compromised position as a means for ridding himself of this man, and has him hung on the very gallows Haman had constructed to hang his rival, Mordecai (7:7–10). Haman had literally been "hoisted on his own petard"!

With all his heart, the king desperately wants to reverse the decree he had made. But Persian law prevents him from doing so. Therefore, on the advice of Esther, Ahasuerus makes a second decree that, when the day of persecution occurs, the Jews may arm themselves and given permission to wage war against their persecutors until their Persian foes are annihilated. Further, the king promoted Mordecai to the leadership of Persia under the king and assigned him the responsibility to implement this decree (8:1–17). The result was that the Jews defended themselves and their enemies were wiped out (9:1–17). And everybody then lived happily ever after (10:1–2)!

The book of Esther is about power—the exercise of power unilaterally to further one's own ambitions and to oppress an entire people. It is also about the exercise of power relationally, demonstrating that, if one carefully analyzes and understands the scope of his or her power, one can work within even the most corrupt system to bring about good. The book of Esther is also about call—how one person, strategically placed and willing to perish in order to bring about justice can both discern and accept God's call and to act out that call in the most astute way possible.

The entire book magnificently demonstrates how human action can achieve God's purposes in the world. The result of Esther's intervention on behalf of the Jews established the feast of Purim as a permanent festival to remind Israel of its deliverance from the greatest empire of its time, just as the Passover was created to remind Israel of its deliverance from Egyptian bondage—the greatest empire of its time. And both stories of deliverance occur because of one person who hears God's call and obeys that call, being willing to deal with the political and economic power of their respective times.

There is one bittersweet note in the book of Esther. The concluding chapter of the book praises King Ahasuerus for being willing to perceive the wrong and to act to correct it. It also praises Mordecai for using his power for the benefit of the Jews and, eventually, for the entire empire. *But it nowhere mentions Esther!* It is as if she had not been a player in this great work of liberation. And yet the entire success of the mission depended entirely upon Esther. It was she who risked her life to come before the king unbidden and to eventually convince him to change the law sufficiently so that the Jews could defend themselves, and to get rid of the horrible influence of Haman. It was Esther whom God had brought to this hour, and she had used that hour to save an entire people from annihilation. And yet the very book that tells her story so graphically doesn't even mention her in the credits at the end, Could that have been because she was a woman?

Barnabas

Another "little" man in scripture was Barnabas. But what a giant this little man was! We are introduced to Barnabas in the book of the Acts of the Apostles, where he is mentioned in chapters 4 and 9, but figures prominently in chapters 11 through 15. After that, he drops out of sight.[45]

Barnabas was a Jew and then later a Christian Jew who lived on the island of Cyprus. He was of the tribe of Levi, but was likely not a priest because he owned farmland (the Torah forbids Levite priests from owning farmland—see Lev. 25:32–34;

---

[45] Barnabas is also mentioned occasionally by Paul in some of the apostles' letters—I Cor. 9:6, Gal. 2:1–13 and Col. 4:10.

Num. 18:23–24; Deut. 14:27–29). We know nothing of either his conversion to Christ nor his call to Christian service. But he had been given an alternate name by the Christians which tells us a great deal about his call. This man's name was actually Joseph, but he was called by the people of the church, "Barnabas" (which means, "Son of Encouragement"). And that describes Barnabas's ministry; his call was to encourage both believers and non-believers around him.

Barnabas was a Son of Encouragement to the Earliest Church (Acts 4:32–37). This scripture tells of the way the earliest Christians lived in community with each other. "Now the whole group of those who believed were of one heart and soul, and no one claimed private ownership of any possessions, but everything they owned was held in common. With great power, the apostles gave their testimony to the resurrection of the Lord Jesus, and great grace was upon them all. There was not a needy person among them, for as many as owned lands or houses sold them and brought the proceeds of what was sold" (4:32–34). And then the text tells us, "There was a Levite, a native of Cyprus, Joseph, to whom the apostles gave the name Barnabas. He sold a field that belonged to him, then brought the money, and laid it at the apostles' feet" (vv. 36–37). Barnabas blessed the earliest Christian community by donating a field. But Acts 4 implies that many divested themselves of their wealth. So why single out Barnabas? No one knows why, but could it be because it was by far the largest gift or the most generous? At any rate, he was seen by the church, from this time forward, as being the person of encouragement among them.

He was the Son of Encouragement to the early Christian leaders (Acts 9:6–30). The next mention of Barnabas in the book of Acts occurs in Acts 9:6–30. The fanatical Pharisee, Saul, who was the great persecutor of the earliest church, had just been converted to Christ. But was this a genuine conversion, or was this simply a subterfuge to enable him to work his way into the Christian community and spy upon them from the inside? Whether leader or follower, no one knew what to think.

But Barnabas took the time to get to know Saul of Tarsus, and became increasingly convinced that his conversion was genuine. So Barnabas urged the church's leaders to take a chance on Saul. "So Barnabas took Saul, brought him to the apostles, and described for them how on the road he had seen the Lord, who had spoken to him, and how in Damascus he had spoken boldly in the name of Jesus"

(9:27). So Barnabas's advocacy of Saul lessened the suspicions of the Christian leaders, and they gradually came to accept Saul as an authentic convert to Jesus Christ.

Barnabas became the Son of Encouragement to the Apostle Paul (Acts 11:1–14:28). Some Jewish Christians shared the gospel with some Gentiles in the city of Antioch, and they converted to Christ. But could Gentiles become Christians, or did Christ come exclusively for the Jewish people? The apostles sent Barnabas to Antioch to investigate the claims of Gentile converts occurring in that city. He did investigate it and saw it to be true. Thus Barnabas realized that the gospel was as much meant for the Gentiles as it was for the Jews. But how should the church act proactively to bring the gospel to Gentiles? And who would be best equipped to lead that evangelistic effort?

"Barnabas went to Tarsus to look for Saul, and when he had found him, he brought him to Antioch. So it was that for an entire year they met with the church and taught a great many people. . . . And the Holy Spirit said, 'Set apart for me Barnabas and Saul for the work to which I have called them.' Then after fasting and praying they laid hands on them and sent them off (to the Gentiles)" (11:25–26a; 13:2–3).

What was actually occurring was that Barnabas was imagining an entirely different public to hear and respond to the gospel (the Gentiles), then identifying one who had the capacity to become a significant leader in such a ministry (Saul), connecting him with established church leadership and gaining their reluctant support, and then organizing both Paul and himself for missionary action—first in the city of Antioch and then in missionary journeys to Greek and Gentile cities (Acts 13:1–14:28). And the proof of the wisdom of his choice of Saul was Saul's decision to change from a Jewish name to a Greek name—Paul—in order to identify with the Gentiles that both Barnabas and he would try to reach with the gospel.

Acts 13:1 through 14:28 tell of the mission of Barnabas and Paul to the Gentiles in the Roman province of Asia (what is today Turkey, Syria, and Iraq). This "dynamic duo" visited the key cities of Antioch (in Pisidia), Iconium, Lystra, and Derbe, and there not only won many Gentiles to Christ but planted churches and built up Christian communities. But another intriguing phenomenon occurred in their joint ministry.

In the earlier chapters of Acts, it was clear that Barnabas was taking the lead. He was Paul's mentor. But as Paul's skills were honed and his vision grew and his knowledge of and capability of communicating the Christian faith developed, the two men increasingly moved into a collegial relationship until, finally, Barnabas yielded first place to Paul (13:2; 14:1, 15:2). Thus a subtle shift takes place in the account of their mission journey, as the phrase “Barnabas and Paul” shifted to “Paul and Barnabas.” Barnabas had turned over leadership of the mission to Paul.

Barnabas is the Son of Encouragement to John Mark (15:1–41). The issue of whether Gentiles could become Christians without first being Jews finally needed to be settled by church leaders. Therefore, James (the brother of Jesus and the administrative head of the church) called a council of Christian leaders in Jerusalem. This first church council met, the positions were argued; those present listened to the testimony of Paul and Barnabas about Gentiles converted and churches planted in Gentile cities. The issue was then adjudicated by James after consultation with the Christian leaders. He declared, “We should not trouble those Gentiles who are turning to God, but we should write to them (welcoming them into the faith). For in every city, for generations past, Moses has had those who proclaim him, for he has been read aloud every Sabbath in the synagogues” (15:19, 20a, 21). The matter was settled with the recognition that Gentiles could become Christians and create churches every bit as much as could Jews.

Paul and Barnabas then returned to their home base of Antioch in Syria. There they ministered. But then Paul said to Barnabas, “Come, let us return and visit the believers in every city where we proclaimed the word of the Lord and see how they are doing” (15:36). Barnabas agreed but wanted to take the young John Mark as part of the traveling party. Paul refused because he had found Mark unreliable. They argued mightily, but Paul would not yield. Therefore, the scripture tells us, “they parted company; Barnabas took Mark with him and sailed away to Cyprus, But Paul chose Silas and set out (to visit these churches)” (15:39–40a). And that is the last we hear of Barnabas.

Barnabas had the capacity to perceive new ways in which the Spirit was moving and then had the faith to step out into *new ministries and new mission challenges*. He was unbelievably innovative in ministry. Barnabas was the first person who was able to act out one’s relationship of faith in Christ to one’s attitude and action regarding his money. He gave away his personal fortune to the Church (4:36–37). He was the first person who was proactive in inaugurating ministry to the Gentile world, perceiving that the gospel was intended for Gentiles as well as Jews (11:19–26).

But perhaps one of Barnabas's greatest capacities was his ability to reach out to *new people* who were otherwise shunned and marginalized by the Church He connected them to church leadership, organized them for action, called them forth, and trained them for leadership, and then was willing to take second place to them. Thus it was Barnabas who was the first person to discern that the young Saul was a leader chosen by God and, in the face of significant opposition from the other Christian leaders, mentored him in ministry, and called him forth to join him in an outreach to the Gentiles that would revolutionize Christianity (11:19–26). Likewise, Barnabas was the first person to see potential in a young Hellenistic Jew, John Mark, whom Paul rejected because of his undependability. Barnabas shaped that young man into the kind of Christian leader who could eventually author the Gospel of Mark, found the Alexandrian Church, and was martyred in Egypt[46] (15:36–39). Eventually, Barnabas had the satisfaction of seeing Paul admit that the man he once rejected as being undependable was, in reality, one who had become of significant value not only to the Church but to the great apostle, as well (II Tim. 4:11).

Barnabas was always stepping out into the new. He perceived a new mission advance or a new person to call forth. But perhaps the most profound reality about Barnabas and his leadership style was his capacity to put the common good before his personal status and position. This was seen most profoundly in his relationship with Paul when he purposely allowed Paul to develop his leadership talents to such a degree that Paul took over the leadership of their shared mission to the Gentiles, and Barnabas voluntarily took second place. How rarely do we see Christian leaders recognize the superior gifts or leadership of their protégées, nurture them to mature leadership, then voluntarily turn over that leadership to them, assuming a secondary role until God calls them into some other ministry? Yet that was the leadership style Barnabas models for us."[47]

---

[46] Phyllis Tickle, *The Divine Hours: Prayers for Springtime* (New York: Doubleday, 2001), 451.

[47] Robert Linthicum, *Building a People of Power: Equipping Churches to Transform Their Communities* (Eugene, OR: Wipf and Stock, 2015), 189–190. Used by permission of Wipf and Stock Publishers, www.wipfandstock.com. For a full examination of the respective contributions to Christianity of Paul and Barnabas, see pp. 186–190 of *Building A People of Power*.

Conclusion

We have thus far examined the biblical perspective of vocation or call from two perspectives. In the previous two chapters, we have looked at God as the One who calls Israel, the Church, and individuals to do God's work in the world. In this chapter, we have looked particularly at each of us as called people. My primary argument in this chapter is that God chooses and calls anyone to carry out God's will in the world. It is irrelevant whether a person is a clergyperson or whether she is a layperson—God calls us. In the case of the four specific people whose story we read, one was a farmer, another was a queen, still another was a lay member of a church, and the other was an investor. What I wished to make clear in this chapter is that God is "no respecter of persons," but rather chooses and calls each of us and all of us to carry out God's mission to us in the world. And that mission assigned to us might be calling a nation to repentance or caring for a leader of the church or intervening in the political arena for justice for a persecuted people or calling forth the best in others. But whatever that mission might be, it is part of God's great, eternal plan for the building of God's kingdom upon the earth. And whether we might be a priest, a pastor, a missionary—or a layperson—is purely incidental to God!

Having now examined the biblical theology of God as the Creator, the One who Chooses, and the One who Calls, and recognizing ourselves as the Called Ones, we are now ready to explore together the biblical doctrine of call (vocation) rather thoroughly. Therefore, the next three chapters will build a biblical theology of call itself, as we increasingly perceive how God has called each of us to become God's presence and witness in the city to which we have been called.

Chapter 5

The Call

The doctrine of "vocation" or "call" is one of the most neglected doctrines in the church today, and the church suffers tremendously from that neglect. We place a heavy emphasis on the necessity of personal faith in Christ, of being a people together in community, and of grounding our faith in the Scripture. We place a very heavy emphasis upon building up the church, of ministering in and to the church. So the Protestant church of today—whether "mainline" or evangelical—has a strong Christology, a solid emphasis on the doctrine of salvation and a thorough ecclesiology.

But the Church ignores a doctrine that runs as a constant theme through the entirety of the Old and New Testaments, a doctrine which, along with the doctrines of creation and redemption, is the primary doctrine moving through the warp-and-woof of scripture. That doctrine is the assertion that God has chosen and redeemed each individual within a chosen people in order that we might serve God and humanity in a unique way. This is the doctrine of vocation.

The reality is that the doctrine of vocation is structurally and missiologically ignored in the church today. We give lip service to the doctrine of the priesthood of all believers, which is in reality a manifestation of the doctrine of vocation. But it is not lived out in the life or work of the church. It is not lived out for a very simple reason. The doctrine of vocation does not serve the institutionalizing of the church!

What is the doctrine of vocation? It is perhaps most beautifully stated by Frederick Buechner: "The place God calls you to is the place where your deep gladness and the world's deep hunger meet!"[48]

The doctrine of vocation can be summarized in one question. Why do you exist? Put theologically, the question is "What is your purpose in life?" The biblical answer is "Your purpose in living is to serve God by serving humanity." You have been created by God to be used by God in a particular way. And all that you have gone through in life, all the experiences you have had, all the problems you have faced, every rejection you have ever faced as a human being, every celebration in which you have shared, every victory you have tasted all has gone into molding you into who you are right now. Why? So that God can use you in a special way.

Every human being has been created by God to serve Christ in the world in a particular way. And when we discover the deep gladness of our own lives—our redemption in Jesus Christ—and we allow ourselves to be open to the pain of the world and gravitate toward that issue of the world that pains us the most, that is where our deep gladness and the world's deep hunger come together. And that is the place where God calls us to serve him.

There is a profound difference between the concepts of "occupation" and "vocation." The word "vocation" is incorrectly used today, because it is used as a synonym for "occupation." It is not! The word "occupation" simply means, "that which occupies our time." And that which occupies the majority of our time is our work. The word "vocation," on the other hand, literally means "calling." It is that to which you have been called.

Now for some people, their occupation and their vocation are the same, so that their occupation has become a vocation to them. But occupation and vocation do not necessarily need to go together. The Christian has the responsibility to discover her or his vocation—that place to which God calls you right here, right now—irrespective of whether that vocation is also one's occupation.

From my teenage years, I felt called into urban ministry. The occupation with which I chose to live out that call was that of a pastor serving urban churches. But three years into my ministry, I was introduced to the world of community organizing. I

---

[48]Frederick Buechner, *Wishful Thinking* (San Francisco, CA: Harper and Row), 119.

gravitated toward community organizing with a ferocity that made no sense to me. I just plain loved it. I continued as a pastor and saw my work as a minister as both vocation and occupation. But my love was for community organizing. I felt such anger at the disenfranchisement and disempowerment of the poor who lived around the city churches I served. I could not stand to see the way that the marginalized had become the victims of the systems of power in Chicago, Rockford (IL), and Detroit.

Nine years after entering the twin ministries of the pastorate and community organizing and as a part of my own personal spiritual pilgrimage, I came to realize why I felt such intense anger at the sight of powerlessness and marginalization and why I felt so called to do something about it (rather than just minding the church store). It was because I had grown up in an orphanage.

In the orphanage, I had no control over my own life. I went where I was supposed to go and did what I was supposed to do. If I disobeyed, I was punished. My whole life was controlled for me, and I had absolutely nothing to say about it. There was not even a way for me to protest! And I felt thoroughly marginalized and helpless.

Powerlessness is one of the world's deep hungers. But I suddenly discovered that it was my deep hunger, too! And when I realized that fact, and recognized that the gospel had good news to my own interior imprisonment and marginalization, then I began to discover a freedom that I had not known before.

My interior work, in the light of my daily work of addressing the world's deep hunger, was my discovery that my vocation really needed to be that of one who sets people free. This could be exercised through my twin occupations as a pastor and as a community organizer. So it was that I saw as God's calling to me the commission to seek the liberation of people from their spiritual bondage, to provide for my parishioners the opportunity to discover new directions for their lives that brought meaning to their existence, and to work with the poor to enable them to successfully stand up for their rights and confront the systems that were seeking to control and destroy them.

The reality is that each one of us has a story to tell. Each one of us has been hurt and marginalized in some way. Each one of us has been distorted in some way by life's disappointments and hurts. And yet each Christian has been, in a profound way, redeemed. The grace of God has somehow been at work in every one of our lives. For many of us, it came as a total surprise, totally unexpected. That's why it's good news. And now what God is calling you to do is to take a look at all your experience, all which has gone into making you "you," and ask yourself "What breaks my heart? And what does that say to me about my own pilgrimage? How can God use me to address the pain that I experienced and I know is there in the world?"

Scripture and Vocation

If Christians are to impact society and their own worlds, we need to rediscover and redefine the doctrine of vocation. We need to ***rediscover*** vocation and point people to the reality that their life matters—that each of us, whether clergy or lay, have been chosen by God to address a pain of the world through the community of the Church. We need to ***redefine*** vocation so that we move it away from occupation—what we do to earn our bread—and direct it toward the understanding of God's sure and certain call upon our lives.

The scripture is full of the belief that God chooses people to serve God in the world. Whether a person is great or small, whether influential or unknown, whether an individual by himself or part of an active community, God calls people throughout the warp-and-woof of scripture. Moses, Esther, Andrew and Peter, Mary and Martha, David or Jeremiah, Paul or Ephaphroditus, Mary Magdalene or Mother Mary, Israel or the Church are all examples of call.

But those to whom I would first direct our attention are the political, economic, and religious leaders of Israel who were in bondage in the city of Babylon. God's call to those exiles is found in Jer. 29:1–14. It is in their story that we find profound insight into what it means to be a people chosen by God for the world.

Jeremiah 29:1-14 and a Called People

Exiled or Sent? The southern kingdom of Judah had been conquered. The city of Jerusalem had been burned to the ground and the temple destroyed. The political, economic, and religious leaders of Jerusalem had been dragged off as captives to the city of Babylon by the conquering king, Nebuchadnezzar. There, in the city of their captors, the former Israelites lifted up their voices and wept. There, in exile, they began to despair that God would ever deliver them from the hand of their hated captors.

It was to those despairing, grieving captives that a letter came from the prophet Jeremiah. And his advice to those exiles is a word we need to hear as we seek to be God's faithful people in this time and place. That letter—and its advice—now appears as Jer. 29:4–14.

> Thus says the Lord of hosts, the God of Israel, to all the exiles whom I have sent into exile from Jerusalem to Babylon: Build houses and live in them; plant gardens and eat what they produce. Take wives and have sons and daughters; take wives for your sons, and give your daughters in marriage, that they may bear sons and daughters; multiply there, and do not decrease. But seek the *shalom* of the city where I have sent you into exile, and pray to the Lord on its behalf, for in its *shalom* you will find your *shalom*. . . . For thus says the Lord: Only when Babylon's seventy years are completed will I visit you, and I will fulfill to you my promise and bring you back to this place. For surely I know the plans I have for you, says the Lord, plans for your *shalom* and not for harm, to give you a future with hope. Then when you call upon me and come and pray to me, I will hear you. When you search for me, you will find me; if you seek me with all your heart, I will let you find me, says the Lord, and I will restore your fortunes, and gather you from all the nations and all the places where I have driven you, says the Lord, and I will bring you back to the place from which I sent you into exile.[49]

Yahweh's initial word to the Israelite political, economic, and religious leaders in Babylonian exile is a harsh word. Through this prophecy, God tells them that they will remain in exile for seventy years (or, in other words, a lifetime!). They will not be restored to their precious city of Jerusalem. Likely, neither will their children. Only in their grandchildren lies the hope that Israel will once again be restored to its land.

Yet God says to them, "For surely I know the plans I have for you, says the Lord, plans for your shalom and not for harm, to give you a future with hope" (29:11). Although they will remain a lifetime and will die in Babylonian exile, God's plans for them are meant for their good. It was as if God were saying to those Israelite captives, "I know what I am doing. It is my plan that you be here. And I promise you that I will bless you in this foreign city. I will make you a rich blessing to all around you. For the

49 Although this translation is from the same translation used throughout this book, the *New Revised Standard Version* (Nashville, TN: Holman Bible Publishers, 1989), I have taken the liberty to reproduce the Hebrew word *shalom* rather than to translate it into "welfare" (used in the NRSV translation), so that we can see how often and in what ways the word *shalom* is used in the text in order to enable us to appreciate the full meaning of the text.

promise I give to you is realized as you live out the plan I have for you here in your exile!"

Here, then, is God's promise for us called to be God's people in today's world. "I have good plans for you." But what is God's plan that we are called to carry out in order to access God's promise? Here according to Jeremiah is that plan:

"Seek the *shalom* of the city where I have ***sent you into exile***, and pray to the Lord on its behalf, for in its *shalom* you will find your *shalom*" (Jer. 29:7).

When one reads this passage from Jeremiah in different translations of the Bible, one becomes aware that two different English words are used to translate a pivotal Hebrew word. Some translators tell the Israelites to work for the good of the city to which God has "exiled" them. Others have the Israelites "sent" to that city. Which is right?

The Hebrew word variously translated as "exiled" or "sent" actually contains the meaning of both words.[50] It would most accurately be translated with the awkward phrase, "I have caused you to be carried away captive." The word means "exiled"—that is, "forced removal from one's country." But the word also means "sent"—"called" into exile by God, almost as if they were people on a mission.

"Why are you in Babylon?," Jeremiah is, in essence, asking "You have been exiled to this city," God in essence is telling the Jews. You Israelites are in this city because you have been brought here by force. Your nation was conquered, your army decimated, your city razed, your temple burned, and you were clapped into chains and marched across the desert to this hated city of Babylon. That is the *circumstance* that brought you to this city.

Why is each of us in the city in which we find ourselves? You may have been born here. You may have decided to move here. You may be in that community because you have a job here or have built a career here. You may be in your city

[50] The Hebrew word is *galah,* translated as "to remove into exile" or "caused to be carried away captive" (as opposed to "exiled," "being taken captive," or "emigrating"). The word suggests a causal nuance or intentionality to it—i.e., that it is not that the people have simply been defeated in battle and exiled, but that God caused their exile to happen. Thus *galah* intimates the intervention of God in history to serve God's purposes through the exiled people., cf., Francis Brown, et al., *Hebrew and English Lexicon of the Old Testament* (London: Oxford University Press, 1959), 162–165; Robert Young, *Analytical Concordance to the Bible* (Grand Rapids, MI: Eerdmans Publishing Co., 1955), 143.

because your spouse or loved one is here. You may have come there to be educated or to retire here. These are the circumstances that have brought you to your community.

"Why are you in Babylon?," Jeremiah asks the Jewish leaders. Through this passage of scripture, God is also saying in essence to the Jewish leadership, "You are in Babylon because I, the Lord your God, sent you here!" I have chosen to defeat your nation, clap you in chains, and march you over hundreds of miles of sand to bring you as a captive to this city. But why would I do this with the leaders of my people?

You Israelites are in Babylon, Jeremiah 29:7 is suggesting, not simply because you were captured but because God wants you here! You are here because God needs his people here—not only in Jerusalem, but also in Babylon—the city of evil. If there is to be any liberation, any redemption, any transformation of that city, it will happen only if God's people are here to make it happen. You are in Babylon by *God's design*!

Why are you in the city in which you find yourself? You are here for one reason and one reason alone. You are in that community because God has called you here. You are in that city by God's design, by God's will. The circumstances that seemed to compel you to come to this community were not the reason that brought you here. Those circumstances were simply the vehicle God used to get you here and to hold you here. But you are here because the Lord God needs you here and called you here. And whether God's plans for you in this place turn out to be plans for your peace and not for your disaster (29:11) depends upon whether you see yourself as being called by God into this community and then choosing to live into that call. *That* was the good news given through Jeremiah to the Jewish leadership living in exile in hated Babylon.

The Task: Seeking The City's Shalom. So God's real question facing every one of us is, "What are you doing here, Christian?" What are you called to do in that city into which God calls you? How is your vocation to be lived out in that place? "Seek the *shalom* of the city where I have sent you into exile, . . . for in its *shalom* you will find your *shalom*." (29:7) Our calling in whatever community into which God has called us is the work of seeking that city's shalom—its peace, prosperity, well-being, wholeness, fullness, reconciliation, transformation. And we seek its peace as God's people through our life together (29:5–6), our prayers for that place (vs. 7), and the practice and proclamation of our faith (vs. 7). That is the primary vocation or calling to which God's people are called.[51]

Ephesians 4:1-16 and an Organized People

But how do you work for the shalom of your city? How do God's people organize themselves and distribute their labor to build their city into an approximation of the kingdom of God?

In 1963, as I was approaching the end of my seminary studies and was preparing to launch forth into ministry, I was assigned a final paper to write. All graduating seniors of that seminary were required to write such a paper, which was designed to integrate much of the learning they had experienced in that school. Each student was assigned a specific passage of scripture, was to translate that passage from its original Greek or Hebrew, to place that scripture in its historical context, to exegete that passage, then write an exposition of it, and finally to turn that exposition into a sermon which he or she would then have to preach to the seminary's faculty. The scripture assigned to me radically changed my entire understanding of ministry and, consequently, the whole way I practiced ministry for the rest of my career. That scripture was Ephesians 4:1–16. Let's look at it together.

How should God's people respond to a city, nation, and civilization that is intent upon destroying the church? The way to deal with such an empire, Paul teaches the church in the book of Ephesians, is neither to flee from it nor to make itself invisible. It is to directly engage that city and nation, and work for its conversion into the Jewish-Christian dream of the shalom community. And the reason why this is the church's task is because this is what the gospel is all about.

The first three chapters of Ephesians present Paul's theological rationale for such a proactive stance toward Rome. Now, beginning with chapter four, Paul places hands and feet on his theology. In this section, Paul presents his practical strategy for the church working toward the transformation of the city of Rome and the Roman Empire. He begins that presentation by stating his primary battle plan. That presentation begins with the first seven verses of the fourth chapter of Ephesians.

---

[51] A similar exposition of Jeremiah 29:1–14 is found in my books, *Building A People of Power (op. cit.),* and *Transforming Power* (Downers Grove, IL: InterVarsity Press, 2003). Used by permission.

> I therefore, the prisoner in the Lord, beg you to lead a life worthy of the calling to which you have been called, with all humility and gentleness, with patience, bearing with one another in love, making every effort to maintain the unity of the Spirit in the bond of peace. There is one body and one Spirit, just as you were called to the one hope of your calling, one Lord, one faith, one baptism, one God and Father of all, who is above all and through all and in all. But each of us was given grace according to the measure of Christ's gift.

What stands out the strongest in the first three verses is the intense relationality of the words he has chosen. He doesn't begin his plan for winning Rome with words about strategy or tactics or action. Instead, he speaks of the mobilized church needing to be a relational church. The words he uses are all relational: "beg," "lead a life worthy of your calling," exercise in your ministry "humility," "gentleness," "patience," "bearing with one another in love," "making every effort to maintain unity," "practice the bond of peace"! If the church is going to successfully work to transform the public life of Rome or any other city, Paul is telling us, it can do so only if it is unified. And you can't be a truly unified people unless you actively seek to build your faith community as a relational body—a relational culture.

Paul then goes on to argue the theological case for unity in verses 4–6. He names seven beliefs of the church that drives it toward unity. They are "one body (of Christ)," accessing "one Spirit," called to "one hope." The Christians worship "one Lord," practice "one faith," observe "one baptism," and are joined together by "one God and Father of all, who is above all and through all and in all." Because God is unified, Paul is stating, the church's very faith must be unified. If we all hold to a common Lord and become one body together, then our differences are as nothing, for our commonality in Christ must overwhelm all our disagreements in theology, polity, or liturgics.

What Paul is stressing here, as the very premise upon which the city can be engaged and won for Christ is that the church cannot effectively work to transform public life if it is not unified in every way. A fighting or arguing church will reach no person or system with the gospel (4:1–6). Thus, Paul is here recognizing that church-based power has to be relational power, not unilateral power. In seeking to win the empire to Christ, the church will be exercising power. But the kind of power it *must* exercise is relational power.

I define power as the capacity, ability, and willingness to act. Any individual, community, or organization can act powerfully if it has developed its capacity, ability, and willingness to act. But most governments, mega-businesses, and giant religions act unilaterally in the exercise of their capacity, ability, and willingness. That is, they use power as "power over," power as "command-and-control." They act from the "top-down" and tell you how to think or act or behave.

That won't work for the church, Paul is saying, because that goes against everything that Christ ever was and how he chose to act. Jesus used power relationally. He built up people. He rescued people. He motivated them to become what they had the potential to be. Thus, Paul realizes that the church's use of power to seek the transformation of the world must be relational power, and come out of a caring, committed, and unified body.

Built upon the foundation of the exercise of relational power by a unified Church, Paul then writes, "Each of us was given grace according to the measure of Christ's gift. . . . The gifts he gave were that some would be apostles, some prophets, some evangelists, some pastors and teachers, to equip the saints for the work of ministry, for building up the body of Christ" (4:7, 11–12).[52] We are all one people under Christ, Paul reminded us in earlier verses, knit together as one body, unified by one Lord, one faith, one baptism, committed to one Lord. But for what purpose have we been made one in Christ? It is in order for us to exercise the unique gifts each of us has been given by God to contribute to the building up of that one body and reaching our city, the empire, and the world for Christ.

Paul has stressed throughout his ministry his belief that God has purposely placed in the church a diversity of gifts so that the body of Christ is fully served and is equipped for mission (e.g., Rom. 12:4–8; I Cor. 12:12–27). But here in Ephesians 4:11–12, Paul takes his thinking considerably further.

---

[52] I have eliminated verses 8–10 from this text because Paul digressed from his main argument in those three verses. His words, "Christ's gift," in verse 7 reminded him of a well-known Christian hymn of that time. That, in turn, causes Paul to begin speculating on a controversial doctrine of that time also mentioned in the Apostles Creed ("he descended into hell") and alluded to in I Peter 3:18–20. It is at this point that Paul realizes how badly he has gotten off the subject, and suddenly in verse 11 turns back to his main theme.

God has given to the church particular leadership gifts that are to be exercised by specific people. Those gifts (and, consequently, those people) are those of apostleship, prophetic ministries, evangelism, pastoring and teaching (vs. 11). What is the "job" of these "apostles, prophets, evangelists, pastors and teachers"? *The mistranslation of the sentence that follows has had a profound impact on the church of the past 350 years—an intent Paul never intended!*

Consider two distinct translations of Ephesians 4:11–12.

"And he gave some, apostles; and some, prophets; and some, evangelists; and some, pastors and teachers; for the perfecting of the saints, for the work of ministry, for the edifying of the body of Christ." (The King James Version)

"It was he who gave some to be apostles, some to be prophets, some to be evangelists and some to be pastors and teachers, to prepare God's people for works of service, so that the body of Christ might be built up" (The New International Version ©1973).

The translation of Eph. 4:11–12 as found in the King James Version (KJV) tells the reader that the work of these named leaders is threefold: to "perfect the saints," to "do the work of ministry," and to "edify the Church." The translation of the same passage in the New International Version (NIV) suggests something entirely different, however. It states quite clearly that the leaders' work is singular: to prepare God's people for the people's works of service, and in this way, the church is built up.

These two translations present two distinct ways of understanding "church." If you hold to the KJV's translation, then you would carry out ministry with the understanding that it is the job of the clergy to "perfect" the Christians, "do the work of ministry," and "edify the church." The clergy have the responsibility of doing the work of the church; the laity is there to listen and obey. That is, the clergy would be the producers and the laity would be consumers.

But if one holds to the NIV's translation, an entirely different understanding of church emerges. The NIV is suggesting that the clergy would prepare the laity to do the work of the church in the world, and the laity would do it. Or, to put it another way, the clergy would prepare the laity for being the church in public life, and the laity would be engaged daily in being the church in the public life of the world!

Which translation is right? This is a crucial question to answer, because the entire way of understanding the work of the church in the world is at stake. The answer to that question lies in the original Greek. And when you consult the original Greek, there is no question which translation is correct.

The Greek has two words that can be translated "to" or "for." One means "in order to" do something; the other means "so that" something can happen—two very distinct meanings. Both of these Greek words are used in this verse, and it is imperative that each be translated correctly in order to capture what it is that Paul is stating in this passage.

If the two Greek words are correctly translated, here's what you will get: "He gave some to be apostles, some (to be) prophets, some evangelists, some pastors and teachers *in order to* prepare God's people for their work of service *so that* the Body of Christ might be built up." Which is the correct translation? The NIV (as well as the New Revised Standard Version, the English Standard Version, and the New Living Translation)! Intriguingly, the latest re-translation of the King James Version (the New KJV) corrects Ephesians 4:11–12 to conform to the other dominant English translations of the scripture.

Why is it important to reflect on this mistranslation of this text and the damage it has caused the church over the past 350 years before it began to be corrected by a plethora of contemporary translations? This mistranslation appearing in 1611 enabled a clergy-dominated church to justify that domination as it stressed the role of the clergy ("apostles, prophets, evangelists, pastors, teachers") as those who implemented the ministry of the church with the laity assuming the roles of consumers and supporters of the status quo. The result was the separation of Christian faith from everyday life and work, leaving the management of the church in the hands of its clergy. It is significant, for example, that virtually all major Christian-based social reform in the eighteenth and nineteenth centuries in Great Britain and the United States came from independent laity-based social action organizations that were forced to operate outside the church and were often condemned by the church as exercising Christianity in an unapproved and unacceptable manner.

What Paul is actually presenting in this section is his essential battle plan. He is teaching that the way the church will transform the public arena of Rome or of any other nation or people is if its leaders ("apostles, prophets, evangelists, pastors and teachers") commit themselves to equipping and enabling the entire body of Christ and each Christian to be effectively engaged in public life. Thus, clergy exist less to *do* ministry than to *prepare Christians to do public ministry*!

In other words, what Paul is saying is that the church should not so much be a sanctuary to which Christians flee when life tumbles in on them as it should be a school. It should not so much be a fellowship station as it should be a training and planning station to take your city for Christ and his kingdom. The church is the seminary that prepares its laity for Christian engagement in the world!

The implications of Paul's insight, if authentically practiced in the church today, are significant. One implication would be that the majority of the effort of the church's members would not go into sustaining the church as an organization or an institution, but in addressing the substantive issues of its society, holding government and business leaders accountable, and being engaged all over that city in shaping its public life. Another implication is that the church would be "dark" during the week because all its action would be happening out in the schools, in the courtrooms, in City Council chambers, and in businesses.

Paul then concludes his presentation of his strategy for taking Rome for Christ. He writes, "We must no longer be children, tossed to and fro and blown about by every wind of doctrine, by people's trickery, by their craftiness in deceitful scheming. But speaking the truth in love, we must be knit together by every ligament with which it is equipped, as each part is working properly, promotes the body's growth in building itself up in love" (4:14–16).

What would it do for the church, if the church were to take Paul's battle plan seriously, and make it what the church needs to be all about? According to 4:14–16, the result will be a congregation that—as a congregation—is really able to engage its city and work for substantive change while being clear about its vision for the world and the church. Such a church will become virile, healthy, united, effective, and—most of all—obedient to God's call to truly be the church as God created it to return the world to what God intends the city, humanity, and the environment to be all about.

Earlier in this chapter, we quoted Frederick Buechner who wrote, "The place God calls you to is the place where your deep gladness and the world's deep hunger meet." So it is that God calls all of us to be God's deep gladness in our cities and neighborhoods. That is what being a Christian is all about. And to enable that to happen for each of its members is what the Church is called to be about.

The Church and Vocation

It is no secret that Jesus was most harsh toward the religious professionals of his day. Most of his scorn and criticism was centered on the religious establishment of Israel. Here is one example:

> Woe to you, scribes and Pharisees, hypocrites! For you tithe mint, dill, and cummin, and have neglected the weightier matters of the law: justice and mercy and faith. It is these you ought to have practiced without neglecting the others. You blind guides! You strain out a gnat but swallow a camel! . . . Woe to you, scribes and Pharisees, hypocrites! For you are like whitewashed tombs, which on the outside look beautiful, but inside they are full of the bones of the dead and of all kinds of filth. So you also on the outside look righteous to others, but inside you are full of hypocrisy and lawlessness (Matt. 23:23–24, 27–28).

Why was Jesus so confrontational with the religious establishment? Could it be that he was so harsh because he saw that establishment precisely as an establishment? Did he see it seeking to preserve its power, wealth and influence and thus accommodating itself to a Roman dominated world? Did he see that religious establishment keeping the people from their God-given responsibility to be priests to the world and a holy nation (Exod 19:6)? Jesus was opposed to the religious establishment because that establishment was keeping the people from God's design for them and dependent upon that establishment.

A Lay-Centered Church

The church Jesus created was a lay-centered church. All of its earliest leaders, for example, were laypeople—tent-makers, bookkeepers, doctors, tax collectors, and fishermen, all of whom had become fishers of people. There was only one early follower of Jesus who might be considered a "religious professional"—Paul (Saul) who was a Pharisee before becoming a Christian (Acts 23:6). The difficulty he had in winning acceptance into leadership in the church could be partially attributed to that "clergy" status.

The earliest church, therefore, was strongly committed to the perspective that all Christians are called to ministry—and not just those ordained to a specific office. By the end of the first century, the church had developed the positions of bishop, elder, and deacon—but these were not offices to be held for all time but instead were purely functional. The work of church leaders was for the primary purpose of equipping all Christians for the work of ministry (as we developed in our exploration of Eph. 4:1–16 above).

So what caused the church to move away from a perception that all Christians were called by God to "the work of ministry" within their specific contexts? What caused the church to move toward an understanding of ministry carried out primarily (and in due time, exclusively) by religious professionals? To answer that question, we need a little history lesson

From Participation to Domination

By the close of the New Testament era, it is clear that the functional positions of the Church's ministry were rapidly moving toward ordained, established, and permanent offices (I Tim. 3:1–13; Titus 1:5–9). Within a century after the end of the biblical age, the offices of bishop, presbyter (elder), and deacon were firmly established, with a concomitant downgrading of the calling of laypeople for ministry. Thus the early church father, Ignatius, wrote early in the second century, "All of you (are to) follow the bishop as Jesus Christ followed the Father, and follow the elders as the Apostles; and respect the deacons as the commandment of God. *Let no man perform anything pertaining to the church without the bishop.*"[53]

Not all Christians took this imposition of authority gracefully. One lawyer wrote in defense of the laity, "Are not we laymen priests also? The difference between the clergy and the people is due to the authority of the church and the consecration of their rank. Thus where there is no clergy you are your own sole priest. For where there are three, there is a church, though they be laymen."[54]

However, the die was cast. As century followed century, the role, position, and status of the clergy increased and the place of the laity declined. By the end of the first millennium of Christianity, the priesthood had become a divine office, and the laity had been reduced to that of a mere observer of the divine mystery of the mass. Thus, the Church no longer believed that all its members had been called by Christ to serve

---

[53] Ignatius, *Epistle to the Smyrnaeans, Documents of the Christian Church*, c. viii (c. 112 AD), ed. Henry Bettenson (London: Oxford University Press, 1957), 89–90. Italics mine.

[54] Tertullian, *De Exhortatione Castitatis*, 7, ed. Bettenson, *Documents*, 100.

God in the world. Instead, only those ordained by the Church as priests represented Christ in their everyday life.

Two forces particularly contributed to that shift. The first was the primacy and then the supremacy of the Roman pontiff, including his divine right "to illumine and clarify what is contained in the deposits of faith obscurely and implicitly."[55] As the Pope had been selected by God to be the Vicar of Christ, so his clergy were likewise ordained to represent the gospel in the world.

The second force was the elevation of the rite of ordination into a sacrament on a level with the sacraments of Holy Communion and baptism. Church historian Jaroslav Pelikan noted, "Supporting all the other sacraments as their validation is the sacrament of holy orders or ordination. . . . The teaching of the church maintains that the sacrament of holy orders confers upon the priest . . . divine grace for the performance of the duties of his office."[56]

It is also important to note that there has been a significant effort over the past century within both Roman Catholicism and within the Anglican traditions to reclaim the vocational ministry of lay people as well. This effort to balance the sacerdotal role of ordained priests with the recognition of the unique ministerial vocation of those who are not ordained has been asserted through the doctrine of the "priesthood of the laity." Thus, Fr. Michael Dwinell has written, "A human being cannot become fully human, fully whole, fully real, fully completed, unless he is both moving into and living out of his priestliness. . . . Regardless of what else we may do with our lives, if the priest part is absent, we (are) less than complete."[57]

Reaction was inevitable to the medieval perspective that ministry was confined to the clergy. And that reaction reached its apex on October 31, 1517, when a monk priest hammered a document to a church door in Wittenberg, Germany, calling the church to accountability. The Reformation had begun.

---

[55]Henry Denzinger, "Pope Pius XII, 'Humani Generis,'" *The Sources of Catholic Dogma* (St. Louis: B. Herder Book Co., 1957), 640.

[56] Jaroslav Pelikan, *The Riddle of Roman Catholicism* (Nashville, TN: Abingdon Press, 1959), 124–126.

[57] Michael Dwinell, *Being Priest to One Another* (Liguori, Missouri: Triumph Books, 1993), 9.

The Reformation was centered on three essential beliefs that all Reformers insisted upon and held in common. Those three beliefs can be summarized in very few words:

* Scripture Only
* Faith Only
* The Priesthood of All Believers

Whether it was Luther, Calvin, Zwingli, or Cranmer, all the Reformers were firmly persuaded that Scripture, and Scripture alone, must be the *sole* authority for Christian belief and faith. As Luther so dramatically put it at his trial for heresy, "Unless I am convicted by Scripture and plain reason . . . my conscience is captive to the Word of God. I cannot and will not recant anything, for to go against conscience is neither right nor safe. Here I stand, I cannot do otherwise. God help me. Amen."[58]

The second belief upon which all of the Reformers agreed was that salvation was by faith alone. They made this assertion upon the final authority they had accepted of Scripture, which teaches salvation by faith alone. The Reformers therefore accused the Church of having fallen into heresy by teaching that a right relationship with God comes by obeying the Law and the rules of the Church (e.g., indulgences). Rather, the Reformers insisted that God had already acted in Jesus Christ to provide forgiveness of sins and eternal salvation to all humanity. Such forgiveness is offered as a continuing gift by God to each individual—a manifestation of God's amazing grace. Our only action, to appropriate such forgiveness, is to receive that gift on faith (thus the formula, "justification by faith").

The third belief all Reformers held in common was the "priesthood of all believers." This was the belief that one class of people—the ordained priesthood—did not have the exclusive right either to forgive sins or to follow holy orders. Every Christian is called to be a minister of the gospel, whether ordained or unordained, the Reformers insisted. And as one who is called to serve Christ in "the muck and the mire" of everyday life, every Christian is commissioned to assume responsibility for the spiritual condition of all around her or him.

---

[58] Roland H. Bainton, *Here I Stand: A Life of Martin Luther* (Nashville, TN: Abingdon Press, 1950), 185.

The Protestant Church has essentially stayed true to the first two basic beliefs of the Reformation. Scripture continues to be the Protestant Church's primary authority. And we continue to assert that we cannot earn our way to heaven but can only receive salvation as a free gift from God. But the Church has significantly distorted the doctrine of the priesthood of all believers. And the reason why that is the case is clear. As the Protestant Church followed the inevitable pathway of creating and maintaining itself as an institution, it soon discovered (as had the Roman Catholic Church before it) that the doctrine of the priesthood of all believers did not result in building the *institution* of the Church. The convenient ignoring of this doctrine in the way that the church goes about being church has been a profound distortion of the doctrine taught by Martin Luther and John Calvin.

The church today tends to understand the doctrine of the priesthood of all believers as the assertion that every person must be his own priest before God—that I must assume responsibility both for my own conversion and my continuing growth in faith. But that is not the doctrine that was taught by Luther and Calvin.

What Luther and Calvin taught was that every Christian is the priest of his or her neighbor. We are not our own priest. Nor is our priest an ordained religious professional who dictates to us our spiritual condition. Rather, ***we are all each other's priests***, hearing confession and granting absolution. We are priest to one another. Luther put it most plainly. "He (the Christian) is a priest not to his own advantage but to serve other men. This service is to bear the sins and iniquities of others, lest they be the chief actors both in their own perdition as well as that of others."[59]

What Luther sought to do was not to remove from the Church the responsibility of participating in the forgiveness of sins. Rather, it was to remove from a particular class of Christians—the ordained priesthood—that exclusive responsibility in order to distribute that privilege upon the entire Christian community. Thus, each Christian was to be each other's priests. And the way each Christian was to best live out being a priest to his neighbor was through the vocation he practiced. Thus, Luther wrote, "All our work in the field, in the garden, in the city, in the home, in struggles, in

[59] Martin Luther, *Epistle to the Hebrews* (Philadelphia: Westminster Press, 1962), 103.

governments—to what does it all amount before God? (God) clothes himself in the form of an ordinary man who performs his work on earth."[60]

John Calvin stressed the importance of the one seeking forgiveness to make both public and private confession. "The secret confession which is made to God is followed by voluntary confession to men, whenever that is conducive to the divine glory or our humiliation,"[61] Calvin wrote. He recommends the pastor to play this role, but leaves open to "any particular individual into whose bosom we are to disburden our feelings" such hearing of one's confession. Calvin then states most specifically, "For as the duty of mutual admonition and correction is committed to all Christians, but is specially enjoined on ministers, so while we ought all to console each other mutually, and confirm each other in confidence in the divine mercy, we see that ministers are appointed to be the witnesses and sponsors of it."[62]

Finally, Calvin refers directly to the vocation of the laity, when he writes, "A vocation is the principle part of human life and the part that means the most to God."[63]

John Wesley, 200 years later, built into his Methodist societies the implementation of this Reformation doctrine of the priesthood of all believers. In those societies, which were the backbone of the Methodist revival in Great Britain, a mature Christian saw to the spiritual formation and moral growth of its members within the context of an intimate fellowship. There, both public and private confession of sin was coupled with instruction in the Christian life and encouragement toward personal holiness. The disciplines of the Moravian movement and the practices of the Anglican Evangelicals, both contemporary with the Methodist revival, all sought to practice the priesthood of all believers in the active forgiving of sin and in the holding of Christians to accountability regarding the nurturance of their personal holiness.

With the reclaiming of the doctrine of the priesthood of all believers came the embracing once again of a doctrine of vocation. If every Christian is called to be every

---

[60] As quoted by Gustaf Wingren, *Luther on Vocation* (Evansville, IN: Ballast Press, 1994), 137–138.

[61] John Calvin, *Institutes of the Christian Religion, Vol. I* (Grand Rapids, MI: Wm. B. Eerdmans, 1957), 543.

[62] Calvin, *Institutes,* 544.

[63] John Calvin, *Treatises Against the Anabaptists and Against the Libertines* (Grand Rapids, MI: Baker Book House, 1982), 78.

other person's priest as she or he goes about everyday activities, then that means that all in which one labors should be dedicated to God as our ministry to humanity.

The vocation or calling we have received from God is both a profound gift from God which provides purpose to our lives, yet it is also our obligation and responsibility. In the catechism for the Church of Geneva, Calvin interprets the phrase, "Give us this day our daily bread" from this perspective. Thus, he wrote, "Although we are to work and even sweat to provide food, nevertheless we are not nourished by our labour or industry or diligence, but by God's blessing only, by which the labour of our hands is prospered, which would otherwise be in vain." [64]

In this section on the doctrine of vocation throughout the history of the Church, we have sought to demonstrate that one of the primary efforts of the Reformation was to recapture that doctrine from centuries of neglect by the Church, in order to restore it to the place of prominence that it held in Scripture. The subsequent history of the Church has been the effort to submerge that doctrine once again because it does not serve the inevitable effort to build the church as an institution. Therefore, our task today—if we want to both have a vital Christian life and a vital Church—is to rediscover and redefine for our own day a doctrine of vocation which can give to every Christian the sense of God's sure and certain call upon her or his life.

Conclusion

In today's world and especially in the city, we are constantly reminded in innumerable ways that we are insignificant and unimportant cogs in the machine, that we have no purpose in life except to make and spend money. People in today's world are often hurting people, many times hopeless people. And that includes people in the church who may find significance for their lives by being in the church. But outside the church and their families, they feel unimportant. The world communicates to them in many ways every day that it will go on with or without them.

The doctrine of vocation declares the opposite! The doctrine of vocation says to people, "You are important. You exist for a purpose. You are not here simply to work or buy, to make money and keep the economy rolling. You are here as a child of God to

---

[64] John Calvin, "Catechism of the Church at Geneva," *Theological Treatises,* Library of Christian Classics Series, Vol. XXII (Philadelphia: Westminster Press, 1964), 126.

be used by God in a particular way in order to contribute to God's redemption and transformation of this city and of the world. You are important to Christ because God has created you to be an integral part of the Kingdom of God. You were created by God and chosen by God and are called by God to serve Christ in the world. And others in this congregation are also crucial, for they, too, have been created, chosen, and called by God. You need to find each other and you need to work together to become Christ's ambassadors in the world. And our job, as a Church, is to enable that to happen and to get out of the way"!

The belief that all of us are called by God to serve God and humanity in a particular way is a basic underlying premise throughout the Bible. I believe the reclaiming of the doctrine and practice of vocation is strategic to the future of Christianity in an urban, secular world. Unless the church learns ways to enable all its members to discover and act out their vocation, as well as have a theology about it, it will not have any substantive future at all. But if it does develop both a theology and practice of vocation that enables everyone to be a Christ to his or her neighbor, then we will make a profound difference in our church, our community, and our city that will "turn the world upside down"!

Chapter 6

Profiles of Vocation

> Now during those days Jesus went out to the mountain to pray; and he spent the night in prayer to God. And when day came, he called his disciples and chose twelve of them, whom he also named apostles: Simon, whom he named Peter, and his brother Andrew, and James, and John, and Philip, and Bartholomew, and Matthew, and Thomas, and James son of Alphaeus, and Simon, who was called the Zealot, and Judas son of James, and Judas Iscariot, who became a traitor (Luke 6:12–16).

Jesus chose twelve men and later (as Luke points out), several women who are to be his disciples. These people are to live with Jesus, learn from him, and work with him. Upon them, Jesus would build his kingdom. But who were these few people in whom Jesus would trust the destiny of his Church?

Those Who Followed Jesus

The people upon whom Jesus would build his church consisted of three groups: the disciples (or apostles); select women; and others who would enter Christianity in its early years but did not know Jesus while he was alive. These are who they were:

The Disciples

Jesus's disciples were his most intimate followers whom he nurtured, taught, and formed into the leadership of his kingdom. *Simon Peter* was a fisherman from Galilee, and the brother of Andrew. *Andrew* was also a fisherman from Galilee. *James*, son of Zebedee, brother to John, was also a fisherman from Galilee. *John* was brother to James, and was also a fisherman. In all biblical listings of the disciples, these four are always grouped together and are always the first listed. Likely, they made up an "inner circle" of disciples upon whom Jesus particularly concentrated.

The other disciples included *Philip*, who was from Bethsaida; his occupation is unknown. *Bartholomew* also went by the name Nathanael and was from Cana in Galilee; his occupation is also unknown. *Matthew*—or Levi—was a tax collector, living in Capernaum; he was a son of Alphaeus and likely James the Less's brother (there were two "James," so one was traditionally called "James the Less" to distinguish him from James, the son of Zebedee about whom we wrote above). *Thomas* was also named Didymus, and was also a fisherman; he became well-known as "Doubting Thomas" because he would not believe Jesus had risen from the dead until he saw the stigmata, but he was also the first to confess Jesus as God (John 20:26–29).

Additional disciples included *James,* the son of Alphaeus, (see "James the Less" above); his occupation is unknown. *Simon the Zealot* was from Cana; he was part of a Jewish violent revolutionary force (the Zealots), seeking the overthrow of Rome. *Judas son of James* was always called such after the resurrection in order to distinguish him (understandably) from Judas Iscariot; he later became known as Lebbaeus Thaddeus by tradition (Thaddeus means "warm hearted") because of the infamy associated with the name "Judas." *Judas Iscariot* was always listed as the twelfth disciple before Jesus's resurrection. He was from Kerioth, and his occupation was unknown. However, he handled the treasury of the Twelve and dispensed alms as well as maintaining their corporate livelihood, which would suggest that he was a bookkeeper or accountant, a money-changer or financial manager by occupation.

There is one other disciple who is not listed as one of the twelve, but needs to be because he was selected by the disciples after Jesus's resurrection to replace Judas. *Matthias* apparently accompanied the Twelve and Jesus but was not selected by Jesus to be one of this inner core. It is said of him, "(Matthias) accompanied us all the time that the Lord Jesus went in and out among us. . . . (and was) a witness . . . of his resurrection." (Acts 1:22) Chosen by the disciples to replace Judas, Matthias is never heard from again, nor do we know anything more about him.

The Women

Unlike any other religious leader of his day, Jesus had a significant group of women who followed him. Women were judged unclean and beneath men in station and character by Jewish society, and therefore rabbis would not even consider allowing them to attend their teachings or be their disciples. Not so Jesus. According to Luke's gospel, he encouraged the participation and leadership of women and had a group of them who joined with the disciple band in living, learning and working alongside them.

There were eight women who receive particular attention from the gospel writers. *Mary Magdalene* was healed by Jesus of "seven demons"; she was from the city of Magdala, apparently had great wealth, was the first to witness his resurrection, and is always mentioned first among the women who followed Jesus. *Joanna* was the wife of Chuza, manager of Herod's household; she, too, was obviously a woman of wealth and power. *Susanna* is one about whom we know nothing except that she is mentioned in Luke 8:3. *Mary*, one of three "Marys" around Jesus, is the mother of James and Joses (the sons of Alphaeus, perhaps?). *Salome* is one about whom nothing is known except she is mentioned in Mark 15:40; she is not to be confused with the Salome who danced for the head of John the Baptist. *Martha*, who with her sister Mary, lived in an unnamed village close to Jerusalem whose house Jesus would frequently visit; their brother was Lazarus, whom Jesus raised from the dead. *Mary* is one of the three Marys and is sister to Martha; she was a diligent student of Jesus. Finally, there is the *unnamed mother* of the sons of Zebedee; we do not know her name, but she faithfully followed Jesus along with her two sons, James and John.

Of course, although she was not a part of the group of women following Jesus, we would not want to overlook *Mary*, the mother of Jesus and of James (James would become a leader of the infant Church—not to be confused with James Zebedee or James Alphaeus). Besides the birth narratives in the gospels of Matthew and Luke, Mary appears in stories of Jesus's adolescence, during his ministry, at the cross, and later in Acts and as a possible source in Luke's gospel account. From Nazareth, Mary was a peasant.

The Later Believers

There are two other followers of Jesus who played pivotal roles in the formation of the earliest Church but who probably never met Jesus during his earthly life. *Barnabas* we earlier wrote about extensively. His name was actually Joseph. He was from Cyprus, and he was a wealthy landowner. He was responsible for organizing Christianity's first outreach to the Gentiles, and discipled both Paul and Mark (the author of the second gospel) when they were young Christians.

Paul (also named Saul) is probably the most prominent and clearly the most formative of all of Jesus's followers in his impact upon the development of Christianity. Paul was born in Tarsus, was raised in Jerusalem, a tentmaker by occupation, a Jew who was also a Roman citizen by birth, and a Pharisee. After his conversion, he became Christianity's main apostle to the Gentiles, making three missionary trips, writing 12 or 13 books, founding an unknown number of churches, and becoming Christianity's leading evangelist and theologian.

This is a quick survey of those who followed Jesus. It is worthy of note that none of these followers of Jesus—except for Paul—were professional religionists (that is, priests, rabbis, or adjudicators of the Law of Moses). All were laypeople! But we can learn much more about the biblical concept of call, not simply by noting their lay origins, but by profiling the vocation of a few of these followers. This we will now do.

A Few Who Followed Jesus

Simon Peter

"I never met a man I didn't like." That famous statement by Will Rogers could only be made by a very likeable man. I would imagine that the same statement could have been said of one of Jesus's most outstanding followers—Simon Peter.

Simon Peter is portrayed in scripture as a big, gentle, impetuous, sometimes bumbling, warm-hearted bear of a man. He was the sort of man who wore his heart on his sleeve, always caring about others, an effusive man, quick to respond to his own feelings, and often putting his mouth into gear before his mind. You really couldn't help but like Simon Peter because he was an innocent—a man of absolutely no guile who genuinely loved people and responded warmly to all of life. It was this warm-hearted, child-like exuberance that was Peter's greatest asset. But Jesus saw that it also had the potential to be the Big Fisherman's greatest weakness.

When one looks at most of Jesus's encounters with Peter before the Lord's crucifixion—his call to become a fisher of people, his invitation to Peter to walk on the water with him, his confrontation of Peter when Simon in one breath confessed him as Messiah and in the next told him that his crucifixion was unacceptable, his inclusion of Peter in Jesus's transfiguration before God—all of these encounters were at least partially designed to push Simon Peter beyond himself.

Simon's personality had served him well before he met Jesus. His warm-hearted, guileless and open manner caused people to be very receptive to him. He was well liked and trusted, and therefore it was easy for him to assume leadership. Consequently, he was a very confident and self-assured person. But then came this miracle-worker, this walker-on-water, this disturbing teacher, this man transfigured before God, and Simon Peter began to discover that his likeable personality had its limitations.

There were two events in Simon's life that did more than anything else to transform him into Peter—the rock upon which an infant church could be built. The first event was Peter's denial of Jesus (Matt 26:69–75; Mark 14:66–72; Luke 22:54–62; John 18:15–18, 25–27). Jesus had been arrested and brought to trial on the grounds of religious heresy and political treason. The sentence for conviction for treason had to be death. Peter, when asked three times if he knew Jesus, denied any knowledge of or any relationship with his Master.

In his denial of Jesus, Peter was brought up against the reality of his great capacity to do evil. A danger that a person faces who gets along well with people is that he starts to believe that he really is a good and decent person. And Simon Peter had fallen into that trap.

But this act of denying his relationship with Jesus brought him up against himself. This act denied the deep friendship and even love between the two men. This act denied everything that Jesus had meant to Peter over the past three years. But worst of all, this act denied Jesus his life—for Jewish law taught that two successful witnesses were required to condemn a person of a crime punishable by death, and Peter's testimony that these accusations against Jesus were false and unsubstantiated likely would have won Jesus an acquittal. For one brief moment, the fate of the Messiah lay in Peter's hands. And Peter let him die!

Why did Peter deny Jesus? The only explanation that makes sense was that he was afraid to be associated with him. He feared for his own skin. So, by his denial, Peter condemned the Son of God to death.

Peter was brought up against himself. He finally saw himself for what he truly was—not affable, not warm-hearted, not guileless but a coward, a betrayer, a murderer of the Christ! Peter had discovered his great capacity to do evil.

The second event Jesus used to transform Simon Peter into the rock was his post-resurrection meeting with Peter on the shore of the Sea of Galilee (John 21:4–19). Peter knew that Jesus had risen from the dead, but he was probably dreading an encounter with the risen Christ. After all, what could he say about his denial?

One morning, while Simon Peter was fishing with the other disciples, Jesus appeared on the shore of that lake where the big fisherman had first met the young rabbi from Nazareth. A second meeting there was now inevitable.

> Jesus was the first to speak. "Simon, son of John, do you love me?"
>
> "Yes, Lord, you know that I am your friend."
>
> "Feed my lambs. Simon, son of John, do you love me?"
>
> "Yes, Lord, you know that I am your friend."
>
> "Tend my sheep. Simon, son of John, are you my friend?"
>
> "Lord, you know everything; you know that I am your friend."
>
> "Feed my sheep. Very truly, I tell you, the day will come when you will not simply be my friend. Someday, you will sacrifice your life for me. Then, you will know that you love me. All I ask of you now is that you follow me"![65]

In this encounter at the Sea of Galilee, Jesus gave to Simon Peter two magnificent gifts. The first gift was the amazing forgiveness and depth of his love. Jesus let Peter know that he held no grudge against him, and would not withhold his love. He simply showed Peter that no matter what the fisherman might have done—even denial, betrayal, and allowing execution to take place—that would not alter

[65] John 21:15–19, my personal translation of this text. Explanation for this translation: In the original Greek of this text, two Greek words are used which are both rightly translated "love." *Philia* means the love of a friend, and *agape* means a deep and committed love. Thus, Jesus asks Peter twice, "Do you *agape* me?" And each time, Peter replies, "I *philia* you." In the third instance, Jesus changes his question to "Do you *philia* me?," which causes the author to note that Peter was hurt because the third time Jesus used *philia* instead of *agape* (John 21:17). To Peter's third response, Jesus replies, "Feed my sheep. Very truly I tell you, when you were younger, you used to fasten your own belt and to go wherever you wished. But when you grow old, you will stretch out your hands, and someone else will fasten a belt around you and take you where you do not wish to go. Follow me!" (21:18)

Biblical scholars are divided in the interpretation of this passage. Many scholars do not draw a distinction between the particular uses of *philia* and *agape* in this passage, focusing upon Jesus's question to Peter being, simply, "Do you love me, and is that love implemented in your actions?" Other scholars, including myself, feel that the author John was drawing a clear distinction between Jesus's expectation of the love he wanted from Peter and the love Peter was honestly recognizing he could give—thus, the significance between the choice of the two words for "love." My justification for drawing this distinction is Peter's honest appraisal of himself (sobered by his earlier denial of Jesus), and Jesus, in essence, responding, "Today, Peter, you may be able only to love me as a friend. But I am telling you, Peter, that the day will come when you will choose to die for me. On that day, you will know that you love me as I now love you. Meanwhile, follow me!" That this is an accurate interpretation of this text is indicated by John's commentary on what would otherwise seem an obscure passage, "He said this to indicate the kind of death by which Peter would glorify God."

Jesus's love for him. Jesus's second gift to Peter was the affirmation that he did not expect Peter to love him back with equal love. Rather, he asked only one thing of his disciple—to follow him! And when Simon quietly and humbly accepted these two gifts after his denial, he was transformed into Peter—the rock!

What a magnificent thing Jesus had done for Peter! The Simon whom Jesus first met at the Sea of Galilee three years earlier had within him the raw material to be the leader of the infant church. He had the personal dynamism, the warmth, the optimistic and enthusiastic personality necessary to rally, support, and lead the Early Church. But that dynamism and power had never been tried in the fire!

But then came the miracles of healing, the walking on water, rebuke after confessing Jesus as Messiah, the transfiguration. And then had come Peter's denial, his Lord's crucifixion, and then their meeting a second time by the Sea of Galilee. God had painfully, even brutally prepared Simon to become Peter, the rock.

Peter had learned, not just intellectually but in the very living of his life, what Christ had to teach him if he were to truly be the spiritual father of the Church. He had to learn of his great capacity to do evil! For if he did not know of his potential for evil, he would have used his warmth and charm to seek his own ends in the Church. He had to learn of Jesus's ongoing and constant love for him, for if he did not know of that gift of love he would seek to get it from others by using his charisma—and thus would divert the Church's loyalty from Jesus to himself. He had to learn of the limitations of his own love for Christ and for others, for only in recognizing those limitations could he accept himself as he truly was rather than placing upon himself the unrealistic expectation of constant love for the Church. Such unrealistic expectations would result in his self-condemnation because his love would inevitably ebb and flow.

Once Peter had discovered his capacity to sin, Christ's ongoing forgiveness and love for him, and the limitations of his own love, he was set free to discover his true calling and in its fulfillment, use his warmth, caring enthusiasm, his tempered guilelessness, even his impetuosity to set the foundations of Christ's church which has endured for 2,000 years.

Judas Iscariot and Paul the Apostle

Every successful reformation needs within it a heart, a mind, and a voice. Each such movement needs someone who can dream and conceptualize the revolution, someone else who can devise a plan for turning that dream into reality, and still a third person who can so articulate that dream to the world that people will follow it. Thus, Thomas Jefferson dreamed and then conceptualized a democratic state not under the tyranny of a king. James Madison developed the constitution that would implement that dream in former colonies freed of that tyranny. George Washington led the people to victory over the forces that would destroy the dream. Thus, one could say that we truly had three "fathers" of our country!

Jesus saw the need of having followers who could be heart, mind, and voice for the kingdom of God. The Apostle John was its heart, likely revealing throughout his ministry but finally writing it up in his Gospel and in Revelation his dream of what the world and the Church would be like lived under the authority and love of the Word of God. Peter was obviously its voice who, with his capacity both to rouse crowds and to love people, wooed thousands of souls into that kingdom. But who was selected by Jesus to be the brains—the mind—the conceptualizer of the Church to proclaim and represent that kingdom to the world? I would suggest that the person chosen was the man named Judas Iscariot!

When we hear the name Judas Iscariot, only one reality floods our minds. Judas—the betrayer! But Judas was not always the betrayer. For three years, he lived and learned and worked with Jesus. He was as accepted and loved by Jesus as was any other disciple. He was not called by Jesus to be his betrayer; to suggest such an idea is to make Jesus the most manipulative of men.

I would suggest that Judas was chosen by Jesus to be the thinker—the conceptualizer among the disciples—the man who, more than anyone else, could build a logical, rational, and consistent faith and church, who could take John's dream of the New Jerusalem and construct a road map to get there, who could help the Church truly find a reason for the faith that was embraced within it.

What is the evidence for this assertion? Consider the following. Judas's seating at the Last Supper was a seating close enough to Jesus that Jesus could whisper to him (John 13:27-30); there was nothing abnormal in that seating or the other disciples—terribly competitive regarding closeness to Jesus (Mark 10:35–45; Luke 22:24)—would have protested. This would indicate that Judas was just behind Peter and Andrew, James and John in stature.

Second, Judas was apparently the disciple who handled the administration and planning of the disciple band, and was trusted with all its money as well (John

12:1–8; 13:29)—no small responsibility! But the greatest argument for Judas as the intended mind of the earliest church were the events surrounding his terrible betrayal.

Consider the apparent absurdity of Jesus's last days! One day, Jesus led a triumphal entry into Jerusalem—an action involving an enormous crowd of people (Matt 21:8–11). Four days later, one of his closest friends betrayed him to the authorities, guaranteeing his death. From the heights of public adulation to total rejection in just four days! What possible explanation could be made for such despicable action on Judas's part?

When Jesus entered Jerusalem on that Palm Sunday 2,000 years ago, it was the culmination of many of the disciples' dreams for Jesus—including Judas! In that ride into Jerusalem, Jesus was fulfilling Old Testament prophesy (Isa. 62:11; Zech. 9:9) and thus declaring himself the Messiah or ruler of the Jews. The prophetic meaning of Jesus's action was not lost on the disciples; they understood full well the symbolism of what was occurring (Matt. 21:1–11, 14–16). Both to Judas and to the other disciples, this public declaration by Jesus could mean only one thing—Jesus as Messiah was about to set up the long-anticipated Jewish kingdom of God. The next logical step in Judas's mind was for Jesus to mobilize the Israelite people into an army, to overthrow both the Roman rulers of Israel and the hated Jewish priesthood, and establish an independent state of Israel. Quickly, God would intervene, Rome would be destroyed, and Jesus would then be ruler of a Jewish empire—the kingdom of God.

But Jesus raised no army; he only gathered his little company of disciples for a meal. He led no attack upon the Roman garrison in Jerusalem; he only criticized the priests in the temple. He didn't seek to recruit the people into a fighting force; he only continued to teach them. He didn't claim the rulership of Jerusalem; instead he wept over that city. Judas realized with sinking heart that Jesus was not doing anything to bring about a revolution against Rome, and the opportunity was slipping through his fingers.

The Christian Church, over its 2,000 years of history, has developed only two theories adequate to explain Judas's apparently baffling betrayal of Jesus. The first theory is that Judas betrayed Jesus to force his hand. By placing him in the position of either losing his life or defending it, Jesus would be forced to take up arms against Rome and the revolution would begin. The second theory was that Judas, seeing Jesus frittering away the little advantage he had, concluded that this man was not the

Messiah after all. He—Judas—had been deceived. In anger and disgust, therefore, Judas washed his hands of Jesus by betraying him.

Whatever theory you choose, the "bottom line" is still the same. Jesus was not acting according to Judas's plan. This was the logical time to mobilize the people and lead the revolution. All prophecy had been fulfilled and a considerable host loyal to Jesus assembled. Yet Jesus was not doing what the Jewish law, the prophets, and the logic of Judas said he must do at this critical moment. From Judas's perspective, Jesus had betrayed the trust Israel had invested in him. Jesus had betrayed the Messianic dream. And for that, he deserved to die!

What Judas little realized was that, in his betrayal of Jesus, he was betraying his own soul. Closed to what Jesus had actually taught and practiced over their three years together, Judas had set himself up for the destruction of his own soul. That destruction would cost Judas his life (Matt. 27:3–10).

But if the dream of God's kingdom would become reality on the earth, the Church still needed someone to give form and substance to that dream. The heart of the gospel lived on in the Apostle John; the voice of the Church was now invested even more strongly in the chastened and matured Peter. But who would be the mind of the Church?

The disciples gathered together and selected a man named Matthias. But God chose a Jewish Pharisee named Paul of Tarsus. After the disciples selected him, Matthias was never heard from again. But God met Paul on the road to Damascus, and proclaimed to the Church, this man "is an instrument whom I have chosen to bring my name before Gentiles and kings and before the people of Israel" (Acts 9:15).

And chosen instrument was what Paul became. This man won more people to Christ, reached more cities and nations with the gospel, and founded more churches than any other disciple. But Paul's greatest contribution to Christianity was his authorship of a number of books written to urban churches and individuals, some of which are now lost, but at least nine and perhaps twelve still exist in the New Testament canon.[66] Those books present one of the most consistent, rational, and

---

[66] Almost all biblical scholars today claim Pauline authorship for Romans, I and II Corinthians, Galatians, Philippians, Colossians, Philemon, and I and II Thessalonians. Some scholars also name Paul as the author of Ephesians, I and II Timothy, and Titus. See A. C. Purdy, "Paul the

logically developed systems of belief that the Christian Church and the world has ever seen. And every Christian has been radically influenced by that system of belief. Paul became the mind of the Christian Church—the mind that Judas had originally been chosen to be.

What was the difference between Judas and Paul? What was the difference that caused one man to become one of humanity's most hated and reviled people and the other to become one of its most profound and influential saints? The difference is very small indeed.

Both Judas and Paul had the same serious flaw. Each man had an enemy within himself. The difference between the two was dictated by the way each of them chose to deal with that enemy.

The enemy—that fatal flaw—was the terrorizing fear that they might be wrong. They both feared discovering that the cause to which they had invested their entire lives would prove to be false. Each of the men protected that fear through the use of anger and hostility. But it was at this point that the difference became plain.

Judas would not admit his fear to himself. He would not deal with the anger, dread, and hostility within himself. Instead, he projected that fear and its protective anger out onto the world. Judas could never say with that famed comic-strip character, "We have met the enemy and he is us"! No, the enemy was always someone else.

First, it was the Romans. If only the Romans could be conquered and God's kingdom of love and justice ushered in, then everyone would live in peace and joy, and Judas's own unidentified fear would be relieved.

Then, when Jesus refused to go to war against the Romans on that fateful Palm Sunday, Judas saw his design for the world crumbling, and the fear that he might be wrong rose as terror in his throat. So it was that he turned against the man who most loved him. Rome was no longer the enemy; Jesus was! And when Jesus died and by his death, revealed to the biblically informed Judas that he was indeed the Messiah, Judas was faced once again with the reality that he was wrong and had made an overwhelming mistake in that betrayal (Matt. 27:3–4). But even with that evidence arrayed against him, Judas could not admit to the enemy within.

Apostle," *The Interpreter's Dictionary of the Bible, K-Q*, ed. George A. Buttrick (Nashville, TN: Abingdon Press, 1962), 602–603.

Thus it was that he turned against God and identified him as his ultimate enemy. But God had not used Judas, choosing him for this crime. Judas was used by his own inner enemy which he refused, even to his last breath, to face. The true tragedy of Judas was that he could never face the darkness in his own soul. Therefore that dark enemy defeated him, and in defeating him, caused the death of the Son of God.

St. Paul was faced with this very same enemy—the fear that all to which he had committed his life could be wrong. And, initially, he handled that fear in the same way in which Judas had. Instead of struggling with his own fear that Judaism might be wrong, Paul lashed out against the Christians, believing that if he destroyed them, he would destroy the threat to his faith and therefore the threat to his own soul (Acts 7:58–8:1; 9:1–2; Gal. 1:13–14).

Then, like Judas, Paul met Jesus (Acts 9:3–19). But something happened to Paul in his meeting with Jesus that had not happened to Judas. Paul faced his own sinfulness (I Tim. 1:12–15), and in that facing, became fully open to everything the Master had to give him. Paul received all Jesus offered to him, and not simply that portion of Jesus's life and message that confirmed and supported his personal convictions. He was willing to give that up to the Galilean. He was willing to risk everything in his life (Phil. 3:7–14), including the fear that crept closest to his heart—the fear that he could be eternally wrong (I Cor. 15:12–58).

The result was that Paul became a man who was able to face his own inner enemy (Rom 8:31–39). He no longer needed to project that enemy out upon the world. Instead, he could admit that the fear that lived *within* was the enemy; he became acquainted with that enemy, faced up to it and committed that fear to God. With such a commitment, Paul was liberated from the tyranny of that enemy within. He was freed from his fear of his fear. He could now be at peace with himself. And because he could be at peace even with his enemy within, he could bring the peace of God to the world.

Mary and Martha

Jesus of Nazareth was being entertained in the home of his very close friends, Mary and Martha. Martha was bustling around in the kitchen, preparing dinner for her honored guest while Mary sat in rapt attention, thoroughly caught up in the Master's words. The longer Martha worked in the kitchen, the more angry she became at the quiet and not very helpful Mary.

Finally, Martha stalked into the room where Jesus and Mary were visiting. In exasperation, she demanded of Jesus, "Lord, do you not care that my sister has left me to do all the work by myself? Tell her then to help me." But the Lord answered her, "Martha, Martha, you are worried and distracted by many things; there is need of only one thing. Mary has chosen the better part, which will not be taken from her" (Luke 10:41–42).

"Mary has chosen the better part." There are few passages of scripture more prone to misinterpretation than this one. It is used repeatedly to justify the contemplative life over the activist life. Yet both contemplative and activist err if they believe this passage indicated Jesus's preference of one way over the other.

Mary was a true contemplative. Today, we would call her an introvert. She was quiet, thoughtful, meditative, the kind of person who would be very intuitive, who would carefully think through what she believed, who would dream great dreams. Her greatest delight would be to spend her time quietly listening to those more spiritually discerning and wise than she. The last thing Mary would choose to do would be that of being the center of attention.

Martha, on the other hand, was a true activist. Today, we would call her an extrovert. She would be a no-nonsense, hard-working, task-oriented person, a woman who would move very quickly and spontaneously out of her feelings, who would laugh easily and cry easily, and sympathize easily and get angry easily. Her greatest delight would be to savor every element of a meal with her friends. The last thing Martha would choose would be that of having an hour with absolutely nothing to do.

When Jesus said to Martha, "Mary has chosen the better part," he was not saying "contemplation is better than action; quiet is more spiritual than hospitality." What he was saying, in essence, was "Martha, you allow yourself to become too caught up in your familiar functions of activism and production. If you are to become a fulfilled, whole person, discovering God's call for yourself, you will need to discover your better part—the part Mary has already found—that of quiet and contemplation."

If it had been Mary who would have complained that Martha was disturbing her quiet by banging pots and pans together, Jesus probably would have said to her, "Mary, Mary, you become so caught up in ministering to your mind that you forget how important the body is. If you are to become a whole person and discover God's call to you, you will need to learn what Martha has already found—that hard work and the enjoyment of a beautiful dinner with your friends is a little bit of heaven. Martha has chosen the better part"!

I believe that within each of us God has placed a deep desire to be a whole, balanced, fulfilled human being. The thinking person envies the one who can play. The intuitive person wishes he could be more spontaneous. The introvert wishes she wasn't so shy. All of those reactions are actually God-given instincts to be a more balanced and integrated person. The envy we feel toward another person is, in reality, the recognition that we need to discover in ourselves that quality we see so well personified in that envied person. The warmth we feel toward another may actually be our soul's hope to absorb from that person the spirit we find in him that so stands in contrast with our own.

This was exactly what Mary and Martha had unwittingly done. Because both of them were so opposite in their personalities, they had gravitated toward each other in order to create a home which was both balanced and functional. But what had originally seemed an effective way to create a full life together had not worked out well.

The trap Mary and Martha had fallen into was that they were preventing each other from choosing the better part. That prevention was not intentional; they had simply fallen into it through each of them exercising only what they did best. Because Mary never took the time to prepare a meal for her guests, she wasn't discovering the joy of hospitality. And because Martha never allowed herself to take the time to sit at the feet of Jesus, she wasn't discovering the joy of contemplation.

The result was that both women were angry at each other, were seeking to manipulate each other into doing what the other wanted done, and were missing the joy and potential blessing of a visit from Jesus. Neither was choosing the better part she needed. And that is exactly the problem with seeking to meet your inner need for wholeness and balance through another person. It simply can't be done!

St. Paul wrote, "We are God's work of art, created in Christ Jesus to live the good life as from the beginning he had meant us to live it" (Eph. 2:10, *The Jerusalem Bible*). It is not two or three or four people who make up God's work of art. Each one of us is created by God to be his work of art, a complete, whole, thoroughly balanced and integrated individual. Each one of us is called by God to become the beautiful person he has created us to be. And we can never discover our calling for what God wants us to *do* unless we are discovering God's call for us to *be*.

We are examining in this chapter the lives of those who followed Jesus while he was here on earth—some examined peripherally, others more thoroughly. As we examine carefully each of their lives, we discover certain common factors. Each one of these followers of Jesus had natural potentials and gifts. Whether it was Peter's warm, spontaneous responsiveness to people, or John's capacity to dream the impossible dream, or Judas's capacity to organize, each follower had great potential within himself or herself; each person was God's very incomplete, unfinished work of art.

But each follower of Jesus also had a fatal flaw. Each of these disciples had something within him or her that kept that person from becoming all he had the potential to be. It might have been Matthew's acceptance of other people's evaluation of his worth, Thomas's doubts and uncertainties, or Paul's fear that the gospel in which he believed could be wrong—or even Martha's unwillingness to be anything else than what her sister believed her to be. Whatever the flaw, there was something standing between each person and Christ, between each person as she was and each person as she had the potential to be, between each person and the embracing and living into that vocation for one's life which Christ meant them to fill. And that flaw was keeping each follower of Christ from becoming a whole, mature Christian and the type of person God needed before he could use her to transform the world around her.

There was still one more common factor. One event—and one event alone—transformed each of these followers of Christ except Judas. And that event didn't transform Judas because Judas chose to exclude it from his experience with Christ.

One event turned around each follower's life, overcame each person's flaw, and liberated each of these followers to become the people who would turn the world upside down. It was not Jesus's words which finally liberated them. It was not his actions that ultimately removed this fatal flaw. It was not even the Master's life which enabled them to become fully functional, balanced people. It was one event filling a three-day period of time which transformed each of these followers into God's work of art. That event was the crucifixion and resurrection of Jesus Christ!

St. Paul wrote, "You were dead, through the crimes and the sins in which you used to live. . . . But God loved us with so much love that he was generous with his mercy: when we were dead through our sins, he brought us to life with Christ . . . and raised us up with him and gave us a place with him in heaven. . . . For it is through grace that you have been saved." (Eph. 2:1, 4–6 *The Jerusalem Bible*)

What each follower of the Christ except Judas discovered at the Master's crucifixion and resurrection was that he or she could not make himself into a better, more balanced person. None of them, by their seeking and searching, could find fulfillment, whether they searched for that fulfillment in another person or by the accumulation of things. Their wholeness could come only as a free gift from God. Their fatal flaw could be removed only by God. The development of their potentials and gifts wouldn't occur by committing themselves to a self-help program but by committing themselves to Christ. As Jesus had gone to his cross, so did each of his followers have to go to theirs—their crosses of wanting to be a leader, wanting to be right, wanting to be sure, wanting to be great, wanting to be popular, wanting to be in control, wanting to be liked. Each of them had to be willing to say to God, "Here I am, Lord, just as I am—with all my potentials, with all my gifts, with all my expectations and hopes—and with all of my flaws and shortcomings. I turn them all over to you. Do with me as you will. Use me as you choose. I surrender all my life to you." Because until they came to the self-emptying place of saying that, they could never discover God's call and intentions for their lives.

Death! Emptiness! Crucifixion! But then comes the first day of the week and an empty tomb. Then comes resurrection! And each follower of Christ was raised from his own spiritual death to become the person that he needed to be in order to be able to do what God was calling him or her to do to enable humanity's experiencing of the kingdom of God!

In Jesus's last recorded encounter with Mary and Martha, Martha is finally sitting at the Christ's feet! Jesus says to her, "Martha, I am the resurrection and the life. Those who believe in me, even though they die will live, and everyone who lives and believes in me will never die. Do you believe this?" (John 11:25–26)

And Martha—the busy and bustling Martha, the newly reflective and rapt Martha, the now whole and balanced Martha answers, "Yes, Lord, I believe!"

Summary

As we look at the stories of those who followed Jesus, what stands out to me is that each person is a unique personality who is chosen and called by Jesus. Each person has great potential and unique gifts, but also a significant enough weakness that it could cripple or even destroy that person in her or his service of God and humanity. Each is profoundly affected by her or his encounter with Jesus, and thus is shaped into becoming the particular servant Jesus needs to serve both him and the church.

What is particularly noteworthy, however, is that Jesus drew them all together to become—as one Body—the totality of what none of them could be as individuals. All these personalities—together—needed to make up the disciple band, the women in leadership, the future leaders Jesus would add to his church. All are needed in order—together—to create a Body adequate for working for the transformation of the world. That is what Paul meant when he called the whole church together "the Body of Christ" (I Cor. 12:12- 13:1).

From these profiles of vocation, we learn that *vocation is built not so much on what we can do as it is on who we are.* Our calling into service of Christ and the people of the world is not so much based upon our performance as it is based upon our personality. God is less concerned with your production than God is concerned with your character—whether you are becoming the person God created, chose, and called you to be. Because only in becoming the unique person you are intended to be will you be used by God in the ways God intends to use you.

In other words, what looking at the apostolic profiles of vocation teach us, is that God needs *you*—you, with all of your particularities and peculiarities, with all of your strengths and shortcomings—as an integrated part of a larger Body of Christ. God wants you—*just because you are you!*

An ancient story told by the church of the first several centuries reminds us of what Jesus invested in his followers and in all of us by calling us to "leave our nets and follow him."

When Jesus returned to heaven after his Ascension, the angels gathered to welcome him and to celebrate his victory over death. Their talk inevitably moved from Jesus's death and resurrection to the building of his church and the great investment made in it to bring the world to Christ and his kingdom.

"But Jesus," said the archangel Gabriel, "these disciples of yours are such fallible, limited people. They don't have much education. They are not powerfully placed. They are unsophisticated and weak of intent and ability. What if they fall short of your intentions? What if they fail in their bringing your gospel and your kingdom to the world? What alternate plan do you then have to reach the world?"

Jesus looked lovingly at his inquisitor, and he responded, "Gabriel, Gabriel my friend. Do you not understand? All now depends upon them and those who follow them. To reach the world, I have no plan other than my people."

Chapter 7

Principles of Vocation

There is one profound difference between human beings and all other creatures on the face of the earth. In fact, some scientists have suggested that this is the unique ingredient that makes a human being human. Apparently, we are the only creatures who ask the question, "Why do I exist?" We are the only creatures who have enough of a sense of the uniqueness of ourselves to wonder, "For what purpose do I exist? Why was I born and why do I live today? Why was I placed on this planet?"

Thus far in our study of call, we have surveyed a large number of people in the Bible—some extremely well known and strategic and some relatively unknown and apparently peripheral to the "heavenly vision." There are two significant observations about these people. The first is that most of the people used by God in the Bible were not religious professionals. Instead, most were laypeople. In fact, when one looks at the scripture, one is shocked to see how few religious professionals were actually used profoundly by God. Essentially, it is the laity who is used by God throughout biblical history.

Second, all those used by God felt called to a vocation of serving humanity in a particular way. These vocations covered a wide spectrum, with different people feeling called to address a broad sweep of human needs. Some saw this vocation as a life's work, such as Jeremiah who felt he had been called to be a prophet from the time he was in the womb (Jer. 1:4–10). Others lived into their call for a short portion of their lives, such as Epaphroditus whose call to serve Paul (Phil. 2:25–30) probably lasted only a couple of years. Some of these laypeople lived out their vocation through their occupation, while others served God and humanity outside their occupation. But what is the common denominator of all these lay people was that they all felt called by

God to a vocation of serving humanity in a particular way—and saw that service as a service of God.

We also studied more closely specific people who had followed Jesus. Although we surveyed all the disciples and all the women who had followed Jesus, we looked intensely at five people: Peter, Judas, Paul, and Mary and Martha. What we discovered was that each of these people was a unique personality with great potential. Each of these people was profoundly affected by an encounter with Jesus that caused them to look at the direction of their lives. Each of them was either molded into becoming the servant of God that Christ was calling them to be—or intentionally choosing to reject Christ's offer of discipleship to them.

Except for Judas, all of the disciples and women were drawn into becoming one body in Christ. Each was his or her unique personality—some being extroverts, others introverts, some feeling-driven people and others thinkers, some were intuitive and others lived by depending upon their senses. But what was unique was that they were all drawn into becoming one Body of Christ, so that that Body had the totality of human experience that none of them could have as individuals. From these profiles, we learned that vocation is not so much built on one's gifts or abilities or skills; vocation is built upon who you are as a person—a unique person made in the image of God so that you can play a particular role for humanity in God's economy.

We have seen how comprehensive is the emphasis on vocation throughout the Bible. We've seen how individual people have been called as the unique personalities they were, shaped by Christ and transformed into a single community. Now we want to reflect upon one single life in order to discover the primary principles of vocation. And we will do this by examining perhaps the clearest and most comprehensive account of vocation that occurs in scripture. To do that, we will look at the life and ministry of the great liberator—Moses!

Moses as Our Model

Moses was a man who seemed blessed by God. The baby of Israelite slaves, Moses was rescued from almost certain death to be adopted by the daughter of the king of Egypt. Raised as her son, Moses was "instructed in all the wisdom of the Egyptians" (Acts 7:22).

The First Principle

God Prepares Us for Our Call by Breaking Our Hearts, Spiritually Forming Us, and Breaking Through to Us.

Growing up in the royal court of Egypt and grandson to the Pharaoh, what would this prince of Egypt have learned (Heb. 11:24–26)? First, there would have been his formal education. The topics to which he would likely have been tutored would have been political science, public administration, military science, the Egyptian religion, history, literature, geometry, geography, and perhaps even engineering and hydraulics.

But there would have been his informal education as well—the "school of hard knocks." As a participant in the life of the royal court and as a military commander, Moses would have learned a great deal about political intrigue, the use of power politics, the relative effectiveness of confrontation versus compromise. In the military campaign Hebrew tradition tells us he led into Ethiopia, he would have learned much about commanding and leading an army, mobilizing a large force of people, setting strategic and tactical objectives, and handling the logistics of limited resources.

Now, if you had asked Moses why he was learning all of this, he would likely have responded, "In order to someday be a competent ruler or administrator of Egypt." But God had Moses learn all these things for an entirely different purpose.

God Prepares Us by Breaking Our Hearts over Human Need. When Moses had reached 40 years of age, the Scripture tells us, he happened into the Israelite slave encampment and saw an Egyptian beating a Hebrew slave. His blood rose at such injustice. Taking matters into his own hands, Moses killed the Egyptian and buried his body in the sand.

Moses thought he had gotten away with his act of vengeance. But by the next day, the deed was known throughout the land of Egypt. Moses, realizing he was now a wanted murderer, fled Egypt and escaped into the desert (Exod. 2:11–15).

In this story, the young Moses is described to us as a person with a strong sense of justice. That commitment to justice is handled in an immature way, because the story suggests a leader who is impetuous, devious, believing that he had the right to judge and to wreck vengeance on anyone acting unjustly.

There is no indication in this scripture that, at this time, Moses identified himself as a Hebrew. One could argue that his defense of the beaten Hebrew slave was because Moses felt a kinship with that slave. However, the text doesn't suggest that. It could be equally argued that Moses acted in the way he did because he was a man who cared a great deal about justice, and he saw an overlord beating upon a slave—so Moses simply acted to stop such an act of injustice.

Nor is there any suggestion in this text that Moses had any knowledge of or relationship with God. It could be argued that, raised as an Egyptian, Moses worshipped the Egyptian gods and was ignorant of the God of the Hebrews. There is nothing in this biblical account to suggest any awareness of—much less commitment to—the God of Abraham, Isaac, and Jacob.

God Prepares Us by Spiritually Forming Us. Escaping from the wrath of Pharaoh, the criminal Moses arrived in the land of Midian, stopping by a well to rest. The daughters of a priest of Midian came to the well to draw water. But then shepherds also arrived and, wanting the water for themselves, drove away the women. Again, Moses's hatred of injustice was raised and he attacked the shepherds, driving them off. The daughters, grateful for his intervention, took him home to meet their father who invited Moses to settle with them. Eventually, Moses married one of the daughters, raised a family, and settled down to the life of a shepherd. Thus had the mighty fallen (Exod. 2:16–22)!

Moses's defense of the daughters of Reuel (Jethro) lends credence to the argument that Moses's attack upon the Egyptian was fueled by his commitment to justice, not to his sense of kinship with the Hebrews. It is a further indication that what drove Moses was the defense of anyone who was being treated unjustly—whether Hebrew slave or Midianite woman. Apparently, both the sense of justice and the tendency toward impetuosity ran very, very deeply within Moses.

Over the next 40 years, Moses lived as a shepherd on the backside of the desert—caring for his father-in-law's sheep, raising a family, and living life a far cry from his former experience of the Egyptian court. Presumably, he believed that this was to be the remaining pattern of his life—that all the glory of being an Egyptian prince lay behind him, and that he would live the remainder of his life and would die as a desert shepherd.

But in the 40 years Moses spent as a shepherd in the desert, he was "back in school"—learning about how to survive in a desert, learning to read the "signs" of a desert, learning the routes to and locations of the oases of life-giving water. He would have learned about animal husbandry, desert health care, and the nature of primitive communities. In his daily life, tending sheep on the backside of the desert, this former prince of Egypt learned much about humility, helplessness, weakness, and the relative meaninglessness of an ordinary peasant's life. But most of all, he would have learned about God and himself.

From his father-in-law and the desert people, Moses was first introduced to the God of the Israelites—the God of Abraham, Isaac, and Jacob. There he learned to embrace the faith of those who trusted in the God of Mount Sinai—the God who was above all other gods, the God who was unknowable, the God who had no name! There is no suggestion in the book of Exodus that Moses knew anything about the God of the Israelites before he lived with this Bedouin family, or even wanted to know. But there in the harshness of the desert, Moses discovered a god of compassion and justice (Exod. 2:23–25).

Now, if you had asked Moses why he was experiencing all that he was learning in his desert existence, he would likely have responded, "In order to survive as a shepherd in the desert." But God had Moses learn all these things for an entirely different reason. And that reason revealed itself on one memorable day that would forever change Moses's life.

God Prepares Us by Breaking Through To Us.

Consider this scripture:

> Moses was keeping the flock of his father-in-law Jethro, the priest of Midian; he led his flock . . . to Horeb, the mountain of God. There the . . . Lord appeared to him in a flame of fire out of a bush; he looked, and the bush was blazing, yet it was not consumed. . . . God called to him out of the bush, "Moses, Moses!" And he said, "Here I am." Then God said, "Come no closer! Remove the sandals from your feet, for the place on which you are standing is holy ground." He said further, "I am the God of your father, the God of Abraham, the God of Isaac, and the God of Jacob." And Moses hid his face, for he was afraid to look at God. Then the Lord said, "I have observed the misery of my people who are in Egypt. . . . Come, I will send you to Pharaoh to bring my people, the Israelites, out of Egypt!" (Exod. 3:1–7, 10)

God had been working in the life and heart of Moses for 80 years to prepare him to be the great liberator and lawgiver of Israel. Over that 80-year period God had worked in Moses, teaching him the wisdom of Egypt and of the desert, awakening within him his deep commitment to justice, and spiritually forming him in the solitude of caring for sheep where much of his impetuosity was tempered with a new humility and wisdom. Now it was time for God to break through to Moses with a clear and unmistakable call. This God did through the incident of the burning bush.

First, in the burning bush, God directly encounters Moses and reveals to him who God is. He identifies Himself with "the God of your father, the God of Abraham, the God of Isaac, and the God of Jacob" (3:6). But God takes Moses a step further in God's self-disclosure to the prince-shepherd.

> But Moses said to God, "If I come to the Israelites and say to them, 'The God of your ancestors has sent me to you,' and they ask me, 'What is his name?' what shall I say to them?" God said to Moses, "I AM WHO I AM." He said further, "Thus you shall say to the Israelites, 'I AM (Yahweh) has sent me to you.'" God also said to Moses, "Thus you shall say to the Israelites, 'Yahweh, the God of your ancestors, the God of Abraham, the God of Isaac, and the God of Jacob, has sent me to you': This is my name forever, and this is my title for all generations" (Exod. 3:13–15).

Second, God moves to new depths in Moses's heart. God shares with Moses a new understanding of who God is and therefore what God is capable of doing in the world.

To the Israelites, a name was crucial. The name of a person symbolized the nature—the very essence—of that person. Therefore, when Moses asked for God's name, he was making a significant request. He was asking God to reveal his basic essence to him. To return to the Israelites with God's name (and thus with God's essence) would give Moses the power he needed.

God's answer to Moses's question, "What is your name?" was this—"I AM WHO I AM." In Hebrew it reads, "God said to Moses, 'Yahweh.'"

Yahweh is God's name. The word can't be translated into English. "I Am Who I Am," the usual translation, is deceptive since it implies a state of being. The actual Hebrew word has more a causal sense to it. "I become what I become," or "I will be what I will be" might be more accurate.

By telling Moses his name, God identified himself and his essential nature. By using this name, God proclaimed that he was neither a regional deity (to be confined to one country over which he had sovereignty) nor a nature deity (controlled by the cycles of nature). Yahweh—*by the very fact that he was named Yahweh*—was the God who was sovereign over history. The name "Yahweh" revealed God as the creator and controller of history.

God told Moses to return to the Israelite slaves with the message that the God who created the world was their God—the God of Abraham, Isaac, and Jacob. Their God, Yahweh, is the God who controls history—and thus, controls the Egyptians! Israel's God, Yahweh, is the God who creates the future—and thus, can create a new people out of a fugitive bunch of slaves led by an escaped convict wanted by Egyptian law. By revealing his name, God told Moses to return to the Israelite slaves with the news that the sovereign king of the whole universe was about to lead them out into freedom—and no principality (even Egypt's pharaoh) could stop them!

Third, God revealed to Moses that he—the humbled Sinai shepherd—was to be God's instrument to free God's people from slavery. The specifics of that call we will examine in the next section.

In this story of the preparation of Moses, we see demonstrated the model God uses to prepare you and me for that purpose for which God created us. God prepares us for that work God would have us do by breaking our hearts, by spiritually forming us, and by breaking through to us. God prepared Moses to be the great liberator of Israel by first breaking his heart over a specific human need—the injustice that those who are powerful practice upon those who are marginalized, defenseless, and powerless. Thus, Moses defended the Israelite being beaten by the Egyptian taskmaster, and he defended the women being driven from the well by the shepherds. God broke Moses's heart, over-and-over again, with the injustice of the world.

But such sensitivity to human need is insufficient to truly discern God's call in one's life. God also put Moses on the backside of the desert for 40 years—a former prince of Egypt, highly educated and experienced in commanding armies, forced to live the life of a nomad and shepherd among the poorest of the poor. And this God did to bring Moses to himself, to make him aware of his own inadequacies and deep spiritual need, and to thus teach him to rely, not upon his own intelligence and zeal and enthusiasm, but to rely upon the Lord.

And finally, God prepared Moses by breaking through to him in a new way and at a specific time. God appeared to Moses in the burning bush, and Moses's life was forever changed. God did two things for Moses in God's encounter with the prince-shepherd. First, Moses had a profound, life-changing meeting with God. Second, Moses discovered God's call upon his life in responding to human need. Our intense awareness of human need and God's spiritual formation of us are steps God takes in our lives to bring us to that moment when God will meet us and declare, "Come, I will send you to Pharaoh to bring my people out of Egypt."

This, then, is the first principle of biblical vocation: God prepares us for our call by breaking our hearts, by spiritually forming us, and by breaking through to us.

The Second Principle

Everyone is Called to Serve God by Ministering to a Deep Hunger of the World, but Discovering and Carrying Out that Call Only Comes Out of God's Interior Work in Us.

A young evangelist, Rev. Robert Pierce, was preaching in cities of China just in front of the advance of the Red Army as it carried out its victorious conquest of that great nation in 1949. One day, as Bob Pierce finished the evangelistic service, he walked into the crowd to greet people, pray with them, and be responsive to them.

Suddenly, a young mother thrust a baby into his arms, said quickly, "Her name is White Jade. Take good care of her," and disappeared into the crowd. Pierce stood there, holding the baby. But what was the young evangelist to do with her?

What Rev. Pierce did was to find an orphanage and take the baby there. He was in for a surprise. The administrator of the orphanage refused to take the baby. "We are completely full," she said, "and we don't have any money to accommodate another child." Pierce emptied out his pockets, but there still wasn't enough to care for that baby. So he did the only thing he could do. He sold his airplane ticket (and his escape) out of China to someone who wanted to flee the advancing Red Army, and thus bought care for White Jade. But now, he had no means to get back home.

That night, Bob Pierce wrote in the flyleaf of his Bible a prayer that came out of that day's experience. This was what he wrote: "Let my heart be broken with the things that break the heart of God."

Bob Pierce eventually got out of China, and returned to the USA. He continued to pray that God would show him how to respond to the pain of orphan children in the world. The result of that prayer was that Bob Pierce felt called to found World Vision. The largest Christian relief and development organization in the world began with the willingness of a preacher to let his heart be broken by the things that break the heart of God.

> Then the Lord said, "I have observed the misery of my people who are in Egypt; I have heard their cry on account of their taskmasters. Indeed, I know their sufferings, and I have come down to deliver them from the Egyptians, and to bring them up out of that land to a good and broad land, a land flowing with milk and honey, to the country of the Canaanites, the Hittites, the Amorites, the Perizzites, the Hivites and the Jebusites. The cry of the Israelites has now come to me; I have also seen how the Egyptians oppress them. So come, I will send you to Pharaoh to bring my people, the Israelites, out of Egypt" (Exod. 3:7–10).

What was breaking God's heart in the story of the Exodus? The oppression of the Israelite slaves. What broke Moses's heart? The oppression of the Israelite slaves.

Throughout his entire adult life, Moses had hated injustice. Whenever he saw oppression of the weak, the marginalized, the powerless, his blood boiled in rage—and he acted (sometimes foolheartedly) on that rage. Now, suddenly, at the burning bush, Moses discovers that what has been breaking his heart for 80 years had been breaking God's heart since humankind had first been created.

Moses now faces the reality that God is calling him—as God's hands, feet, and mouth—to do something about such injustice! So Moses realizes that the vocation for which God had been preparing him all his life was to confront the political, economic, and religious systems and the spiritually oppressive powers of Egypt (symbolized in the person of the Pharaoh), to defeat them in Godly battle (the plagues, the Passover), and to lead the oppressed Israelites into freedom!

But the Moses who stood before the burning bush was not the Moses who had killed the Egyptian tormentor or rescued the Midianite maidens. God had been at work in Moses's life in his 40-year exile in the desert. And God was now meeting powerfully with Moses at the burning bush. Over the years, Moses had matured, as God had done an interior work in him, so that even his deep hunger for justice had been seasoned.

> (God said,) "So come, I will send you to Pharaoh to bring my people, the Israelites, out of Egypt." But Moses said to God, "Who am I that I should go to Pharaoh, and bring the Israelites out of Egypt?" (God) said, "I will be with you; and this shall be the sign for you that it is I who sent you: when you have brought the people out of Egypt, you shall worship God on this mountain"(Exod. 3:10-12).

In Moses's response to God's call to him, we see demonstrated the significant change that had occurred in Moses's spirit over his 40-year desert exile. In the desert—and now, on Mt. Sinai, God has become more than just a name to Moses.

The Moses of an earlier year would have leapt at God's call to confront Pharaoh and to lead the Israelites into freedom. That would have been a natural and even inevitable response, given his combination of commitment to defend the cause of the poor and oppressed and his impetuosity. But at the burning bush, we see Moses shying from that call of God's. He immediately questions his capacity to accomplish that action. His response demonstrates that he has become more realistic and honest regarding his abilities. It indicates his willingness to accept the role as a shepherd that fate seems to have dictated to him. But it also indicates his growing maturity in his relationship with God.

Moses realizes that, if God is not in the plan to set Israel free, that plan is doomed to failure. The call to liberation must come from God. And that God must be the God who can defeat the Egyptian gods and can set Israel free, because He is the God of history. If God is indeed Yahweh, then that comes as amazingly good news for Moses, for it is that God who can send him to Egypt and can empower his struggle with Pharaoh. Only if Yahweh is indeed Yahweh, and only if Yahweh has authentically called him to do this work, will Moses even begin to consider the possibility of doing it.

Moses would never have discovered that what was breaking his heart was also that which was breaking God's heart if his hasty, ill-conceived action in Egypt had not failed and he had been forced to flee for his life. It was his 40 years in exile that brought Moses to himself and prepared him to discover that God had placed in his heart, all along, that rage against oppression that God also felt. And it was only in the spiritual and literal desert of his seemingly ruined life that Moses could discover the purpose for his life. Second, you are called to serve God by ministering to some need or brokenness in the world, but discovering and carrying out that call only comes out of God's interior work in you.

The Third Principle:

A Call Always Comes as Frighteningly Good News for Which We Feel Incompetent and Overextended.

> (God said,) "Come, I will send you to Pharaoh to bring my people, the Israelites out of Egypt." But Moses said to God, "Who am I that I should go to Pharaoh, and bring the Israelites out of Egypt?" . . . Then Moses answered, "But suppose they do not believe me or listen to me, but say, 'The Lord did not appear to you.'" . . . But Moses said to the Lord, "O my Lord, I have never been eloquent, neither in the past nor even now that you have spoken to your servant; but I am slow of speech and slow of tongue." . . . But (Moses) said, "O my Lord, please send someone else!" (Exod. 3:10-11, 4:1; 4:10; 4:13)

When God tells Moses he is to set free the Israelites, Moses responds, "Who am I that I should go to Pharaoh, and bring the Israelites out of Egypt?" (Exod. 3:11) Obviously, the once-proud Moses had been humbled.

Actually, Moses's sense of incompetence is somewhat laughable. Overwhelmingly intimidated by God's call, Moses uses every excuse in the book to get out from under this unsought obligation. First, he says, "Suppose they do not believe me or listen to me?" God demonstrates to Moses the power God has bestowed on Moses to carry out that task; he instructs him to throw a stick on the ground and it becomes a snake, to put his hand in his cloak and it becomes leprous, to pour water on the ground and it becomes blood. Isn't that going to impress Pharaoh and Israel?

Stripped of that excuse, Moses says, "O my Lord, I am slow of speech and slow of tongue." God gives to Moses the eloquent Aaron to be his mouthpiece. Finally, in desperation, Moses whines, "O my Lord, please send someone else." Now he has gone too far. And God simply commands, "Go, and I will be with you!"

This would not have been the response of the young Moses. The young Moses would have leapt at the opportunity! Now, the aged Moses hesitates, waffles, stutters, and is clearly both uncertain and intimidated by the demand God is placing upon him.

But why is it important that Moses be intimidated by his call? As long as Moses thinks he is competent to carry out this call, he will seek to carry out that call in his own strength. If, on the other hand, he is intimidated by the complexity and size of what he is called to do, then he'll always be dependent upon God.

Feeling overextended or incompetent is the sure and certain sign that you are called to a particular work for God. If you feel, "No way can I do that," then it is probably God's will that you do it. It is tremendously important that we be intimidated by our call. If we are not overwhelmed by what God is asking us to do, we won't be dependent upon God. Instead, we'll trust in our own abilities—as did Moses when he killed the Egyptian. And you can see what a mess Moses made out of it when he trusted in his own abilities.

A friend of mine uses the phrase "frighteningly good news" to describe call. Your call will come to you as "good news" because it is a call to address that which you are deeply heart-broken and concerned about. But it will also come as "frighteningly" good news because it will look overwhelming. Third, God's call to us always comes as frighteningly good news for which we feel incompetent and overextended.

The Fourth Principle

God Always Adequately Prepares and Gifts Us for Our Call—Although We May Not Perceive It.

God always adequately prepares and gifts us for that call. Although we may feel intimidated by that call, God is not intimidated. God has selected just the right person to carry out that work—you—and God has adequately prepared, gifted, and graced you for that work. This truth God demonstrates to Moses in a most tender and compassionate way.

> But Moses said to the Lord, "O my Lord, I have never been eloquent, neither in the past nor even now that you have spoken to your servant; but I am slow of speech and slow of tongue." Then the Lord said to him, "Who gives speech to mortals? Who makes them mute or deaf, seeing or blind? Is it not I, the Lord? Now go, and I will be with your mouth and teach you what you are to speak" (Exod. 4:10-12).

Isn't that beautiful? Moses feels overwhelmed and inadequate to the task. But God very tenderly says to him, "Moses, I made your mouth. I gave you the capacity to speak far beyond your expectations. If you step out in faith and do what I am calling you to do, you will discover a capacity in yourself to articulate your thoughts you never dreamed possible. Trust me to call forth and use the gifts that lie dormant in you—for I have filled you and skilled you in order to use you to change the world!"

This is a theme that occurs over and over again in scripture. A person must first be humbled before her call, so that she sees himself as inadequate. Then, out of that sense of being overwhelmed, God in essence says to her, "Look, I have adequately gifted you to carry out this call. Go and do it!" God shows us that the sign that we are, indeed, adequately qualified and gifted for the task, is that the task deeply intimidates us!

If you are called to do a particular work for God, God has already prepared, gifted, and graced you for that task. But we likely do not perceive it. The gifts are all there but likely they have not been called forth, precisely because it is the living into that call that calls forth those gifts.

Thirty years ago, I sensed that God was calling me out of the pastorate and into an international ministry, working to empower the urban poor and to equip urban pastors around the world. The invitation of World Vision International to head up their international urban ministry effort provided the opportunity to live out that new call that was such "frighteningly good news." When I began my ministry with World Vision, I felt very adequate and competent to be the pastor of a local church. But the work to which I was being called made me feel overwhelmed and very much out of control!

Out of that sense of helplessness, I became terribly concerned that each training event of pastors I led throughout the world would be done "just right." Consequently, I would write out detailed presentations consuming reams of paper! But one day, a Brazilian pastor whom I greatly trust said to me, "Bob, you know your stuff. Why do you need all that paper? Just share what you already know!" So, taking his admonition seriously, I threw away my reams of paper and started to teach with just a few notes in front of me.

What I discovered was that all this writing of detailed material was actually a crutch that was getting in the way of my authentically communicating with people. When I prepared carefully beforehand but spoke extemporaneously, I found my presentations greatly improved. The situation and the urging of a good friend called forth the gift that had been in me my entire ministry, but which I had never discovered or perceived about myself because I had never been pushed to "try out my wings."

So the fourth principle of vocation is that a person who is called is already prepared, gifted, and graced for that task—but may not perceive it and may not have had those gifts called forth. If a person perceives himself as adequately gifted but is not intimidated by his call, he will become arrogant. If, on the other hand, she is intimidated by the call but does not perceive herself as adequately gifted, she will become overwhelmed—and will likely not enter into that call. So to truly live into a call, one needs to feel both overextension (to keep you humble) and recognition that you are adequately gifted (to keep you motivated).

The Fifth Principle:

We Need Each Other to Effectively Carry Out Our Call.

When Moses lamented that he was intimidated to face this overwhelming assignment on his own, God replied,

> What of your brother Aaron, the Levite? I know that he can speak fluently; even now he is coming out to meet you, and when he sees you his heart will be glad. You shall speak to him and put the words in his mouth; and I will be with your mouth and with his mouth, and will teach you what you shall do. He indeed shall speak for you to the people; he shall serve as a mouth for you, and you shall serve as God for him (Exod. 4:14–16).

Further, God said to Moses:

> Go and assemble the elders of Israel, and say to them, "Yahweh, the God of your ancestors, the God of Abraham, of Isaac, and of Jacob, has appeared to me, saying: I have given heed to you and to what has been done to you in Egypt. I declare that I will bring you up out of the misery of Egypt, to the land of the Canaanites, the Hittites, the Amorites, the Perizzites, the Hivites, and the Jebusites, a land flowing with milk and honey." They will listen to your voice; and you and the elders of Israel shall go to the king of Egypt and say to him,

"Yahweh, the God of the Hebrews, has met with us; let us now go!" (Exod. 3:16–18a)

Moses, Aaron, and the elders were all necessary to each other in order to carry out the call to "let the people go." Moses was the visionary leader, the one chosen by God to lead Israel out of bondage and to win the struggle against Egypt and Egypt's king. But Aaron was both priest and the voice of the revolution. Moses refers to himself as "slow of speech and slow of tongue" (Ex. 4:10); tradition states that Moses had a speech impediment—probably a stutter. Therefore, he needed someone who could speak more eloquently before the Pharaoh than could he.

The elders were also strategic to this liberation effort. First, they blessed it, and confirmed Moses's leadership of it (4:28–31). They willingly followed Moses, and of course their action became example to the entire nation. The elders maintained the discipline of the Israelite resistance. And once the Israelites had been set free and had moved into the desert, it was the elders who maintained the life and the discipline of the community.

All of these leaders were necessary to enable Moses to carry out his call. Together, they became a leadership team. Together, they also became a community of believers, encouraging and supporting each other in their common commitment to carry out the call that had begun with Moses but now had become their call as well. Only by working and being community together could Israel be freed from Egyptian slavery.

So it was that Moses never went to Pharaoh alone. Rather, in every confrontation with the Egyptian king, Aaron accompanied Moses and the elders of Israel stood behind Moses. When Moses led the children of Israel across the Red Sea and to freedom in the Sinai desert, it was Aaron who conducted their worship; Joshua and Caleb who organized and marched the people; Miriam who led the people's celebrations; Jethro who helped Moses to delegate authority; and the elders of Israel who met with him, prayed with him, and supported him through the 40 years of wilderness wanderings. Moses was God's man to lead the Israelites to freedom, and God had prepared him and developed his gifts over 80 years of internship to carry out that leadership. But Moses did not and could not have done it alone. Aaron, Miriam, Joshua, Caleb, Jethro, the elders all joined with Moses in working, leading, and praying together to bring about the greatest nonviolent resistance and freedom movement in the history of the world.

So we cannot stand alone, either. We need each other to discover and carry out our respective calls to serve God by serving people. It is only within a community of believers that we can discover our purpose for living, where we can support each other in that ministry to which we are mutually called, and in which we can care about each other's spiritual sustenance and formation.

One person can't effectively minister to a deep hunger of the world to which she has been called. In order for such ministry to occur, it must be undertaken by a community of believers who respond to the call of the one, embrace that call as their call, care about each other's spiritual sustenance, and work together to carry out that call.

The story of Moses is the story of a man who was obedient to the heavenly vision given to him. Although he was at times rebellious, resistant, angry, and impetuous (even as an old man), Moses was faithful to the call given to him by God at the burning bush on Mount Sinai. And here was the result:

> The Lord (Yahweh) said to Aaron, "Go into the wilderness to meet Moses." So he went; and he met Moses at the mountain of God and kissed him. Moses told Aaron all the words of the Lord with which he had sent him, and all the signs with which he had charged him. Then Moses and Aaron went and assembled all the elders of the Israelites. Aaron spoke all the words that the Lord had spoken to Moses, and performed the signs in the sight of the people. The people believed; and when they heard that the Lord had given heed to the Israelites and that he had seen their misery, they bowed down and worshiped (Exod. 4:27–31).

And Israel was set free!

Conclusion

These are the five primary principles of vocation presented in the scripture. As we have demonstrated from our extended study of scripture over the past several chapters, every human being has been created and chosen by God to serve the deep needs of humanity in a particular way. From the example of Moses, we learn that the process God uses to bring us to action on our call is fivefold:

1. God prepares us for our call by breaking our hearts over a human need, bringing us to Christ and spiritually forming us, and breaking through to us in decisive ways;
2. We discover our call by exposure to human pain, but primarily through deepening our relationship with God;
3. An emerging call always comes as "frightening good news" for which we feel overextended and/or incompetent;
4. Each of us so called is adequately prepared, gifted, and graced by God for that task—but we may not perceive it and may not have had those gifts called forth or confirmed;
5. One person can't effectively minister to a need of the world to which he or she has been called unless that call is carried out within a community of believers who also feel themselves called, support each other in that call, and care about each other's spiritual sustenance.

The story of Moses demonstrates to us that God has a purpose for every single human being's life. God prepares us for that purpose both by our everyday life experiences and by our growing relationship with God. God will make clear to each of us God's call upon our lives. Such a call will always come to us as intimidating, frighteningly good news. Over the years, God has gifted and prepared us to carry out that call upon our lives. God has given us each other to sustain, encourage, and work with us as we seek to be faithful to that purpose for which God created and has called us. In the next five chapters, we will explore how we can each discern our specific call within the larger call of the church, and act upon it.

We began our reflection in this chapter with my observation that the human being is the only animal that asks, "For what purpose do I exist?" The biblical answer to this eternal question is quite specific. You and I exist to serve God by serving humanity in specific, concrete ways. God created and chose you and is now calling you to let your heart be broken with some human or world need that breaks God's heart. And until you allow your heart to be broken with the things that break God's heart, and allow yourself to be open to the call of God's Spirit, you will live your life dissatisfied and in relative meaninglessness. Our hearts will always remain restless until they rest in our faithful following of God's call to us.

In the story of Moses, we see demonstrated the magnificent process through which God takes every human being who is willing to discover and carry out God's call upon her or his life. Dear reader, this is the magnificent work that God wants to do in you and through you, as he calls you to his city! That is the purpose for which you exist! Now—discover that call.

PART II

Your Call: Discovered & Lived

Chapter 8

Nurturing My Deep Gladness

So how do I discover my call?

Thus far, we have discovered that God not only created, chose, and called Israel, the church, and individuals to join with God in the creation of God's society in the cities of the world (the kingdom of God). We have also made the wonderful discovery that God created, chose, and is calling each of us as well. Further, we have discovered that God chooses and calls us no matter who we are, whether we are doctors or trash collectors, political leaders or parents at home, students or the elderly, farmers or business people. God not only calls clergy to follow God, but also calls every layperson as well. And that call from God is every bit as authentic as is the call to any bishop, seminary professor, missionary, or ordained priest or minister.

Every human being has been created, chosen, and called by God to serve God in the world in a particular way. This is our vocation, our "calling"—irrespective of what might be our occupation. Each of us is a unique personality who is chosen and called by Jesus, is adequately gifted to carry out that call, and is given a community of believers to share in the achieving of that call. So our vocation is not so much built upon *what* we can do as it is on *who* we are in our relationship with Christ and each other.

Finally, we have discovered that God calls us to our specific ministry by breaking our hearts over a human need, bringing us to an ever-deepening relationship with Christ, and breaking through to us in decisive ways. We discovered that a sure sign of God's call to us is that this call always comes as "frighteningly good news" for which we feel overextended or incompetent. But God has given us the gifts we need to carry out that call and has given us each other, so that we work together to achieve this call. So, if we are being faithful to the biblical message, we embrace together this commitment to discovering and living into our call to serve Christ in the world—no matter who we are or what we do to earn money!

As we look at biblical history, we realize that there are those who have had God's call virtually thrust upon them (think Moses or Paul or Timothy). Others have seemed to know their call almost from birth (think Samuel or Jeremiah or Jesus). But for most of us, discerning our call has been a lengthy and slowly emerging awareness of why God has placed us here on earth.

The good news is that every one of us has been created, chosen, and called by God—not only to follow Christ in the restoration of the world into His Kingdom—but also to live out that Christ-following in very specific ways.

So the question we must now ask is, "So how do I identify my call?" The whole process of our spiritual formation is for the purpose of helping us to more clearly discern and then to effectively live into God's answer to that question.

So, in the next four chapters (including this one), we will seek to give some biblical directives to discerning and living into our individual call. And the place to begin that discernment is with some basic biblical principles on how God tends to work in our (and in everyone's) life.

Caution—God at Work!

We often see signs upon construction sites that alert us, "Caution—Men at Work!" Well, what are the signs of God at work both within and through us? Is there a pattern that God uses when he is at work in our lives and in the life of our church? How does God enable us to hear God's call to us and to respond to it?

What I have discovered over 60 years of urban ministry is that, if I wanted to live out God's call on my life, I had to pay equal attention to both my spiritual formation (what I call the "journey inward") and the living out of my mission in the world (the "journey outward"). I had to continuously be open to God's work in me both in my spiritual formation and my hands-on living into my work of ministry. And this I had to do, not only as a pastor, but as a teacher, a mission executive, a community worker, and as a parent and husband. These two journeys (the journey inward and the journey outward) morph into a single journey through a call to the city. It is this process of both continuing to discern and to live out one's call that we will examine over the next four chapters.

But where do we begin? We begin with gaining an understanding of what God is doing—how God is at work both to enable us to find our rest and our work in Him. This is the rhythm of the Christian life. Here is the rhythm that underlies our discernment and acting out of our call.

Do One Thing!

One of the most important insights each of us needs in order to successfully carry out that mission to which God calls us is **to do one thing!** We are not called by God to be committed to dealing with all the needs of the city, but to *address only one pain of the world.*

A need does not constitute a call. The city is full of human pain—collapsing marriages, abused children, poverty, injustice, orphans, environmental pollution. Wherever we turn our heads, we, as sensitive Christians, are going to see intense human suffering. As the whole body of Christians in the city, we are to be concerned about all its human need.

But one of the most important truths I learned as a Christian is to trust the Body of Christ—to trust the Church! God doesn't call any given Christian to be committed to addressing the pains of the city. God calls an entire church to be so committed! And the call of another in the church is not necessarily the call that I have received. We must trust God that he has created, chosen, and called his people in our city to address every one of these needs. We must trust that God's church—the body of Christ—will discover each of those needs it is to address and then address them. Our individual responsibility is to discover our particular call and the particular need in the city that God wants us to address. That is the only need for which we can be responsible. This leads us, then, to our second proposition.

The Way Out Is In

The way we discover the human need to which we are called is not by becoming absorbed in addressing that need but by paying attention to living the contemplative life. Our first tendency, when we realize that we are called to be responsible for engaging one primary need of our city, is to begin searching among all the city's problems to see what need tugs most at our heart strings. Now it is possible that what might tug at our heart strings might be the need we are called to encounter. But it is far more likely that what will tug at our heart strings will be those needs in the world that are projections of hidden problems or issues within ourselves that we have never resolved. If those feelings are projections, we will not find God's call through that tug. The only way to discover God's call is not to look out but to look in. We must begin to examine our own lives in Christ. As our fellowship with God deepens, the Lord will reveal the call. This brings us to the third proposition.

Discover the Big Three

We discover God's call and begin acting upon it by reaching inward. There we discover ourselves, begin to love God, and build a Christian community. Each one of those elements of the journey inward is strategic to discovering God's call to us.

Discovering our inner selves is strategic because only as we come to know our inner selves truly can we discover what causes us to act the way we do, what it is we project upon others, what are those weaknesses within us that need to become strengths, and what are those strengths that so dominate our personalities that they need to become comparatively weak. The ancient Delphic maxim first uttered about 3,000 years ago, "Know thyself," is equally true today. Socrates elaborated on that simple statement by reminding us, "The unreflective life is not worth living!" To honestly explore and come to understand who you are is the first and continuing task of any intentional human being. And to undertake such exploration requires one to live a reflective life.

Coming to know and love God is the second necessary element of our journey inward. As we come to know and love God through his Son, we understand more clearly the gifts of God's grace that liberate us, the expectations God has for us as our Creator and ruler, and the possibilities that are open to us when we seek and follow God's will. Remarkably we discover God and our inner selves the same way—by spending time in solitude before the Lord, by daily allowing the Scriptures to speak to the way we choose to live and prioritize our lives, by praying contemplatively, both aloud and meditatively, and by journaling. In following such disciplines, we cannot help but find ourselves growing both in self-understanding and in a deepening relationship with God.

Building of Christian community. The chance of accurately hearing God's call simply by ourselves, however, is slim, because such an introverted approach contains the danger that instead of discovering God we would hear our own self-deceptions. An equally strategic ingredient in hearing God's call to us is participation in a strong, intentional, caring Christian community. God's call will come to us clearly when we practice the solitary disciplines of discovering God and ourselves, but do so only as a part of a supportive, loving community of faith. It is as we journey together through the Christian experience with a small, sustaining group of fellow believers that we will be prepared to hear God's call to us. Such a group cannot be large; in the New Testament it is rarely over 12 people. It must be a group small enough to enter into that search for God's call with us and to care genuinely and deeply that everyone hears their call. As a result, the group must exemplify deep, godly love which brings me to the fourth and final proposition.

The Way In Is Out

We more deeply grow in our relationship with God, self, and others by obeying our call to address a specific pain of the world. As we enter into ourselves, as we fall increasingly in love with God, and as our support community deepens in its life together, God's call will come to us. As we begin to obey that call, we will find that portion of the body of Christ that is in the same mission as that to which we are called. These people will join with us and will enable us to live into that call. In this group, we can plan our strategy to address that issue or pain. The group will call forth from all its members the unique and special gifts each one has to contribute to the undertaking of that common mission. As a part of that group, we move out in mission to the city and world.

At this point, we discover that we are caught up in the most beautiful continuing spiral. Our journey to carry out our common mission to the world will bruise us, exhaust us, and try us deeply (if it does not, then we aren't truly engaged in that mission). We will then turn to Christ and we will find ourselves deeper in Scripture. We will want to be in prayer with God, we will cry on each other's shoulders, and the bonds of love will grow between us. In other words, by carrying out our call to a need of the world, we will be motivated to grow spiritually.

As we grow spiritually, we will find ourselves absorbed in our mission—that purpose for our lives for which God has created, chosen, and called us. Consequently, our lives will take on a meaning and a joy that we never knew possible. We will have begun to follow God's strategy for the church that—if faithfully followed—can only result in a profound transforming of our city!

In other words, what I am essentially saying is, "the way out is in! And the way in is out!" Our way into action, if it is to be authentic, biblical, called-based action, must come through our reflection. And our key to experiencing meaningful, life-transforming reflection must come through our action. And it is at the point of both our journey inward and our journey outward that our identification and living into our call occurs. As I noted earlier, Frederick Buechner best defines the theology of call by referring to it as "the place where your deep gladness and the world's deep hunger meet."[67] This statement captures the point that I am seeking to make. Our embrace of our call and our living into it occurs at the junction between that deep hunger of the world to which our soul most responds and our discovery of our deepest gladness with which we resonate. The way out is in! And the way in is out!

The way to reach outside ourselves is to reach within: to discover ourselves, love God, and participate in Christian community. The way to journey inward (to grow in our relationship with God, self, and others) is to journey beyond ourselves and commit ourselves to a pain of our city; discovering the pain to which we are called, uncovering our gifts and moving out in mission. We grow by going. And we can go only to the degree that we grow (you can't lead someone to a deeper awareness of God than you yourself have experienced).

This is the rhythm of the Christian life. This rhythm catches us up into increasingly effective ministry fueled by the way we continually foster our own spirituality. This journey is not a one-time journey inward and outward. It is a an ongoing rhythm—a continuing journey of ever-increasing growth in Christ and ever-more-effective mission in the world—moving from strength to strength. The journey never stops, until AFTER you have made that final journey to the heavenly home awaiting you![68]

So, let's get on that journey!

Nurturing Our Deep Gladness

Over the remainder of this chapter and the three that follow, I will be presenting some strategies and offering some vehicles you can use to help you more clearly discern your call. But I do so with some fear and trembling because I would not

---

[67] Buechner, *Wishful Thinking*, 119.

[68] Much of this section has been taken from my book, *City of God; City of Satan—A Biblical Theology of the Urban Church* (Grand Rapids, MI: Zondervan Publishing House, 1991), 235–240. Used by permission of Zondervan, www.zondervan.com.

want you to assume that, if you perform certain maneuvers or artifices, you will somehow have disclosed to you God's will for your life. What I am sharing, instead, are some vehicles I personally have found useful in helping me to more clearly perceive or articulate my understanding of God's call to me. My hope is that they might be helpful to you, as well.

Likewise, I would not want you to assume that this is a "one-off" task—that, somehow, if you are able to articulate once that deep gladness of your life or the world's deep hunger to which you feel particularly called by God, that somehow that means the matter is all solved, and you don't need to consider it again. Oh, yes you do! This spiritual awareness is not a product to be purchased and placed on the shelf of your life. It is a process—a never-ending process—sort of like the important reality that you need to both act in loving ways and to say "I love you" to your spouse, and not operate on the assumption that going through the marriage ceremony said it all for time and for eternity.

So all that being said—let us now move on to considering how to discover and nurture our deep gladness!

We must first begin with the realization that although grace is free, spiritual maturity takes work! To be able to hear God speak to us and to respond to God requires spiritual sensitivity on our part. But such sensitivity doesn't come about by simply hoping it will occur. We must pay attention to our own personal spiritual formation and must support one another in our corporate spiritual growth. Spiritual growth takes work.

Our formation as spiritual beings exists for one purpose: to enable us to hear God's call and to deepen and sustain us as we work to carry out and to be obedient to that call. For us to both discern and to then live into our calling, we need to become increasingly sensitive to God's interaction with us, to become increasingly aware of our own maturing interior self, and to enter into supportive, accountable relationships with other Christians. Perhaps one of the best examples in scripture of maturing spiritual discernment leading to an increasing clarity of mission is the story of Mary, the mother of Jesus.

From Virgin to Woman to Virgin Again

> In the sixth month the angel Gabriel was sent by God to a town in Galilee called Nazareth, to a virgin engaged to a man whose name was Joseph.

> And he came to her and said, "Greetings, favored one! The Lord is with you. . . You will conceive in your womb and bear a son, and you will name him Jesus. He will be great, and will be called the Son of the Most High; . . . He will reign over the house of Jacob forever, and of his kingdom there will be no end." Mary said to the angel, "How can this be, since I am a virgin?" (Luke 1:26–28, 31, 33–34)

Mary was a virgin when she conceived Jesus. But what is a virgin? Why, someone who has never engaged in sexual intercourse! But what do we then mean when we refer to a virgin forest or virgin oil or virgin metal—or even Virgin Airlines? What, then, is a virgin?

The word "virgin" actually means a person or an object not altered by outside human intervention. Thus, a virgin forest is one which has not been cut by humans. Virgin metal is that metal produced directly from ore. The word "virgin" literally means "one-in-one's-self," one who is fulfilled, whole, complete in one's self. Thus, to the ancient peoples, virginity was both a state of mind and a state of one's body. The true virgin was a woman who was "one-in-herself." And that oneness, that wholeness was symbolized by her physical virginity, free of sexual union with a man.

A reading of the Gospel of Luke makes it clear that Mary was this kind of virgin—likely a teenage girl, but also a woman with a wisdom and commitment to God far beyond her tender years.

"My soul proclaims the greatness of the Lord," Mary sang,
"and my spirit exults in God my savior,
because he has looked upon his lowly handmaid.
Yes, from this day forward all generations will call me blessed,
for the Almighty has done great things for me" (Luke 1:46–48 *The Jerusalem Bible*).

This poem, Mary's "Magnificat," is one of the most profound hymns in scripture. It reflects so beautifully the spirit and attitude of the woman pregnant with the one who would become Jesus.

"From this day forward all generations will call me blessed," Mary sang, "for the Almighty has done great things for me" (1:48b-49).[69] Earlier, when the angel had appeared to her to announce that she would be the virgin mother of the Christ, Mary responded, "I am the handmaid of the Lord; let what you have said be done to me" (1:38). The openness and freedom Mary evinced towards God was remarkable. It shines with a clarity which could hardly comprehend the pain, the struggle, the rejection that awaited her. She was caught up in the exciting naiveté of initially discovering God's will for her life, and she yielded to it without reserve. Her cousin, Elizabeth, in seeing such unconditional acceptance, could not help but observe, "Blessed is she who believed that the promise made her by the Lord would be fulfilled" (1:45).

Jesus was then born, Mary and Joseph returned to Nazareth, and the years swiftly sped by as the baby born in that manger grew into a man, and the teenage mother grew into a woman. As Jesus grew, "Mary treasured all these words and pondered them in her heart" (2:19). But finally the day came when the adult Jesus came to his mother and told her it was time for him to begin that ministry to which God had called him. And it was then that a profound change became apparent in Mary.

Mary had always believed the angel's words, "You will conceive in your womb and bear a son, and you will name him Jesus. He will reign over the house of Jacob forever, and of his kingdom there will be no end" (1:31, 33). Over the long years of Jesus's growth to manhood, Mary had believed that the angel's promise would be fulfilled by God. In faithfulness to that vision, she was willing to be still and to wait for God to work. But as the years went by, she began to dream about how that great work of God would be accomplished through her son. Without even realizing it, Mary slowly moved from waiting on God to accomplish his promise to anticipating the process God would use.

Mary did this by uncritically accepting the traditions and beliefs of her people. Like so many of her contemporaries in Israel, Mary accepted those prophecies about the Messiah which saw him as a conquering king, while ignoring those Old Testament declarations that suggested a Messiah as a suffering servant, dying for the sins of his people. Thus it was that because Mary apparently could not accept a suffering messiah,

---

[69] *The Jerusalem Bible* (Garden City, NY: Doubleday and Co., 1966).

she moved from being still and waiting for God, to deciding in her own mind how Jesus ought to work. And thus it became inevitable that Jesus and Mary would be in conflict with each other!

It comes as a shock to realize that the relationship between Jesus and his mother was antagonistic during his ministry. Every encounter between Jesus and Mary during that ministry was strained. She asked Jesus to turn water into wine at a marriage feast, and he retorted "Woman, what concern is that to you and to me?" "What concern is that" was a Semitic expression which is best translated, "mind your own business" (John 2:4). She and her sons came to Jesus to persuade him to abandon his ministry, and he replied to the crowd, "Who are my mother and my brothers? . . . Whoever does the will of God, is my brother and sister and mother" (Mark 3:33, 35).

It was this most cutting remark which gives us the basic clue concerning the essential conflict between Jesus and his mother. "It is not she who birthed me who is my true mother," Jesus in essence was saying. "It is she who does the will of God!" By this statement, Jesus was implying that his mother was, out of a concern for the well-being of her son, no longer trusting that he was following God's intentional course for the Messiah (which she knew he was). Thirty years earlier, Elizabeth had said to her, "Blessed is she who believed that that there would be a fulfillment of what was spoken to her by the Lord" (Luke 1:45). And Mary had so believed that promise that she had now fallen into the trap of trying to dictate to Jesus what kind of a Messiah he ought to be. To the degree that she had allowed Israel's conventional wisdom about the Messiah to become her focus, to that degree Mary was veering from God's plans for achieving that purpose. She wanted Jesus to receive the promised crown, but God had willed that the path to that crown would lead through a cross!

Yet, despite all Mary's planning, it was the cross Jesus received. The inevitable did happen. What Mary most feared came to pass. She stood before the cross upon which her beloved Son was hanging—that Son given as a gift to her, that Son who came on angel's wings, that Son of such great promise. And as she stood before the cross and openly wept, her hopes for Jesus lying shattered around her, a most beautiful thing happened. Hanging on that pain-racked cross, Jesus said to his disciple, John, "Here is your mother," and to Mary, "Woman, here (now) is your son." "And from that hour," the scripture tells us, "the disciple took her into his own home" (John 19:26–27). Jesus's compassion and love for his mother shown through in that final hour, and the desperate Mary knew that she was accepted.

This, dear reader, was the journey of Mary's soul, as described in the scriptures. That journey of the soul was a journey from virgin to woman to virgin again. The first-century philosopher, Philo of Alexandria, once wrote "When a virgin lies with a man, she becomes a woman, but when God lies with her soul, she who is a woman becomes virgin again."[70] Thus it was with Mary. As a young girl, she could be one totally dedicated to God's call upon her life, and thus at peace both with herself and with her unmarried pregnant condition (despite how society might interpret it). But such being at-one with herself was at an unconscious level, a child-like faith, an innocence that accepted what life and God had given her.

But then Mary became a woman. Her baby grew up, and as he grew, became independent of her. And the course that he saw for his life opposed the course that she had seen as inevitable to fulfill the angel's prophecy. In the tension created by Jesus's resolute following of God's plan for him, Mary allowed herself to be seduced from her relationship with God. She allowed her natural mother-love to compromise her trust in God's call both to her and to her son. And she became obsessed by her need to control both her own life and her son's life according to the way she understood how God was at work. As she fell to that temptation, the serenity and peace of her former virginity slipped away, and we see a Mary portrayed by scripture as harried, tense, manipulative, and insistent. And that change in her nearly drove an unbridgeable wedge between herself and her son.

But at the cross, all was changed. For it was at that cross that which Mary had most feared for her son became a reality. And with broken heart, Mary faced into that reality. She began seeing God's will as it truly was. And she realized Jesus had been right all along.

And then that new realization was confirmed by the impossible fact that JESUS ROSE FROM THE DEAD!

Thus, at the foot of the cross and then before the open tomb, Mary found herself moving into a new virginity, a wiser virginity, a virginity now conscious, aware, tempered with pain and struggle and grief. And thus it was that Mary again became the virgin who "treasured all (that God had done) in her heart" (Luke 2:51).

---

[70] Helen Luke, *Fire and the Cow* (Three Rivers, MI: Apple Farms Community, 1969), 12.

So it was that Mary became example to us all of the need to treasure, the need to ponder, the need to trust, the need to be still and silent before God and to wait on God's timing and will. For it is out of such pondering, such stillness, such trusting that one becomes virgin—one who is "one-in-herself," the whole and fulfilled human being who is at peace with herself and at peace with God, and therefore can be peacemaker to the world. Thus, Mary teaches us that spiritual formation is not a one-time thing, an angel appearing and a baby being born. It is the recognition that we may hear God's call distinctly at a specific moment in our life and obediently live into that calling, doing the work God has called us to do. But we can, over time, not discern the growth in that call, and so—without intending to do so—move away from God's will for us. But God is faithful to continue God's work in us and will (sometimes painfully) call us to discern how God has matured that call, and thus follow it. And this is the process of moving from "virgin" to "mother" to "virgin again"!

Disciplines for Our Spiritual Formation

Fortunately, the Church has more than 2,000 years of experience in awakening people to their deep gladness through spiritual formation. It has been doing it since Jesus first interacted with his disciples. And the church has discovered a number of vehicles for enabling us Christians to both grow in our relationship with God and to more greatly discern both our own personal deep gladness and the deep hunger of the world to which we are particularly called to engage. Let's look at some of those disciplines of the Christian life.

Worship. A friend of mine attended early morning prayers at King's College Chapel at Cambridge University a number of years ago. He found a seat in the quire[71] of the massive chapel and waited for the service to begin. Suddenly, the back doors were thrust open and a full procession, in full liturgical garb and with the processing choir singing, began down the center aisle of the nave, and then into the quire. My

---

[71] The sanctuary or worship center of the King's College Chapel is divided into two sections, the nave (with all seats facing forward, like an auditorium) and the quire (with seats facing each other along the central aisle). By such an arrangement, the sanctuary can be effectively divided in half, with the nave and quire used together for high-attendance services, and the quire used exclusively for low-attended services such as the Daily Office (see below). Because this service of Lauds would have a light attendance, it was being held in the quire.

friend rose and turned to face the procession—and then realized that he was the only person present, outside of those in the procession!

The procession entered the quire, and the full choir and worship leadership took their assigned places. Then a most remarkable thing happened. The full service of Lauds was celebrated, with the choir singing and incense wafting and chanting and scripture reading and a sermon occurring—and yet, he was the only person sitting in the congregation!

The service ended, and the choir and leaders of worship recessed in full splendor down the aisle and out to the patio. My friend got up, walked alone out of the chapel, and found the entire worship leadership party standing on the patio and visiting with one another. So he walked to the dean of the chapel and said, "Thank you for conducting that entire service just for me." But the dean looked hard at my friend, and then said, "Oh, we didn't do it for you!"

That's the whole point of the most important act of the Body of Christ. Worship is not done for our benefit! It is done for God! We are not the recipients of worship; we are not customers or observers at worship. We are not an audience to be entertained. We are the worshippers! And it is God who is the true audience. It is God who is glorified by our worship, no matter how masterfully or poorly we may do it! And God is pleased with that worship—no matter how masterfully or poorly it is done.

It is precisely because worship is the one act that Christians can do which is entirely directed toward God and is not for our benefit that it is a primary vehicle that contributes to our spiritual formation and the enforcing of our sense of call. We can be enriched by participating in worship. But we are enriched precisely to the degree that we have worshiped God! Such worship of God is conducted by us in three ways.

Corporate Worship. A central way the church has worshiped from its very origins with Jesus and his disciples has been corporate worship. It is absolutely essential both to the formation of our congregation and of us as its members. Worship is the one act that we do together. And it is its very regularity that is the particular blessing that it provides for us. As I pointed out above, corporate worship is for God to enjoy. But that does not mean that we do not benefit from participating in it. Participating in worship deepens our relationship with God, our relationship with each other as a community of faith, and can contribute to both our spiritual formation and to our greater perception of and living into our mission call. Therefore, weekly corporate worship should be the primary and most basic spiritual discipline that we follow as children of God.

The Daily Office. A second vehicle for worship is the Daily Office. As its name implies, this is either corporate or individual worship done daily. The word "office" is used for such worship because it often follows a prescribed course or pattern of worship.[72] The celebration of a daily office first developed in monastic communities in the third and fourth centuries, but is now conducted throughout the entire Body of Christ.

The Daily Office comes out of a celebration of the rhythm of worship and work (spiritual formation and call, journey inward and journey outward). The most celebrated of the offices are "Lauds" (morning), "Midday" (noon), "Vespers" (end of the workday) and "Compline" (just before bedtime). The offices consist of a standard organized rhythm of prayers, the recital or chanting of the psalms and the readings of scripture, conducted in a very meditative, reflective style, including time dedicated to simply sitting in silence. Thus, it enables one to "come away" from the hustle and bustle of everyday life to spend quality time with God each day and to still one's soul. Most of the Christian traditions (Roman Catholic, the Orthodox Church, Anglican, and many Protestant churches) publish the Daily Office for their particular constituency.

The Daily Office plays an important part in my personal spiritual worship. I celebrate "Lauds" almost every day, using a Protestant form of the Daily Office entitled *The Divine Hours*.[73] Lauds provides for me a structure for my prayer time, an opportunity to immerse myself in and journaling upon the scripture of the Daily Lectionary (see below), and the occasion to remember and celebrate the lives of Christian martyrs, saints, and servants throughout the history of the Christian church (an integral part of most daily offices—so that one doesn't fall victim to thinking that Christianity begins and ends with ourselves!).

---

[72] Today, the word "office" is normally used to denote the room in which a particular kind of service is provided (like a "doctor's office") or business is transacted (like a "lawyer's office"). But in earlier usage, "office" was focused almost entirely upon the performance of that service.

[73] Phyllis Tickle, The Divine Hours: A Manual for Prayer (New York: Doubleday, 2001). Tickle's Divine Hours is in three volumes (Prayers for Springtime; Prayers for Summertime; and Prayers for Autumn and Wintertime), and consist of the daily offices of Lauds, Midday, Vespers, and Compline for each day of the year.

Personal Devotions. One should not worship God solely in community. It is important for all Christians to have a "personal time" with God. Normally, the conducting of personal devotions is a daily time set apart by a Christian to spend such time with God—a time of prayer, journaling, and biblical reflection for those who don't prefer the more liturgical Daily Office. Holding personal devotions regularly (preferably daily) is as essential to our individual spiritual formation as is corporate worship for the building of the Body of Christ. It is crucial to structure this time (otherwise, time will get wasted). Whereas the Daily Office provides its own internal structure, holding personal devotions does not—so it is important to develop the structure to that quiet time that best works for you.

Before I discovered the Daily Office about 25 years ago, I found that the rhythm for my daily devotions that worked best for me included, first, a time of just settling in, a time of quiet and of rest. I discovered that if I skipped this step, I would not be able to be present to God in that quiet time but would instead quickly move through the steps I had set. So, nestled in my favorite chair with a hot cup of coffee and viewing through a window its restful scene, simply was necessary to enable me to move out of the agenda of the day and into that quiet time to be spent with God.

Following that quiet time, I would then spend time in the scripture which I was studying (I would normally do one biblical book at a time). I would normally read one chapter and then ask how it was speaking to me. I would then write in my journal what I heard, and from that do some journaling. Then, I would conclude that quiet time in prayer. Although I presently prefer the structure of the Daily Office, I also found this more "free-wheeling" approach to a daily time with God tremendously enriching as well. And in that time, I would discover that I was gaining both increasing clarity on God's then-present mission call to me and my spiritual enjoyment of the Trinity.

Prayer. When I think of prayer, what I most often think of is what a friend of mine calls "Gimme-prayers." And this is the extent of the praying of most Christians. Oh, we may spend a little time in adoration of God and in confession of sin, but pretty quickly we get to the main point of our prayers: "God bless me; God bless my family; God bless my church; God, please make someone well; please provide a job for my friend; help another in her marriage; please bless our city, nation, government, and the world. Amen."

Do you see what's common in all these prayers? They are all "Gimme-prayers"—God, grant me this request, grant me another, and still another! The church has a name for such prayers. They are "simple prayers." That is, they are the prayers that the youngest and most immature Christian will pray. They are, at the same time, the initial kind of prayer that even the most mature Christian will pray. These are the prayers of people that come "from their guts"! Such prayers are all about our needs, our wants, our issues and concerns.

Simple prayer is both an important part of one's spiritual formation and one's growing awareness of why God has created, chosen, and called us. It is appropriate for us to pray simply when we need to simply pray!

There are, however, five primary forms of prayer that the church has traditionally embraced. We should engage in all five types of prayer and in relatively equal emphasis in order for our prayer life (whether individual or corporate) to be truly balanced. Let's look at those five elements of prayer.

Praise and adoration. This is prayer that has nothing to do with us and everything to do with God. There is no "gimme" in this type of prayer. It is fully and totally focused upon God, and the praise and adoration of God just as God is and does—and not for any benefit we might gain by praying as such. The focus is fully upon God and a celebration of God's majesty, love, and justice. A traditional example of such prayer is the *Te Deum*, which begins:

> We praise thee, O God; we acknowledge thee to be the Lord. All the earth doth worship thee: the Father everlasting. To thee all Angels cry aloud; to thee Cherubim and Seraphim continually do cry, "Holy, Holy, Holy, Lord God of Sabbaoth: heaven and earth are full of thy Majesty."[74]

Do you see anything about us in such prayers? It is all about the glorifying and praising of God!

Confession. This is another important element of prayer, particularly in the light of our celebration of the majesty, sinlessness, and grace of God. It is the recognition that we fall far short of that glory—even if we are the nicest person one

[74] The Book of Common Prayer of the Protestant Episcopal Church in the United States of America (New York: James Pott and Co., 1892), 7.

could ever imagine! Confession is the heartfelt and honest confession of our shortcomings before God, the claiming of the redemption of which we are assured in Jesus Christ, and the requesting of forgiveness from God (since it is God whom we have most offended by our deeds, not others or ourselves). Here is a classic example of a prayer of confession.

> Almighty and most merciful Father: we have erred and strayed from thy ways like lost sheep. We have followed too much the devices and desires of our own hearts. We have offended against thy holy laws. We have left undone those things which we ought to have done. And we have done those things which we ought not to have done, and there is no health in us. But thou, O Lord, have mercy upon us, miserable offenders. Spare thou, those, O God, who confess their faults. Restore thou those who are penitent, according to thy promises declared unto mankind in Christ Jesus our Lord. And grant, O most merciful Father, for his sake, that we may hereafter live a godly, righteous, and sober life, to the glory of thy holy Name. Amen.[75]

Thanksgiving. The prayer of thanksgiving is significantly different than the prayer of adoration. The prayer of adoration is all about God and our praise of God for simply being God. The prayer of thanksgiving is not only about God but also about us and our gratitude for God's forgiveness of our shortcomings which have been confessed to him. It is also the expression of gratitude for God's blessings of us, and for the grace-filled nature of God. It is essentially our continuing "thank-you" to God. A beautiful prayer of thanksgiving written by Martin Luther is this one:

> Lord God, heavenly Father, we know that we are dear children of Thine and that thou art our beloved Father, not because we deserve it, nor ever could merit it, but because our dear Lord, Thine only-begotten Son, Jesus Christ, wills to be our brother and of his own accord offers and makes this blessing known to us. Since we may consider ourselves his brothers and

---

[75] Book of Common Prayer, 25–26.

> sisters, and he regards us as such, thou wilt permit us to become and remain children of Thine forever. Amen.[76]

Supplication. This is one of two types of "gimme" prayers. But it is prayed in the light of our recognition of God's holiness and love, the confession of our sins, our assurance of forgiveness through the blood of Jesus Christ, and our thanksgiving for that unmerited forgiveness. Supplication are prayers for ourselves. The word, "supplication" is from the Latin *supplicates* that means "to make a humble entreaty," and was primarily used to refer to one bowing before the emperor and making a request of him. When considering both the prayers of supplication and of intercession (which follows), I find it useful to envision myself in a grand throne room (which is what the cathedral was meant to depict—the throne room of God) making entreaty of the holy God that is described by Isaiah the prophet as "the Lord seated on a throne, high and exalted, and the skirt of his robe filled the temple" (Isa. 6:1, *The New English Bible*).[77] In other words, I'm not having a cozy chat over wine and by a warm fireside with my best friend, but am in a throne room making entreaty both for myself and others before the emperor of the universe. One prayer of supplication is this one:

> Lord Christ, crucified for us, help us to love as you have loved; help us to live as you have lived. Help us to be neighbor to those in need as you in your mercy were neighbor to us and suffered and died for us. In your name we ask it. Amen.[78]

Intercession. Here, one is praying for others. You are still in the great throne room, still appearing before the Lord and emperor of the universe. You are permitted to be before him, making entreaty, not because you deserve so to be, but only because of the sacrifice paid for your redemption by God the Son—Jesus Christ our Lord. But keep your proper place. You are still the (now-redeemed) supplicant, and God is still God—not your buddy! But whereas in supplication, you are making

---

[76] Martin Luther, as included in Clyde Manschreck, *Prayers of the Reformers* (Philadelphia: Muhlenberg Press, 1958), 9.

[77] *The New English Bible* (UK: Oxford University Press and Cambridge University Press. 1970).

[78] Caryl Micklem, *Contemporary Prayers for Public Worship* (Grand Rapids, MI: Eerdmans Publishing Co., 1967), 44.

requests for yourself, in intercession you are making a plea for others. A surprising prayer of intercession is this one:

> We pray, O Lord, as Christ taught us, for our enemies, that both their hearts and ours may be drawn to God the Father of all of us, and filled with a desire to serve Him, that peace may be re-established on the foundation of justice, truth, and good will; through Jesus Christ our Lord. Amen.[79]

These are the five elements of prayer—praise and adoration, confession, thanksgiving, supplication, and intercession. And only all five elements together make prayer truly whole and complete.

There are other types of prayer. But all fall under at least one of these categories of praise, confession, thanksgiving, supplication, or intercession. Some of those prayers are spoken in magnificent, carefully crafted liturgies. Others are solely expressed by the heart, no matter how poorly said. Some may be prayers of deep introspection and self-reflection, such as the prayer of *examen.* Others are prayers dealing with one's spiritual *formation.* Still others may be *sacramental prayers* as one participates in the celebration of one of the sacraments. Others can be prayers of the *daily office*; still others can be prayers from within the practice of *silence*, or of *meditation,* or of *contemplation.* Richard Foster, in his landmark work on prayer,[80] lists 20 distinct types of prayer that fall under the acts of adoration, confession, thanksgiving, supplication, or intercession. But the point is, however we might choose to pray, prayer is an integral and highly strategic part of our spiritual formation, meant by God for our own spiritual development as giving us opportunity to praise, thank, confess sins, or make our requests known to God.

Immersion in Scripture. Christians are "People of the Book"! The Bible is not a book among books. It is THE book of the Christians and of the Jews. Over 450 years ago, Swiss Christians declared of the Bible, "In this Holy Scriptures, the universal Church of Christ has the most complete exposition of all that pertains to a saving faith,

---

79 *The Book of Common Worship*, The General Assembly of the Presbyterian Church in the United States of America (Philadelphia: Office of the General Assembly, 1946), 329–330.

80 Richard Foster, *Prayer: Finding the Heart's True Home* (New York: HarperCollins Press, 1992).

and also to the framing of a life acceptable to God."[81] That is why Christians should study it, reflect upon it, allow the Holy Spirit to speak through it to them, and immerse themselves in it. The Scriptures contribute to both our personal spiritual formation and our increasing discernment of our call and mission in four ways: through biblical study, the use of the Daily Lectionary, biblical reflection (which is different than study), and through practicing Lectio Divina. Let's look briefly at all four.

Bible Study. There is a profound difference between Bible study and reflection upon scripture, and it is important to note that difference. Bible study is exactly what it says it is; it is the study of the Bible. It is an academic exercise. Its primary purpose is to be instructed by the Word. In Bible study, one is approaching the Bible as one's teacher; you are examining it in order to learn from it! This is a very necessary and important act for every serious Christian, and should be undertaken every day—because, no matter how much you study it, you will always discover more in every study. Insight piles upon insight, as one's grasp and appreciation of God's work in one's life, in the city, and in the world grows with regular, systematic study.

There are many ways to study the Bible. The most obvious is to study it book by book—to work with the depths of a given book of the Bible, before moving on to another. The use of resource material is particularly helpful here, such as the 31–volume *Polis Bible Commentary*[82] (which examines scripture from an urban, mission, and global perspective) and William Barclay's 17–volume exposition of the New Testament scriptures, *The Daily Study Bible Series*.[83] There is also my four-volume, *The Gospel of Shalom: A Political Reading of the Lectionary Scriptures*.[84]

---

[81] Heinrich Bullinger, "The Second Helvetic Confession" (1561), *The Book of Confessions* (Louisville, KY: The Office of the General Assembly of The Presbyterian Church [USA], 5.002, 1999), 53.

[82] *The Polis Bible Commentary* has a minimum of two authors for each book: a biblical scholar and an urban mission practitioner; it is currently in production; already-published books of this series are available from its publisher, Urban Loft Publishers.

[83] William Barclay, *The Daily Study Bible Series* (Louisville, KY: Westminster/John Knox Press, 1975, 2004). This commentary is also available as a multimedia CD (Logos Research Systems, Inc., 2001).

[84] This commentary on most of the Bible is available online at www.rclinthicum.org, and is free. It is not available in print.

There are other ways of studying the Bible, besides the study of specific books. Another way is to work with a theme throughout scripture, such as the theology of *shalom* or the kingdom of God, or even the city in scripture (be prepared to discover that the Bible is essentially an urban—not a rural—book!). Still another type of study is to examine the life of a given individual or a group or clan or vocation. There are as many ways to study the scripture as there is one's capacity to think creatively. But it is important to study the Bible, if one is to be serious about perceiving and faithfully living out one's call to the city.

The Daily Lectionary. The lectionary is a selection of scripture for each day of the year over a two-year period of time.[85] Each day's entry normally consists of an Old Testament lesson, a Gospel lesson, an Epistle lesson, and a Psalm. It is so designed that, if one faithfully follows the lectionary, she or he will have read through much of the Bible over that two-year period.

The daily lectionary is, in reality, a further development of the weekly lectionary. The weekly lectionary is designed to be used in Sunday worship, so it is primarily designed for corporate use rather than individual usage. There exists a Common Lectionary which is used by the Roman Catholic and most Protestant denominations, so that all participating churches are reflecting on the same scriptures at their respective Sunday worship. There are three advantages in using the lectionary in public worship. First, it guides the church to study a spectrum of scripture of selected passages on the same subject in the Old Testament, Gospels, Epistles, and Psalms on each Sunday. Second, when it informs the sermon preached, it keeps pastors from "riding theological hobby-horses" because it covers the entire witness of scripture. Third, it both symbolizes and expresses the oneness of the Body of Christ as churches of different traditions gather around the same scriptures in their respective Sunday worship.

Although it is meant for individual rather than corporate use, the daily lectionary provides the very same advantages. It becomes another way of studying and reflecting upon scripture. Consequently, it integrates easily into the use of the Daily Office or of personal devotions. Thus, in my daily quiet time, I use the Lauds segment

---

[85] Whereas the ***daily*** lectionary is for a two-year period, the ***weekly*** lectionary (intended for the Sabbath worship of the church) is for a three-year period, divided into Cycles A, B, and C.

of the appropriate Daily Office to structure my devotional time with God, but add to it that day's scriptures from the Daily Common Lectionary. Those, in turn, are the scriptures that I study, reflect upon, and pray.

Biblical Reflection. There is another way of working with scripture, a way that I have found makes the Bible come alive in my hands: to relate personally to the scripture passage. Relational biblical reflection is a means to live into the Bible, to use the Bible for deepening self-knowledge, building community with others, and relating personally to God.

I relate to the Bible devotionally in two ways. First, I spend a significant amount of time with one passage of scripture—usually seven sessions (one week). Second, when I work with that scripture, I first do an exegetical study. And then I begin to work with the scripture by putting myself into it. For example, if I am studying Jesus's parable of the sower (Matt. 13:1–9; Mark 4:1–9; Luke 8:4–8), I might ask myself the question, "What kind of soil have I been this past week: trampled, rocky, thorny, rich? Why have I selected that soil as representative of my life? In the light of the type of soil I have been, what do I need to ask of the Sower for myself?" I have discovered that, by living this way into scripture, I have given it permission to deal with me in a profoundly personal way that cannot possible occur when I am approaching it academically.[86]

Lectio Divina. Perhaps the most transformative of the ways of reflecting upon scripture is conducting *Lectio Divina.* This is a means of meditating upon scripture that was first developed in the Benedictine Order in the sixth century, but is now used widely throughout both Protestant and Catholic Christianity. *Lectio Divina* ("Divine Reading" in Latin) is a way of relating to scripture through the exercise of four steps. Those four steps, taken one-by-one, are to read the particular scripture ("lectio"), then to meditate upon it ("meditatio"), then to pray over your reading of this scripture ("oratio"), and finally to reflect or contemplate on that passage ("contemplatio").

In order for this exercise to be effective, it is terribly important to take time and to move slowly and deliberately through the process. Often, the individual reads

---

[86] Much of this section has been taken from my book, *City of God,* 245–246. Used by permission of Zondervan, www.zondervan.com.

the designated scripture slowly three times, allowing several minutes to elapse between each of the three readings. Meditation will often be around identifying specific words or phrases in the scripture that speak to you, and then reflecting upon those words. That, in turn, offers opportunity to allow oneself to live into that word. Thus, rather than talking about the peace of Christ, one seeks to share in and experience that peace in him/herself. Thus, *Lectio Divina* provides the practice of an exercise that allows one to more clearly and contemplatively experience and live into the practicing or reflecting upon one's call.

Journaling. An exercise I find to be particularly supportive of such devotional work is journaling. Journaling, of course, is simply the writing down of both the insights coming to you from your work with scripture and the experience of living into that scripture. It can also include your interpretation of what God is doing in your life through that day's activities. And, of course, it can also play the role of a diary, recording important activities of that day, both in relationship to your spiritual formation and of the living into your call. It can be a repository of poems, hymns, or psalms you have enjoyed or written. Finally, a journal can include your recording of dreams you have had the previous night, insightful conversations, or imaging you have done. Your journal is you sharing on paper what God is telling you day-by-day and how God is at work in your life.

Keeping a journal of your spiritual journey can be a profoundly enriching experience. Writing in that journal during your times of solitude and when you are living into Scripture, recording in that journal how God has revealed God's self to you that day, and expressing in written world the struggles of your soul is a penetrating mechanism for enabling you to understand your spiritual journey. At the time, journaling provides the means for working with your soul that comes only through writing down your insights and the process of the forming of your spirit. Later on, it provides a record of what God has been doing in your life. Thus, I have 23 volumes of my journaling in my library, dating back to March 1, 1974. I find particular delight in reading portions of my journal, reminding me of segments of my life and of how God has worked in my life that I have otherwise long since forgotten.

One of the journaling disciplines that I have followed occasionally has been to sit down with my journal on New Year's Day, and to prayerfully read all of my entries for the year that has just ended. From the vantage point of year's end, I am always deeply moved to see how God has been at work in my life that year. I would not have the chance to come to this awareness if it were not for that daily record of my spiritual journey and of the living out of my call.[87]

Spiritual Autobiography. I have personally found this discipline of particular value. Writing one's spiritual autobiography (and editing it over the years) can be an extremely revelatory experience, particularly highlighting areas of one's life on which work needs to be done. This can best be done by actually writing down your autobiography, but if you are not a strong writer, then speaking it out loud in a disciplined way (perhaps by recording it) or by doing it electronically can be an effective way of creating your spiritual autobiography.

But what is a spiritual autobiography? A conventional autobiography is simply the telling of one's own life's story (first this happened, then this, then this). But a spiritual autobiography takes that reflection a step further. Using the significant events of your life as the superstructure upon which to build your autobiography, you examine each event to ask the question, "What was it that God was seeking to do in my life at this point?" Then, you reflect upon what came out of that action of God upon your life (were you receptive; was this a major "Aha" moment for you; did the incident bring about significant change in your life; did you avoid God's challenge?).

An excellent example of a spiritual autobiography is the one written by the apostle Paul (which is also an indication to us that a spiritual autobiography need not be long). If Paul had simply written his autobiography, he would have written something like this: "I was born as Saul of Tarsus, a biblically orthodox Jew. I studied for and became a rabbi of the Jewish faith. But then I was converted to Christianity, changed my name to Paul, and became an apostle to the Gentiles, founding churches throughout the Roman Empire." But instead, he wrote a spiritual autobiography, indicating how God had worked in his life. This is what he wrote,

> I (was) circumcised on the eighth day (of my life), a member of the people of Israel, of the tribe of Benjamin, a Hebrew born of Hebrews; as to the law, a Pharisee; as to zeal, a persecutor of the church; as to righteousness under the law, blameless. Yet whatever gains I had, these I have come to regard as loss because of Christ. More than that, I regard everything as loss because of the surprising value of knowing Christ Jesus my Lord. For his sake

---

[87] Linthicum, *City of God,* 246.

> I have suffered the loss of all things, and I regard them as rubbish, in order that I may gain Christ and be found in him, not having a righteousness of my own that comes from the law, but one that comes through faith in Christ, the righteousness from God based on faith. I want to know Christ and the power of his resurrection and the sharing of his sufferings by becoming like him in his death, if somehow I may attain the resurrection of the dead (Philippians 3:5–11).

What is particularly significant about this writing of his spiritual autobiography is how Paul then uses that writing to restate and further develop his calling.

> Not that I have already obtained this (level of spirituality) or have already reached the goal; but I press on to make it my own, because Christ Jesus has made me his own. Beloved, I do not consider that I have made it my own; but this one thing I do: forgetting what lies behind and straining forward to what lies ahead, I press on toward the goal for the prize of the heavenly call of God in Christ Jesus (3:12–14).

Silence, Solitude, and Retreat. These are three distinct spiritual disciplines, but because they are often practiced together (for example, silence is an essential discipline of a solitary retreat), I am grouping them as one discipline with three primary ingredients. So, let's now look at each of these ingredients.

Silence as a spiritual discipline is the intentional withdrawal of one's self for a designated period of time from the world of human discourse. This can be for a lengthy period of time (for example, going on a silent retreat for a week) or a short period (for example, spending 10 minutes at the beginning of one's daily devotion by sitting in silence as a way of centering down into a meditative mode as one removes one's self from normal activity). It is coming away from the ordinary discourse and activity of the world in order to focus upon one's inner self and one's relationship with God. Silence can also be used as a group discipline, particularly for the period of time between the concluding daily office of the day ("Compline") and the beginning of the first daily office of the next day ("Lauds"); this is traditionally called "The Great Silence" and is practiced in most monastic communities as well as in many group retreats.

I find however I might practice it, that silence is a very necessary part of any spiritual exercise I might undertake. This is true whether it is the beginning of my daily devotional time or whether I am beginning a personal or group retreat. I appreciate it immensely when I worship at a church when the congregation gathers in silence rather than in boisterous visiting with one another; that period of silence before worship helps me to prepare my soul for that corporate meeting with God. It is a very necessary means of enabling the transition to occur in my soul, brain, and body from activism to being still before the Lord.

Solitude is a distinct discipline from that of silence. It is true that if I were to be alone in solitude, there would have to be silence. But the two are distinct. Solitude is the intentional coming away from the bustle of everyday life in order to be alone. But this is not the aloneness of simply being absent from people. For example, I might be alone in my hotel room when on a trip, but such being alone would not be practicing the discipline of solitude; it would simply be living into the reality that I am deprived of any companionship for that evening. Solitude, on the other hand, is the intentional act of being alone for the purpose of spending reflective, contemplative time with one's self before the Lord. This includes not reading—even of the Bible! To read anything is, *ipso facto*, to be engaged in a conversation with another, even though that conversation is not audible. So being in solitude is intentionally being alone with God, with no outside stimulation asserting itself (except for the outward reality of being in the place where you are practicing that solitude). Solitude is an important discipline for a Christian to practice from time to time; I have discovered it to be an occasionally necessary discipline.

Retreat is the physical removal of one's self from one's everyday life to a dedicated and removed space in order to be in communion with God and perhaps others. Today, we think of the word "retreat" as meaning a forced withdrawal from an enemy or from a position. Thus, "retreat" means to us either a military action or a wise escape from an argument we are losing badly. But the word "retreat" actually is from the Middle English word "retret" which meant "to withdraw"—thus meaning to temporarily remove one's self from everyday life.[88] A term used in both the secular and

---

[88] Merriam-Webster's *Collegiate Dictionary, 11th Edition* (Springfield, MA: Merriam-Webster, 2007), 1065.

religious world, a retreat is seen as the coming away from the demands of everyday life for dedicated focus in a removed setting. Retreats primarily fall into two categories: a planning retreat and a spiritual retreat. It is about the spiritual retreat with which we are concerned.

Like most Christians, I have always found spiritual retreats to be very real nourishment to my soul. To be able to temporarily escape the demands and pressures of daily life in order to focus upon relationship with God and others is thoroughly enriching. The church board of one urban church I served provided me with the opportunity to take four one-week retreats each year (once a quarter), either as solitary retreats or with others. Most of the time, I went to a nearby Jesuit monastery where I entered into their monastic rhythm of worship and work, and most of these retreats would be in silence (the only time we would speak would be in the worship of God). Some were solitary retreats (where I was the only retreatant). But I always found them to be both immensely refreshing and insightful, as I would discover new insights about myself, my call, ministry, or church by spending this dedicated time with God.

Spiritual Direction. Spiritual direction (sometimes also called "spiritual friendship") is the conducting of a spiritual mentorship in which a person covenants with a more mature Christian to guide that person in his or her spiritual journey. Usually, the person receiving the spiritual direction (we'll call him/her the "mentee") contracts with the spiritual director to meet with the mentee and help him/her set a spiritual course through the storms of life. This is normally for a designated amount of time (e.g., two years). The spiritual director often asks the mentee to list spiritual disciplines for which the mentee wants to be held accountable. Then the two meet regularly (most often, once a month) both to consider together how it has gone in meeting those disciplines and to talk together about the mentee's spiritual journey. Of course, this can also be a time for the spiritual director to teach, advise, and pray for the mentee. I found being in a relationship with a spiritual director particularly helpful early in my spiritual journey. The director held me accountable, not only for disciplines one would normally consider "spiritual" (e.g., a daily devotional time, writing in my journal, etc.), but for other disciplines I felt it was important for me to keep (e.g., reserving one evening a week to take my wife on a date and one day a week to do something fun with our entire family).

But how to find a spiritual director? Of course, you can ask a mature Christian whom you respect and you feel has much to teach you about the Christian life. But there are also a wide assortment of spiritual director networks that identify certified spiritual directors in your community, according to the type of spiritual director you would desire (e.g., Catholic, Evangelical, interfaith, Mennonite, Jewish, etc.). You can identify the network of your choice through a Google search under "spiritual directors."

Life in Community. One of the most pivotal spiritual disciplines is the building of our life together within a Christian community. Because this is such an important discipline, we will not develop this discipline here but will rather devote an entire chapter of this book to the building of our life in community. So we refer you to Chapter 10 for that examination.

Calling Forth of Gifts. Likewise, the calling forth of gifts is so strategic to both the discerning of our call and our spiritual formation, we will also devote an entire chapter to that discipline. So we refer you to Chapter 11 to explore that discipline.

In Conclusion. Using any or all of the above spiritual disciplines will enable us to more greatly strengthen our self-understanding, nurture our relationship with God and increasingly build our life in community. This, in turn, can increase our discernment of God's ever-present and shifting call to us to serve God in the world in the specific ways God wishes to use us. Thus, the increasing discovery of our own deep gladness will keep on leading us to an increasing discernment and embracing of that hunger of the world to which we, both individually and corporately, may be called.

Getting Started

Discovering your own deep gladness is, on the one hand, a lifelong task, because you, your personal spirituality and the nuances of your call keep on changing. On the other hand, what you have already experienced in your formation as a spiritual being is sufficient for you to have clarity about what God's call to you is right here, right now to address a specific hunger of the world. So we urge you to undertake two actions right now. We urge you to reflect upon who you are and what God has been doing in your life to bring you to the point God has brought you to right now—because in that journey already lies a call. But we also urge you to "keep on keeping on"—to be intentional about continuing your journey inward and the nurturing of your own deep gladness.

In this chapter, we have sought to give you both the theological orientation to better understand that journey, as well as some specific vehicles you can use to enhance your spiritual formation (and, therefore, your growing clarity upon God's call to you to address a deep hunger of the world). I have also included in the appendices of this book (Appendix I-1) an exercise that I have used often in workshops which participants have found helpful in clarifying their deep gladness and thus more clearly discerning their calls. Consequently, I commend it to you for your use, as well.

And now, on to the discovery of that deep hunger of the world that God most desires that you address!

Chapter 9

Discovering My Deep Hunger

"The place God calls you to is the place where your deep gladness and the world's deep hunger meet!"[89]

The journey inward that enables our spiritual formation to take place will increasingly reveal that our "deep gladness" is not an end in itself! One doesn't grow in Christ in order to grow in Christ! One grows in Christ in order to be more spiritually sensitive to God's call to us to address that "deep hunger" of the world to which God specifically calls us. The rhythm of the Christian life leads us to respond to the world's deep hunger, and to respond to that hunger in a particular way. Our spiritual growth exists primarily to prepare and sustain us as we discover God's call for our life and then live into that call. Likewise, our faithful living into and practicing that call to address the world's deep hunger will result in overextension so that we will run—not walk—to times of spiritual formation.

If our work in the world for Christ and His Kingdom doesn't drive us to seek spiritual refreshment, then it is likely inauthentic. And if our spiritual formation doesn't drive us toward a lived-out greater commitment to the addressing of the world's deep hunger, then it too is inauthentic. Exclusive focus on mission will burn us out! And a focus solely on spiritual growth will rust us out!

I think that was driven home for me in an encounter I had with Mother Teresa in 1982. My son (who was then 18) and I were part of a group of pilgrims who journeyed to Calcutta, India, to work and worship with the religious order Mother

---

[89] Buechner, Wishful Thinking, 119.

Teresa had founded—the Missionaries of Charity. To our disappointment, the sisters told us that Mother Teresa was away on a trip, so we would not meet her. But then, unexpectedly, she returned—and she wanted to meet both with our group and with each of us individually.

When I had the privilege to meet with her, I introduced myself and told her how delighted I was to visit with her. But then she cut through all the appropriate niceties by focusing on me as if she could see through me, and asked, "Young man, do you love Jesus?" I was stunned, but I managed to stumble out a "Yes, I do!" But still fixing me in her glare, she said, "Yes, you do—but do you love Jesus in the distressing disguise of the poor?"

If I did not love Jesus in the distressing disguise of the poor, then I didn't love Jesus! As Mother said later to the group, "We here at this house meet Jesus twice each day—in our worship at Mass and in the faces of the poor with whom we minister!" Spiritual formation occurs so that one might minister in Christ's name. And our ministry to others occurs so that we will be drawn closer to Jesus. The journey inward must result in empowering our journey outward. And our journey outward must drive us to continue our journey inward.

Why am I stressing this? Simply because I see today's Protestant, holiness, and Pentecostal churches, especially in the first world, becoming greatly enamored with spiritual formation and in the exercise of spiritual disciplines. But I rarely see a recognition that such formation must be done for the sake and benefit of the world.

Understanding Your Call

Thus far in this book, we have examined the doctrine and practice of God's call to each human being (whether clergy or lay) and to all humanity from several perspectives. We have acknowledged that God creates, chooses and calls us to serve God in the world by working for God's kingdom. We have discovered that God's call is extended to laypeople as well as clergy—that it is meant for absolutely everyone! We are all uniquely created, loved, and chosen by God. Further, we have affirmed that our hearts remain restless until we embrace and begin to act out that vocation as God's call to us. We believe that God has created both the Church and Israel to provide us with the communities of call with which we can be a part, in which we can be nurtured and taught, and through which we can live out our vocation to the world. Finally, we have articulated the first primary principles of call (which we saw epitomized in Moses) as:

1. God prepares us for our call by breaking our hearts, spiritually forming us, and breaking through to us;
2. Discovering and carrying out God's call to us only comes out of God's interior work that God keeps on doing within us;
3. Call always comes to us as frightening good news for which we feel incompetent and overextended;
4. God always adequately prepares and gifts us for our call—although we may not acknowledge that we are so gifted;
5. We can't effectively minister to that deep hunger of the world to which we have been called, except as supported by our community of faith.

In the light of the above, the question then becomes, "If all this is true, then how can I discern and live into that calling that God is extending to me?" And we began to answer that question in the previous chapter. That chapter sought to demonstrate to us that one can't discern and effectively live into his/her call simply through responding to human need. That process of discernment requires intentional spiritual formation on our part, both as an individual and within a supportive community of believers.

But now, in this chapter, we are ready to move to the most important question of this book. "Since the witness of scripture is that we are all called by God to serve God by serving humanity in a particular way, then how can I discern and live into my unique call?" How can we discover our call? And once we have discovered it, how then do we act it out in the real world? Answering that question begins with recognizing two realities about any person's or any community's call.

Calls Don't Stand Still

Calls keep changing! It is likely that there is a continuing common theme to your call. But as you spiritually grow and the world changes and the acting out of your mission moves forward, your call also keeps changing. That call will likely have at least one continuing focus, but how that focus is acted out will keep on changing. So any discernment you have of your call is a discernment for this time and place only. In due time, it is likely to change—particularly if you do a good job of doing your job!

Perhaps the best way for me to explain this principle is to tell you my own journey discovering and living into my call.

As I stated earlier in this book, I lived most of my childhood and youth in an orphanage in Philadelphia's inner city. I became a Christian in 1950 at 13, while attending a revival meeting held at an Episcopal Church when I was away from the orphanage during the Thanksgiving holiday. Because I lived on an enclosed campus, I could not become a part of any church but rather depended upon radio preachers for my spiritual sustenance and instruction. What I heard was that, as a Christian, I had the obligation to share the gospel (or at least the little that I knew of it). So it became my mission to win students to Christ and to form a little group of young Christians reading the Bible together and supporting one another.

After graduating in 1954, I became an active part of an independent Bible church, and my understanding of my mission extended beyond personal witnessing to doing street preaching. And I began to consider the possibility of becoming a pastor or evangelist. But I also felt deeply drawn to the city as my venue for ministry.

In 1955, I enrolled at Wheaton College in the suburban Chicago area, and immediately felt drawn into that great city. I joined a ministry working in one of Chicago's high-rise projects where poor African-Americans were "warehoused." This ministry included calling in their homes each week, and therefore building deep relationships with many. It was out of this experience that my call became increasingly clear to me. It was a call to ministry among the urban poor and powerless. And it was a call to work with people to set themselves free, both spiritually and economically. Toward that end, I very intentionally looked at Protestant denominations that were Reformed (like me) in theology. And it became clear that the Reformed denomination in the late 1950s that had the greatest ministry and financial commitment to urban ministry was The United Presbyterian Church in the USA. So I became a Presbyterian.

After graduating from college, I intentionally chose a seminary that was well-known at the time for training students for urban ministry—McCormick Theological Seminary in Chicago. Studying at that school as well as direct engagement in hands-on ministry both confirmed to me that I was called to urban ministry, and also gave me the systems-analysis training that I would need to later be engaged in urban work that would not only feed the hungry but would organize people to build a sustainable alternate economy.

In 1963, I was ordained into the ministry and pastored churches through 1985 in Milwaukee, Rockford (IL), Chicago, and Detroit. In my early years, I understood my call to urban ministry to include working with my congregation and the neighborhood to address what the church (and I) perceived as the outstanding problems of that community, developing projects and sustaining them and each other through a supportive community of faith. By 1968, I was well aware of the inadequacies in this approach, and thus both my perception of ministry and my understanding of my call began to change.

The real problem of my inner-city neighborhoods, I began to realize, was not poverty or poor housing or lack of jobs or welfare. The real problem was powerlessness—the people of my neighborhoods had no real say over their own lives and families. And that powerlessness was as much spiritual as political and economic. So I came to embrace the principles, values, and strategies of broad-based community organizing—and have found that a happy home ever since! Building around the "Iron Rule" of organizing ("Never do for others what they can do for themselves"), my call to urban ministry began to shift to the building of relationships with the people in the community and in the church to work together on problems common to us all, and to share the gospel as good news of self-determination for all of us.

Then, in 1975, I was called to a large and wealthy church near Detroit, and my understanding of my call consequently expanded. I still felt very much called to urban ministry and to the empowerment of the poor, powerless, and ethnic minorities. But I discovered two realities at that church. I discovered that the rich are poor as well.[90] And I also discovered that, while I knew well how to organize people for action, I was not equipped to provide solid spiritual support because I lacked spiritual formation myself. So I began to work with a theology of money and power, encouraging people to become aware of and face into the tyranny of their money upon their lives. I entered, first with fear and trembling, but later wholeheartedly into my own spiritual formation (see the previous chapter) which, of course, reflected itself in my ministry.

Then, a major change occurred. As I mentioned earlier, my son and I went on a pilgrimage to Calcutta and other Asian cities to work with their poor. I came back with an awareness of the poverty of the urban world and how the economic and political systems of both the west and the east have contributed to making it so wretched for so many. The result was some substantive soul-searching and

---

90 Mother Teresa later said to me that the poorest people she had ever met were rich Christians from the USA because "their material wealth gets in the way of their spiritual poverty, and they don't even know it"!

experimenting with my personal ministry over a three-year period, and then the decision to leave the pastorate for an entirely different kind of ministry.

In 1985, I resigned my pastorate and accepted the call of World Vision International to equip World Vision field offices and urban communities around the world to organize to address their most substantive physical, economic, political, social, and spiritual problems. This, of course, meant a major shifting in my sense of call. It was still a call to urban ministry. But it was a call to cities throughout the world, not just in the United States. And it was a call away from my personal "hands-on" engagement in ministry in order to become the teacher, trainer, mentor, and systems-organizer to others who would multiply that "hands-on" ministry in my stead.

I continued that ministry through 1995 in 28 slums and squatter settlements in 21 world-class cities in 14 Asian, African, and Latin American countries. In those slums, we created 53 people-owned businesses, the building of over 6,000 homes, and the planting of scores of churches, as well as health clinics, schools, water and sanitation systems, libraries, paved streets, and political action groups. During this time, I taught over 17,000 pastors and mission leaders in 120 urban ministry consultations and workshops. And writing for publications became an expectation of my job. As I like to put it, "World Vision gave me a world vision!" Thus, my call expanded to include the cities, Christian pastors, and the urban poor of the world.

In 1996, I left World Vision to direct the Hollywood-Wilshire Clusters of Churches in Los Angeles, and to later become president of Partners in Urban Transformation and a lecturer in community organizing at Eastern University in Philadelphia. I see this period from 1996 through 2009 as a transition period for me, moving from the heady world of international ministry back to local work, continuing in a teaching and administrative role, but also being able to return to some concrete organizing and pastoral care at the local church level. And thus my sense of call adjusted appropriately. The saying, "Think globally and act locally" comes very much to mind, because this new call brought me back to grass-roots, hands-on ministry—and yet the global experience, orientation, and commitment permeated that ministry.

I officially retired from ministry in 2009. But God has been gracious in these declining years. God gave me the joy of a final pastorate, as I filled the pulpit at First Presbyterian Church of Pomona (see Chapter 1) in the two-year interim between their installed pastors. First Church was, for me, everything I have always wanted in a church. It was as if God was giving me my heart's desire for my final pastorate.

During this time, I have also had the privilege of sharing in the creation of a new community organization in the Inland Empire-San Gabriel Valley portion of the Los Angeles metropolitan area—an area politically independent of L.A. but consisting of over 4,000,000 people (including a sizeable minority of disenfranchised Hispanic people). ICON (Inland Communities Organizing Network), an affiliate of the international (IAF) Industrial Areas Foundation, is that organization that both First Church and my home church—LaVerne Heights Church—have played a role in creating, as we organize to address concerns of the people around crime and safety, unsafe streets, public education issues, environmental pollution, sufficient jobs, eldercare, and end-of-life options. I have been able to work with my home church on the strengthening of their unique structure for mission—ministry groups (which you'll read about in Chapter 12). And how has my call adjusted to this latest period of my life? Well, it's still a commitment to urban ministry and the urban church, and to setting people free. But it is increasingly a call to quiet and unobtrusive support behind the scenes, and far less "front-and-center" leadership. It is quietly seeking to be of support to others who are now taking my place.

And what of the future? Well, I am now 80 at the time of this writing—so I don't know how much future is left for me! But I know that my call will continue until my last breath. How it will continue, I do not know. I anticipate it will be quiet support—of encouragement, unobtrusive work, and prayer. And, hopefully, this will continue until that day comes when this life will be over—and I will wake up in the arms of Jesus!

Thus, calls do not stand still! They change as we change. This means that one never answers for all time, "What is my call?" Although it is possible that one may have the same general call for the entirety of his adult life (e.g., "setting urban people free"), it will adjust and evolve as one lives life and as that life changes. So what that means is that, in regard to our call, we are always becoming. We are always moving into the future to meet God there. We are always becoming what we are always becoming. And that is the joy of the gospel!

Where's Your Call Coming From?

As we developed earlier in this chapter and book, awareness of your call comes out of both your personal spiritual formation and the particular concern for humanity to which you most resonate. This is nowhere as evident as it was in Israel's greatest prophet, Elijah.

I Kings 19:1–15 is one of the most awe-inspiring and powerful stories in the Old Testament. Elijah the prophet had just won the contest between himself and the 850 priests of Ba'al where Yahweh had answered with fire and proven himself God. Elijah had won a great victory for God as the people declared, 'Yahweh, he is the God!" Inspired by the victory, the people then purged their country of the 850 priests of Ba'al. That, in turn, brought a severe response from Queen Jezebel. "So may the gods do to me, and more also, if I do not make Elijah's life like the life of one of the dead priests of Ba'al by this time tomorrow," she vowed (19:2, NRSV). And Elijah decided that it would be most discrete to make himself scarce!

Angry, depressed, frightened, and thoroughly confused, Elijah fled into the wilderness. Why had God let him down? Why was he facing such major persecution and defeat after so splendid a victory? How could such a reversal of fortune have happened so quickly?

Wandering in the desert, the sun beating down on him, Elijah came to a ravine in which there was a large bush. He threw himself down in the shade of the bush, and looked out over the deathly stillness of the wilderness. He reflected on all that had happened to him over the past few days—the great victory he had won, the cheering people, the defeated monarchs—and then this totally irrational, inexplicable reversal of public opinion. And now he, the prophet who had won such a great victory for Yahweh, was fleeing for this life in the desert. So Elijah cried out to God, "It is enough! O Lord, take away my life, for I am no better than my ancestors" (19:4).

But God wouldn't accept such despair. Rather, God acted! First, God told Elijah, "Return to your origins." The text tells us that, after his angry cry, Elijah sat under the shade bush dejected and resigned. There he fell asleep but was suddenly awakened by the touch of another person. There before him stood a messenger from Yahweh. "Get up and eat," he commanded offering Elijah bread and water. "Get up and eat, otherwise the journey will be too much for you" (vs. 7). What journey, the prophet wanted to know? And the messenger turned and pointed in the direction of Horeb—Mount Sinai!

Mount Sinai—the most holy spot in all of Israel's history. Mount Sinai—where God had met with Israel and had covenanted with them to be their god if they would be his people. Mount Sinai—where the Israelite life-style of justice, equitable sharing of wealth, and relationship with God was given through the Ten Commandments. God was commanding Elijah to go to Mount Sinai, to return to the origins of Israel's and his own faith.

"Return to your origins." Remember the 2,000 years of the life of the church and the 3,500 years of our spiritual parent, Israel. Remember our spiritual formation and our mission outreach, uniting entire nations around the world in the worship of Yahweh and, for us who are Christians, embracing that God in the man Christ Jesus. It reminds us, as well, of our own personal origins in the faith, how God has worked and moved in our own lives, drawing us to God's self. When we look at that history, no matter how dark the present might be, we cannot help but pray, "Lord, you have been faithful in the past. You will be faithful in my future. I can trust you in this present dark moment!"

Second, God told Elijah, "Meet with me." When Elijah arrived at Mt. Sinai, God said to him, "Go out and stand on the mountain before the Lord, for the Lord is about to pass by" (vs. 11). Elijah did as he was told, and the text then states, "There was a great wind, but the Lord was not in the wind; and after the wind an earthquake, but the Lord was not in the earthquake; and after the earthquake a fire, but the Lord was not in the fire; and after the fire, a sound of sheer silence" (vv. 11–12).

This is a significant statement. In most appearances of God that appeared in the Old Testament, God was accompanied by fire, wind, thunder, lightning, or earthquake (e.g., Judg. 5:4–5; Pss. 18:7–15; 68:7–8; Hab. 3:15). But in this passage, God comes as "a sound of sheer silence" (the Hebrew actually says, "the sound of a soft whisper"), in the most gentle and eerie stillness.

And Elijah found Yahweh there. Elijah found Yahweh, not as the God of power, the God of violence, the God of mighty works—but as a God of intimacy, of quietness, a God who personally cared for his much-maligned prophet. Elijah learned first hand, in meeting God as a still, small voice what another prophet would later share with the whole world—that "in returning and rest shall ye be saved; in quietness and in confidence shall be your strength" (Isa. 30:15, KJV).

If there is anything that I have learned in my personal spiritual journey, it is that God comes to us in "the sound of silence." We cannot hear God's call to us or receive God's comforting touch when we are caught up in the rush and pressure of life. God has become real to me only to the degree that I am willing to leave my schedules and appointments and demands and deadlines, and make room for God. God comes only as we take time to be still and to enter into that space of quiet within us all.

It is then and there, when Elijah, beaten down by the conflict of his urban mission, was willing to be still and to wait upon God that God finally spoke to him—not in the midst of Elijah's fury. And God said, "What are you doing here, Elijah" (vs. 13)? Elijah boldly answered God, "I have been very zealous for the Lord, the God of hosts; for the Israelites have forsaken your covenant, thrown down your altars, and killed your people with the sword. I alone am left, and they are seeking my life, to take it away" (vs. 14). To this complaint, God simply responds, "Go, return!"

Third, God told Elijah, "Return to the battle—and I will give you one to share in that battle." In the final part of this story, Yahweh told Elijah to return to Israel. He informed the prophet that the struggle ahead of him would be even more intense than that which lay behind him. God gave Elijah specific instructions as to what he was to do. But then God did one thing more. He told Elijah to find a young man named Elisha, the son of Shaphat (v. 16). For Elisha would become Elijah's companion, mentored by Elijah and would work alongside the older prophet until Elijah's homecoming. Then Elisha would continue to carry out the reforming work Elijah had begun in Israel.

The way in is out. The way out is in. Seeing that Elijah was exhausted with the demands of carrying out the work to which he had been called, God graciously provided for that prophet's interior revitalization through his spiritual formation. He met with God in "the sound of silence." And having been spiritually refreshed, Elijah was then sent forth by God to rejoin the struggle!

Return to your origins. Meet with God there. Return to the battle. These are the ways God equips us to be God's means to bring God's transformation to the world!

Discovering Your Call

Pay Attention to Your Discontent

When I returned to the United States after my time both with Mother Teresa and from that 1982 mission trip to Hong Kong, Bangkok, and Calcutta, I found myself returning with a great deal of unease. I had seen and worked among a level of human suffering I had never encountered in any US city. My mission perspective had been forcibly expanded as I wrestled with what it meant for me to experience Jesus "in the distressing disguise of the poorest of the poor." And what I soon discovered was that this disease did not go away. I soon realized it was not supposed to go away! This was God's way of calling me into a new dimension of my call to set people (perhaps even myself) free—a dimension I could not yet identify. So what was I to do?

I soon learned the importance of simply living into my discontent. Rather than dismissing it or waiting for it to dissipate, I began to realize that all that God was calling me to do at that time was simply to live into that discontent. So I entered with a renewed gusto both into my Detroit pastorate but in particular the community-outreach dimension of that pastorate. Over the previous several years, our church had been pivotal in the forming of People in Faith United (PIFU), a congregation-based community organization in the poor Detroit neighborhood abutting the parish area of my church. And I had been active in the formation of that community organization.

But now I entered into it with renewed energy. I became involved in PIFU's effort to negotiate with a major Detroit automobile company to build a truck factory in "PIFUland," and helped train PIFU resident members to lead those negotiations—the result was the building and operation of that factory reduced unemployment in that PIFU community from 74% to 7%. Then I became involved in the PIFU Housing Corporation and asked the church to grant me a year's leave of absence so that I could head the formation of that corporation. They agreed, and I led PIFU in creating a housing restoration and building effort that enabled residents to buy their homes through a "sweat-equity" agreement negotiated between local banks and the State of Michigan. For two additional years, I continued this intense involvement with PIFU (after returning to my church from my one-year leave of absence), not knowing where this divine discontent would end up taking me—but simply living into it and turning it into practical action. Where this would all end up I would not know for three years. But as I looked back at that time from my later vantage point of going to work for World Vision, it was as if God was saying to me, "This is how you develop a poor urban community's economics, Bob. This is how you both build houses and the finances to get them built. This is how you help shape a holistic community." Why God was teaching me all this, I had not the foggiest idea. But that he was so teaching me, there was never a doubt.

Often it is paying attention to and living into your discontent that is your first step toward discerning a new call or a significant adaptation of your call. An awareness of one's call or the perception of a change in one's call does not come quickly. It normally takes a significant period of time; in my story shared above, it took three years. So, often, the first sign that God may be leading you in a new way is your vague discontent with what you are doing at present (even though it is a legitimate call). Living into that discontent and purposefully moving in experimental directions is the way to become open to the new into which God might be leading you.

Continuing Your Journeys Inward and Outward

Essential to that process of discernment must be the continuing of your personal spiritual formation and your willingness to both identify and begin to act upon your sensitivity to human need. Let's look briefly at both of these.

Explore Your Sensitivity to Human Need. During such a period of experiment and discernment, you need to act your journey outward in two ways. First, you need to "keep on keeping on"; you need to remain invested in and working upon your ministry to the world to which you feel called. You should not yet abandon that ministry. But, second, you need to also explore that human need toward which you feel "strangely warmed." For example, in the story above I kept on being involved in the work of PIFU and of our church's engagement in PIFU. But, at the same time, I realized that a new dimension of human need had opened to me as a result of my pilgrimage to be among the poor of India, Thailand, and Hong Kong. I knew that I couldn't abandon my church and family and move permanently into the Two-thirds World, but I knew I had been "strangely warmed" by it. Therefore, I had to pay attention to it. I paid that attention in two ways. First, in undertaking the work that was coming my way at PIFU, I knew I was learning much about how to do economic housing and community development. And second, I could study about the urban third world. In doing this, I was exploring my sensitivity to urban human need.

Focus on Your Journey Inward. Simultaneous to such an exploration, it is crucial that one continue one's journey inward. Your spiritual formation remains most important, so you need to pay attention to that journey. I think at such a "sorting-out" time in one's life, the vehicle of journaling becomes particularly important, because it is in the act of journaling that one can write down (and thus remember) both what one is experiencing through both journeys, but also particularly how they are integrating together. For example, I discovered that working at that time with the biblical themes of the "stranger," the Sabbatical Year and Jubilee, and of systemic justice in the Bible was very helpful in my bringing theological meaning and biblical insight into my struggle to respond to international urban need.

Live Into Your "In-Between" Time

It is important to embrace that "in-between" time, particularly in deeply reflecting upon changes in expectations. One of the clearest indicators for me that God was truly calling me into something new that I did not yet perceive was an incident that occurred early in my third year of this portion of my journey. I was contacted with an invitation to consider the call to the pastorate of a specific church.

This was an urban church that, normally, I would have died for in an American city that I truly liked. But I found myself responding with less than enthusiasm. I realized that I was totally disinterested in the job! It simply didn't excite—or even intrigue me at all. Reflecting upon my feelings, I began by "beating myself up." What's the matter with me? Don't I recognize a marvelous opportunity when it is offered me? I wrestled with my lack of enthusiasm.

But soon God began to deal with me as I worried and debated and journaled upon my lack of interest. Yes, this was the kind of position most pastors would yearn after—the appropriate final step in the building of a ministerial career. But I began to realize it wasn't for me. God was calling me to something else. And what God was calling me to, I began to realize, was not the pastorate of another church (the only career choice I had ever considered), but something outside the pastorate entirely. By living into that ambiguity, I began to realize that God was calling me out of the pastorate. But what was God calling me into? I didn't have the foggiest idea! But I was forced by God to "read the signs of the times"!

Expect God to Move in Unpredictable Ways

One night, my wife Marlene and I were sitting in our living room, reading. She was looking at a magazine published by World Vision International.[91] Soon after we married 26 years earlier, we had sponsored an orphan child through World Vision and had continued to support a number of children through that relief and

---

[91] World Vision International is one of three World Vision corporations in the United States, responsible for conducting the work of World Vision within and through the United States. World Vision Inc. coordinates World Vision's ministry in the United States and raises funds. World Vision Relief and Development receives government contracts, and World Vision International is the central body that coordinates World Vision's work around the world. It was WVI that was seeking to develop an urban ministry innovation in key urban areas throughout Asia, Africa, and Latin America, and was therefore searching for the person to lead this effort (called the "Urban Advance").

development agency. One of the benefits of doing this was receiving the monthly World Vision magazine. So Marlene was reading it, when suddenly she tossed the magazine over to me, saying, "Bob, they seem to be describing you in this 'help wanted' announcement." I caught the magazine and began to read the page to which Marlene had turned it.

It was indeed describing me! The announcement said that World Vision was looking for an ordained pastor with at least 25 years of urban pastoral experience, particularly among the poor, along with experience in housing, economic, and community development, and a well-developed biblical theology of the urban work of the church. To top it all off, it was desirable if the candidate also had some grey in his or her hair (indicating experience and, hopefully, wisdom)!

But I didn't want to go to World Vision! I was a Presbyterian pastor. And if I wasn't going to continue to serve the church in a pastorate, I would at least serve it by working in its urban ministry, or in a teaching or management position. I wouldn't go outside the church to a faith-based, independent, mission agency—for goodness sakes!

"But, Bob, they are describing you," Marlene observed. "You ought to at least take a look at the position." So I contacted them. And a few weeks later, Marlene and I were on a plane, flying from Detroit to Los Angeles. When we arrived, we had dinner with our host, then a morning introductory meeting with the organization's executive leadership. Marlene was then escorted to see some of the sights of southern California and, over the next several days, some potential housing. And I continued in meetings with WVI leadership.

That afternoon, Marlene—who is far more spiritually sensitive than am I—found her way to a nearby church where she sat in its sanctuary and cried and cried and cried! She knew that I would take the job, and so she mourned the passing of that way of life we had known for most of the 26 years of our marriage. It would be several months before I made the final decision to accept World Vision's offer, but she knew from that morning meeting that it would be a fait accompli. So my calling of working for the empowering of the poor changed from the pastorate to working with a faith-based mission agency. And God had completed my transition!

I have told you this story in order to illustrate the main point I am seeking to make. My call was, in reality, much bigger than even I understood. I thought it was a call to the pastorate. But it was a call to the world—and to the empowering of the urban poor of the world. But to bring about that new understanding on my part so that I would act upon it as God desired, God had taken me on a trip that would turn my world upside down, then got me to pay attention to and act upon the discontent awakened through that trip, and to do so through deepening my personal journeys inward and outward, living into that in-between time so that I began to perceive that my career priorities were changing, and then to move in an entirely unpredictable way to bring me to the decision that changed the tack of my life. It took God three years to break through to me so that I would appropriately act upon it! And that is what God may do in your life as well!

Getting Started

You may be well along in discerning and acting upon God's call to you to serve God in a particular way in the world. Or you may just be starting. If you are just starting, there is an exercise that I have used in workshops on call. It is found in the Appendix as worksheet I-2, "Discerning My Call." You may find it of help.

And now, on to the centering of our personal spiritual formation and call in the Christian community—which we will explore in the next chapter.

Chapter 10

Building My Life in Community

Dietrich Bonhoeffer is best known today as the German church leader who, in the waning years of the Second World War, joined an effort to assassinate Adolf Hitler, and paid for that effort by being executed himself. He is therefore justly viewed as one of the great Christian martyrs of the twentieth century. But perhaps Bonhoeffer's greatest contribution to Christian theology and practice was found in his leadership of the Church Training Center in Finkenwalde, Germany, from 1935 through 1940, when it was closed by the Gestapo. This was no ordinary seminary. It was a small core of clergy coming from and then dispersing throughout Germany to live out Christian community and to work for justice and reform in Hitler's Nazi Germany.[92]

While the leader of this seminary, Bonhoeffer wrote two remarkable books that have become classics of Christian devotion. *The Cost of Discipleship* prepares the reader for the rigors of living as Christians in a world opposed to it. *Life Together* presents the essence and necessity for living in Christian community. Both remained unpublished in the United States until after the Second World War.[93] As we reflect together in this chapter on building Christian life in community, reflect upon these words from these two books:

---

92 For the best books on Bonhoeffer, read Eric Metaxas's *Bonhoeffer: Pastor, Martyr, Prophet, Spy* (Nashville: Thomas Nelson, 2010) or Mary Bosanquet, *The Life and Death of Dietrich Bonhoeffer* (New York: Harper and Row, 1968).

93 Dietrich Bonhoeffer, *The Cost of Discipleship* (New York: Macmillan, 1963); *Life Together* (New York: Harper and Bros., 1954).

"One is a brother to another only through Jesus Christ. Not what a man is in himself, his spirituality and piety, constitutes the basis of our community. . . . Our community with one another consists solely in what Christ has done to both of us."[94]

"When Christ calls a man, he bids him come and die. For God is a God who *bears*. The Son of God bore our flesh, he bore the cross, he bore our sins. In the same way his followers are also called upon to bear, and that is precisely what it means to be a Christian!"[95]

There is no such thing as a solitary Christian, Bonhoeffer told us. Either you are a Christian participating in a Christian community—or you are no Christian at all! To be a "Christ-one" (the literal meaning of the word "Christian") is to be at one with other Christians. And the only thing that causes you to be one with other Christians is your common dependence upon, allegiance to, and being called to salvation and service by Jesus Christ. That is what we are exploring when we reflect together on the spiritual discipline of living in Christian community together.

The Bible on Christian Community

There is perhaps no more thorough examination of the necessity for Christian community (even among people who don't like each other) than Paul's teachings on such community in his first letter to the Corinthian church.

I Corinthians 12:12–31

This penetrating exposition on Christian community begins, "Just as the body is one and has many members, and all the members of the body, though many, are one body, so it is with Christ. For in the one Spirit we were all baptized into one body—Jews or Greeks, slaves or free—and we were all made to drink of one Spirit" (12:12–13).

Paul presents his argument for the diversity and unity of the Church by using the analogy of the human body. In this, he is not alone. The image of one body with many members was a popular image of Paul's day. For example, both Josephus and Dionysius of Halicarnassus who were contemporaries of Paul, use the image of a human body with many members to present their arguments for Jewish and Roman

---

[94] Bonhoeffer, *Life*, 25.

[95] Bonhoeffer, *Cost*, 99, 102.

unity respectively (Josephus, *The Jewish War*, 4:406; Dionysius, *Ant. Rom.*, 6:86). What is both unique and brilliant about Paul's use of this metaphor, however, is how he takes a popular image and skillfully applies it to the church, especially in linking people's exercise of their calling by God and the gifts invested in them by God to the image of the church as one body with many members.

Paul begins his development of this metaphor by indicating that it is the sacrament of baptism which symbolizes both entrance of the individual into the church and each person's incorporation—in one's uniqueness—with the entire community of faith. Baptism, Paul makes clear, is both a water ritual and the receiving of the Holy Spirit. Baptism replaces circumcision in the Jewish community as the sign of admission into God's covenant people (Col. 2:11–14). Thus, it is the act of baptism that symbolizes each new Christian's incorporation into the Body of Christ. Paul then continues,

> Indeed, the body does not consist of one member but of many. If the foot would say, "Because I am not a hand, I do not belong to the body," that would not make it any less a part of the body. And if the ear would say, "Because I am not an eye, I do not belong to the body," that would not make it any less a part of the body. If the whole body were an eye, where would the hearing be? If the whole body were hearing, where would the sense of smell be? But as it is God arranged the members in the body, each one of them, as he chose. If all were a single member, where would the body be? As it is, there are many members, yet one body. The eye cannot say to the hand, "I have no need of you," nor again the head to the feet, "I have no need of you." On the contrary, the members of the body that seem to be weaker are indispensable, and those members of the body that we think less honorable we clothe with greater honor, and our less respectable members are treated with greatest respect; whereas our more respectable members do not need this. But God has so arranged the body, giving the greater honor to the inferior member, that there may be no dissension within the body, but the members may have the same care for one another. If one member suffers, all suffer together with it; if one member is honored, all rejoice together with it (12:14–26).

What is intriguing about this scripture is the unique combination of theologizing and pastoral care exhibited by Paul in it. He is, at one and the same time, both presenting a profound theology of the relationship between the whole and the parts in the community of faith (vv. 14, 20) and at the same time, responding pastorally to the hurts and sense of rejection on the part of many of the members of the Corinthian church (esp. vv. 21–25).

It is important to remember that the Corinthian church of that time was a church divided into four parties: the Apollos party, the Pauline party, the Petrine party, and the Christ party (I Cor. 1:10-17). The Pauline party was made up of those whose allegiance lay with Paul. They were most likely the original converts through whom Paul founded the Corinthian church in his one-and-a-half-year ministry there. Most of those converts would have likely been slaves, freedman, and peasants.

The Apollos party was formed around Paul's successor as pastor of the Corinthian church. That pastor, Apollos, is well known in scripture and was a highly articulate Alexandrian Jew, greatly influenced by Philo of Alexandria and, consequently, the philosophy of Stoicism (Acts 18:24–28). Apollos was eloquent, philosophical, and intellectual in his presentation of the gospel (I Cor. 2:1–5; II Cor. 11:5–6; 12:11). Therefore, he likely attracted to him a different class of Corinthians than did Paul—the more highly educated, wealthy, and sophisticated people. Likewise, the preaching of Apollos was likely lost on Paul's converts.

The Petrine (or Cephas) party was likely made up of Judaizers who had entered Corinth. They were Christians who believed that adherence to the Jewish Law was necessary for salvation. They identified with Simon Peter because, even though Peter had opened the way of the gospel to the Gentiles (Acts 10:1–42), he apparently never felt comfortable around Gentiles (Gal. 1:11–14). Therefore, unintentionally, Peter became the rallying point for those who desired to make the Corinthian church Jewish.

The Christ party was the most pathetic of all. This party was made up of those who didn't fit in to any of the other three factions, and so created their own party in order not to feel left out. It is intriguing that, by calling themselves the Christ party (that is, those loyal to Jesus Christ, rather than Paul, Peter, or Apollos), they practiced the ultimate "one-upmanship" in order not to feel excluded.

As one can imagine, the intellectuals and elite belonged primarily to the Apollos and Petrine parties, while the ordinary and uneducated peasants belonged to the Pauline and Christ parties. This reality was magnificently expressed in both the prophetic role and the pastoral role Paul exhibited throughout both letters to the Corinthian Church.

Thus, in I Corinthians 12:4–11, Paul deals firmly with those who think too highly of the spiritual gifts they claim they have (that is, those who made up the Apollos and Petrine parties). But in the scripture we are now considering, especially in 12:20-25, Paul writes to those who are intimidated by the Christian powerful and consequently have the lowest estimation of their own worth. It is the members of the Pauline and Christ parties who seem the weaker and less honorable, but in reality Christ has chosen them to be those whom he perceives as being most indispensable to the church and are consequently most honored by the Savior. Paul reminds those beaten down and intimidated people that "God has so arranged the body, giving the greater honor to the inferior member, that there may be no dissension within the body, but the members may have the same care for one another" (12:24–25).

Paul cautions the Corinthian Christians not to judge their brother and sister Christians on externals, but instead challenging them to recognize that often God chooses the weaker, less powerful, or influential people through whom to work God's will. It is precisely their humility that God uses to have a greater impact upon the church.

Then, in verse 26, Paul presents his principal of reciprocity (cf. Rom. 12:15; II Cor. 11:29; Gal. 6:2). "If one member suffers, all suffer together with it; if one member is honored, all rejoice together with it." We are all bound together into one "body," Paul declares, not divided into four parties. We are not meant by Christ to be competing entities. Therefore, if one part of the body is injured or ill, in a profound sense the whole body is injured or ill (one says, "I am ill," not "my stomach is ill"). Likewise, if even the lowliest member is honored by the body, that is an honor for all who name the name of Jesus Christ!

Paul then applies his argument specifically to the Corinthian Church:

> Now you (Corinthians) are the body of Christ and individually members of it. And God has appointed in the church first apostles, second prophets, third teachers, then deeds of power, then gifts of healing, forms of assistance, forms of leadership, various kinds of tongues. Are all apostles? Are all prophets? Are all teachers? Do all work miracles? Do all possess gifts of healing? Do all speak in tongues? Do all interpret? But strive for the greater gifts (12:27–31a).

Here, Paul once again names gifts necessary to the effective and productive functioning of the Body of Christ, but he does so by making some significant distinctions with the previous list of gifts he gave in I Corinthians 12:8–10. First, he creates a different list of gifts than that in verses 8–10, listing for the first time the gifts of apostles, teachers, and deeds of power, and by excluding the earlier-listed gifts of wisdom, knowledge, faith, and the discernment of spirits. By not limiting his second list to the first, Paul has greatly expanded the exercise of gifts legitimately exercised within the church.

Second, in 12:27–31, Paul mixes offices and functions. He names some gifts as being "apostles, prophets, teachers." But he names other gifts as "healing, assistance, leadership, tongues." That is, some of the list consists of offices to be filled and others consist of functions to be implemented. What's going on here?

In present day English, an office is seen as a position of authority to exercise that authority for a public purpose (or the room in which one officially exercises that authority). But to Paul, an office was a task one assumes to be done for another person. Thus, in this list, Paul is in essence saying that there are Christians who "apostle," others who "prophesy," others who "teach." He sees the office as a function, not as an official position. Therefore, such a list of offices is consistent with a list of functions.

Finally, by including offices among the gifts, and placing them in an order of importance, Paul has differentiated from his earlier list in 12:8–10. He states that the highest gift is that of "apostlizing"; the second is "prophesying"; the third is "teaching"; the fourth is "healing" the sick; and so on down the list, ending with the gifts of speaking in tongues and interpreting that speech. By placing tongues at the bottom of the list, as he also did in 12:10, Paul is intentionally marginalizing this gift—not because it is bad but because of the havoc its misuse has brought about in the Corinthian church. It is, in this listing, the lowest of all gifts of the Spirit.

Paul then concludes his statement on gifts with the admonition, "But strive for the greater gifts" (12:31a). Of course, we will look more carefully at our discernment of our gifts in the next chapter, but I have included it in this exposition of I Corinthians 12:12–31 because it is an integral part of Paul's examination of the nature of the church as community.

I Corinthians 13:1–13

This is Paul's famous love poem. It is a beautiful statement of the nature of selfless love, and especially Christian love. But it is also meant to follow directly I Corinthians 12:12–31 (which we have just examined), and thus has a very strategic place in this letter.

As noted above, the Corinthian Church was divided into four unequal parties—the Pauline, Apollos, Petrine, and Christ parties. Each of the parties had its own agenda for the Corinthian Church, and was pushing that agenda with no compromise and with no inclusion of the other parties. The result was a "superiority complex" on the part of some and a sense of being marginalized and powerless on the part of others.

A crucial part of that struggle had been around the "spiritual gifts" of prophecies, tongues, and knowledge (knowledge not being accumulated information or wisdom, but special insight and discernment given by the Holy Spirit). In I Corinthians 12, Paul had argued that these spiritual gifts are given by God to the church to build up and edify the church, and to better equip it for outreach to the world. Those gifts are distributed as God chooses throughout the church (not exclusively to a given "party"), and exist for the strengthening and edifying of everyone. Therefore, Paul advises the Corinthians, embrace the gift that God has placed within you, use it for the good of the entire church, and do not covet the gifts of others.

But Paul takes his readers one step further. He urges them to embrace the gifts within them. But he then states, "And I will show you a still more excellent way" (12:31b).

That "more excellent way" is the gift of love—the one gift that every member of the church needs to embrace and exercise. Thus, Paul begins his great chapter on love as the supreme gift of each Christian—a love for one another that excludes no one and embraces everyone. In other words, what Paul is telling the church is "You don't have to *like* each other, but as Christians, you do have to *love* each other." Let's examine Paul's insight more deeply.

I Corinthians 13:1–3 begins the poem by stressing that love is the supreme gift God awakens in every Christian. If one has prophetic powers, understands all knowledge, speaks in heavenly language but does not treat brother and sister Christians as loved siblings, then he is nothing more than "a noisy gong or a clanging cymbal." He is worthless!

But what is "love," and how does it differ from "like"? Paul moves on in verses 4–7 to describe what he means by the word "love." It is important to recognize that those who spoke Greek at the time of Paul distinguished between three types of love—erotic love, companionable love or friendship, and self-giving love; so it was crucial that Paul define here what he meant by love. The kind of love that the Corinthian Christians are to practice toward one another, Paul declares, is self-giving or godly love. It is a love that is patient with one another, kind, not envious, not boastful, not arrogant or rude. It doesn't insist on its own way. It is not irritable or resentful, doesn't rejoice in the exposure of wrong in other people but believes the best about them, hopes for the best in people, and endures persecution, condemnation, or ridicule.

Thus, Paul is saying by the very words he uses, when we speak of the church being a loving church, we don't mean that we should encourage people to be erotically attracted to each other, nor do we mean that we get along with each other ("liking" or "enjoying" each other). Rather, we are to love each other in the way God through Christ has loved us![96]

Paul then compares and contrasts the love we are to have toward each other with other virtues (vv. 8–10). All the "gifts of the Spirit," Paul contends, are temporary gifts. They are given to strengthen the church and its world mission during this period of transition between the first and the second comings of Christ. Whether one speaks of prophecy, knowledge or tongues, they will all "come to an end."

But love—God's love reflected through us—is another matter entirely. Love will never end. Love will be as much in God's kingdom when it comes in its totality as it is needed today. It is the one virtue given by God that is everlasting. Therefore, it makes sense to concentrate on nurturing this gift within ourselves and each other.

Paul then concludes his poem,

> "When I was a child, I spoke like a child, I thought like a child, I reasoned like a child; when I became an adult I put an end to childish ways. For now we see in a mirror, dimly, but then we will see face to face. Now I know only in part; then I will know fully, even as I have been fully known.

---

[96] The Greek word for erotic love was "eros." The word for brotherly love or friendship was "philia," and the word for Godly love was "agape" (*ah gah pay)*. The word for love used throughout I Corinthians 13 by Paul is the Greek word, "agape."

And now faith, hope, and love abide, these three; and the greatest of these is love" (13:11–13).

Paul uses two metaphors here to communicate his concern: the metaphor of child and adult, and of seeing either a reflection or reality. Living centered in and boasting of our station ("I'm of the Apollos party"; "I'm of the Petrine party") or our gifts is like living as a child; it is childish and is not the stuff of mature Christians. Living centered in love for God's people and the world is the stance of the mature Christian. Likewise, living centered in ourselves and our own gifts, and living in a party spirit is like viewing life through a mirror (a mirror in Roman times was made of burnished bronze and thus gave both a dim and distorted reflection of the person); living in love is like seeing a person face-to-face. Thus, to settle for satisfaction with one's gifts is to settle for second-place. Likewise, to settle for party identification ("I'm a Baptist"; "I'm a Bible-believing Christian") is to settle for less than God wants for us. To strive after that "more excellent way" of Christian love is to strive after the very essence of Christianity.

Thus, Paul ends, "faith, hope, and love abide, these three; but the greatest of these is love." Authentic Christian faith comes down to three ingredients: a right relationship with God ("*faith*"), *hope* that God is indeed the ground of our and humanity's very being, and *love*. All three are crucial, but it is *agape* love that is eternal, for *agape* love is the indispensable characteristic of authentic Christian life. Therefore, Paul is saying to the Corinthian Christians, do not long after the gifts of the Spirit; do not be proud of your religious status or organization. Long after the exhibition of *agape* love in your life. For you can exhibit only what you are allowing God to grow in you—God's love for the city and for the world, and for all who inhabit the same (especially those who name the name of Jesus Christ—whether you like them or not)!

Living in Community

What Bonhoeffer states directly and that to which Paul alludes in I Corinthians 12– 13, is that although it is possible for a person to identify one's own call by one's self, you can't sustain the living into or the implementing of that call by yourself. There is no such thing as a "solitary" Christian. A "Christ-one" must be in community with other "Christ-ones" in order to be fully Christian! Both the implementation and sustenance depends upon life in community.

But what do we mean by "community."? Community does not mean "hail-fellow-well-met." It does not mean people who enjoy each other or like to "hang out" with each other. It is conceivable that you might not particularly like some of the people in your Christian community. But what it does mean is that you are bound to each other with cords of Christ-like love! Therefore, Christian community is not a gathering of "warm fuzzies" but instead is a disciplined body of Christian believers who seek to live out with utmost seriousness, the Church as the Body of Christ.

The Christian Community

The Church, both in its worldwide and in its local form (a congregation of that body, whether affiliated with a denomination or not) is the lived-out body of Christ. What we all have in common is just one reality—we all belong to and have embraced Jesus Christ as our Lord and Savior. We are, as Paul so eloquently puts it, of "one Lord, one faith, one baptism, one God and Father of all" (Eph. 4:5–6a). We are not supposed to be of one nation, one political party, one ethnic group, one educational level, one liking of the same sort of music, etc. In fact, to the degree that any given local manifestation of the Body of Christ holds in common any other characteristic than that of belonging to Jesus Christ, to that degree that local church is heretical! Commonality in anything other than Jesus Christ diverts us from our authentic oneness—our being mutually embraced by Christ. That was the problem the Corinthian church had when it allowed itself to divide into the Pauline, Apollos, Petrine, and Christ parties. Something other than Christ became that church's way of identifying and understanding itself. "Our community with one another consists solely in what Christ has done for us" (Bonhoeffer above).[97]

Because we are to be one in Christ, the Christian community is called to a common mission—to be "Christ-ones" to the world! And that mission, in order to be authentic, must be acted out both corporately and individually. That is, to be Christ-like to the world is the mission of the whole church. And that mission is acted out, both

---

[97] Bonhoeffer, *Life*, 25.

through the corporate actions of the church in the world, and through the individual witness and work of each of its individual "Christ-ones"!

This is why it becomes so important for Christians to discover and then live out their particular call into the world. That call is never a solitary call. It is always a call within community, in which one undertakes one's call within the larger context of the call of his or her local community of faith. Each of us has our own particular call but, together, all those acted-out calls meld into one mass call, with each assisting in the carrying out of that congregational call. That is why it becomes so important for each local congregation to perceive and act upon their own corporate call (see Chapter 12). Also, that means that anything that gets in the way of the discerning and carrying out of that congregational call ("I'm of the Petrine party"; "I'm of the Apollos party") becomes diversionary to the mission of that church and of God's choice and call of it.

That is why Paul gives such space to the discussion of the importance of the discernment and acting out of our respective gifts (see Chapter 11). Because community exists around a common mission in Christ, then it is necessary for an adequate supply and distribution of the gifts necessary to successfully carry out that mission, to be given to each local church. Thus, God has brought together all the gifts in all the people necessary to carry out that ministry, as well as those common gifts necessary to maintain that community. Exercised in that community are all the gifts needed by that community to both sustain its life together and to carry out its mission in the world. Therefore, we can only talk in a limited way about discovering God's call unless we start talking about the relationship between the individual and the congregation.

What I am simply saying is this: The sign that a church is serious about empowering its people to live out their vocation is that church's commitment to building the kind of life together that can become the cradle in which that church's mission outreach is born. The sign of the seriousness and intentionality of that church's members is their expectation that there be such group life, along with their willingness to enter into it so that each person can find God's call upon his or her life.

In other words, unless a given church has less than 12 members,[98] the sign of its commitment to being Christ's presence in their city is their development of small groups of spiritual and missional discernment.

The Practice of Christian Community

What does a small group do that no other size group can do? A group of 12 or less people is the best size of a group for people to hear and to be heard! Have a group larger than 12, and at least a few in the group will fall silent. Have a group of 6 or under, and people will feel the pressure of giving input. Have a group around 10 to 12, and everyone has the opportunity to share and yet not enough pressure to feel that he or she must share more than they care to share (in order to keep the conversation going).

There is a reason why most of the major movements of Christianity have been built around small groups. Not only Jesus had his 12, but each of Paul's churches was small enough to meet in the parlor of a home. Later on, Christians created small monastic communities to both support each other in their faith journeys and to preserve early Christian learning. Calvin had his Geneva Academy (which spread the Reformed faith throughout Europe), Wesley his "methodical" small groups (which gave rise to them being called "Methodists"), and Bonhoeffer his Church Training Center. The church only got into trouble when it got large.

The genius of the small group is its potential for sharing and, thus, support. That support can build into the sustenance of Christians in their individual and corporate walk with Christ, and in their growing effectiveness in living out their respective and common missions in the world. Such support includes standing present to each other, encouraging each other, weeping and laughing with each other, sharing out of scripture, and struggling through life. Support includes holding each other accountable to our respective spiritual formation and our acting out our mission in the world. Support includes calling forth the gifts of each other through helping one another to discover, identify, affirm, and develop those gifts, as well as reflecting and acting together on our individual missions, the mission of that small group, and the

---

[98] There is a reason that Jesus chose twelve people to become his "front-line" of disciples. Twelve people is the ideal number for a group to share, learn, reach out, and work together for the good of the world.

mission of their church. Support includes dependence upon and rejoicing in God's work in our midst and in our worship as a group. And support includes enabling each other to move out into God's call into mission. These make up the work of a small group that very few, if any, other larger groups can achieve in the church. It is a unique ministry of enabling, equipping, encouraging, and implementing being Christ to the world.

One of the objectives of much of the elected leadership of the church I served in Detroit was to increase the engagement of its members in both neighborhood and citywide issues; I, of course, concurred with them. But the question was "How?" We explored the strategies used by other urban churches that had been successful in enabling that to happen in their memberships. We soon began to notice that, in most of these situations, the common denominator was the development of small groups. Since our church was over a thousand members, this required us to put together a strategy for different kinds of small groups. Our basic small group was the mission group (see Chapter 13). Each of these groups was built around the carrying out of a specific call; that is, each group was founded by a church member who felt called to a particular mission in our neighborhood, city, nation, or world, shared that call with church members and created a group to implement that mission from those who responded to that call. A second type of small group was built upon the model of our mission groups but were ministry groups in which people were called to a ministry within our congregation (such as children's education, a senior citizen's luncheon, and congregational care). A third were those that focused on spiritual formation, including study groups, Bible study groups, and even one group studying the personality theorist C. G. Jung. A fourth type of group was one concerned with creating and bringing about four spiritual retreats a year for our church members that would deepen their life in Christ and their relationships with each other.

The point was that our large church had created a strategy that, in essence, "broke up" the church into many small "churches" while still retaining the worship community as a large congregation. About one-third of the congregation participated in these small groups, and in these small groups people contributed to the building of our life in community as a church, deepening people's spiritual formation and enabling them to be engaged in mission in very specific ways. As a consequence, our committee structure was reduced from 14 committees to 4 administrative committees (personnel, buildings and grounds, finances, Endowment Fund)—thus freeing people for participation in both the small groups and mission efforts of our church.

Getting Started

John Wesley is reported to have said to recent seminary graduates, "Young men, find companions or make them. The Bible knows nothing of solitary religion."[99]

It is easy for the concept of life in community to become very mysterious or esoteric—but it is not. Through the creation and living into the life of small groups, discovering what God wants for your life and how God is calling you into mission becomes very real, concrete, practical, and joyous! The healthy small group which sustains its members as they carry out their vocation is the zenith of a journey that begins when one decides to know God's will, and begins the journey into relationship with God, self, and a community of faith. Upon having found God's call, the group becomes the foundation from which all of the rest of life is lived and new journeys are taken out into mission in the city and world. The group also becomes foundational for the growing of a deeper relationship with God, self, and others. The result is the sense of knowing and living in the assurance that you are fulfilling that purpose for which you have been created by God, in the midst of a people created and sustained by that same God.

If you are already in a small group, are considering joining one, or are simply contemplating what it means to live in community, may I urge you to make use of the exercise I-3, "Living Into Community," which is found in the Appendix.

And now, on to a deeper discovery of the gifts given to you by God!

---

[99] Retrieved from www.imarc.cc/buletiw/wesleyq.html.

Chapter 11

Calling Forth My Gifts

In the previous chapter, we examined the importance of the church acting out being the community of Christ—not so much an institution, as a living, breathing Body being Christ to the city through its life together, its spoken witness, its ministering to the needs of the city's people, its praying for the city, and its engagement "for Christ and His Kingdom" within the public life of the city. But in this chapter, we want to concentrate upon one particular function of the church—the function it must play if ordinary people are to be called forth and shaped into city-changing called Christians!

A particularly strategic role of the church, especially in its small groupings (where true community is birthed and nurtured), is the identifying and calling forth of the gifts of each person so that he or she will embrace those gifts and use them to carry out their calling in the city. That will be the topic of this chapter.

The Gifts for Vocation

It is extremely difficult for us to both perceive and truly appreciate our own gifts—much less call them forth and activate their use! That is why the community of faith, as realized in a small group, is so essential to help us own our own gifts, and to recognize how our mutual giftedness supports the corporate carrying out of our church's mission in the city.

In other words, you are not only created, chosen, and called by God into the city and to a mission in that city. And you are not only one person who is part of a larger body of "Christ-ones" who work together to carry out Christ's call to the transformation of that city. It is also true that God has invested specific gifts in you. God wants you to claim and use those gifts to carry out that ministry to which God has called you. In other words, God has already placed within you the gifts you need to carry out your city-transforming work. You just need to identify them, accept them, and then actually use them for Christ and His Kingdom!

But what do I mean when I say that we are all gifted Christians? Well, when the Bible speaks about the gifts of God's people, it is referring to three very distinct categories of gifts. And all of us possess some gifts from each of these three categories. So let's look at the Bible on the gifting of God's people, so that we can better identify and use the unique gifts God has given to each of us.

Natural Abilities or Talents:

You have likely had the occasion where you have heard someone sing or preach magnificently in your church. And later, when you and others are talking about their song of praise or their sermon or talk, one of your group has said, "She has a natural gift!" Such natural gifts are given to each of us—skills that God has placed within us that seem to come forth with little effort. This is part of the spectrum of the gifting we receive from God.

This is beautifully developed in Matthew 25:14–30 and I Peter 4:10-14. The Matthew passage is one of Jesus's most famous parables—the story of three slaves given money by their departing master to invest to increase the worth of his estate during his trip away from it.

This parable is close to being an allegory. Jesus suggests he is the master going into the "far country." The slaves are his disciples. The property the master invests in them is the Kingdom of God. The long time that the master is away is the period of time between Jesus's going away (his death and resurrection) and his return (the second coming). The rewards the faithful slaves receive are the commendation and investment that Jesus makes in them as the result of their faithfulness. Being cast into outer darkness is not a description of hell but rather the judgment the unfaithful slave receives for not following a "long obedience in the same direction."

In this parable, the three unnamed disciples are given the same mission—to take the gospel they have been given and to invest it in the world so that there are measurable returns from that investment. Although the original meaning of "talent" is a stated amount of money, it is now taken by the church to mean a skill or ability that is used by the servant to enhance the gospel in the world. Thus, this parable is telling us that if we want to be seen by Jesus as a "good and trustworthy slave," we need to take the abilities and skills that God has invested in us and use them for Christ and His

Kingdom. We all have different abilities—some of us more than others (ten or five talents or just two).

The parable thus asks the question, "What will we do with this investment Jesus has made in us?" Will we become proactive, working hard for the kingdom, willing to risk the gift invested in us in pursuit of the transformation of at least our little corner of the city? Will our faithfulness to Christ and His Kingdom be expressed through our commitment to focus our lives on the sharing of the vision of the city as the city of God and working for it in everything we do? Or will we be like the third slave who hides in the ground the great treasure Christ has invested in us, afraid to chance anything on the dream of the kingdom, and thus end up being no good to ourselves, to the world, or to Christ? What will we choose to do with Jesus's investment in us? Peter speaks directly to that to which Jesus alludes. The apostle writes in I Peter 4:7–11:

> The end of all things is near; therefore be serious and discipline yourselves for the sake of your prayers. Above all, maintain constant love for one another, for love covers a multitude of sins. Be hospitable to one another without complaining. Like good stewards of the manifold grace of God, serve one another with whatever gift each of you has received. Whoever speaks must do so as one speaking the very words of God; whoever serves must do so with the strength that God supplies, so that God may be glorified in all things through Jesus Christ. To him belong the glory and the power forever and ever. Amen.

We all have abilities and skills, Peter states. Some of us are skilled at praying, others in caring for those in need. Still others have the gift of hospitality, for others it is speaking, and for others, serving. But whatever is our ability or skill, Peter declares, "serve one another with whatever gift each of you has received." The number of skills is unimportant. The depth of those skills is unimportant. What is important is the use of those abilities for the good of the Body of Christ, and for all those who make their home in our city.

Thus, the first kind of gift which all of us enjoy are the particular talents and skills that lie dormant within each of us. Rather than being overly modest about them, our task as Christians is to acknowledge them, work at improving and honing them, and then using them for the sake both of the people of our church and of the city (whether Christian or not). The task of the church, particularly in its setting of small groups, is to recognize the "diamond in the rough," call forth that skill, and urge its occupant to own it, hone it, and use it for the sake of the world.

Spiritual Gifts

But beyond our natural abilities and talents, the people of the church—both lay and clergy—are also invested with "spiritual gifts." These are unique gifts that are absolutely essential both to build up the Body of Christ and to enable that Body to engage with and work for the transformation of the world—including the city into which a given church has been planted.

Perhaps one of the most profound statements about spiritual gifts that appears in scripture is Paul's careful examination of them in Romans 12:1–8. This includes the placing of spiritual gifts into the larger context of the life and mission of the church. Let's take a look at that passage.

Romans 12:1–8 signals the major shift of the book of Romans from theology to ethics, from right thinking to right actions. And Paul makes that transition through a most magnificent statement.

> I appeal to you therefore, brothers and sisters, by the mercies of God, to present your bodies as a living sacrifice, holy and acceptable to God, which is your spiritual worship. Do not be conformed to this world, but be transformed by the renewing of your minds, so that you may discern what is the will of God—what is good and acceptable and perfect (Rom. 12:1–2).

Paul calls on all Christians "to present your bodies as a living sacrifice, holy and acceptable to God, which is your spiritual worship." Whether these Roman Christians were formerly Jews or Gentiles, both groups knew about their worship being centered in sacrifice. If any were Jews, their entire worship of Yahweh was built around the sacrificial system in which temple worship was centered in providing burnt offerings of meat or grain, doves or fruit, to God as their "spiritual worship." Likewise, if these Christians were former pagans, then whether they worshipped Roman or Greek gods or were of a mystery religion, that religion was centered on the provision of sacrifices to those gods at their respective temples. So Paul is calling them to Christian discipleship from out of the context of what they knew—their former religious practices.

All Christians, Paul is stating here, are called "to present their bodies as a living sacrifice." The words used by Paul would automatically create a cognitive dissonance on the part of the readers, almost a contradiction in terms (like "jumbo shrimp" which literally means "big little"). A sacrifice, *by its very nature of being a sacrifice*, is dead. To sacrifice something means to kill it—whether it would be the slaying of an animal or a bird, the harvesting and burning of grain, or the plucking of fruit. By any of those acts—slaying, harvesting, plucking—one is killing that object. The offering that makes the sacrifice a sacrifice is the surrender of the life of that object—and then surrendering that sacrificed life over to the god. Therefore, to speak of a "living sacrifice" was a contradiction in terms for anyone raised in either the Jewish or Gentile worship context.

But what Paul is saying here is that one is "to present your bodies as a living sacrifice." Dramatically reversing the imagery, Paul is stating that what is precious to God is not a dead animal or fruit but a living person who consecrates the remainder of his life to living out Christ's love and practicing his Christian faith in his city. Authentic Christianity, Paul is declaring, is the living of redemptive love in front of the world, consecrating mind and soul and heart and strength to serve not one's own objectives, but to serve Christ and His Kingdom. This is authentic worship!

The particular word Paul uses here that is translated worship is *latreia*, the noun of *latreuein*. *Latreuein* actually meant "to work for hire or pay." It is the exchange of your skill, your bodily strength, your intellectual capacity for the pay that the employer would give to you. It is a negotiated action in which both employee and employer participate ("I agree to do this for you if you pay me that amount of money"). *Latreuein* was never used for slave labor; it requires, instead, mutual agreement. Therefore, it was used for "that to which a person would give his life." Because it was used of one's vocation or "calling" in life, it evolved into the "serving of the gods" or "worship."

But Paul also states in this passage that his appeal to us Christians to worship God in such deliberate ways should be done because of "the mercies of God." The doctrine of grace that Paul had so carefully presented earlier in the book of Romans was presented, Paul now reveals, so that we can live out God's grace through our love for the poor and needy and our commitment to the powerless and oppressed in a sinful city.

So Paul is stating here that our calling in life, as Christians, is to center our work, our life, and our entire purpose in the service of God—body, soul, and mind—and to do this through our service of humanity through our political, economic, social, and spiritual involvement. "Whatever you do," Paul is in essence saying, "do it for Christ and His Kingdom!" Such action on our part is our worship which is "holy and acceptable to God." For authentic worship is the offering of our everyday work for justice, equity, and engagement of the city to God.

Paul furthers his argument by writing, "Do not be conformed to this world, but be transformed by the renewing of your minds, so that you may discern what is the will of God—what is good and acceptable and perfect" (vs. 2).

The Greek word translated "conformed" is the word *suschematiczesthai*, from which we get the word "scheme" or "the creation of a temporary plan of action or program" (sometimes suggesting that there is something crafty or secret or hidden about that plan). Whereas the NRSV translates this phrase "do not be conformed to this world," other translations try to capture the unique nuance of this virtually untranslatable Greek word by phrases such as "do not conform to the pattern of this world" (NIV), "do not model yourselves on the behavior of the world around you" (Jerusalem Bible), or "don't become so well-adjusted to your culture that you fit into it" (The Message).

In essence, what Paul is saying is "If you are going to be a living sacrifice for God, working to transform your city into Christ's kingdom, then don't allow yourself to be seduced by the priorities, standards, and assumptions of that city. Life isn't about building one's own power. He who dies with the most toys doesn't win. Success and achievement and admiration are not the standards to which we should give our lives. Don't get "sucked-in" by this world."

Rather, "be transformed by the renewing of your minds, so that you may discern what is the will of God—what is good and acceptable and perfect." The Greek word translated "transformed" is equally intriguing. *Metamorphousthai* means "the ultimate change that creates the essential shape" of something. Obviously, it is the word from which we gain the English word, "metamorphosis" which means "to undergo systemic change" which, once occurring, can never be reversed (e.g., a caterpillar to a butterfly). This is captured in the same translations of the Bible which we previously examined. Thus, the NRSV translates the phrase, "be transformed by the renewing of your minds"; the NIV translates it the same way; the Jerusalem Bible translates it, "let your behavior change, modeled by your new mind"; and the Message states it, "fix your attention on God because you'll be changed from the inside out." That is, God has not done a cosmetic change on you (*suschematizesthai*); God has done a life-changing and irreversible transformation of you (*metamorphousthai*) so that you have come out of your conversion experience, not with a body tuck here or there, but as a totally new creation that is called to center your life on "what is good and acceptable and perfect" to God!

This, then, is our mission—to work for Christ and His kingdom by giving our lives to the living out of God's shalom community. This is truly authentic worship. But how do we actually carry out that mission? That is what Paul addresses in verses 3–8.

> For by the grace given to me I say to everyone among you not to think of yourself more highly than you ought to think, but to think with sober judgment, each according to the measure of faith that God has assigned. For as in one body we have many members, and not all the members have the same function, so we, who are many, are one body in Christ, and individually members one of another. We have gifts that differ according to the grace given to us: prophecy, in proportion to faith; ministry, in ministering; the teacher, in teaching; the exhorter, in exhortation; the giver, in generosity; the leader, in diligence; the compassionate, in cheerfulness (vv. 3–8).

How does the Christian family work together for Christ and His kingdom by our engagement in the political, economic, and spiritual life of our nation and city as well as in the life of the church? We carry out that mission in two ways, Paul suggests, and the two ways are integrated into each other.

First, we practice living out God's intentions for our city by the relationships we foster with one another in the church. "Do not think of yourself more highly than you ought to think." Do not have an exalted or unrealistic perception of yourself. You are less important than you think you are—especially within the Body of Christ. If you center upon your own assessment of your exalted worth in the church, then you will not appreciate the roles everybody else has but will see yourself out of proportion to the others. You are a part of a team and not its star! Not even Paul is a star! The only star should be Jesus. Whatever is your role on the team, you play it and play it to the best of your ability.

Second, "think with sober judgment (about yourself)." Know yourself; have an honest assessment of your own capacities and your own abilities, and don't overextend yourself (an exhausted Christian helps nobody's mission). Accept yourself and who you are. Accept the gift or gifts you have been given, neither taking pride in them nor minimizing them. You are who you are. You are exactly the person with the capabilities and the attitude that God needs in the place to which God has assigned you. So embrace that place, and work diligently within it.

The important reality Paul is urging his readers to see is that the Church is one body, and each of us members is filling a particular niche within that body. "For as in one body we have many members, and not all members have the same function, so we, who are many, are one body in Christ, and individually we are members one of another" (vv. 4–5). As William Barclay so beautifully puts our task, "Paul is here saying that a Christian must accept himself; and even if he finds that the contribution he has to offer will be unseen, he must make it, certain that it is essential and that without it the world and the Church can never be what they are meant to be."[100]

In the light of what Paul has written about the importance of realistically seeing your place within God's kingdom and seeking to be faithful in filling that position as fully as possible, the apostle then goes on to talk about the importance of the spiritual gift(s) given you by God.

"We have gifts that differ according to the grace given to us" (12:6). The work to which God assigns us as part of the work of the church in the city is not based upon what we would like to do nor upon God's arbitrary choice of what we are to do. Instead, that assignment is made based upon the gifts with which God has chosen to endow us.

The Greek word translated "gifts" is the word *charisma*. We talk of the "charisma" of a person. But the English use of the word "charisma" misses the point of the Greek. In English, "charisma" means the dynamism with which some of us are filled. Some people have charisma (sex appeal, dynamism, attractiveness) and some of us do not. Some of us are mighty stallions, and some of us are bell cows. So we celebrate the people who have "charisma" and wish we had some as well.

But the Greek word *charisma* means "the gift of God." That is, our charism is the particular capacity or ability given us by God for the building up of the life of the

---

[100] William Barclay, *The Letter to the Romans* (Philadelphia, PA: Westminster Press, 1975), 160.

church or the carrying out of that life in mission to the world. Paul names some of those charisms in this scripture. Some of us are called and gifted by God to be "prophets"—that is, those appointed by God in the church to speak truth to power. Some of us have the gift of *diakonia* (from which we get the word, "deacon"), called to provide practical, caring service to people both within and outside the church. Others have the charism of teaching, assuming the responsibility of expositing the scripture and to explain our acting out of God's call. Still others have the gift of exhortation—that is, preaching the gospel—again both to believers and unbelievers.

Others of us have a ministry of money; that is, God has given such people much of the world's goods, but that is for the purpose of being both stewards of that wealth and to redistribute that wealth in order to enable the church to more effectively work for the spiritual, social, economic, and political transformation of the world. Still others have the gift of leadership, but like Jesus, the ultimate task of leaders is always to build the leadership potential of others. Finally, Paul tells the reader that a key charism of church people is compassion—simply caring for people and helping them realize that they are not alone in this dark world!

These are the spiritual gifts that Paul lists in this chapter in Romans. But he shares other gifts in other passages. In I Corinthians 12, for example, he adds to the above list the charisms of "wisdom" (that is, truth-telling); "knowledge" (that is, teaching truth); "faith"; "gifts of healing"; "working of miracles"; "discernment of spirits" (that is, the gift of reflecting and weighing what others say, and then speaking to it); "tongues"; and "interpretations of tongues."

In I Corinthians, Paul concludes his examination of spiritual gifts with the reminder,

> All these (gifts) are activated by one and the same Spirit, who allots to each one individually just as the Spirit chooses. For just as the body is one and has many members, and all the members of the body, though many, are one body, so it is with Christ. For in the one Spirit we were all baptized into one body—Jews or Greeks, slaves or free (12:11–13a).

Whether Paul is writing as he does here in Romans about God's call to us to work for God's shalom in the city of Rome or in I Corinthians about the interior "body-life" of that church, what Paul is essentially seeking to communicate is this: It is not about you! It is about Christ! It is not about who you are or the gifts you might have or the strategic place you might hold in the church. That is all as nothing. It is about God, God's formation of the church, God's vision of his kingdom and the city as God intends for all humanity, God's call to Christ to initiate that kingdom through his life, death, and resurrection, and God's creation of the church to work for that kingdom in the political, economic, and religious life of the society into which God has placed it. It is all about God! So step away from the center you never did occupy and accept your rightful place at the foot of the cross, there to worship and to be used by God as God determines, so that the cross might be lifted high and all the world drawn to the One who is making all things new!

To summarize, therefore, there are both "natural" gifts and "spiritual" gifts. "Natural" gifts are the natural abilities or talents we have which are honed by practice and study. For example, one might have a natural proclivity toward music and the playing of the piano, but even the most gifted person (e.g., Mozart as a little child) requires continued practice and the learning of music theory in order to become accomplished. This is a "natural" gift.

Likewise, there are "spiritual" gifts. These are gifts given to us by the Holy Spirit. These gifts are "charisms"—gifts invested in us by God which normally we can exercise immediately upon our recognition (or in spite of not recognizing) of them. As introduced above, those gifts are:

- Apostolic ministry (that is, the gift of planting the church or organizing for mission in a broad and comprehensive way);
- Prophetic ministry (that is, proclaiming truth to power; the sharing of wisdom);
- Teaching (expositing the scriptures and teaching the faith; the sharing of knowledge);
- Exhortation (encouraging and building up the believers);
- The service of others (practical caring for people; compassion);
- Leadership (organizing people for action and calling forth leadership in others);
- Faith (the capacity to believe God implicitly);
- The ministry of money (gift of generating and distributing money to address society's needs and/or to fund the work of the church);
- Healing (the healing of souls, minds, and body);

- Miracle working (working for miraculous transformation in people's lives);
- Discernment of spirits (reflecting and weighing what others say, and then speaking to it);
- Speaking in tongues (giving direct messages from God);
- Interpreting tongues (translating spirit language into intelligible language, so that everyone present understands the message; Paul forbids tongue-speaking unless interpretation also occurs).

All of these are gifts given to each of us to carry out unique ministry in the church. The assumption is that the Holy Spirit gives a spectrum of both natural and spiritual gifts to every church in order to enable that church to both build the interior life of that church and to carry out its mission in the neighborhood, city, and world to which it has been assigned. But there are also gifts that we are to hold in common.

Gifts in Common

Although all individuals are given both natural and spiritual gifts to exercise in that church to which they have been called, the scripture is clear that there are certain gifts that all Christians are to exercise *in common* in all the churches. One scripture that particularly develops this theme is Galatians 5:1, 13–25.

Paul has developed in the first four chapters of his letter to the Galatian Church his argument that authentic Christian faith does not seek to win God's redemptive favor by obeying the Mosaic Law or by doing good deeds. Rather, salvation is a freely given gift of God that we appropriate by receiving. Thus, we are saved, not by our good works (whether moral deeds or obedience to the regulations of the Law), but by Christ's work upon the cross that we actively embrace. Thus, we are the recipient of salvation, not its initiator. We are not transformed by the redemptive power of Christ's death because of our actions, but because of his!

Now, in Galatians 5:1–25, Paul shifts his focus to develop how a faith incurred by God's saving action is to be lived out in the world. How is faith to be lived out in life? Paul begins, "For freedom Christ has set us free. Stand firm, therefore, and do not submit again to a yoke of slavery" (5:1). You are called, Paul is insisting, to live what you believe. You are given at the cross authentic freedom in Christ. Do not fall prey, therefore, to trying to earn favor with God by doing good works.

> For you were called to freedom, brothers and sisters; only do not use your freedom as an opportunity for self-indulgence, but through love become slaves to one another. For the whole law is summed up in a single commandment: "You shall love your neighbor as yourself." If, however, you bite and devour one another, take care that you are not consumed by one another (vv. 13–15).

Paul has spent considerable effort in demonstrating to the Galatian Christians that they do not need to obey the minutia or the principles of the Mosaic Law in order to earn salvation from Christ. Rather, salvation is a gift given to us by God for us to receive. But how do we respond to that gift? We can say, "Since I am free of the Law, then it is perfectly all right for me to not observe the requirements of the Law instructing me not to steal, kill, commit adultery, or covet." In so saying, we can begin to live a life without moral or ethical constraint.

But that is to misunderstand both the Law and the nature of genuine faith in Christ. The freedom we have in Christ does not mean that we have liberty to sin, but freedom from sin (Rom. 6:1–7:6)! Freedom from sin does not provide us with the opportunity for self-indulgence. Rather, to be free from sin means that a greater obligation is laid upon us—the entire intent of the Law lived out in the command, "You shall love your neighbor as yourself" (Lev. 19:18; Matt. 5:43–47; 22:34–40; Mark 12:28–31; Luke 10:25–28; Rom. 13:8). If a church is a divisive and embattled church where pagans see you "biting and devouring each other," then these pagans must conclude that this is not an authentically Christian church, for its Christians are not exhibiting the marks of a Spirit-filled people who have truly received Christ's free gift of salvation. People are to say of us, "Behold, how they love one another"—not, "behold, how they love to fight with one another"!

Paul then goes on to spell out the marks of those who are still living in enslavement to the Law and those who have been truly set free by the Spirit. Those who still remain dominated by the Law and its works are those who commit "fornication, impurity, licentiousness, idolatry, sorcery, enmities, strife, jealousy, anger, quarrels, dissensions, factions, envy, drunkenness, carousing, and things like these" (vv. 19–21). The list is very artfully crafted to begin with the most gross and obvious sins but moving steadily towards more subtle and less obnoxious sins, so that one suddenly realizes that he may not be fornicating or worshiping idols, but if he is quarreling or being jealous, he is still living in sin. He is every bit as guilty of the "sins of the flesh" as is his more wanton neighbor. And such actions, engaged in repeatedly, should cause one to wonder whether or not he truly has embraced the grace of God.

In contrast with these "marks of the flesh," Paul then presents the signs that one has authentically received Christ as Savior and is exhibiting the "marks of the Spirit": "love, joy, peace, patience, kindness, generosity, faithfulness, gentleness, and self-control" (vs. 22).

Paul is not suggesting that occasional acts of strife, jealousy, or anger indicate one is not a Christian, nor that if one is not always exhibiting love, joy, patience, or self-control, it is clear that one must not be a Christian. To argue that is to return to a belief of salvation by one's good works, and not by God's grace. But what Paul ***is*** arguing is that one should look at the general tenor of one's life, and if one sees nothing but "works of the flesh" and little propensity toward the "fruits of the Spirit," one must take solemn evaluation of one's self. For to be a Christian means that one has become a part of a community of faith and that if one is acting out the "works of the flesh," one is slashing away at the fabric of that community's life, and that should give pause to us. For our task as those who have received the free gift of transformation through Christ is to live out that transformation within that community, thus becoming a "Christ-one" to one another and to our city.

What, then, are the gifts that all of us should be practicing throughout out the entirety of our lives. Those gifts are love, joy, peace, patience, kindness, generosity, faithfulness, gentleness, and self-control (Gal. 5:22). These are the "fruits of the Spirit," the gifts that should be manifested in all Christians.

The Common Elements of All the Gifts

As we reflect on our "natural," "spiritual," and "common" gifts we explored above, we can see that there are some common themes running through all these gifts. What are these common elements?

God gives our gifts. All gifts that we have are gifts given to us by God. We haven't earned them. We don't deserve them. Many gifts we do not even expect to have. Each gift is a God-given gift. But our task is to recognize that gift, and then develop and use it for the glory of God and the building up of the life and mission of the church to the city.

Gifts enable us to carry out our call. There are no extra gifts. God doesn't have a quota of gifts he must distribute. Every gift we exercise is a gift given to us to enable us to carry out the call assigned to us by God. Other gifts are superfluous, and will eventually erode away.

Each gift is for the Body. Each of our gifts has been given to us by God for the purpose of the energizing of the body of faith. The purpose of the gift is to either build up the body of Christ or to strengthen its service to the pains of the world.

Each gift is called forth by the community. We can rarely recognize our own gifts—primarily because ego gets in the way! It is the community of faith that can see gifts in us we can't ourselves discern. A primary responsibility that our faith community has is to identify and then call forth our gifts, making sure that we both develop and make use of those gifts for Christ and his kingdom (more about this below).

No gift is to be used for ourselves. We shouldn't use our God-given gifts that are meant for the building up of the life and mission of the church to use for our own self-aggrandizement. We are not to try to benefit from our gifts. They don't exist to make us big or famous or important. Some people do get recognition for the exercise of their gift, but that should never be their motivation in using it. Rather, they should give all the glory to God!

The Calling forth of Gifts

An essential role that the Body of Christ is expected to play is that of the calling forth of each Christian's gifts. Each gift is called forth by the community of faith. Why and how is that done?

Why Gift-Calling is a Task for the Church

It is hard for us to call forth our own gifts. It is not a task for us to do by ourselves, for that can lead to unconscious prioritizing, unrealistic expectations, and self-deception. The exercise of unconscious priorities come from our preconceived perspectives of what ought to be top priority in the church and what is not. Each of us have those people in ministry—both contemporaries and historical figures—whom we particularly admire, and we can unconsciously select their gifts as the gifts we want to exercise ourselves, and then allow that unconscious content to shape our expectation of our own ministry and gifts. Likewise, we can have unrealistic expectations of ourselves, and therefore not look honestly at who we are, what we treasure, and what skills we actually have or gifts we covet. As a result of all this unconscious content, we are not the best people to determine for ourselves what are our gifts. Rather, we quickly embrace the gifts we want to assume. The potential for our self-deception is particularly high when it comes to discerning our gifts.

Who, then, is best equipped to name my gifts? It is not me! Rather, it is that portion of the Body of Christ with which I most associate. The Christian people who know me best and are being honest about me are likely the best people to both perceive and to call forth my natural, spiritual and common gifts.

One of the reasons the group is best able to call forth my gifts is that they don't have the same expectations for me that I have of myself. I have been known to avoid identifying my own gifts for fear that if I do, I will then be obligated to use them. We fear what our gifts might demand of us. So it is easy to avoid such demanding gifts and to settle, instead, for something safe, secure, and below our capacity.

Likewise, most of us sell ourselves short. Before the world, we might project an image of having our act together. But, in reality, we are like a swan that may be looking serene as it sails along the stream, but it may be rapidly paddling below. We are more prone to see our weaknesses than to see our strengths. The power of a discerning group is that they can often see as a strength that which we might identify as a weakness. Their calling forth of that weakness may enable us to deal with it and thus make it into a strength.

But how can a church realistically call forth the gifts of its members? If a church is only 10 or 20 or 50 members, one can see how that could happen. But in a church of 500 or 1,000 or 2,000 people, how would that be possible? The answer is, "It's not possible—unless the church is sub-divided into small groups." The calling forth of others gifts can most effectively happen only in the most intimate of supportive groups. A large organization—precisely because it is anonymous—cannot know people well enough to call forth the gifts of its people. Only a small group can do that. And this is one of the reasons why small groups are so strategic to the truly effective city church. So how do the small groups of a church call forth the gifts of the members of those groups? That is what we will consider in the next section.

The Small Group as Key to Gift-Calling

The small group (8–20 members) is the most potent means a church has to name and call forth the gifts of each person in that group. The assumption regarding such a group is that it has been together for an extended period of time. The calling forth of gifts cannot happen well if the group has only recently been organized, or exists for just one or a few meetings. Continued, long familiarity with each other is necessary for gifts to be accurately identified.

Likewise, the best small group to call forth groups is a group that has been developed around a specific single mission focus. In that type of group, it is assumed that everyone in the group feels called to the mission of that group; otherwise, why would they be in the group? In such a group, the calling forth of gifts becomes a powerful tool for the group's effective carrying out of that mission. So there is strong motivation in such a group for each member to be playing that role within the group and on behalf of the group that God intends that member to play.

If the group believes that God has called that group into being and has called each member of it into that group, then they must assume that all the gifts that are necessary to carry on the life and mission of that group are already contained within that group. This is not to say that all the spiritual gifts and natural gifts listed above are contained in that group. Instead, it is to say that all the gifts *necessary to maintain the life and mission of that group* are within that group. Thus, there may be spiritual or natural gifts named in scripture which do not need to be a part of that group in order for it to carry out its life and mission, so they won't be there. But if all the people in the group are meant by God to be in that group, then all the gifts that are needed for that group to function well are contained among those people (whether they recognize those gifts or not). A task facing the group, therefore, is to identify, call forth, and develop those gifts that group needs to both carry out its mission and to build its life together.

The work of the group in regard to its members' gifts are threefold, as noted above. They are to ***identify*** the gifts both needed by the group and the gifts contained (however raw and undeveloped they might be) within the group. They are to ***call forth*** those gifts in each other, encouraging their use. And they are to ***develop*** those gifts. They are responsible for urging each person to practice and thus build up those gifts by using them within the group. The group becomes each person's first laboratory for practicing those gifts. Thus, the group is responsible, not only to name the gifts, but to give space within that group for the named gifts to be exercised by the individuals named with those gifts. In other words, the group is responsible for nurturing those gifts, both building up and holding each person accountable for the performance of those gifts within the group.

You will discover that it is relatively easy to name skills and abilities of each person—particularly after you have gotten to know them well and as they function within the group and the larger church. It is much more difficult to identify each person's spiritual gifts. That requires a much longer relationship with them, a discernment of the roles they play best in the group, and the particular focus of their spirituality and its formation. This means that this requires the group to work intensely with each person over an extended period of time, encouraging that person to carry around within them the data the group has either named or called forth from them. It means allowing the person considerable time to reflect on the naming of a gift, and of the testing of that gift to see whether that has been an accurate call by the group. It means allowing time for that person to practice that gift within the group, whether it focuses on the building up of the spiritual life of the group or the carrying out of its mission (both are equally important).

If it seems surely a gift to be used in the mission of the group, then that person can be consecrated to the Lord to carry out that call in the group and in the Body of Christ. He/she can then practice that gift with a sense of the group investing in him/her the right and obligation to practice that gift on behalf of that group, that church and, perhaps, the larger Body of Christ (the topic of mission groups will be explored in detail in Chapter 13).

As I noted earlier, the church I pastored in Detroit had a number of small mission groups to enable members of our church both to be engaged in hands-on ministry and for their spiritual formation. The group to which I belonged was the PIFU Mission Group—our church's "core team" of those involved in People In Faith United, our local community organization. We decided to work intentionally with the calling forth of the gifts of the group's members, so we went on retreat together over a weekend.

During that retreat, the leader of the retreat led us through a particular exercise which asked us to go off by ourselves and do two things: first, prayerfully select the animal that we thought most captured the essence of our giftedness, and then, second, to do the same for every other member of the mission group. When we returned from this individual exercise, we would share the results and see what would emerge.

Off by myself, I prayerfully considered the animal that I felt most captured my essence. There was no question what I would choose. It was a powerful, glistening stallion!

We gathered as a group, and we listened to the reports. Finally, it became my turn. I shared my choice—a strong, swift stallion. Then it was everyone else's turn to share. I was stunned by their response. All but one chose a bell cow or lead cow! I was scandalized!

The leader asked me how I felt about the group's choice, and I let them know how wrong they were! But then one member of our mission group, who had earlier farmed before moving to Detroit, said, "Bob, I don't think you understand what a bell cow is, or how strategic it is to the herd. A bell cow is not just any old cow. It is the cow that is recognized by the herd as the wisest and most reflective of the cows in its choices. The bell cow leads the rest of the herd both to pasture and back to the barn again at the end of the day. That cow has to be very sensitive to the conditions around her, making sure that every cow can negotiate the path she is taking and they are following, and to be aware of every danger. Without the bell cow to lead them, the herd is helpless! They will just mill around, uncertain where to go. That is the leadership we see in you. And that is why we chose a bell cow to typify your leadership."

I learned something very valuable that day about my leadership style, gifts, and call. I wanted to be a great stallion—the charismatic leader to whom everyone is drawn and who is the center of the corral. I had followed that vision of leadership for years, wondering why it just didn't seem to fit me. But the kind of leader the group saw in me was that of a bell cow, who can think imaginatively and plot out the best routes, who enjoys working behind the scenes making things happen, and who nurtures others for leadership. Once I could see that difference, and embrace my role as a "bell cow" leader, then my life and ministry began to experience an authenticity it had previously not seemed to have. Little did I realize when that gift was discerned when I was a pastor, that it would be precisely the style of leadership that would work best in my work as an urban mission coordinator at World Vision, as a teacher at Eastern University, and as a mission executive. It is this kind of discernment by the group that is the gift of the church in forming us as lay and clergy ministers of the gospel in the cities of the world.

Getting Started

So how do you get started in discerning and calling forth the natural, spiritual, and common gifts of each other? First, we must recognize that we can't likely call forth our own gifts with any degree of accuracy, because we are so dominated by our dreams of what we would like to be (a great stallion). It is the small group in the Body of Christ that can best call forth the gifts we most need to successfully carry out our individual and corporate call to mission.

But if we acknowledge that the calling forth of gifts comes from the group, what should the group do to begin that process? How do we get started? The first step is for the group to intentionally decide to assume that role—but only after they feel they have gotten to really know one another, warts and all. The second step is to determine whether you wish to do this internally, or whether you need someone to lead you from the outside.

The third step is to take the step—to actually do it. That includes working with each person regarding their perceived self-image and working with the others to share what they observe. One of the most helpful scripture passages regarding gift discernment is Exodus 3:1–4:17 in which Moses receives God's call to "let my people go" but seeks to decline it because he perceives himself as inadequate. God, in response, calls forth Moses's gifts while acknowledging Moses's inadequacies and compensating for them. Perhaps the worksheet in the appendix—Worksheet I-4—may be of help in doing that.

The final step is ownership. People must own both the call they have received from God, and the recognition of their gifts. That recognition must feel authentic. So, once a person is able to integrate their call, their community, and their giftedness, then they can be off to Egypt to proclaim to the Pharaoh, "Let my people go!"

PART III

Your Church's Call: Organized For Action

Chapter 12

Discovering Your Church's Call

We have just explored the means that both laypeople and clergy have to discover their particular call from God. But it is not just individuals that are called. In reality, local congregations are also called. They are called in very specific ways. When a church both lives into its particular call and, at the same time, enables its members to discern and live out their specific calls which enable that church's call to be carried out, then the combination has been created that will lead to remarkable city-changing power—both for that church and for each of its members.

In this section of this book, we will examine the call of a local urban congregation—the congregation in which you participate. In this chapter, we will discover how a local church can discern the unique call from God which it is meant to embrace. In the next chapter, we will explore the structure that both enables that congregation to carry out its mission and to enable its members to live into and carry out their call within that larger call of their church. And in Chapter 14, we will examine a means by which that shared carrying out of call can bring about substantive and systemic change in your neighborhood and, sometimes, even to your entire city. In the final chapter, we will then knit the strands of this book together into one integrated tapestry of urban Christians in an urban church effectively building the shalom of their city. So, let's now begin by examining how a church can discern its unique call.

A Church that Found its Call

"Should our church focus our life and mission on Jesus as Lord or Jesus as Savior?" That was the question that one of the elders of my home church asked at our congregation's "Discernment Retreat" more than 20 years ago. The ultimate answer to that question would change the life of our congregation.

LaVerne Heights Presbyterian Church (LVHPC) is a relatively small, middle-class congregation in a small city in the Los Angeles metropolis (besides Los Angeles city, the Los Angeles metropolis is made up of 123 additional cities, each "cheek-by-jowl" of each other and forming one giant urban sprawl). In 1992, our pastor had left and we were in the process of searching for our next minister. We began by conducting a mission study, seeking to determine how God might now be calling us as a congregation. Because I was guiding urban mission studies in both a number of World Vision national entities throughout the world and in several American denominations, the church leadership asked me to lead that mission study of our congregation.

The process I chose was built around a "Discernment Weekend," which would seek to engage a high percentage of the congregation in a weekend retreat on March 13–15, 1992 (all members would be invited to attend). That retreat had included time for each member to work with selected scripture (see below), to reflect on their individual insights on God's mission call to our church, then had worked in small groups, and now had brought everyone together in a single discernment gathering. We were getting up on newsprint ideas from the people and the various small groups regarding our mission. Someone then said, "At the heart of our mission, we need to be committed to Jesus Christ as our Savior." I dutifully wrote that on the newsprint. And then came that question from another member—"Should our church focus our life and mission on Jesus as Lord or Jesus as Savior?" That question became a divine moment!

"What's the difference?" somebody asked. "What's the difference?" the questioner replied. "The difference is the entire thrust of our church. Are we primarily going to be about converting people to Christ or are we going to focus on making disciples for Christ? "Savior" says one thing; "Lord" says something quite different!"

Thus began the debate. And it was a debate that continued for about two hours. It was one of the most stimulating examples of lay theologizing I had ever witnessed. So I just sat back and let it happen.

Out of that two-hour debate and the hour it took afterward for the congregation to actually sculpt the resultant mission statement, the LVHPC membership gathered that day wrestled through what kind of church they believed God was calling our church to be. As the debate went on, it became steadily clearer that what the members felt most drawn to was the development of a church focused upon the building of Christian disciples who would be focused on discerning and carrying out God's call to the world. Here is the mission statement that those retreatants created that weekend:

> As a people committed to the Lord Jesus Christ and empowered by the Holy Spirit, we nurture and equip each other to be disciples who perceive and carry out God's call to our mission: to share the Gospel and address community and world needs to the glory of God.[101]

This was to be the new marching orders to our congregation. It saw the mission to which LVHPC and all its members were called to be "to share the Gospel and address community and world needs" for God's glory. And it saw the way to accomplish that call was to "nurture and equip each other to be disciples" so that each of us could "perceive and carry out God's call to our mission." And this could only be accomplished if we remained "a people committed to the Lord Jesus Christ and empowered by the Holy Spirit"; we could not do it in our own strength.

This mission statement has had the most profound impact upon LVHPC's consequent development. It is a church with a clear sense of mission and direction. It carries on eight distinct service and justice missions in its city, the eastern edge of the Los Angeles metropolis, and throughout the world, with a financial commitment of 20% of the church's operating budget. Besides children's and youth education, the church now has 15 groups studying scripture once a month or more, with over 70% of the congregation participating.[102] A strong network of both lay and clergy support cares for members in both the tragedies and triumphs of their lives. The primary vehicle by which the church eventually lived into this mission, we will examine in the next chapter!

The Called Church

Each urban church should have its own specific call to mission in the city. That corporate call should enhance and help implement the individual call of each of its church members. This insight of the specific call of Christ to every church is beautifully presented in Revelation 2:1– 3:22.

---

[101] The Session, LaVerne Heights Presbyterian Church, *1992 Mission Study of the LaVerne Heights Presbyterian Church* (Mission Study Committee, author p. 3, 1992).

[102] LaVerne Heights Presbyterian Church. *Annual Report, December 31, 2015 (2016).* Also, additional research by Robert Linthicum.

The book of Revelation is actually a letter written to seven churches in their respective cities in Asia Minor. The book consists of two parts. The first part (1:1–3:22) presents specifically to each of the seven churches the unique challenge facing each one of them as they seek to maintain both their witness and their existence in the hostile environment of the Roman Empire. The second part (4:1– 22:21) presents to those embattled churches what will eventually happen to the Roman Empire and to any other empire that worships another god than Jesus Christ, and how Christ will ultimately win (and the church with him). The seven urban churches to which John is writing in this letter are the churches in Ephesus (2:1–7); Smyrna (2:8–11); Pergamum (2:12–17); Thyatira (2:18–29); Sardis (3:1–6); Philadelphia (3:7–13); and Laodicea (3:14–22).

Each message to each of these churches follows the same pattern. First, each message is written not to the city nor to the church but to the "angel"[103] of that church (2:1, 8, 12, 18; 3:1, 7, 14). Second, the unique nature of each of these cities is stated succinctly. Third, each message deals with how that specific church has responded to that city as it has sought to carry out its ministry there. Finally, each message states what it is that Jesus wants that church to do in order to either carry on its ministry there or to correct the directions it is heading. Therefore, it is a profound message to all urban churches of today, both in its content and in the process it follows in analyzing that church and challenging its ministry.

What John tells the reader is that three of the seven churches (Ephesus, Smyrna, and Philadelphia) had been faithful thus far in their Christian witness in coming up against, impacting, and influencing their cities for Christ and his kingdom. Four of them had been more converted by their cities than converting them (Pergamum, Thyatira, Sardis, and Laodicea). But all had been called to be faithful to the gospel (as opposed to being successful), whatever the priorities or seduction of their respective cities. The church being faithful to the gospel in the city might not look like the church being faithful in another city. "Being faithful" meant different ministry

---

[103] The use of the "angel of the city church" motif is the way that John developed the idea that both a city and a church has its own unique spirituality, so to address the letter to the "angel" of the church is to be focusing upon the interior spirituality of each church as it comes up against the spiritual essence of that city. For a more full treatment of the corporate spirituality of the city, see my book, *City of God*, 73–78.

foci in different situations.[104] But all the churches were called to "keep their eyes on the prize" and thus be faithful to their calling.

Thus, Revelation 2:1– 3:22 first reminds the church that we can't isolate ourselves from the city but must directly interact with that city's spirituality and the way those priorities are lived out in the political, economic, cultural, and religious life of that city. Second, it reminds us that our essential task in our ministry in the city is to be faithful, and not seek after success. But faithfulness is determined by a discernment of our task in the light of the spiritual warfare going on in that city.

Third, we learn from this study of Revelation 2– 3 that each church is faithful by discerning and then living into its specific call. What is the correct call for one church is not the appropriate call for another church. We are not to be imitators of each other, but of Christ. Our church will be effective in its urban ministry, therefore, only to the degree that it is clear about its own particular call, and then seeks to carry out that call in its city.

Finally, we learn from Revelation 2– 3 that each of us, as member Christians of a given specific Christian fellowship or church, are called to that church, chosen and gifted for that church, to play an integral role in the carrying out of the mission of our church and of the Body of Christ in our city. Our individual calls are not haphazard calls. Nor are they to be practiced in a solitary individualism. Our personal calls are, in some way, integrally related to the call of our congregation. So it becomes our responsibility to perceive that relationship, and then to carry out its implementation in and through our lives.[105]

How Your Church Can Discern God's Call to Its Mission

But if all of this is true, then how do we work with our church in helping it to discern its unique and specific call to the city? That is what we will explore in this section.

---

[104] Thus, the church in Sardis would be faithful if it were to wake up to the way its city had seduced it, whereas the church in Thyatira would be faithful if it would reject its own popularity among the intelligentsia of that city.

[105] For a more thorough examination of Rev. 2:1–3:22 as a template for the church's faithful ministry in its city, read my book, *City of God,* 294–313. This material includes an examination of the message to each of the seven churches, as well as conclusions that are drawn from the whole.

There are several different ways a church can discern God's call to it. The use of the spiritual disciplines shared in Chapters 8, 9, and 11 can all be used to be directed in this way. Likewise, a team or committee can be dedicated to this task, exploring this issue by study of that church, its neighborhood or parish area, models of other churches, and the use of the spiritual disciplines. But the vehicle that I have discovered that seems to be most helpful in enabling a church to discern its call is the mission study.

Mission Studies

Mission studies are designed to enable a church to determine its primary focus or mission as a church. So, by its very nature, it ought to cause a church to look thoughtfully at its life and work, and out of that plus its theological tradition, articulate the next essential focus of that church.

There are a number of available mission study designs. If your church belongs to a Protestant denomination, it is highly likely that your denomination either has an official mission study form or access to various mission study designs. If your church is an independent church, there are mission study designs which you can access on the web, and from other sources. I created my own design, which I have used in over 200 urban churches and mission agencies (see below). So there are lots of designs available to your church.

But how do you know what mission study design to choose? What separates a good mission study design from a poor one? There are several characteristics that I believe are essential to have in any truly effective mission study design, as follows:

- The purpose of any good mission study is to enable the congregation to both articulate and to be challenged to implement God's new call to that congregation; the question is, therefore, to what degree this considered design accomplishes that task.
- The articulation of that new call should be the primary emphasis of the mission statement. Consequently, that statement should not present theological, liturgical, or polity convictions, but rather be a statement that is a clear, specific, concrete, and measurable mission statement (it is hoped that the design should also develop mission, life together, and institutional objectives, a structure for

implementing the same, etc., but the primary focus needs to be a mission statement).

- The mission study design needs to directly involve the members of the congregation in the formation of that mission statement; otherwise, there will not be ownership on the part of church members.

One Way A Church Can Discern Its Call

As I pastored inner-city churches, I very early realized that each church needed to be able to discern and articulate a clear understanding of why God had brought them as a church to that time and place. What was the particular and specific call that God had extended to them as a congregation, at that moment in history? Beginning in 1963, I worked at developing a process to enable a congregation to move through that process of discernment. As you can imagine, that process has changed considerably over the years, as I "tweaked" this and "messed" with that. But in due time, it assumed a clear three-step process built around the formation of a mission discernment committee made up of members of each church. When I went to work in 1985 for World Vision International, I adapted the process to be used by mission agencies (primarily, World Vision national entities like World Vision Keyna and WV India and WV Brazil that were committed to developing an urban mission thrust). It was finally published as *Church: Discover Your Calling* and distributed by the Presbyterian Distribution Service (PDS# 72380-96-003).[106] It has been my privilege to lead more than 200 churches and mission agencies through this mission discernment process, and most of the stories in this book are from a few of the churches that used this design.

The vehicle I developed to enable churches to discern their particular call has three primary steps to it. The first and the third, we will only mention briefly here. But it is the second step that we will here examine more closely.

After the discernment committee is appointed, the first step has to do with research. That research is in two forms. The first is statistical information on the

---

[106] Robert Linthicum, *Church: Discover Your Calling* (Louisville, KY: Presbyterian Distribution Service, The Presbyterian Church [USA], 1993). Out of print; no longer available.

congregation and its parish area.[107] The second is in the interviewing of key community players and officials, and most (if not all) of the church members.[108] The objective of this step is to get to know both the congregation and its parish residents, including both the strengths and weaknesses of each. Of course, another task is making the necessary arrangements for the Discernment Weekend (where the congregation's call is usually articulated).

The second step is the Discernment Weekend itself (which we will examine below).

And, of course, the third step is to complete all the work that was not completed at the Discernment Weekend, and then to write up the report. Once the report is completed, then it is approved by the official decision-making body of that congregation, and becomes the new "marching orders" for that congregation.

The Discernment Weekend. The intention of the Discernment Weekend is to gather all the members of the congregation so that they may reflect upon and determine God's next call to this church, as it continues its ministry in the city. This congregational retreat is normally over a weekend, from Friday evening (beginning with dinner) through Sunday afternoon. According to the financial and numerical capacity of the congregation, it can be held at a retreat center, a nearby college, or even in the church building itself.

Attendance is paramount! I have discovered that the success by which that call is embraced by the membership of that church is directly proportional to the number of church members present for this weekend retreat. I believe that the most effective number needs to be, about 70% of the congregation for a church under 200, about 50% for a church between 200 and 500, and about 25% for a church above 1,000 members. So that means a robust recruitment campaign.

---

[107] You should be able to get from your denomination, church association, or mission agency a template of the statistical profile used within that body by its churches for researching churches and the neighborhood around a church. These are often associated with the mission study process recommended by that body. It is wise to gather the statistical data most used within your denomination, association, or agency. Using their profile will most likely accomplish that objective.

[108] The holding of intentional conversations with the members and friends of your congregation and with community leaders is the most important activity in conducting a mission study that truly reflects the convictions and desires of your congregation. Instructions for doing this and a full template for holding such intentional conversations is presented in my book, *Building A People of Power* (Eugene, OR: Wipf and Stock, 2015), 117–146.

There are five primary objectives for a Discernment Weekend. They are:

1. A (hopefully entertaining) summary of the information gathered both from statistics and from individual neighborhood and church membership visits, including a profile of the congregation ten and five years ago and today, a profile of the parish area or neighborhood, and implications of that information.
2. Shared biblical reflection on God's call to the church (see *"The Last Temptation of Christ"* below).
3. Determination of God's new mission call to this church.
4. Creation of mission objectives to enable that call to be carried out by this church.
5. Creation of interior (life together) objectives and the management of the church's resources, in order to make the implementation of mission objectives possible.

How, then, are these objectives accomplished? An examination of the agenda for a Discernment Weekend presents the process for accomplishing these objectives (see Appendix II-1). As you can see, the weekend consists of a combination of committee reports, individual biblical reflection on the part of each retreatant, small group work, plenary sessions of joint decision making, and work in the already-existing administrative and programmatic bodies or committees of the church. Tying all this together is the retreat leader, who has a clear overall vision of what the retreat can be, acts as host and convener, but who also acts as the retreat processor, taking people through the steps they need to take both individually and together, while allaying their anxieties.

Looking at the retreat schedule, it becomes obvious that the most important portion of this Discernment Weekend is the period of individual, small groups, and plenary creation of a unified mission statement. So we will spend the remainder of this chapter on exploring that portion of a mission discernment retreat.

Discerning a Church's Mission Call. The actual process for enabling a congregation to discern that call into which God is presently calling that church consists of the following steps (time segments are assigned to the steps as the ideal time in which it takes to complete each step):

9:00 Plenary Bible study (see *The Last Temptation of Christ* below)

9:45 Individual biblical reflection (see Appendix II-2 for form to be used)

10:45	Sharing in small groups about the individual reflections
11:30	Plenary sharing from small groups
12:30	Lunch
1:30	Preparation for mission focusing, led by retreat leader
2:00	Work on mission focusing in small groups
2:45	Plenary report-backs from small groups, and conclusions drawn
3:10	Assignment to writing team to compose mission statement from plenary and small groups reflections
5:00	Writing team presents draft of mission statement; editing and final approval occurs.

The scripture that will be studied individually, in small groups, and in the entire group is John 12:20-27. This study should occur in four distinct ways over a total of three-and-a-half hours of time. This seems like an excessive amount of time dedicated to the study of a specific scripture passage in a relatively short retreat, but it is absolutely strategic to discerning a church's call. So it is time well spent!

The study begins with its introduction (see *The Last Temptation of Christ* below), which is presented by the retreat leader. In her/his presentation, the leader will present the background to the event recorded in this passage, focus upon the opportunity afforded to Jesus to escape the cross by going to Greece to teach, and then center on the way—and even the actual words—of Jesus's response to such a tempting offer. It is Jesus's response that becomes the potential response of those in this congregation wrestling with God's call into the future that God intends for it. All of this, the retreat leader makes clear in her/his start-up presentation.

After the presentation, each person at the retreat is given a worksheet (see Appendix II-2) and asked to go off by him/herself, center down, meditate, reflect on this scripture passage, and then ask the key question of this retreat. The particular passage is John 12:27: "Now my soul is troubled. And what should I say—'Father, save me from this hour?' No, it is for this reason (i.e., purpose) that I have come to this hour. Father, glorify your name." The key question is, "For what purpose do I believe God has brought us as a church to this hour?"[109] Why has God had our church go

[109] Linthicum, *Building,* 45.

through its years of ministry—the good, the bad, and the ugly—and we have now come to this moment? For what purpose? Why have we been brought to this hour?"

I don't know why it is so. But for some strange reason, this question gets people to look at their church with entirely different eyes than they normally look at their church. I have seen it happen over and over and over and over again—hundreds of times. Asking the question this way somehow frees people from their conventional and "knee-jerk" ways of talking about the mission of the church, and gets them thinking creatively. They begin thinking "outside the box" of their own imagination.

During that quiet reflection time, we ask the people to journal on their answers to that question, then to bring that worksheet back with them, and share it in small groups. It is there, in these small groups at 10:45, that the second miracle occurs. People listen to each person's sharing of their response. And they begin to discern congruence between what different people are sharing. The leader of each of the small groups asks the question, "From this exercise, into what kind of ministry does it appear that God is calling us as a congregation?"[110] And when the small group makes its decision, it is time for them to bring that good news back to the plenary gathering of all the retreatants.

At the 11:30 plenary, each small group is asked to share its conclusions. These are noted on newsprint or Powerpoint projection. Then the entire group looks at the reports, and begins looking for common or similar responses. Usually, by working with the reports this way, the conclusions of the reports can be narrowed to only one or two basic ideas.

After lunch, everyone returns to the plenary so that the leader can review the few common themes gleaned from the work of various small groups. S/he stresses the importance of reducing these themes further, so that the retreatants can discern a common mission focus for this church. With that, s/he sends the people back to their respective small groups. In each of the small groups, each group returns to the statement it brought to the plenary at the 11:30 hour, and it asks of itself the question, "In the light of (a) what we have written in this statement and (b) what we have heard from the other groups as they shared this morning, what do you think should be the

---

[110] Linthicum, *Building,* 45.

mission focus of our church?"[111] Working with the ideas shared, each group seeks to create a single mission focus statement, write it on a fresh sheet of newsprint, and return to the plenary with it.

At the 2:45 plenary, the lists are reviewed, and then the leader asks "What is the single idea (or primary ideas) that runs through all these statements?" People's responses are written down on a newsprint or on Powerpoint. Then, once this time of sharing is completed, the leader will ask "Is there one statement among these statements that says it best?" or "Are there a few statements that seem to particularly say it well?" or "What phrases, words, or statements seem to particularly state the primary ideas or that particularly capture your attention?"[112] The choice of question depends upon how many ideas you are working with. If, for example, there is only one basic idea being expressed in different ways by the small groups, you can ask the first question. If, on the other hand, there are three basic ideas in contention, the third question is likely the best.

After this segment is completed, it can be assigned to the writing team that takes all the ideas, worries with words, and hopefully comes up with their recommended mission statement. While the writing team works on this task, everybody else goes on to work on other tasks (such as working together on the implications to the church of implementing the mission focus that has been selected).

At 5:00, then, the writing team returns to the plenary and presents the statement they have created, the entire group worries with words, and by this process, the final mission statement is created and approved by the plenary. And that gives that church both its new mission focus and the call that God is giving it to step out into the next risky steps of faith to which God is calling it!

The Last Temptation of Christ. The heart of the process for discerning a church's mission call is both the individual and group study of John 12:20-27—a study we might call "The Last Temptation of Christ." In order for this passage to do its particular work at discerning a church's call, it is important to present in the opening plenary the following material, in order to place that passage into context and give it

---

[111] Linthicum, *Building,* 47.

[112] Linthicum, *Building,* 47.

understanding, so that the people can most effectively apply it to their church's life and mission.

This scripture begins with the words, "Now among those who went up to worship at the festival were some Greeks. They came to Philip, who was from Bethsaida in Galilee, and said to him, 'Sir, we wish to see Jesus'" (12:20-21).

The Greek word here translated "Greeks" is crucial to the understanding of the import of this story. It is the Greek word that should be best translated "Gentile." It is *not* the Greek word for Jews who spoke Greek or lived in Gentile countries, nor does the word mean Greeks who were Jewish proselytes. It means "pagans," "Gentiles"—those outside the influence of the Chosen People, and therefore in the eyes of the Jewish officials of that day, those rejected by God. These "Greeks" presumably have not come to Jerusalem to participate in the Passover festival but specifically and intentionally to meet with "the Son of Man." Thus, it is these "non-Jewish Gentiles" who come to Philip and ask to speak with Jesus.

It is also intriguing to note that the two disciples to whom they go to gain entry to Jesus have Greek names—Philip and Andrew. Did these Gentiles feel they would make more headway by going to apparently Greek-influenced disciples? We do not know. But the very placing of this story at this point in the Johannine narrative serves to illustrate clearly the truth of the Pharisees' comment, "Look, the whole *world* has gone after him" (John 12:19), for now even non-Jewish Gentiles are seeking Jesus out!

The text does not tell us whether or not these Gentiles ever got to see Jesus. But what did happen was a response by Jesus to their request, brought to him by Andrew and Philip—a response that seems thoroughly inappropriate! To their request that he visit with these Gentiles, Jesus responds:

> The hour has come for the Son of Man to be glorified. Very truly, I tell you, unless a grain of wheat falls into the earth and dies, it remains just a single grain; but if it dies, it bears much fruit. Those who love their life lose it, and those who hate their life in this world will keep it for eternal life. Whoever serves me must follow me, and where I am, there will my servant be also. Whoever serves me, the Father will honor (12:23b-26).

This is a strange response to a simple request by Gentiles to speak to Jesus. One would have expected on Jesus's part a simple response of "Yes" or "No." But, instead, Jesus launches into what only can be called a "rant" about a living or dying grain of wheat. But if one puts this story in the larger context, then one can begin to perceive Jesus's anxiety and his consequently strange reaction.

What did these Gentiles want to see Jesus about? The scripture doesn't say. But what makes the most sense is that these Gentiles were coming to ask Jesus to leave the dangers of Jerusalem and return with them into Gentile territory. There, Jesus could be safe, and would be free and even welcomed to teach and heal as he so obviously felt led. It is intriguing that the Synoptic Gospels report that Jesus spent significant time (some would estimate around one-third of his time) in Gentile territory beyond the borders of Galilee.

Thus, in these Gentiles' offer lay the way out of the death that would otherwise inevitably await Jesus if he continued his attack of the Jewish authorities—and that, quite soon! Should he accept the offer? Would he accept the offer? Could he not now "save face" while rapidly de-escalating his conflict with the Jewish clerical aristocracy, doing so by accepting the request of a people who wanted him to teach and heal in their country? It must have been terribly, terribly tempting—especially to a young man who really was dreading the thought of dying (cf. Luke 22:41–46). It was, in reality, the last temptation of Christ!

Jesus rejects their offer of escape. Using the metaphor of wheat, Jesus states that it is only through his dying that humanity will live. It is only through his crucifixion that those committed to him will be birthed into a new community. If he becomes fixated upon preserving his life, Jesus observes, then all will be lost—the kingdom, the world, humanity. On the other hand, if he is willing to face into his own death, then all humanity will be redeemed. This is Jesus's answer to his last temptation. To take the easy way out would be to be disobedient to that vision and call that God had given to him, not just at the beginning of his ministry, but at the very beginning of time (John 1:1–14).

It is at this point that Jesus then utters one of the most poignant lines that appear in scripture. "Now my soul is troubled. And what shall I say—'Father, save me from this hour'? No, it is for this very reason that I have come to this hour. Father, glorify your name" (12:27–28a).

This is one of the few places in John when you truly see into the inner anguish of the man himself. Here you see Jesus in the very raw! He is a young man—33 years old. He doesn't want to die! He wants to go on living, serving others, building a community, healing the broken, making humanity whole again. Here is the opportunity to do so. With all his heart, he wants to cry out, "Father, save me from this hour"!

But he will not utter such a cry. Jesus will stay the course. He will play out the drama that lies before him. HE *MUST* DIE! For unless he dies, there is to be no redemption of humanity.

So Jesus makes the decision to stay in unyielding confrontation with the political, economic, and religious powers of both Israel and of Rome until they do their worst and destroy him. To die is his purpose in life. So he calls upon God to sustain him in what he must now do.

Jesus's key statement in this passage is, "It is for this purpose (some translations read "reason") that I have come to this hour." That is, Jesus's purpose was to die—and to die redemptively. He was born to die!

So it is that we can ask the question of each person participating in this discernment process, "For what purpose has God brought your church to this hour?" But in order to ask that question, we must first ask each person to answer, "How is my soul troubled over my church?" And we must ask, "Why has God preserved us as God's people here, maintaining a loving congregation and a home—not only for ourselves but for our community?"[113] What is accomplished for most churches participating in such a discernment process is that it allows the people who are working both corporately and individually with this scripture to let go of their own particular agenda for that church and to become open to hearing from God's Spirit what God's intentions are for the life and mission of that congregation (see Appendix II-2 for worksheet we suggest be given to each person reflecting upon this scripture).

Getting Started

So, how is your congregation to get started? I would suggest the following steps:

- The governing body or the appropriate decision-making group or person should make the decision that the church participate in such a discernment process.

---

[113] Linthicum, *Building*, 53.

- Either a group or an individual be given the responsibility to select an actual mission study process to be recommended for this purpose. Be sure that this mission study process is built upon three premises: (a) the process should be focused upon enabling a congregation to articulate God's mission call to it; (b) it should result in the creation of a mission statement that will articulate that new call (or reconfirm an old call); (c) the mission study directly involves the members of the congregation in the formation of that mission statement.
- The decision-making body (or person) of the church approves the use of that mission study design and commands that it is to be implemented.
- A team or committee is appointed to manage the implementation of that mission study. That team would not so much do the mission study itself as it would organize the congregation to do that study by the process the study presents.
- Begin the study process.

And may you, as a congregation, more clearly perceive God's call to you as a community of believers, and out of that perception, more clearly discern the strategic role each of you as individual believers play in the implementation of that mission design for Christ and His Kingdom!

Chapter 13

Little Groups That Can Transform Your City

In the previous chapter, I shared with you the story of how the LaVerne Heights Presbyterian Church—my home church—came to a clear discernment of God's particular call to it. That call was to "nurture and equip each other to be disciples who perceive and carry out God's call to our mission: to share the gospel and address community and world needs to the glory of God." The carrying out of that call was based upon that church being "a people committed to the Lord Jesus Christ and empowered by the Holy Spirit." As you will recall, this call was developed at an all-congregational retreat on March 13–15, 1992, and was embraced by the whole congregation.

But now we have to ask an important question. That question is: "How did it all work out for you, Church?" Well, let's see what happened.

A Difference-Making Church

Based upon that mission statement, the LVHPC congregation then continued at that retreat to build objectives and strategies for its life and ministry for 1992 through 1995. Because it felt wedded to its already existing committee structure, it sought to fit these new objectives and strategies into that structure with the instruction to make it work. But this action was, in essence, an act of "putting new wine into old wineskins." It became increasingly apparent, as time went on, that the church's traditional structure was, at its best, unwieldy in implementing an effort to concentrate upon building Christian disciples who would become increasingly aware of their call and could live out that call. It became clear that there was not the means by which people could act out their call within the church if that call didn't conform to the priorities of the church's structure. So what should the church do?

When the mission statement was originally approved by the congregation, it was given a three-year testing timespan (1992–1995) before evaluation of it would happen. So, in 1995, the ruling body of the church (it is named the "Session") examined the struggling of the church's mission implementation and recognized the problem. It became clear to the Session that either the church structure should be changed or its mission call abandoned. Abandoning God's call to LVHPC was not an option, so it was the structure that had to be changed.

One of the beauties of the Presbyterian governance system is that, although each church is required to have a Session ultimately responsible for the carrying out of that church's mission outreach, life together, and institutional maintenance, the Session can choose to organize its congregation however it pleases to accomplish that end. It is not required to have any committees at all. Therefore, LVHPC had the right to organize itself in any way that the Session thought was appropriate in order to best carry out its mission.

Consequently, on Dec. 28, 1995, the Session appointed a task force representative of the church to examine alternative structures and recommend to the Session the structure the church ought to follow to best carry out its call. Because I was serving part time on the church staff as its "parish associate,"[114] the Session assigned me to provide staff support to that task force.

Over the ensuing year, our task force looked at a number of structures used by churches to enable them to carry out their respective calls. But we found ourselves particularly drawn to the structure used by the Church of the Saviour in Washington, DC—the structure of "mission groups." Church of the Saviour (COS) was an ecumenical, intentional congregation in inner-city Washington.[115] It was a unique

---

[114] The position of "parish associate" enables an ordained Presbyterian minister who is not currently serving a church to provide Session-specified pastoral services to a congregation, with or without pay (I was serving without pay). It is designed to allow an ordained minister who is serving a mission agency, teaching in a seminary or college, serving as a chaplain, or is retired to still be connected to and providing pastoral service to a local congregation. At that time, I was working full time for World Vision International as its director of WVI's "Urban Advance," an organizing effort in African, Asian, and Latin American cities, but becoming a "parish associate" provided me a way to continue in pastoral ministry.

[115] For books on COS, see Elizabeth O'Connor, *Call to Commitment: the Story of the Church of the Saviour* (New York: Harper and Row, 1963); Cosby, *Handbook*; and Henri Nouwen, *Life of the Beloved: Spiritual Living in a Secular World* (New York: Crossroads, 1992). Also, read about the

church for its time (it began in 1946) when small, incarnational, nondenominational churches with committed laity working with and for the urban poor were rare.

In very short order, COS carried out an amazing array of missions that were both extremely diverse and significant in their impact upon the poor, the Washington elite, and the church throughout the world. Thus, the church targeted a specific impoverished and overlooked neighborhood in Washington, and there developed a housing corporation, a clinic, a job-placement service, a coffee house/bookstore, a training center, and a worshiping congregation. Its "For Love of Children" (FLOC) became a national model for giving detention center children a new start in life. Its Wellspring ministry provided spiritual direction for pastors throughout the United States and its Ministry of Money enabled the wealthy to use their money to advance God's kingdom in cities around the world. Most intriguing was the heavy emphasis the church made upon each member's spiritual formation, particularly in its tying of such growth to those members' engagement in working for justice in their city.

What particularly drew our team to COS was its structure of "mission groups." Rev. N. Gordon Cosby, the COS pastor, defined a mission group as "a small group of people conscious of the action of the Holy Spirit in their lives, enabling them to hear the call of God through Christ, to belong in love to one another, and to offer the gift of their corporate life for the world's healing and unity."[116] Necessary to both the formation and the maintenance of a mission group, Cosby pointed out, was both the group itself and all its members engaging in an inward journey and an outward journey. That inward journey needed to be focused upon "growth in the life of meditation and contemplation rooted in the Scriptures," "growth in self-understanding," and "growth in community."[117] The outward journey was to be an expression of that group's inward journey (and vice versa) to be carried out in "presence, service, and verbal witness."

This seemed to be what we were looking for, if we were going to authentically live into the call we had received from Christ to be "disciples who perceive and carry out God's call to our mission to share the gospel and address community and world

---

Church of the Saviour in the introduction to this book; this book's bibliography includes many books about COS; particularly see books written by Elizabeth O'Connor.

[116] Cosby, *Handbook*, 54.

[117] Cosby, *Handbook*, 54–55.

needs to the glory of God." So our team began reading everything we could find on COS, followed by talking with some of its lay leaders and paying a visit to the church and a few of its mission groups.

On April 20, 1997, the team made its final report to the Session, recommending the structure of mission groups for our church—but with a change of name to "ministry groups." The Session heard the report as good news, and the process began to shift LVHPC from a structure of committees to a primary structure and practice of ministry groups. That transition was completed by September 1, 1998, and the first ministry groups came into being.

Since their start-up in 1998, LVHPC has had 14 ministry groups, 8 of which continue today (we built into our ministry group structure the means for a group to voluntarily dissolve when it had completed its task, so that groups weren't continued beyond their natural lifespan). The present ministry groups include:

- Connect (ministering to visitors, helping them to connect with the congregation and to provide opportunities for church members to connect with each other);
- Creation Care Task Force (raising awareness of environmental care through the church's recycling and green waste programs, education, biblical reflection, hiking opportunities, and beach clean ups);
- Dorcas (making and donating items to people in local hospitals, nursing homes, the homeless, helping agencies, PCH orphan children, and "memory boxes" for mothers whose infants have died in birth);
- Homelessness (providing breakfasts for Pomona homeless as well as goods and housing care);
- ICON (Inland Communities Organizing Network: a broad-based organizing IAF affiliate), addressing systemic issues in elder rights, neighborhood safety, environmental pollution, jobs, and education—see Chapter 15;
- Missions (coordinating LVHPC's missions outreach to mission organizations around the world, to local community outreach, working hands-on in housing construction and clean water, and supporting denominational missions);
- Pomona Hope (working with Pomona First Presbyterian Church's community development corporation, providing funding and church

volunteers for its children's tutoring and after-school program, summer enrichment program, and community garden);

- Providence Children's Home (supporting the development of this orphanage near Nairobi, Kenya, through fundraising, regularly sending work teams, and raising nearly a half-million dollars to complete the building of the orphanage).

Please note that ministry groups cover a spectrum from evangelistic and service projects to community development and systemic change efforts. A total of 93 members of this church, 43% of the membership, are in its ministry groups, and about another 30% participate in some way in their programming. To learn more about LVHPC's ministry groups, you can visit the church's website, www.lvhpc.org and follow the footnote instructions[118] in order to see a video on this unique means for engaging the members of this congregation in mission and to impact the world around it for Christ and his kingdom.

Mission Groups—A Way to Transform the City (and Your Church)

Both my experience and my intuition tell me that the most effective way for an urban congregation to seek the effective transformation of its neighborhood and city is through little groups of God's people who both feel called by God to the city and are living out that call together in a specific way. The place to begin in seeking the transformation of our city is with the little action groups within a congregation that gain their power through each group's members recognizing the call of both that group and each of its members to work in specific ways for that city's transformation.

How American Congregations Have Organized Themselves.

Historically, American congregations have organized their interior life and institutional development as a congregation and the carrying out of their mission in four distinct ways. Let's take a moment to look at those ways.

---

[118] Go to the home page of the LaVerne Heights Church, www.lvhpc.org. On the home page, scan down the page to the picture entitled "Ministry Groups." Clock on the "View" button. Up will come the video, "What Is A Ministry Group?," which you can then view at your leisure. You can also watch a second video on ministry groups, "What's A Church to Do?" "What's A Church to Do?" is meant to be a short motivational piece of just a few minutes. "What Is A Ministry Group?" is meant to be instructional, and is fifteen minutes in length.

The Church as Pulpit. This approach to "doing church" in the city focuses the work of that church upon the preaching of the Word and the worship of God. It is the Sunday worship and, in particular, the preaching of sermons and the teaching of that church's pastor or pastors that is its primary (and sometimes exclusive) function. The congregation comes together primarily for worship one or more times a week. The church building is "dark" the remainder of the week, as activities and programming are kept to a minimum with self-designated people assuming responsibility for predictable functions of the church ("since we want to have a reception after Joe's funeral, call Aunt Mabel who always does the receptions here").

In this design, there are few or even no committees (although there may be ongoing fellowships like a Woman's Association or a Men's Breakfast). The church is built around the pastor, whose primary role is to preach and teach, and perhaps represent the church at public functions. In this scenario, the pastor is seen primarily as a "prince of the pulpit," and the life of the church is centered in him or her. The governing board of the church acts as a "committee of the whole," as it carries out its role as the primary decision-making and pastoral body of the church.

This understanding of church was the early structure of the city church from American colonial times through the 1930s. It worked well as preaching centers in "mainline denominations" in the cities of the eighteenth through the early twentieth centuries. It still exists in selected independent megachurches, if the pastor holds a national preaching reputation (often enhanced by television). Although formerly the dominant model in America's cities, it is now virtually gone from the urban scene except in its megachurch form, but can still be found in some isolated and primarily rural areas of our country today. Although it worked well as a conveyor of the gospel to an unredeemed world, it is a most inadequate model of church today in urban communities that are at risk or where the people need emotional, mental, social, and physical as well as spiritual support. And it does not help people to discover and live out their call to serve Christ in the world, because they have been effectively turned into an audience rather than a congregation.

The Program Church. The majority of urban churches today fall into this category. This type of church was an inevitable evolution, given the inadequacy of the pulpit church to truly engage with the late twentieth- and twenty-first-century city.

The program model sees the church essentially as a corporation or institution in which committees are created and function under the authority of the church's governing board to implement that board's decisions regarding the life, ministry, mission outreach, and institutional development of that church. Church members are recruited to serve on these committees, either indefinitely or for a prescribed period of time. The underlying doctrine upon which the committee structure is built is the emphasis upon order and the wise stewardship of the church's resources (including its people), since the church is seen primarily as an ecclesiastical institution.

The governing board sees itself, not primarily as the spiritual leaders of the congregation (either individually or corporately), but rather as a board of directors. The role of the pastor in the program model of church, therefore, is that of being chairman of the board and the church's chief executive (and often, operational) officer. The "buck stops with him/her." It is hoped that the pastor is a good preacher, has a winsome personality, and cares for her/his people—but the pastor's final responsibility is the smooth operation AND EXPANSION of that ecclesiastical institution.

This approach to church works best in midsize to large congregations, with significant financial, building, and people resources. It operates poorly in small, struggling congregations with a limited number of people and financial resources. This structure began emerging in large denominational churches in the 1930s but accelerated significantly after the close of the Second World War when Christianity exploded in the suburbs of the cities. Today, the vast majority of both denominational and unaffiliated congregations operate upon this model, although there is increasing dissatisfaction with it (that dissatisfaction is what has likely prompted you to read this book this far!). Although this approach often builds a fine institution, it is not likely to enable people to discover and embrace their call, never mind build a call together within that congregation.

The Mission Church Model. The mission church model sees the church essentially as an intentional community of people drawn together by God for the engagement of the world. In this model, the structure of the church is often built around "mission groups" or small groups of church members and friends both working together on a commonly identified mission and building a life together in Christ. That twin emphasis exists in mission groups because its people see themselves as being called together by God to both address that mission and to build together their relationships with God and Christ.

The primary doctrine around which a mission model of church is built is the doctrine of "call" or "vocation"—the biblical belief that every person (and not just clergy) is called by God for a particular ministry in the world, and that fulfillment comes in finding and living into that call with others also so called.

The essential role of the governing board of a church that functions around the doctrine of call and acts out that doctrine through mission groups is a pastoral role. That is, the governing board exists to encourage and hold mission groups accountable for the carrying out of their stated missions, and to coordinate the overall ministry of that congregation. The primary role of the pastor is to be an enabler/encourager of people in their discovery of their own calls and of their mission groups, as well as being a discerner/prophet capable of always perceiving the next risky steps of faith to which that congregation may be called by God. This approach to organizing the life and work of a church began with the ministry of the Church of the Saviour in Washington DC in the late 1940s, and became an alternative way of organizing Protestant urban churches since the 1960s. However, this approach has been influenced by the living out of called mission in small groups from the early Benedictine monasteries of the sixth century through the Methodist "Holiness Clubs" in the eighteenth and the small group renewal movement in Protestantism in the 1950s.

It is the mission group structure that we will now examine for the remainder of this chapter as the primary vehicle by which each Christian can discern and live out their call to be transforming good news to both their congregation and to their city.

What Is A Mission Group?

A mission group is a small group of church members and friends who gather together for a period of time both to undertake a common mission and to build a strong life together.[119] Every phrase in that sentence is important.

First, a mission group is "a small group of church members and friends." In itself, a mission group need not be large—just enough people to plan and to organize the ministry of that group. However, it may offer the opportunity to many more members and friends of the church to participate in that mission on a short-term basis. But the mission group itself need only be large enough to plan and implement its work.

---

[119] Much of the ensuing material on mission groups is dependent upon an internal document within the LaVerne Heights Presbyterian Church, *Handbook for Ministry Groups,* authored by myself and used with permission of the church. The handbook was first published in 1998, with revised editions in 2010 and 2015.

For example, one church built around mission groups has an annual Vacation Bible School that reaches hundreds of children and families in its neighborhood who are unchurched. To do that, the mission group planning this VBS recruits from that church a volunteer staff of over 70 working as teachers, traffic guards, worship leaders, treat makers, prop builders. and who-knows-what-else. But the actual mission group itself is composed of only eight people who begin nine months before the Vacation Bible School occurs to prepare for it. So a mission group needs to be only "a small group of church members and friends."

Second, a mission group operates for a "period of time." It should not be envisioned by the church's governing board that once a person commits him/herself to a mission, that this commitment continues "till death do you part." Each mission group member has the opportunity to decide at appointed times (usually once each year) whether she or he wishes to continue service in that group.

Likewise, the mission group should always be nothing more than one year from extinction. At the same time each year, the members of each mission group ought to enter into a time of prayer and discernment to see whether they should continue for another year. If they decide to do so, then they begin working on their next year's ministry. But if they decide that God is telling them that it is time to close that mission, they are free to do so—and the church takes time both to celebrate the ministry of that group and to hold a funeral!

Third, each mission group "undertakes a common mission." What marks a mission group as a *mission* group is that it is not essentially about maintaining the church or the church's programs. It is about enabling the church to move forth into mission into its community. As a part of that mission, it might mean maintaining the church or a program of the church, but that is not its focus. Its focus is always outreach into the community, that city, or "the uttermost parts of the earth."

Now, the mission of each group is distinct from the mission of any other group in that congregation. You might have one group that is focused on children, another on Spanish-speaking ministries, another on adult spiritual formation, another on the church's community-development initiative, another on evangelism, and another on building the power of a local community organization of which that congregation is a part. But what all mission groups in a church have in common is that they are all carrying out a ministry to someone. Each mission group is about ministering in Christ's name to someone in the church, in the community, or in the wider city or world.

To put it another way, a given mission group is responsible for carrying out the Church's ministry in its chosen area of mission, and is dedicated to that task by the congregation. That mission group is the "keeper of the vision" for that ministry. Although other mission groups or other church entities may share in the carrying out of that mission, they do so under the guidance and authority of this particular mission group.

Fourth, each mission group "builds a strong life together." Each mission group does exist to carry out a specific mission. But it exists for another reason as well—"to build a strong life in Christ together." Each mission group needs to be concerned about the spiritual growth of each member of its group and of the group itself. And why is it important that each group pay attention to its growth in Christ as well as its mission? Simply because you can take people spiritually no further than you yourself have gone! You cannot effectively minister to a pain of the world unless you are also ministering to your own deep pain. A mission group is not a program or a mechanistic structure. It is an organic body, people living in relationship with each other, with their common mission and with God. And if they are not, at least to some degree, right with God, they cannot hope to bring about the full righting of their neighborhood or city!

Therefore, the interior work of a mission group would include a time for Bible study or reading another book together. But this time for spiritual formation should also include prayer for each other, sharing of concerns from the lives of the participants in the mission group, and sharing mission concerns.

In building a life together of mutual support and accountability, in growing together in our Christian faith, and in carrying out that ministry together to which we as individuals feel particularly called, we should grow in our commitment to Jesus Christ, in our empowerment by the Holy Spirit, and in becoming stronger disciples who are carrying out God's call to us to be his Church in the world.

Organizing Between a Congregation's Mission Groups

In operating its ministry groups since 1998, the governing body of LaVerne Heights Church came to realize that it was important for there to be coordination between the ministry groups. Precisely because people felt called to their particular mission and ministry group, the Session discovered that the benefit of ministry groups was the high level of commitment and conviction on the part of its members. But a concomitant problem was that a leader or group could very easily lose a sense of relationship and balance with the other groups. It was inevitable that each group would push its own agenda. The LVHPC Session resolved this difficulty by creating a coordinating body made up of the moderators of each ministry group—the Moderators Council—and by creating a coordinating position that sometimes was a paid staff position and at other times a volunteer position filled by one or two church members. Let's look briefly at each.

The Moderators Council. The LVHPC Session determined in 2005 to have the moderators of all the church's mission groups meet together quarterly to coordinate efforts and to make common plans. The Session assigned to the staff person for ministry groups the responsibility of chairing these meetings, and to report to the Session the actions generated by these meetings (see below). After nearly five years of this informal operation, the moderators found that this structure was very helpful, and thus recommended to the Session the continuance of these working relationships, which was approved by the Session.

The tasks of the Council are twofold. First, it is responsible for providing opportunity for moderators to share with each other what is happening in their respective ministry groups (so that all can stay informed about the work of all), to rejoice together around victories, and to reflect together about identified issues and problems.

Second, it created the means for the planning of common activities and events that the Council perceives as strengthening the work, life, and witness of the ministry groups (such as an Alternative Christmas Fair, training events, and opportunities to share the work of individual groups with the congregation). The tasks description of the LVHPC Moderators Council is found in Appendix III-1.

The Coordinator for Ministry Groups: Since 2005, there has been at least one person either employed by LVHPC or a volunteer, who provided oversight and direction to the church's ministry group effort. Whether staff or volunteer, this person has always been directly accountable to the senior pastor of the church as his/her supervisor and to the Session for policy purposes. Besides moderating the quarterly meetings of the Moderators Council, the coordinator has made sure that common tasks are performed (such as the preparation by each ministry group of an annual self-evaluation of their work and the setting of new goals and budget requests), that the congregation is kept well informed on the work of their ministry groups, and to provide support, counsel, and when needed, intervention in the work of each group. The tasks description of the LVHPC Coordinator for Ministry Group is found in Appendix III-2.

How to Get A Mission Group Started

How would a person who feels called to a mission find out if there are others in the congregation who also feel so called? And how would they organize themselves into a mission group? Here is the process that I would suggest:

Issue a Call to Mission. An individual or group of church members might become convicted about or feel called toward a particular human need, and sense that God is calling them to issue a call to mission. The pastor would be approached by this person or group, the call to mission would be shared with the pastor, and arrangements would be made for this individual or group to share this call with the congregation.

If, after the call has been shared in worship or in a public gathering, a minimum of three people would have responded to that call, this is an indication that the congregation has sufficient appetite to undertake this mission. Thus, the mission group would have passed its first step in becoming organized. Less than a three-person response would indicate a lack of congregational appetite in this proposal.

Create A Mission Proposal. The people who had responded to that call would meet together, and at that meeting (or as many subsequent meetings as might be necessary to complete this step), they would do the following:

1. The whole group talks about becoming a mission group and would agree to build a life together and seek to carry out their mission;
2. The whole group formulates a tentative mission statement that would explain the mission concern that had brought them together;
3. The group selects, from their midst, people to play the following roles, necessary to keep a mission group operating:

   Moderator: Responsible for managing the group, checking on the maintenance of the group disciplines, chairing the group in the making of decisions, and representing the group before the church's governing body, congregation and at the Moderators Council;

Spiritual Director: Responsible for leading the Bible studies or book study of the group, seeing that individual nurturing was taking place, coordinating the nurture ministry of the group, and seeing that the worship of God occurs in the group;

Mission Director: Responsible for providing leadership to and supervising the work of the mission group in regards to its mission;

Treasurer: Responsible to maintain any necessary records of both fundraising and the distribution of those funds in a way that was agreeable with the church's governing body

4. Out of all the work done in #2 above, the nascent mission group would create a mission proposal for the church's governing body. This proposal should include the tentative mission statement of the group, a list of those who have indicated their desire to be a part of this group, a list of the selected leaders of the group (moderator, spiritual director, mission director, treasurer), and its request that the governing body give initial approval to this proposed mission group and its mission. The group would then submit that proposal to the governing body.

Receive Initial Validation. Having accomplished the above, the group would present its mission proposal to the board, along with its request for validation. Having satisfied themselves that all of the above steps have been taken and that the mission is a valid call for this church, the governing board would grant initial validation to the group and would constitute it as a mission group of that church. The new mission group would then take the following steps in the formation of their group's interior life and in their mission development.

How to Develop the Interior Life of the Group:

No mission group will simply automatically develop a nurturing interior life. It must be intentionally nurtured, if it is to happen at all. The process I have discovered that seems to work the best is to set the parameters of the exercise of that group's interior life, and to set those parameters at the very first meeting of the group after it has been approved by the congregation's governing body. So, at that first meeting, the group would begin the development of their interior life by taking the following steps:

Establish the Schedule. Each mission group should determine how often it would meet. I have discovered that the timing that best sustains a group's mission effort is to meet once each month. Therefore, at its first meeting, the frequency, day, and time of these meetings should be decided upon.

I suggest that a typical meeting schedule should include about 40 minutes for Bible study or book study, about 10 minutes for prayer and worship together (including prayer for the group's mission), and about 10 minutes for sharing both personal and mission concerns and for individual and group prayer. But each mission group needs to determine for itself the schedule that will work best for them in their building of their interior life.

Establish the Disciplines. Each mission group should decide whether it wanted to hold each member of the group accountable to the exercise of specific disciplines. Following are some examples of conceivable disciplines:

a. To faithfully attend each meeting of the mission group;
b. To participate in the planning and implementation of the mission of the group;
c. To participate in the Bible study, sharing, worship, and prayer life of the group;
d. To pray weekly for the other members of the group;
e. To spend personal time daily in Bible reading and prayer.

Begin. Having done the above, the mission group would then begin their regular meetings and thus begin the building of a life together.

How to Develop the Mission of the Group:

After the mission group has begun its regular meetings, it would start work on planning and carrying out the mission for which the group had been created in the first place. This could be accomplished by taking the following steps:

Developing the mission proposal. It is important that the mission group both understand the people and condition to which they would seek to minister, and decide what they intend to do to minister in regard to those people. Consequently, it should plan to spend about 50 minutes of each meeting, *in addition to the interior life activities,* in developing this mission proposal. In order to understand the problems and how they should minister, the following steps for preparing the mission proposal are suggested:

a. Research the problem. Find out all you can about the need or issue, including the causes of the problem and what experts think are the appropriate steps to be taken to deal substantively with this problem. Statistical research can be done, but nothing beats actually talking to the people and discovering what they perceive are their problems, joys, and challenges.

b. Decide what the mission group wants to do about these challenges. Decide how long you want to initially work on the project and then formulate goals which you honestly think you can accomplish in that period of time (a goal is the end toward which the group's effort is directed).

c. Determine the objectives you want to achieve in the first year of work of your group, and the strategies or program you will need to implement to meet those objectives (an objective is a strategic step that needs to be achieved in order to move toward the accomplishing of a goal). Figure out the steps you will have to take to get the strategy or program started. Figure out the tasks you will have to assume to keep the program functioning.

d. Decide how you will evaluate the program when you have reached the end of the period the program is to run (or if it's a continuing effort, when will be the dates when you temporarily stop and evaluate how the work is going). How will you tell whether you reached the goals you set, and whether the program was really effective? (See the section on evaluation below)

e. Develop a start-up budget and operating budget for any new mission, or an operating budget for any continuing ministry. Indicate expected sources of income and the plans for raising the same.

f. Write up a mission proposal, including "a" through "e" above.

Receive Final Validation. If the permission to proceed given to your group by the congregation's governing body requires you to report back for final approval, then present this mission proposal and plan of action, and present a report on their progress in developing a continuing interior life within the mission group. If the governing body is satisfied with the proposal and report, final validation can be given and the group becomes a full-fledged functioning mission group of your church.

Mission Begins. The mission group would now begin implementing its project according to the guidelines of the project proposal. If there is a coordinating moderator's council of the church's mission groups, then this group's moderator would become a part of that council.

On Maintaining a Mission Group

Once final validation has been received and the actual work of mission has begun, the mission group will need to assume the task of sustaining itself. This sustenance seems to cut in four directions.

The Offices Certain tasks must continue to be implemented in order for a mission group to remain vibrant and strong. Those tasks can probably best be carried out by having each individual in the mission group perform a specific office (see I Corinthians 12:4–11), according to how they feel called. As we pointed out earlier in this chapter, the offices we feel are minimal to the maintenance of any mission group are:

Moderator:	leadership of the group, including maintaining its disciplines;
Spiritual Director:	responsible for the study and nurturing life of the group, as well as its worship;
Mission Director:	responsible for coordinating the mission project of the group.
Treasurer:	responsible for managing the financial affairs and bookkeeping of the group.
Ministers:	everyone in the group when each is involved in the work of the mission project.

The Balance of the Group's Interior Life and Mission Thrust. There will always be a temptation for the mission group to become unbalanced, either placing too much attention on its mission project or stressing its interior life to the exclusion to its mission. To maintain this balance month by month, we would recommend the following:

a. Always be sure to maintain your discipline of regularly scheduled meetings;

b. Maintain the disciplines of the group as developed in the section entitled, "How to Develop the Interior Life of the Group";

c. Be sure that at each meeting, time is spent in study, prayer, and in sharing together from one another's lives;

d. Be sure that at each of these meetings, time is spent sharing concerns about the mission project and people's work in it, making plans for the exercise of that mission and praying for those concerns as well;

e. Regularly evaluate how closely the mission project is following the project proposal, including whether the actual work of the project is getting done on the schedule set down in the proposal (are you actually doing what you said you would do when you said it would be done?).

Group Accountability. A mission group will be effective only to the degree that its members are accountable to each other. Through the disciplines and the group process, each individual should be encouraged and supported to maintain the commitments s/he made in joining the mission group. Through the evaluation process presented in the mission proposal, the entire group should feel accountable to the church's governing body to fulfill what it said it intended to do, as well.

Evaluation

Now we come to the hated "E" word! But evaluation is absolutely necessary to maintain the integrity and effectiveness of the group. A people unwilling to honestly evaluate their work and correct their mistakes are destined to repeat those mistakes over and over again. And that, in turn, will slowly (or maybe not so slowly) move the group away from the accomplishment of their vision. So, what is the most painless and yet most responsible way to evaluate a mission group's work?

At least once each year, each mission group should prepare an evaluation of its life and work. That evaluation (and requests for the coming year) should be submitted to the congregation's governing body; otherwise, there is no accountability. The evaluation done by each mission group could be coordinated through the Moderators' Council.

There are several reasons for doing this evaluation. First, it is to keep the governing body abreast of the work and recent developments in each mission group and is to enable that body to evaluate both intent and performance. Second, it is to provide that discipline to the mission groups that cause them to be accountable to themselves and each other, and to evaluate their own progress or regress as individual groups. Third, it can assist the governing body in drawing up a realistic budget for a new year. And fourth, it can create common expectations on the part of the governing body and each mission group as to the intentions of that mission group for its next operational year. An example of an evaluation design, and budget and goal development for the ministry groups at LVHPC is contained in Appendix III-3.

On Joining, Leaving and Dissolving a Mission Group

No mission group will exist forever. As it was once born, so each mission group should eventually die. The decision to intentionally die should be done at the completion of a given project, when a mission group would evaluate with the congregation's governing body its work and would decide that it was time to dissolve the group.

Dissolution might occur for one of several reasons: the mission may be completed; the mission will never be completed, but the mission group has made a sufficient contribution to that work; the mission has failed; the people wish to withdraw; interest by the Church in the mission has waned, etc. There is nothing wrong with dissolving a mission group. It is, rather, a natural and inevitable step and should, in time, occur.

When a mission group comes to the end of its time, it is important that a celebration of its life and ministry should be held by its members, alumni, and the church, and it should be honorably retired.

No individual will continue in a group forever. During the lifetime of a mission group, it is also inevitable that individuals will both be entering and leaving that mission group. How should that occur?

Some people will enter the mission group by responding to the initial call of mission. They would enter as stated in the earlier parts of this chapter, participating in the formation of the interior life, the disciplines, and the actual mission project. We would suggest that, after the mission proposal is completed, all of these "initial" members be given the opportunity to permanently join or to withdraw. By exercising this option, the group will enable members to depart gracefully, if the project that evolved might not be in agreement with their vision of that call to which they initially responded.

Each year, each mission group should celebrate the anniversary month of their founding. That month, celebrated annually and publicly, would provide an ideal time for new members to join the group and any present members who so decide to leave the group. Thus, it provides a socially acceptable way for people to both come and go in the mission group and should be recognized as such by the congregation.

At LVHPC, each of our ministry group's anniversaries is celebrated by the congregation at worship in the following four ways:

1. The month before the group's anniversary month, the moderator shares with the members of the ministry group both its upcoming anniversary (so that they can plan for it) and offers to the ministry group's members the option of leaving the group on that anniversary.
2. On its anniversary month, the ministry group has exclusive access to a designated bulletin board in the narthex (lobby) of our church's worship center; there it can post a display of its current ministry.
3. At a given Sunday worship service (jointly determined by the pastor and ministry group moderator), the ministry group shares with the congregation its mission, sounds a call to the congregation for any members or church friends to join the ministry group, and gives recognition to and celebrates the work of those members who are now leaving the group.
4. Following that Sunday worship service, the ministry group then has the right to have a table on the patio for our church's coffee hour and for the remaining Sundays of that month, sharing the work of the group and exploring with people their interest in joining the group. In the light of such exploration, the group would then follow up with church members and friends who express an interest in developing a relationship with the group.

In ways like this, a mission group can be open to receiving new members at its anniversary date and to release present members on that same date. No one should be permitted to join a mission group unless s/he agrees beforehand to abide by all the disciplines and regulation which that mission group has developed and which every other member is expected to observe. Those who are leaving the group need to be publicly recognized for their contribution to the group and sent forth to minister elsewhere through that church.

Getting Started

Perhaps, after reading this chapter, you would like to birth one or more mission groups in your congregation. How can you do that? I would suggest following the steps listed below. But before taking the first of these steps, I would recommend that you first talk with your pastor and with the leadership group of your church to get their permission to proceed with the idea. That permission can move in one of two directions. It could be permission for your congregation to have mission groups (thereby automatically giving you permission to proceed with the implementing of that to which you feel called). Or it could be a more limited permission—simply giving you the permission to solely call your desired group into being to test whether this would be a good strategy for the congregation to eventually follow throughout its life and mission.

Having received the permission of the pastor and governing board to proceed with the implementation of this idea, I would then suggest you take the following steps:

1. **Sound your call to the congregation.** This usually happens at a Sunday worship service, when you share your vision with the congregation and ask whether there are others who would like to explore with you the possibility of starting a mission group to carry out its designated mission.
2. **Hold a meeting with people interested in starting this mission group.** Usually, this occurs with a Sunday luncheon meeting which is attended by everyone who would like to explore the formation of this mission group. The idea is discussed, decisions are made, and *if three or more people agree to working together on this mission, the mission group is tentatively formed.*
3. **A representative of your mission group and the pastor bring to the governing board your request for the formation of this group.** This is a tentative formation, gaining the agreement of the board to the idea of your mission group and

acknowledging that there are sufficient people to form that group. Your mission group then selects members to act as the moderator of the mission group, its spiritual director, and its mission director.

4. **The mission group prepares a plan of action for the carrying out of this mission.** This plan includes the long-term goal, the first-year objectives to begin movement toward that goal, implementing strategies, budget, and any intentions to raise money to meet that budget (including your expectations for church support in its annual budget). Once prepared, this report is presented to the governing board.
5. **The board gives final approval to the mission group to carry out its mission** in the name of your congregation. You now meet regularly to implement and administer your mission and to build the common life of your group. Reports of the same are to be submitted monthly to the board. Your mission group has the right to bring action items to any board meeting. And the mission group will be responsible for preparing an annual evaluation of its life and work for the board.

And now, you are off-and-running!

Conclusion

Earlier in this book, we quoted Frederick Buechner as saying, "The place God calls you to is the place where your deep gladness and the world's deep hunger meet."[120] Each Christian is called both to grow in his relationships to God, others and self—in other words, discover one's deep gladness. And each Christian is called to serve Christ in some meaningful way in the world—that is, discover that deep hunger of the world to which that Christian responds.

Most Christians who seek on their own to discover that deep gladness and deep hunger are not successful in their endeavor. They either become focused on seeking to minister to others or become fixated in pursuing their own spirituality. Thus, in the case of the former, they "burn out" and in the latter, "rust out."

---

[120] Buechner, *Wishful Thinking*, 119.

The mission group approach shared in this chapter provides a tested sound and scriptural way to enable an urban congregation and Christian individuals to integrate our inward and outward journeys, and thus discover and live into God's call upon our lives. Mission groups will provide the means by which you may follow the disciplines necessary to build a spiritual life together with others and identify that ministry to some hurting segment of the world to which God calls you. In this way, we will together make our faith live in the city into which we have been called by God. We will be strengthened in our Christian discipleship and we will share the gospel and address human need there. Thus, we will find ourselves both as urban people of the cross and as Christian individuals growing in our commitment to the Lord Jesus Christ and empowered by the Holy Spirit, to the glory of God the Father. And we will likely change our city!

Chapter 14

Reshaping the Systems

One Sunday after worship, when I was pastoring First Presbyterian Church of Pomona, CA (see Chapter 1), a member of our congregation approached me, mad as mad could be! She told me that she had just discovered that a trash recycling company had very quietly bought land just a few blocks from her home and from First Church with the intentions of building a waste collection station in that neighborhood. She had discovered that this proposed project was within a one-mile radius of nine public and parochial schools, would add 610 heavy-duty truck trips per day to the roads, put significant pollution into the area, and would process 1,500 tons of trash per day both from Pomona and eleven other cities. That trash company, she reported, was quietly seeking the permission of the city authorities to approve this station without letting the neighborhood know about it. What should she do about it, she asked?

Well, what could she do about it? I suggested that the place to start was to find out whether there were other members of First Church who would be concerned about this potential danger as well (80% of the congregation lives within a few miles of the church).

So, at the next Sunday worship service, this member shared her concern with the congregation. Were they interested in doing something about this threat to their neighborhood, she asked? To my surprise, more than half of that church's members indicated interest in working on this issue with her. So they got to work, gathering data on the proposal. They confirmed the information she had been given. They further discovered that the city's Environmental Impact Report raised serious health concerns about the project's environmental risks. And when they talked to many of the people living in that neighborhood, they discovered that they, too, were concerned enough to want to do something about it. But what should our church and the community do?

Recognizing this was a much larger issue than they could tackle alone, the church came to the regional broad-based organization of which the church was a member—ICON (Inland Communities Organizing Network, an affiliate of the Industrial Areas Foundation (IAF)—see "Networks" below). Would ICON work with them to organize to stop the station? ICON's response? "Of course, we will work with you on this issue; that's what we're all about!"

ICON is the broad-based/community organization of the IAF within the Inland Empire sub-region of the Los Angeles metropolitan area. The Inland Empire lies immediately east of the Los Angeles metropolis, runs 45 miles from west to east, and has a population of 4,300,000—making it the fourteenth largest city in the United States—if it were a single city rather than the 28 smaller cities that it actually is. ICON is a people's cooperative, made up of institutions that build their power upon their members (e.g., churches, Catholic parishes, synagogues, schools, PTAs, unions, and small businesses). And Pomona's First Presbyterian Church is a member of this cooperative.

What did ICON do about this problem? They organized and trained the people both of First Presbyterian Church and that neighborhood to oppose this measure and mobilized the other ICON member institutions throughout the Pomona Valley to accompany them in that opposition. In less than six months, they got over 3,000 letters written to the Pomona Planning Commission. They held three major rallies with hundreds registering their opposition, and between 388 and 428 people attended the three Pomona Planning Commission hearings. Faced with such community protest, the Planning Commission voted to reject the request of the company.

But the matter wasn't over yet, because the waste transfer company had the right to appeal this issue to the Pomona City Council. And appeal they did. So what then happened?

The Pomona City Council decided to hear the appeal and to rule on the matter. And that was when the politics really got nasty. We discovered that years before the waste transfer people made the request for approval of the waste transfer station, they had made significant financial contributions to some city council members' re-election campaigns as well as to various community groups. When ICON discovered this, they knew that the Council would likely rule in the company's favor. Knowing they might not win outright, ICON decided instead to see how many concessions they could get. So ICON, First Church, and neighborhood leaders met with the company.

At the hearing, the City Council approved the trash company's request to allow them to build a waste transfer station on that disputed property. But the council also concurred with the demands ICON brought before them and to which the company reluctantly agreed. Those demands included requiring all garbage trucks to meet the highest standards of environmental protection, re-routing those trucks so that none drove by the nine schools in that community, reducing the number of cities using the station to just one—Pomona itself, and the employment of an environmental officer by the city who would supervise the implementation of a "Clean and Green" campaign. Therefore, by this agreement, the trash company got their waste transfer station, but the neighborhood was protected from the environmental and traffic hazards that the station would otherwise had brought into that neighborhood. Thus, both sides won!

But that didn't end First Church's and ICON's commitment to change this situation. Over the next three years, ICON, First Church, and others wrote a new waste and recycling ordinance, got the city to conduct a comprehensive inspection of all the waste and recycling facilities in the city, got the City Council to approve the ordinance and to ban the development of any further waste and recycling businesses. This is how a small church and a people's cooperative can work to bring about justice in the systems of a city!

What Does It Mean to "Do Justice"?

The prophet Micah defined authentic relation as being "to do justice, to love each other tenderly, and to walk humbly with your God" (Micah 6:8, my translation). This is perhaps the single clearest biblical statement of what it means to "do Torah"—to obey the Law of Moses. "Loving each other tenderly" and "walking humbly with God" are clearly self explanatory. But what does it mean to "do justice"?

The Torah defines three ways of "doing justice." And the remainder of the Old Testament and of New Testament ethics concurs with those three ways. Let's look briefly at them.

First, ***service*** is a key way that God's people are to "do justice." This element of working for justice focuses upon the direct provision of human services to people, such as feeding the hungry or clothing the naked. So food pantries and clothing distribution centers and medical care clinics fall into this category. The provision of services is the most obvious and the most numerous of the ways that the church does justice toward others.

The provision of services is a strong emphasis in scripture. For example, in the Torah, each Israelite family is commanded, during their celebration of the annual Feast of the First Fruits. In other words, every Israelite family was expected to set aside from their earnings for a given year 10% of their income which they, in turn, were to give to the most vulnerable people in their village or city—the orphan and widow (Israel's poorest of the poor), resident aliens from other countries, and religious leaders who had no means of support (the Levites). This was a primary way that the people of Israel were to fight poverty in their community. Each family was to directly share a designated portion of their wealth (the tithe) with the most vulnerable people of their city or village. In this way, all would be adequately cared for, and poverty would take on a human face—specific people known to specific families for which each family had assumed responsibility. This provision of service was simply seen as an expected duty of every Israelite family—no questions asked and no exceptions made!

Likewise, when 5,000 men (besides women and children) gathered to be taught and healed by Jesus, and he observed that the day was long spent and the people were hungry and no food close at hand, he challenged his disciples "You give them something to eat." They responded, "We have nothing here but five loaves and two fish." The scripture then says,

> And Jesus said, "Bring them here to me." Then he ordered the crowds to sit down on the grass. Taking the five loaves and the two fish, he looked up to heaven, and blessed and broke the loaves, and gave them to the disciples, and the disciples gave them to the crowds. And all ate and were filled; and they took up what was left over of the broken pieces, twelve baskets full (Matt. 14:16–20).

It is clear from this story that Matthew did not intend it to stand alone. It was meant to resonate with the Jewish reader's recognition that justice came for Israel at a desert Mount Sinai where the Law was given, the nation of Israel was born, and the people fed with manna and quail (Exod. 16:1–36). It reminded them of the comparable miracle enacted in the feeding of the people in the wilderness when they faced certain starvation. And Jesus's miracle reminded them that the celebration of the Festival of

First Fruits was first created by Israel while they were still in the wilderness to remind them that they had once been slaves in Egypt and that, consequently, they needed to care for those who were widows, orphans, aliens, and Levites in their midst.

But it is also particularly worthy to note the precise words Matthew used to describe Jesus's feeding of the 5,000. Jesus "took" (that is, lifted up) the bread, "blessed" it, "broke" it, and "gave it" to the people through his disciples. This telling about this miracle is repeated in each of the four gospels (Matt. 14:13–21; Mark 6:30-44; Luke 9:10-17; John 6:1–15)—signaling its importance. Further, the very same words—"took," "blessed," "broke," "gave"—is used for Jesus's feeding of the disciples at another banquet—the Passover meal before his death when he instituted the sacrament of the Lord's Supper (Matt. 26:26–28; Mark 14:22–24; Luke 22:19). Finally, the very same words are used in Luke when Jesus ate with the two disciples at the inn in Emmaus after his resurrection (Luke 24:30-31) and in John when the disciples ate breakfast with the resurrected Jesus on the shore by the Sea of Galilee (John 21:9–14). Coincidence? I don't think so, for these are all sacramental moments of a generous Savior serving his "flock."

An essential message that is given in scripture regarding the "doing of justice," therefore, is that such "doing" includes the generosity of God's people, being willing to serve those in need —whether they deserve it or not!

How does the doing of service work out in the life and ministry of the church? A legitimate and necessary part of both the church and its members doing the work of justice is that of providing services. Jesus declared, "I was hungry and you gave me food; I was thirsty and you gave me something to drink. I was a stranger and you welcomed me; I was naked and you gave me clothing. I was sick and you took care of me; I was in prison and you visited me." And when asked when we did these things, Jesus replies, "Truly I tell you, just as you did it to one of the least of these, you did it to me" (Matt. 25:35–40). The church and many of us in the church are called by God to the providing of ministries of mercy. And it is in such provision, that we are doing justice for Christ and his kingdom!

But there is a second way that the Torah and the Bible teach that God's people are to do justice.

Second, ***self-reliance*** is also an essential way that God's people are to "do justice." Justice is not completed by giving a person a fish. Justice must also include teaching him to fish, so that he can feed himself. Both the Law of Moses and the Bible as a whole teaches that, whereas service is essential and strategic, it is not sufficient. Something more is needed. And that something more is "self-reliance."

One of the most beautiful stories in scripture is the story of Ruth—the Moabite widow who returns from the country of Moab with her elderly mother-in-law, Naomi, back to Israel to seek to survive in the homeland of the Hebrews. There, she meets and marries Naomi's "kinsman," Boaz, and thus becomes the great-grandmother of King David—one of Israel's most important leaders.

Destitute and weak from starvation, Ruth tells Naomi what she will do to find food for them. "Let me go to the field (of Boaz) and glean among the ears of grain" (Ruth 2:2). Naomi gives Ruth permission, and the younger woman goes to the fields owned by Boaz, and there gathers the grain at the corners of the field that had not been harvested. She then picks that grain to make meal for Naomi and herself. Boaz notices her, and instructs his servants to leave behind plenty of grain, to supply Ruth with water, and to make her work as comfortable as possible. Of course, from this comes a lovely romance, ending up in Ruth's marriage to Boaz and the salvation of Naomi's family.

What is particularly significant about this story, however, is the assumption of its author (and of Boaz) that the corners of the field should not be gleaned, but should rather be left for the likes of such poor people as Ruth, so that they might glean it instead, and thus have enough to eat. Where did Boaz get this idea that this was the appropriate thing to do?

Boaz got this idea from his reading of the Torah! Leviticus 23:22 says, "When you reap the harvest of your land, you shall not reap to the very edges of your field, or gather the gleanings of your harvest; you shall leave them for the poor and for the alien. I am the Lord your God" (Lev. 23:22, cf. Lev. 19:9–10, Deut. 24:19–20). Further, Deut. 24:21–22 declares, "When you gather the grapes of your vineyard, do not glean what is left; it shall be for the alien, the orphan, and the widow. Remember that you were a slave in the land of Egypt; therefore I am commanding you to do this."

Boaz was simply obeying the Law of Moses. He was not being particularly generous—just doing what was expected of any good Jew! But what is particularly significant in this scripture passage is its implied suggestion that it is not simply the responsibility of the farmer and the husbandman to leave some of his grain or grapes for the poor. It was also the responsibility of the poor to glean their own grain and to pick their own grapes. That is, the Law was devised to provide opportunity for people to help themselves—but if they were to be helped, it required their action as well as the action of others. Something was not simply being given to them. They were expected to work for their provisions. They were to harvest that grain or grapes, and then use them for their and their family's benefit. That's why Boaz instructed his field hands not only to leave some gleanings behind, but also to supply water and a place to rest for Ruth. The Torah expected self-reliance on the part of the poor and alien by accepting responsibility for themselves.

The same concept is picked up in the Gospels of the New Testament. Whereas in some miracles, Jesus required nothing of the one receiving the intervention, in other miracle stories, the one being healed was expected to take action as part of the healing process. Thus, Jesus frequently said to people, "Your faith has made you whole" (e.g., Matt. 9:22; Mark 10:52; Luke 17:19). In other words, it wasn't Jesus that made them whole but their faith—and Jesus acted as a conduit for that faith! Likewise, at the wedding at Cana, the servants had to pour forth the water for it to become wine (John 2:7–8), and the beggar at the Pool of Siloam had to bathe his eyes in that pool after Jesus smeared mud on his face in order to be able to see (John 9:11). And, most intriguing, sometimes another person or persons had to do something in order for still another to be healed. Thus, it was Jairus's insistence that Jesus come raise his daughter from the dead that led to her resuscitation (Luke 8:40-42, 49–56). And when Jesus raised Lazarus from the dead, he instructed the people present, "Unbind him, and let him go" (John 11:44). Thus, the people played a strategic part in the raising of Lazarus.

The clear message of scripture is that we are to be a part of a miracle. God doesn't often do it alone. He depends upon our participation. An integral part of doing justice is the participation of the person to whom justice is being done. It is not those needing justice that are the problem. It is the work of those needing justice that are a part of the solution.

How, then, does today's urban church enable people to be self-reliant and to join with the church in the rebuilding of their neighborhoods.? Such ministry includes the forming of community development corporations and projects, doing economic development and job placement and training, and the building of affordable housing (sometimes with down payments earned through "sweat equity"). These are all ways the church has moved beyond the provision of services to mobilizing both its own people and the people of the neighborhood to work together to address essential needs of the people.

But what if the problem is far greater than what the provision of services or the calling forth of people's self-reliance can change? You see, it is just to give a person a fish so that he doesn't starve to death. It is even more just to teach him to fish so that he can feed himself. But that is often still not enough. Teaching one to fish (and even supplying the equipment to fish) is not sufficient IF powerful people, institutions, or groups control all the fishing holes and will keep even the small fisherman out. When the very systems of the city are arrayed against the "little guy or gal," then more is required of the church. And that "something more" is the bringing about of systemic change!

Third, ***systemic change*** is, in particular, the most strategic way God's people are to "do justice." The Torah was written in the light of Israel's experience as slaves in Egypt. The political, religious, and economic systems of Egypt were arrayed against the Israelites who lived in their midst. In fact, those systems were so biased against Israel that the Egyptians had forgotten how well those systems had been served by the Israelite Joseph 400 years earlier when he had delivered Egypt from certain famine and had built their wealth. And the power of those systems was personified in the person of the Pharaoh of Egypt.

There is no person today who occupies a comparable role in society as Pharaoh did in Egypt. He was, of course, the ruler of Egypt with almost tyrannical power. But he was also the center of the wealth of Egypt (in essence, even Egyptian freedmen generated wealth for Pharaoh's benefit, because that wealth ultimately belonged to him and he had a right to claim it). And most important of all, he was the living personification of the chief god of the Egyptian pantheon, a god in-and-of-himself. Therefore, in his single person, the Pharaoh represented all the systems that made Egypt, Egypt!

And then one came proclaiming, "Let my people go"—and organized God's people to carry out that proclamation in their leaving of the land.

God's deliverance of Israel from Egypt and its Pharaoh became the definitive experience for Israel as it worked to shape its nation. God had taken Israel out from Egypt. But the entire history of Old Testament Israel was their struggle to take Egypt out of Israel. What sort of society should Israel create for itself? How would they build a society where the king could not be an autocratic ruler, where prophets could stand over against the national political and economic order and call it to accountability, and where wealth was shared rather than hoarded by either one man or a few powerful families? How could Israel live out being a shalom community rather than an unilateral autocracy? Israel did this through its Law of Moses, the Torah, lived out through the celebration of the Sabbath.

Most of today's societies are built around the multiples of ten. But Israelite society was built around the number seven—simply because God had created the heavens and the earth "in seven days." Thus, Israel regulated its life together around the Sabbath Day (one day of rest, worship, and family enjoyment every seven days), the Sabbath Week (seven festivals seven weeks apart), the Sabbath Month (the Rosh Hashanah/Yom Kippur/Sukkot celebration), the Sabbatical Year (celebrated once every seven years), and Jubilee (the super-Sabbatical Year observed once every seven Sabbatical years). All of these calendar-forming events were designed to remind Israel of its origins, worship and give thanks to God together, and to manage the economy![121]

The celebration of the Sabbatical Year was to ***repair*** wealth distribution; it was a mid-course correction of economic practice. The purpose of the Jubilee was to ***redistribute*** wealth; it was a highly intentional legislative reversal of fortune!

At each Sabbatical Year, each Jewish family, from king to peasant, was to: (a) allow their farmland to lie fallow (in order to be able to restore itself); (b) forgive the debts of all people who owed you money (and to have your debts also forgiven); and (c) to free all slaves (Deut. 15:1–18). This was an effort to repair the excesses and injustices that might occur over the previous seven years, thus making a "mid-course correction" of the Jewish economy.

The purpose of Jubilee was far more radical (Lev. 25:8–55). This observation was to happen every 49 years, on the assumption that the economy would inevitably, over time, favor the wealthy and powerful at the expense of the peasant and "people of the land." Therefore, Jubilee not only required the fallow land, forgiving of debts, and freeing of slaves that the Sabbatical Year required, it also required the redistribution of

---

[121] For a thorough systemic analysis of Israel's political, economic, and religious systems, celebrations and legislation, see my chapter-by-chapter analysis of Deuteronomy in my book, *Deuteronomy—A Commentary,* The Polis Bible Commentary (Skyforest, CA: Urban Loft Publishers, 2017), especially Ch. 3, "There Shall Be No Poor Among You" and Ch. 4, "On Feasts, Fasts and Funds."

land. Every 49 years, each owner of land had to divest himself of that land and return it to its original family! Thus, it was impossible to inherit land and build wealth down through the generations—because it had to be returned to the family given it by Joshua when Israel first entered the land. So this was an intentional redistribution of wealth, a radical legislated reversal of fortune. No wonder this radical requirement was the law most often ignored (see II Chron. 36:20-21).

Although the Jubilee is most thoroughly presented in Leviticus 25:8–55, its allusions are throughout both the Old and New Testaments, and particularly echoed in the Deuteronomic festivals of Passover (Deut. 16:1–8), First Fruits (16:9–12; 26:1–15), and Booths (16:13–17) (also called "Tabernacles"), and in its legislation of the Sabbatical Year (Deut. 15:1–18).

Thus, the Jubilee was essentially a means to organize the nation and people of Israel to guarantee systemic change in the economy, governance, and religion of that people of God. The Jubilee moved Israel from focusing entirely on providing service to one another (e.g., feeding the hungry) or building the people's self-reliance (e.g., leaving grain for the poor to glean) to that of enabling the people and the people's political, economic, and religious systems to undertake regular, measured, structural systemic change!

It is important to recognize that this commitment to systemic change was not exclusive to the Old Testament, but also appears throughout the New Testament—and most particularly in the life, ministry, death, and resurrection of Jesus Christ! Thus, in his inaugural sermon, Jesus declared his mission as being "to bring good news to the poor. . . . to proclaim release to the captives and recovery of sight to the blind, to let the oppressed go free, and to proclaim the year of the Lord's favor" (Luke 4:18–19). The term, "the year of the Lord's favor," was a synonym for "the year of Jubilee," and mixed with the statement, "to let the oppressed go free" indicated Jesus's commitment to the radical change of Israelite society. Thus, Jesus saw himself as having been sent by God on the mission, not only of serving people ("to bring good news to the poor"), and to teach self-reliance ("let the oppressed go free"), but also to work for systemic change ("proclaim the year of the Lord's favor"—i.e., "It's Jubilee time"!). Jesus was committed to the radical change of Israel and of the world.

But this was not just words proclaimed by Jesus. This was action—the actual work of Jubilee! This is perhaps most clearly presented in Jesus's death and resurrection. St. Paul magnificently articulated the redemptive nature of Jesus's death and resurrection. But redemption does not encompass the entirety of what Jesus accomplished through that act.

Jesus's death and resurrection also was an act designed to invalidate the unjust systems of both Jewish and Roman society and to replace them with a Jubilee world. This was most obviously presented in John 19:31–42.

John tells us that Jesus's death "occurred so that the scripture might be fulfilled, 'None of his bones shall be broken'" (19:36). And again, John states, "They will look on the one whom they have pierced" (19: 37b). The first reference comes from two Hebrew Bible passages—Exodus 12:46 and Psalm 34:20. The first passage is about the Passover Lamb, sacrificed for the sins of the people, stating "You shall not take any of the animal outside the house, and you shall not break any of its bones." Psalm 34:20 is about the Righteous One who receives the afflictions of his people, and whose flesh is eaten as a sacrament or holy ordinance that brings healing to the people.

The second scripture is quoted from Zechariah 12:10. This passage is within the context of the victory of God's people over the "shepherds" of Israel's systems who are only concerned about "devouring the flock of the (people)" in their lust for power and greed. There will be one who will stand against these leaders of Judah, Zechariah declares, and these leaders will dispose of him because of the threat he poses to their power. When they do so, however, "the inhabitants of Jerusalem" will look upon the one "they have pierced, they shall mourn for him, as one mourns for an only child, and weep bitterly over him, as one weeps over a firstborn" (Zech. 12:10b).

What John does here, therefore, is to interpret Jesus's death as a sacrifice and liberation of humanity, an act of atonement (the Pascal Lamb). And he places the blame for his death on the leaders of Israel's systems and the Romans (who did the "piercing"—John 19:34). They conspired together to rid the nation of the man whose death would become redemptive and liberating to the people oppressed by those systems. And then, in the resurrection stories, not only of the Gospel of John but of Matthew, Mark, and Luke as well, these evangelists demonstrate that the world government that believed itself invincible, and demonstrated the same through the crucifixion of its worst criminals, could not "keep a good man down." Even one executed by hanging on a cross could rise from the dead, and in doing so, demonstrate that Rome did not have the power of life and death over him or over any of his followers. The Christians had become free of the intimidation of either Rome or Israel's leaders. And, therefore, they could freely work for the liberation of any system so that it might be just, caring, and godly, particularly for the benefit of the poor, powerless, and marginalized. Neither Rome nor Israel's leaders—nor any other power (or Power)—could intimidate them!

In other words, John is saying that the political, economic, and religious systems of Judah and Rome, in ridding themselves of the man who was such a threat to them, set into motion a movement that would remain a "thorn in their side" until both structures had been overthrown and removed from the world. They had set into motion the events that would ultimately destroy them when they sought to destroy Jesus!

Service, Self-reliance, and Systemic Change

What does it mean to "do justice"? The scripture lays out three essential means for working for justice in the city: service, ministries that build self-reliance, and working for systemic change. We have reviewed all three above. I would particularly want to point out, however, that one doesn't get to choose between the three. If we are truly to make a difference in the city for Christ and His Kingdom, we can't take the least controversial or the most popular means and build our calling and ministry around that means. We don't get to choose! I would contend that EVERY legitimate Christian ministry in the city must—at times—provide service to those who are hurting. Every such ministry must build self-reliance among those who have been made powerless, are poor, or are marginalized. And every ministry must, if it is to be faithful to the call of the people of God, stand up against the "principalities and powers" and work for radical change within that city's political, economic, and values-sustaining (i.e., "religious") systems—whether it be the city council, a major industry, or the board of education. If you are not so engaged, then you are simply not being faithful to the gospel!

It is intriguing, when one examines the ministry (mission) groups of LaVerne Heights Church presented in Chapter 12, that all of these groups fall into at least one of these three means. Thus, the work of service is the focus of LVHPC's Connect, Dorcas, and Homelessness Ministry Groups; the building of self-reliance is the primary objective of that church's Missions, Pomona Hope, and Providence Children's Home groups; and the working for systemic change in either the Los Angeles metropolitan area or the United States is the work of that church's Creation Care and ICON (Inland

Communities Organizing Network) ministry groups. That fact, to my mind, indicates a church well balanced in its outreach to its city, region, and the world.

Service, self-reliance, systemic change—these three are the essential ways that both a Christian's and a church's call is acted out in the world. It doesn't require much imagination to perceive how to serve people or even to help build their self-reliance. But the church can be rather unimaginative and not very proactive in working for systemic change. So let us now focus the remainder of this chapter on the effective and successful implementation of systemic change. How can called Christians in a called church truly transform the political, economic, values-setting, as well as religious culture of its city?

Making Systemic Change Happen

If a church or laypeople within a church feel called to working for systemic change, how can they live out such a call? I have found that, by far, the most effective way to carry out such a call is through involvement in community or broad-based organizing. But what is community organizing?

What is Community Organizing?

This is community organizing:

The Ramona neighborhood in the Inland Empire of southern California is a "no-man's land." It is an unincorporated area of 41 blocks cut off from the rest of San Bernardino County by the cities of Montclair and Pomona that surround this neighborhood with industry. Because it is "out of sight" of the rest of the county, it neither gets the attention it needs nor its fair share of county services. Its occupants are primarily poor and working class Hispanic people, most of whom do not speak English. It has only three public streetlights for its 41 blocks, few sidewalks, and pot-holed, deteriorating streets. Consequently, children on their way to the nearby Ramona Elementary School are forced to walk down the middle of trash-strewn and broken-up streets, seeking to avoid potholes and puddles of standing water.

The Inland Communities Organizing Network (ICON), to which my church, First Church-Pomona and other congregations and peoples-institutions belong, is working among the mothers of this neighborhood. These women have organized themselves to successfully demand from the county both "no parking" signs and sheriff policing. And those parents and ICON are now negotiating with the regional power company to bring more street lighting into the neighborhood.

This is community organizing:

"Beginning in 1983, . . . East Brooklyn Congregations (EBC: a broad-based community organization of 24 churches and community groups) broke ground on the first of thousands of affordable Nehemiah homes that would be built in Brooklyn and the South Bronx. . . . Today, EBC still continues to build affordable homes and apartments in the Spring Creek section of East New York. All across Brownsville and East New York, more than 3,500 Nehemiah homes have been built to provide decent and affordable housing to African-American and Hispanic buyers for decades. Another 1,000 similar homes were also built in the South Bronx. More than 1,200 affordable apartments have been built or renovated." The work of EBC and its partner organizations has added over the past 35 years about 300,000 homes and apartments for people who would otherwise be unable to purchase housing in New York City."[122]

This is community organizing:

"Organizing refocused us as a congregation. We felt we were thrashing about with no clear understanding of what we should be about. Our involvement in ICON organizing provides us ways to build our relationships with each other in our congregation, spending significant time reflecting with each other, and bringing us to the realization that we are actually quite committed to our city. The result of such sharing together was our addressing those concerns most urgent to us: crime in our church neighborhood, safety for us and our neighbors, the creation of a healthy environment in which to live, workforce development, and improving public education for our children. Our biggest surprise was to discover that such involvement 'outside our church' richly enhanced our worship and life together 'inside our church,' as we came to an increasing clear understanding of who we are called by God to be."[123]

This is community organizing:

A congregation that was a member institution in a citywide community organization was having a difficult time in building its leadership. Most people in the congregation were willing to help but intimidated with the thought of providing leadership. So members of that congregation's organizing core team decided to offer a

---

[122] Rev. David Brawley and Father Francis Skelly, "Turning Vacant Lots into Affordable Housing" press release. Retrieved from the IAF website, www.industrialareasfoundation.com.

[123] Testimony from a person associated with First Presbyterian Church of Pomona. Used by permission.

course for selected church members in leadership development. After receiving permission of the church's pastor and its governing board, the core team contracted with the lead organizer of its community organization to teach a leadership development course for those selected church members. She did, and it was immensely successful. The course sought to inspire people with the challenge of assuming leadership and focused on leadership not as some unique charism that only a very few have but rather having relationships with people who will work with that leader ("a leader is a person with followers"). It even taught people how to chair a committee or moderate a meeting, using "Robert's Rules of Order." The course ended up being offered multiple times at that church, and the result was many church members willing to assume leadership roles both within that church and within that community organization.

This is community organizing:

"The most recent affirmation of our organizing efforts came from a member who has been in the congregation for 40 years. It was very clear to him that since our congregation began doing broad-based organizing five years ago, the culture of the congregation has been changing. 'The church is a lot more relational since we started doing this organizing stuff,' he recently said.

What did that church member mean by 'relational'? Most congregations like to say they are friendly—and many truly are. But 'relational' is much more than that. Relational means people have a genuine curiosity about other people—a curiosity that asks, 'I wonder what this person's story is? I wonder what he or she finds interesting or needful about faith.' Those kinds of wonderings created a different conversation with new arrivals and long-time pew sitters. Organizing continues to change the culture of our congregation in ways that surprise, challenge, and delight us."[124]

What, then, is community organizing? "Community organization" is the generic term used of organizations built around common principles, values, and strategies that are committed to the building of the power of the people and of their institutions in order to enable them to negotiate on a "level playing field" with the principle political, economic, educational, healthcare, and values-sustaining institutions of a given city, region, state, or nation.

---

[124] Used by permission of Rev. Julie Roberts-Fronk, First Christian Church of Pomona.

A community organization is an instrument of ordinary people and their institutions that is committed to building and using the power of those people in order that they may successfully advocate for their interests and issues. The authentic institutions of the people (as opposed to the political or economic institutions) consist of their religious congregations, unions, social networks, clubs, and community groups. The objective of organizing is to sufficiently impact the political, economic, educational, and social systems of a city or region so that those systems are less likely to focus solely on building the financial and political power of their operators or owners, but instead follow policies that contribute to the building of the quality of life of ordinary people. To the degree that a community organization is successful in accomplishing this objective, to that degree it is truly practicing justice!

All community organizing is built around its "Iron Rule": "Never do for others what they can do for themselves." Effective organizing recognizes that to do something *for* a person often makes them more dependent. Only enabling people to take charge of their own situation builds their power. Therefore, the primary purpose of community organizing is to build the capacity, ability, and willingness of ordinary people to shape their destiny together. The strategy of organizing is used in order to enable the people of a given community to:

- Analyze and understand the issues (perhaps even better than do the systems of power);
- Determine their own solutions;
- Implement the actions to carry out those solutions;
- Evaluate the results;
- Move on to determine and then tackle the next issue facing them as a community.

Thus, in one city, many poor neighborhoods were without street lights. This encouraged crime and kept families isolated from one another. The people organized through their community organization to negotiate with the police and city council, culminating in a public action involving 500 people. The result? The city allotted $1,200,000 to install 5,000 street lights in that city's poorest areas, and crime plummeted!

At its best, community organizing simultaneously accomplishes three things. *First,* it enables the people and their institutions to substantively address the issues with which the people are struggling. *Second,* it requires the political, economic, educational, and social institutions that manage that society to make decisions on behalf of the people that is consonant with the desires of the people. *Third,* it builds the people's confidence in themselves to work together to shape their corporate future, including strengthening their people's institutions.

It is community organizing that leads to transformation of a community because it results in people's attitudes toward themselves being changed. Once people learn how to and experience standing up to both public and private institutions that would otherwise dominate them, they perceive themselves as being powerful and competent. And that results in the government and outside agencies recognizing that the people are a force to be taken seriously. Organizing results in people building respect for themselves, and for the systems developing respect for them as well! This is accomplished by training, equipping, and developing ordinary people into leaders who can both reflect and act powerfully together to build their future as a community. Thus, community organizing is the democratic ideal practiced in everyday life!

The Heart of Organizing: Using the Power of the People

No Christian nor church can hope to substantively impact and change its urban community unless it learns to use power. The word, "power" is a "dirty-word" among many evangelical Christians. Or the word is domesticated by using it only in terms of the work of the Holy Spirit within and among us. But "power" is far more powerful than that! So you can't hope to make any difference in your neighborhood, city, or region unless you learn how to use the people power that is at your disposal.

But what is "power"? What do we mean by this word? Well, my definition of it is really quite simple: "Power is the capacity, ability, and willingness to act." Now look carefully at that definition, and note what it does not say. It does not assign to the word "power" any negative or repugnant connotations. Power is neither good nor bad. It is nothing more than the means to get something done. What makes it good or bad is not the exercise of power itself but the purpose for which that power is exercised. Hitler exercised power to dominate, repress, and even exterminate people. But Jesus used power to build the kingdom of God and to transform human beings. It isn't power that is evil but the motive driving the person or group using that power.

What does it mean to say that power is the "capacity, ability, and willingness" to act? Taking action successfully is the intended consequence of exercising power. You want to achieve a specific result! But why do I use the words, "capacity, ability, and willingness" to condition the successful action? It is because it requires all three of these attributes to bring about an effective action. Let's look at each of these attributes:

- "capacity" is having the resources to act;
- "ability" is the skill to take the action you would like to take;
- "willingness" is the drive to actually do what needs to be done.

You need all three in order to be able to act powerfully—whether you are an individual, a church, or a community group or club. And the objective of any good community organization is to build within you and each of its leaders both their capacity and ability to act in concert together, while motivating their willingness to act. This is the heart of community organizing.

There are only two types of power in the world. There is the power of money, and there is the power of people. The two are often in conflict with each other, because when the power of money and of people is aligned, you will have a dictatorship. It is the power of people that organizing concentrates upon building, because of the two, it is the most powerful and most often leads to justice for even "the least of these."

The power of money is the power, primarily, of institutions. It is funded by money and all that money can buy—whether that's tanks and guns, television advertising time, or political campaigns. The power of money rarely represents the interest of the people. Rather, by its very nature, it represents the priorities of those who possess that money or the means to obtain that money. Consequently, by its very nature, it is power that is exercised unilaterally—power that is exercised from the "top-down," with the chosen few determining what the situation should be for the many below them. It is designed to benefit most of all those who are in control of that power, although those sophisticated in the use of unilateral power know that it is wise to divest one's self of a minimum of that money to make the people below you happy with your investment in them (so that they don't rebel).

The power of people is a different kind of power. It is, by its very nature, relational, because it is essentially concerned about the welfare of (minimally) a designated group of people or (maximumly) all people. Consequently, it is about justice for all (or some), and the calling forth of the capacity, ability, and willingness of its people to take charge of their situation and create a world compatible with their values. It is this power that community organization is essentially concerned about building among its constituency—both within its own organization and in all the member institutions that make up that community organization.

This is not to say that all unilateral power is evil and all relational power is good. Unilateral power can be exercised in ways that deeply care for the well-being of the people subject to it (e.g., a government healthcare policy). And relational power can become very intolerant and manipulative ("I care about only those people who agree with my convictions"). But on the whole, the power of money can most easily become dominating and maintaining of the status quo, and relational power can most easily lead to working for justice and mercy. It is the objective of good community organizing to build the people power of its constituency, and of all the people within the neighborhood, city, or region to which it is committed.

The Principles of Organizing

Organizing takes place through the exercise of distinct principles. Here are some of them:

The World as It Should Be: One cannot bring about profound change in a society unless one is clear about the kind of society toward which one wishes to work. The world as it should be is posited by community organizing as a relational culture practicing a politics of justice, an economics of equitable distribution of wealth so that poverty is eliminated, and an environment of sustainability.

The World as It Is: One also can't bring about change unless one has an accurate, even brutal analysis of society as it currently is. Organizing posits a present world of political, economic, and social systems exercising unilateral power that results in the practice of a politics of oppression, an economics of exploitation and a culture of control that is designed to serve the self-interests of the systems and to maintain them in power.

The Task of Organizing Is to Build Power: The chief objective is for people without power to build and demonstrate their power in such a way that they will be taken seriously by the political, economic, and cultural controllers of power who will choose to enter into good faith negotiations with the people out of their own enlightened self-interest

People Power Is Built on Relationships: Unless confronted to change, economic, political, and cultural power actors will exercise unilateral power (that is, "power over," "power down upon") that is backed up by laws, force exercised through police and the military, economic arrangements and pressures, and cultural norms and conventions that were created by those unilateral power actors to maintain themselves and their heirs in power. The only kind of power that can oppose unilateral power without creating warfare or revolution is relational power, painstakingly built upon the trust created over years of sharing together in the struggle to make life just.

All Organizing Is Reorganizing: The world is already clearly organized by those in power for their advantage; the organizing task of the people through relational power is to reorganize the way power is exercised. Such "reorganizing" goes on constantly because every organizing effort will inevitably seek to serve its own ends to the exclusion of other claims. Therefore, those exercising power must do "actions" not only upon the establishment but also upon themselves and each other.

The Objective Is an Exchange of Power: Any action that is designed to reorganize the status quo results in an exchange of power. That is, those holding unilateral power have something the people exercising relational power want. And those holding relational power want the acquiescence or cooperation of those holding unilateral power. The objective is for each group to get from the other group what each group is seeking. That is the exchange of power. It is redistributing of power because those holding the power recognize that it is in their self-interest to share some of that power.

The Action Is in the Reaction: The objective of any action conducted by the people is to get a reaction from the systems or the people with which they are dealing. It is to place a demand before the systems, each other, or one's self that requires a response. How that person, group, or system reacts and responds determines the next step the organizing effort will take.

Power Precedes Program: Most Christian ministries and secular institutions assume power is built through programming. Nothing is further from the truth. Programming uses up, depletes, and exhausts people. If one carefully builds the power of the people first by organizing them relationally rather than through programming, they will build their own depth that can generate either actions or programs that will be sustained.

Never Do for Others What They Can Do for Themselves: This is called the "Iron Rule" of organizing—the foundational concept upon which organizing is built. The primary objective of organizing is to motivate, equip, and train people to take charge together of their situation, determine what they intend to do about it, and organize themselves to take action and/or to create the actions or programs in order to deal with the systems to get what they want.

Negotiations and Confrontation: The primary tactic of community organizing is negotiation—the art of people and systems reaching a settlement together that achieves the objectives of both, and in which an exchange of power has occurred. However, most business and government targets will not negotiate with the people until they have witnessed a display of power that will motivate their desire to negotiate. Confrontation is a primary tactic for bringing a target to the negotiating table, as are the tactics of agitation, civil disobedience, and demanding accountability.

The Pedagogy of Action and Reflection: The vehicle for learning and for building relational power is the interaction of action and reflection. No action is ever undertaken without considerable reflection beforehand (not just tactical planning, but theoretical reflection on the nature of power as used by the target, the operation, and objectives of a given governmental, educational, or business system, etc.). No action, once undertaken, is complete until a full evaluation of it has occurred so that success can be celebrated and mistakes can be identified and corrected. When a spiral of action and reflection takes place in the organizing effort, every action will become more substantive than the action before it, and every reflection will become more profound and deeper than the reflection before it.

The Task Is Building Leaders: An essential task of organizing is to build leaders who have developed the capacity, ability, and willingness to act and to lead their communities in acting powerfully to bring about the kind of change that will both strengthen the people and serve their development as a human community. All the organizing steps and theories of building relational power are the means by which the leadership capability of the community's people is called forth and they live out in their own life and work the Iron Rule as a people.

Building Community Is the Ultimate Objective: Community is a group of people with a continuing experience, tradition, and history who support and challenge each other to act powerfully, both individually and collectively, to affirm, defend, and advance their values and self-interest. This is the primary purpose of community organizing—to create out of a victimized, marginalized, destructive collection of people a community whose quality of life is such that people find fulfillment and joy in living there. The power of the oppressor must be replaced by a quality of corporate life that is of such superiority to either that of the formerly oppressed or of their oppressors that it brings purpose, direction, joy, and fulfillment to all who experience it. That is the chief end of organizing.[125]

But Isn't It Political?

It's according to what you mean by the word "political." If you mean by "political," engagement in public life—then, yes, organizing is political. If you mean by "political" the pressing of a particular party agenda (like that of the Republican or Democratic parties) or a particular candidate for office, then organizing is decisively not political! To put it another way, no good broad-based organizing is about partisan politics. They never run nor even advocate a particular person or political party for office. Instead, they are an equal-opportunity agitator which seeks to call any elected, appointed, or self-selected leader to accountability—no matter what happens to be his or her particular political position.

Organizing places a primary emphasis on making the systems of any society—its political structure, its business community, its schools, health, and social service institutions—work for the benefit of all the people. Because that is where it places a major emphasis, it is easy for people to believe that organizing is about the expansion of these systems. In reality, it is not about their expansion but their accountability to the people—and their use for the common good (not the good of a selected few). Therefore, organizing follows neither a "liberal" nor a "conservative" agenda but rather its own agenda—that of making the systems work for the good of all!

Community Organizing and Community Development

If you want to really annoy me, use the titles "community organizing" and "community development" interchangeably! They are not interchangeable. They are two very distinct disciplines and must be appreciated as such, if both are to work for the good of the urban poor. So what is the difference between community organizing and community development?

There are four ways humanity can respond to human need. They can provide social services. They can advocate on behalf of those unfortunate. They can undertake community or economic development. Or they organize the people to create their own

---

[125] Much of this material has been taken from my book, *Building A People of Power*, 171–173, and is used by permission.

destiny. In my opinion, community organizing must be the foundation upon which development, advocacy, or social services must be built. If it is not built on an organizing foundation, I believe the work that will be done in any of these fields will be seriously—even fatally—flawed, because it operates on an inadequate conceptual base.

Each of these disciplines is committed, eventually, to the empowerment of the people they serve. At its best, community development and economic development seek to involve the people they are seeking to serve in the deliberative and planning process of development, the choice of projects, the building of strategy, and the implementation of that strategy. Advocacy seeks to stand for the people and to defend them before the "principalities and powers" because the people apparently don't have sufficient power to stand on their own. Social services provide ministries of mercy to the people—food, clothing, shelter, health care, education—in hopes that the people will learn to eventually stand on their own feet.

But all three fields have a serious flaw at the heart of their mobilizing work. That flaw is the assumption that the problem essentially lies with the poor. All three fields assume that these poor people are unable to provide for themselves what they need in order to survive this situation, and therefore an outside agency needs to come in to build up the capacity of the people and make them capable of being competitive in the real world. From the perspective of these three fields, the problem essentially lies with the people.

Community organizing analyzes the situation in a profoundly different way. To any community organizer, the problem doesn't lie with the people. The problem lies with the systems of power in that city and country. The way the political, economic, educational, social, healthcare, cultural, and religious systems of any city are organized, some hold the power and others seek that power or are victims of that power. Those who hold the power have "stacked the deck" to guarantee that the elite remain in power and others exist to serve that power base.

This was most profoundly stated more than a century ago by Frederick Douglass, the escaped African-American slave who had experienced much of his life what he here taught. He wrote:

> Power concedes nothing without a demand. It never did and it never will. Find out just what people will submit to, and you have found the exact amount of injustice and wrong which will be imposed upon them; and these will continue until they are resisted with either words or blows, or with both.

> *The limits of the systems are prescribed by the endurance of those whom they oppress.*[126]

The poor aren't incompetent! They are powerless! That they have survived for thousands of years under the oppression of political, economic, and social tyrants is testimony to their resiliency and their extreme competence in coping. Our task is not so much to teach them how to compete in a world still controlled by those already in control. Nor is our task finally to provide the charity they need to help them struggle to stay alive. The task must be that of working with them to build the significant power they already have at their fingertips but which society has never identified as power—the power of each other—and to develop their skills and capacities to use that power so that the systems realize they must make room for them and take seriously their concerns. Then, in that context of an empowered people, that community can make use of the principles and practices of economic development or community development or even advocacy and social services to help build the power of that community and make it truly powerful in the power equation of that city or state.

Organizing Networks

There are four major organizing networks throughout the United States, and elsewhere in the world. Those networks are (in alphabetical order) DART (Direct Action and Research Training), the Gamaliel Foundation, IAF (the Industrial Areas Foundation), and PICO (People Improving Communities through Organizing). These networks are gatherings of numerous neighborhood, citywide, or regionwide community and broad-based organizations (like ICON, One LA, or EBC, mentioned earlier in this chapter). The networks exist in order to strengthen the capacity of the local "on-the-ground" community organization to do the best job it can in enabling its member institutions and the people to shape their future in each city.

An independent, stand-alone community organization can often do significant work. But it stands alone, without support from other sources, and always faces the threat of co-option by the systems of its city or the danger of irrelevance. The

---

[126] A letter of Frederick Douglass to an associate, written in 1849. Italics mine.

networks, instead, provide to each of their member organizations three crucial advantages.

First, each network provides significant standards both for itself and for its member affiliate organizations. By its nature, it creates an accountability structure. Each network contracts with each of its member affiliates, providing both support and performance and convictional standards. Thus, each affiliate knows what is expected out of them and what to expect from the network. These standards are crucial for maintaining quality control. But each network also is pastoral toward its affiliate, so that if it is unable to maintain the standards expected of it, the network will work with it to correct the situation. So, for example, the local IAF affiliate to which my church belongs, ICON, was struggling to remain viable; the IAF sent to it, on a part-time basis, its most-skilled organizer who spent a year with us working us through that difficult "patch" while helping us rebuild our viability.

Second, each network provides training opportunities to each of its affiliates. These training events include national events, regional and affiliate events, and even training events for each local member institution. Those events cover everything from working on honing organizing strategies and skills to conducting serious biblical, theological, sociological, and political studies led by leading scholars from across the world. Thus, for example, the DART network holds an annual clergy conference, where its clergy gather for strategic planning, depth reflection in their respective theological traditions, and for building deeper relationships with each other.

Third, each network has a large team of trained, experienced organizers, as well as a vehicle to enable the honing of organizers' skills and capacities as they advance in that system. The network can place in each affiliate organization the best and most qualified lead organizer and organizing specialist staff that can best serve that affiliate. Thus, each affiliate is guaranteed getting quality organizers to guide their work and a means for that organizer to be both supported and held to accountability by that network.

There are community organizations that are not an affiliate of one of the four primary networks. But I do not envy them their independence. When I began participating in community organizing as a pastor in 1967, there was simply membership in the IAF or being a part of an independent community organization without any affiliation. Two of the three organizations in which my churches were members were independent. It was not fun! We had no standards to operate by, except for standards we would set ourselves; those standards often proved too exacting (so that we were always failing) or too vague (so we could not measure our weaknesses until they became overwhelming). Training in one of the two community organizations was non-existent, so that we just struggled along. In the other, training was more rigorous, simply because our organizer had come out of the IAF and simply continued to use their training in our organization. But the biggest problem was the "care and feeding" of our organizers (some of whom needed major guidance), because there was no larger network to nurture and discipline them.

The moral of the story is that, if your congregation gets involved in the work of a community organization, be sure that it's an organization that is an affiliate of one of the four major organizing networks. The names, contact information, and a little about each of these networks is listed in Appendix IV of this book.

Organizing and Call

If you personally feel called to dealing with injustice, and/or if your congregation has a call to fighting for the rights of the poor, powerless, or marginalized, community organizing provides the best vehicle for carrying out that call. At its heart, all community and broad-based organizing is committed to systemic change. It is committed, not in mitigating the situation, but permanently and substantively changing it. And it now has nearly three-quarters of a century of experience in bringing about change in some of the most resistant urban environments in the United States—and, indeed, in the world. If you really feel called to the abrogation of injustice, you need to move beyond the provision of social services and mercy ministries, beyond advocacy, and even beyond community and economic development to working for systemic change through the means of community and broad-based organizing. So I would urge you to explore the four networks and the possibility of both getting involved personally and seeking to involve your congregation in such organizing. For nothing else is adequate for the call that God has placed before you!

Getting Started

So, how can you get started in engaging in community and broad-based organizing? There are two ways:

First, if your church is in a large or midsized city in the United States, there is a high likelihood that at least one of the organizing networks has an affiliate in your city. Each of the networks has on its website a full list of all its affiliated organizations. So, with a little bit of research, you can determine whether such a connection exists in your city.

If there is, then—JOIN IT. Check it out. Visit its website. Attend its public meetings. Meet with its lead organizer. Talk with him or her about the work that affiliate is doing in your city; which churches, religious institutions, and community groups belong to it; and what are the issues it is currently organizing around. Then see if there is any appetite at all in your church to explore a possible relationship with that organization. Consider the possibility of creating a mission group in your congregation to act as the core team of that organization, and thus provide the connecting tissue between your church and that community organization. So—make it happen!

Second, if there is no network-affiliated broad-based or community organization in your city, then get it organized. But how do you go about doing that? I would suggest these steps:

1. Study the four networks carefully, and determine the network that you would most like to have affiliated with the local community organization you envision occurring in your city.
2. Contact that network, and learn from them the process they expect a potential affiliate to go through and the conditions that must be met to become an affiliate; also find out if they will provide any help for that organizing process.
3. Have individual meetings with people in your congregation who you think would be interested, and see if they would be willing to explore with you this possibility of developing a local community organization.
4. Visit with pastors and community leaders you know that represent other relational institutions to see if there is an appetite to explore this possibility.
5. Pull together a little team to visit the nearest affiliate of that network, and check out their life together and work. Visiting for a few days, spending time with their lead organizer, and particularly talking with pastors and leaders in that organization will give you some sense of the energy that working with that network and doing grass-roots organizing can generate.

6. Work closely with the network to begin the process of pulling together the local institutions, the people and the money that would allow the network to send an organizing team to your city to work with you and the others to make this effort happen.

All of this may sound somewhat intimidating. But keep in mind that this is the process that has been followed countless times to bring the more than 300 community and broad-based organizations into existence today throughout the United States! If they can do it, you can do it also!

What it all comes down to is this—don't just sit there; make something happen! Whether there is a network affiliate in your city or not, make it happen! Until your city has a viable community or broad-based organization in it, it will be extremely difficult for you to make a systemic difference in your city. And that is what God calls us to be about—to turn our city upside down for Christ and His Kingdom!

Chapter 15

Living Out Vocation

"What are you doing here, Christian?" God's question to Elijah is now God's question to us, as we seek to "live and move and have our being" in that city into which God has called us. Together, in this book, we have reflected upon the city-changing power of called laypeople. Now, I would like to end our visit together by focusing briefly on the three basic themes of this book: the city itself, the church as God's body in the city, and us as God's people created, chosen, and called to the city to be "Christ-ones" there. So let's look at each of these three themes.

The City

The City is a Fascinating Place

I grew up in the (then) third-largest city in the United States—Philadelphia. For me, that growing-up time included its tragedies (such as the death of my father and the necessity faced by my mother of giving up legal claim to my brother and me so that we would become wards of the State of Pennsylvania and assigned to the Girard orphanage). But as I look back on those 18 years of growing up in Philadelphia, I find that most of the incidents I remember all proclaim, "This city is a fascinating place in which a boy can grow to adulthood!" Here are just a few of my memories:

As a little boy required to take summer afternoon naps, lying in my bed looking at the shifting shadows of leafy trees through the sunlight playing on my bedroom wall, I heard the clip-clopping of draft horses' hooves and the sing-song cry of vendors driving their wagons, "Pastries today; lots of fresh rolls, croissants, and muffins"; "watermelons, cantaloupe, fresh strawberries"; "iced fish, snapper, flounder, scallops, and clams."

Running up the great staircase fronting the Philadelphia Art Institute decades before Rocky Balboa did it!

The snowstorm shut down the city, but us boys from Sections 7–12 built a snow fort that withstood the attack of the snowball legions from Sections 1–6, as we won the great snow war!

Eating Philly's famous food like sticky buns, giant pretzels with mustard, bagels and Philadelphia Cream Cheese, scrapple (don't ask), shoo-fly pie, hoagies, and of course, Philly Cheesesteaks!

My brother and I repeatedly pulling our Red Flyer wagon filled with metal cans to the Bandbox Theater to contribute to the war effort (WW II) and getting free passes for four hours of Saturday matinees (cartoons, news reel, the Phantom serials, a cowboy movie, the feature) and coming out with the most marvelous headache!

Having the whole orphanage elementary school invited to a Phillies major league ball game, and getting to meet Robin Roberts, the Phillies ace pitcher!

Spending all day with my brother hiking the Wissahickon Creek Trail (one of its entrances being just a few blocks from our home).

Getting into the cafeteria line at the Automat, with row upon row of goodies in cubicles behind little glass doors, dropping our dime into the appropriate slot, having the door spring open so that I could reach in and take out a big slice of huckleberry pie (you haven't lived if you haven't eaten huckleberry pie!), putting the plate on my tray. and shutting the door—but then waiting to see the mysterious hand come from the other side into the cubicle with another serving of huckleberry pie for the next customer.

Riding all day on the city's public transportation trolley cars, by riding each car to the end of its line and then using your day's pass to hop on another going in a different direction (you see a whole lot of the city that way)!

Standing in awe before the REAL Liberty Bell!

Taking a boat down the Delaware River and passing the city's massive Navy Yard, seeing all the destroyers and battleships, and even an occasion aircraft carrier in port!

Being part of a group of Girard boys meeting President Truman when he visited Girard for its centenary, and giving him a "hum mud" ("hum muds" are giant ginger cookies peculiar to Girard that we either ate or used as money [as in "I'll give you three hum muds for your baseball card of Richie Allen"]).

During our summer vacation, going with my brother to the local drugstore where we would sit at the lunch counter and eat free liverwurst and onion sandwiches (the store owner knew that we were orphans) and then getting to sit cross-legged on the floor in front of the magazine rack and reading the comics.

Standing in the falling snow at midnight after the Christmas Eve service in front of the Market Square Church and singing with the choir, "Silent Night."

Getting my first kiss (from a *girl*, not my Mom)!

Even for a poor boy, the city was an absolutely fascinating playground. And it is fascinating still. From 1987 through 2003, I had the privilege of being a visiting professor on the Philadelphia campus of Eastern University. At least once every year, I got to return "home." And in my free time when I wasn't teaching, guess what I did! I visited family and friends of long ago still living in Philly. I ran up the stairs of the Philadelphia Art Institute again, visited most of the sites of my youth, stood in front of an office building occupying the site where the Market Square Church used to be, and even visited the orphanage where I had grown up and thrilled at the fact that it was still caring for poor boys (and, now girls), preparing them for a productive life when before they were without hope. So don't forget what is fascinating about the city—especially when you come up against its darkness!

The City is an Unforgiving Place

As I think back to growing up in the city as a child and then a youth, I realize that the city was to me a place of wonder. I simply accepted it as my environment. In fact, I assumed that for the vast majority of human beings, a city was everybody's environment (except for the few unlucky ones who had to grow up on a farm)—a place of high adventure and boundless new experiences. I simply was unaware, as a child, of the dark side of the city. Even when my wallet was lifted when I was Christmas shopping as a boy of nine, it did not register upon me that the city can be a most unforgiving place; it was just one evil individual that stole my Christmas money.

In what ways is a city unforgiving? Perhaps the best statement in scripture that describes the dark side of the people and the structures that occupy the city was made by Jesus in his penetrating parable of the rich man and Lazarus (Luke 16:19–31).

In this parable, Jesus tells of a rich man "who was dressed in fine linen and who feasted sumptuously every day," as well as a poor beggar named Lazarus who sat at the rich man's front gate. Jesus is clearly making a contrast between Israel's urban elite and its urban poor. He begins by examining the rich man. He tells the listener that the rich man "dressed in purple and fine linen." These are the clothes, not only of the very rich, but of the nobleman as well. Clothes dyed purple were clothes normally reserved for nobility because the dye was extremely rare and costly. And Egyptian "fine linen" was the most luxurious cloth available in the ancient world. Thus, Jesus is telling his hearers that this man is extremely wealthy, is likely a noble, and is therefore very, very powerful.

But Jesus also makes clear that this rich man's problem is not only his wealth and his power. He is further guilty of the most conspicuous consumption of it as well. Thus, he tells the listener that this man "feasted sumptuously every day." That is, he not only threw banquets for his fellow urban elite. He threw banquets every day for himself and for whoever might grace his table.

By the very way Jesus describes this man, he is making a statement about the wealth and power of the Jewish elite in the city of Jerusalem. He is telling us that the elite control the political, economic, and religious systems of the city and nation—and are using that control to primarily benefit themselves.

Jesus then creates the contrast to this rich man in the person of Lazarus. He tells us that "a poor man named Lazarus" lay at the rich man's gate at the entrance to his estate, was covered with sores, "longed to satisfy his hunger with what fell from the rich man's table" and was subject to the dogs licking his sores. This is as miserable an image of a man that Jesus could possibly draw.

Lazarus is a destitute beggar, part of the "expendables" of Israelite society. The expendables of Israel, made up of orphans and widows, the destitute, beggars, and shepherds were the detritus of the nation, those who had been cast aside by the elite as the inevitable victims of the way that society was organized. They had likely fallen from peasantry into destitution. The lot of Israel's peasants at the time of Jesus was tenuous at best. Because even the most successful farmer, artisan, or merchant would realize only about 12% profit from his or her labor, she or he had no significant savings or wealth behind him/her. Consequently, a single reversal of fortune (such as severe sickness, an economic downturn, or even the wedding of a daughter) could plummet the peasant into the "expendable" class, where he or she would struggle to stay alive. This was what Jesus was telling those who listened to his parable by calling the man a beggar.

Jesus goes on to tell us that Lazarus was at that rich man's gate in order to gather that which might fall from the rich man's table to assuage his hunger. Lazarus is looking for just a few crumbs in order to sustain his life. In Israelite society, there were no napkins at an elegant dinner party. What would be used would be the loaves of bread. At a sumptuous party, one would take a pita-like or tamale-like circle of flatbread, tear it in order to use it as a utensil upon which to scoop up the food (and eat the bread with the food) and reserve a portion of the torn bread upon which to wipe one's hands as one dined. Having wiped one's hands on the bread, one would then toss the used piece onto the floor. Servants would later sweep up all the pieces from around the dining table and would toss it out the door onto the street for the dogs to eat. That was what Lazarus was waiting for—the bread "napkins" to be tossed out the gate and onto the street, so that he could fight the dogs for it.

There are, however, indications in the text that something highly imaginative is about to happen. Jesus names the beggar "Lazarus"—and this beggar is the only primary character in any of Jesus's parables ever given a name. The rich man, on the other hand, is nameless (the name "Dives" given to him was not a name given to him by Jesus; "dives" is simply the Latin for "rich"). The name "Lazarus" means "helped by God" or "God has helped"; although that name seems in stark contrast to his actual life. Perhaps God is about to do something that changes all that.

Both Lazarus and the rich man die. Jesus tells us that the rich man "died and was buried"—that is, he had had a proper funeral, with an adequate time for mourning and likely as ostentatious a send-off as had been his life of conspicuous consumption. Lazarus, on the other hand, "died and was carried away by the angels to the bosom of Abraham." In other words, Lazarus received no proper burial. Given his position in society, his body was likely cast upon the garbage heap of Gahanna outside Jerusalem and burned.

But the story doesn't end there. Lazarus awakens from death to find himself in "the bosom of Abraham." And he finds himself an honored guest in this heavenly place, for he is seated at Abraham's side (vv. 23b, 22). So, not only has Lazarus died and gone to heaven; he is God's most honored guest there! Lazarus had indeed been "helped by God."

But for the rich man, the story is quite different. "In Hades, where he was being tormented, he looked up and saw Abraham far away with Lazarus by his side" (vs. 23). In first century Jewish thought, "Hades" was a place where sinners were sent who had not received just judgment for their sins in their life on earth; it was a place of great pain, judgment, and punishment. The "sins" of this rich man, obviously, had been in wallowing in his wealth and his conspicuous consumption, brought about by his commitment to and benefiting from the very political and economic forces that both made him wealthy and thrust people like Lazarus into grinding poverty. More than that, he had refused to address the social ills of the people (like Lazarus) that had been in his face. Instead, he had chosen to ignore their need rather than to use his money to right the wrong. This was beautifully captured by Jesus when he mentions that the rich man recognizes Lazarus sitting at Abraham's side. From the rich man's perspective, he should be at Abraham's side; yet here was this beggar in the place of honor at the heavenly banquet!

The reaction of the rich man to this scene is intriguing. He commands, "Father Abraham, have mercy on me, and send Lazarus to dip the tip of his finger in water and cool my tongue; for I am in agony in these flames" (vs. 24). Even in death, where society is clearly turned upside down, the rich man can't help but treat Lazarus like a servant. That rich man still saw himself as a privileged elite, free to give orders, and to expect them to be obeyed by the likes of an expendable like Lazarus.

Of course, the rich man gets a rude awakening from Abraham. Abraham explains that in God's kingdom, the ways of the world—even the kosher world of the Torah—are turned upside down. "Remember that during your lifetime you received your good things, and Lazarus in like manner evil things, but now he is comforted here, and you are in agony" (vs. 25). At the very least, this rich man should have extended the compassion of hospitality to the beggar at his gate (cf. Amos 5:12–15), but he could not even do that. Therefore, he is sentenced for penance to Hades, "and between you and us a great chasm has been fixed."

The rich man tries to bargain with Abraham. He uses his family as his bargaining chip. "At least send Lazarus to my five brothers so that he may warn them, so that they will not also come into this place of torment" (vv. 27–28). He still sees Lazarus as his servant. He does not recognize that Lazarus was also his brother, as a fellow human being and as a fellow Jew, as precious to God as was he.

Abraham retorts, "They have Moses and the prophets; they should listen to them. For if they do not listen to Moses and the prophets; . . . neither will they be convinced even if someone rises from the dead" (vv. 29, 31).

The Law and the Prophets, the writings of the Old Testament, the entirety of Torah itself makes clear what is the obligation of every Jew, Abraham responds to the rich man. "He has told you, O mortal, what is good; and what does the Lord require of you but to do justice, to love kindness, and to walk humbly with your God" (Micah 6:8). It's all there—in plain view. God's longing for all of us is to act justly toward each other, to share wealth equitably, to change a society to eliminate an "expendable" class as well as men enslaved by conspicuous consumption, and "to walk humbly with your God." If the powerful, wealthy, and influential in society won't be convinced that they must be centered in working for the common good (including committing their wealth to that purpose), and see that as the very essence of their relationship with God, then even one rising from the dead will not convince them—even if it be Lazarus or Jesus![127]

What this parable so magnificently does is to get to the heart of the essential problem of the city. In essence, the problem is not simply that people treat each other badly. It is that people made wealthy and powerful by the city treat the urban poor badly. And that evil is not simply an individual evil. It is a systemic evil. It is that the city is at the center of the rule of a nation, the creation and distribution of the wealth of that nation, and the articulation and acting out of the values of that nation. And this is all incorporated into the very ways that that city's (and, consequently, that nation's) political, economic, and religious systems function. They function in order to sustain the most powerful and wealthy in their conspicuous consumption and do so by laying the burden to generate that wealth and power upon the backs of the ordinary folk of that city. They are careful to award those ordinary people sufficiently so that the people are seduced into supporting and cooperating with those powerful (out of self-interest). But it is inevitable that there will be Lazarus's created by such a system—those who don't make it. This is what is so dark about the city. And this is where Jesus's parable is of such good news, because it promises us that there will someday be a great reversal when Lazarus will sit in Abraham's bosom and rich men will beg for a drop of water because they neither used their wealth to care for the poor nor sought to build an urban system that would "do justice, love mercy, and walk humbly with God."

---

[127] The writings of William Herzog and Derek Engdahl on this parable have been particularly helpful in contributing to my understanding of its political implications. See William Herzog II, *Parables as Subversive Speech: Jesus as Pedagogue of the Oppressed* (Louisville, KY: Westminster/John Knox Press, 1994), 114–130, and Engdahl, *Chasm*, 129–232.

The Church

The City is the Graveyard of Churches

The perception does not have to be defended that the city is hard on churches! As I argued elsewhere in this book, the Protestant city church has gone through three very clear stages in its interaction with the city—first, as a preaching point (from colonial times to the early twentieth century), then as the programming church (the twentieth century), and now, today, the missional church. Of course, these transitions have not been sudden shifts in ecclesial practice but rather have occurred slowly and over extended periods of time. But the nature of the Protestant church has changed over the decades and centuries in the city (the Roman Catholic and Orthodox Churches have been less marked in their transitions because they are essentially sacerdotal churches focused around the celebration of their sacraments which the faithful continue to believe that they need to receive—and thus are less likely to abandon one congregation for another).

The decline in denominational city churches over the past 50 years has been marked. Even as given churches have shifted from pulpit-centered to programming to missional churches (or not), the decline has continued in almost all denominations. Thus, the loss of church membership in primarily city denominational churches between 1965 and the beginning of the twenty-first century is really quite shocking. Membership and attendance in American Baptist city churches have declined by 6%, the Evangelical Lutheran Church by 10%, the Methodist Church by 25%, the United Church of Christ by 34%, the Episcopal Church by 38%, the Presbyterian Church by 41%, and the Disciples of Christ by 57%.[128]

So what is taking the place of declining city churches? Well, first of all—*nothing!* As our society becomes increasingly secular, fewer and fewer people are affiliating with a church, or even worshipping. So the city itself is becoming increasingly a secular place.

Second, there are church efforts that have appealed to city dwellers, and those efforts are gaining an increasing percentage of the church-going public. These efforts

---

[128] "Where Did All the Presbyterians Go?," *Presbyterians Today* (Louisville, KY: The Presbyterian Church [USA], July/August 2002), 13–14; also see Richard N. Ostling, "The Church Search," *Time*, April 5, 1993, for comparable statistics for the period 1965–1990.

fall into three groupings. There are denominations that are still experiencing growth. There is the phenomenon of the megachurch. And there is the growth of the missional church. We will explore the missional church in the next section. But in this section, let's take a brief look at growing denominations and with the megachurch.

There are denominational churches experiencing growth. Churches that seem to be thriving in the city are primarily sacerdotal, evangelical, or charismatic churches, particularly as cities become increasingly Latino and Asian. The Roman Catholic Church grew by 38% between 1965 and 2000, the Southern Baptist Convention by 48%, the Seventh Day Adventist Church by 142%, the Mormon Church by 162%, and the Assemblies of God by 350%![129] The growth in the Roman Catholic Church is almost entirely caused by the significant increase in the Latino population of the cities. As Latinos move from Latin American countries into US cities, they naturally gravitate toward the church of their youth, their language, and of their mother country. An indicator that this is so is that in the Los Angeles Archdiocese (whose archbishop is a Latino), priests are not placed in parishes unless they speak fluent Spanish! Where growth has occurred in Assemblies of God, Seventh Day Adventist, and Southern Baptist churches, it seems to be caused by their embrace of missional church values. We will explore that phenomenon in the section below, where we will examine the missional church as emerging church.

Growth occurs through megachurches. All of us are familiar with the megachurch phenomenon. This is the giant congregation, usually built around a highly dynamic pastor-preacher. Mostly found in cities or in close-in suburbs to cities, the megachurch includes large campuses (often with sanctuaries or auditoriums seating 2,000 to 10,000 people, and equipped with TV equipment and giant screens), packed sanctuaries and parking lots, and a plethora of programs and activities. Worship is not often liturgical but rather is more a performance that the congregation watches, akin to a pop concert. The larger the city, the more megachurches it has. But the common reality is that there are very few megachurches in a given city commensurate with the city's population. From my perspective, this gives a megachurch an apparent measurement of success that it really doesn't deserve. Let me explain.

---

[129] "Where?," Presbyterians Today, 13–14.

In the city of Los Angeles, there are very few megachurches that are affiliated with a denomination—and when they are, they are usually the anchor church of that denomination (for example, the seat of the local bishop of that denomination). Most of the few true megachurches in or near Los Angeles are independent churches; that is, they do not belong to a denomination, but are a "stand-alone" church. Most of them have weekly Sunday attendance between 2,000 and 10,000—an apparently-impressive gathering!

But consider the context. In the city of Los Angeles, there are (for example) 36 Presbyterian USA churches.[130] Between all 36 Presbyterian churches, they have a combined attendance on any given Sunday of 10,000. So, if all the Presbyterian churches in Los Angeles were somehow merged into one church and every Presbyterian joined that church, its Sunday attendance would be over 10,000. Voila! A Presbyterian megachurch! Thus, when we compare an independent megachurch with a denominational church, we are actually comparing apples with oranges. The success of the megachurch is more apparent than real when you are thinking in terms of reaching an entire city for Christ and His Kingdom!

Because the megachurch most often depends upon the ministry of its dynamic pastor, it is in reality a very fragile institution. Simply consider how quickly the "Crystal Cathedral" in Garden Grove, CA, collapsed after the retirement and death of its famed senior pastor, Dr. Robert Schuller. It was a ministry built upon him, and when he was no longer present to give it direction, it soon came apart. This is the fragility of any megachurch.

So the future of the church in the city no longer lies with its megachurches or with its denominational loyalty. It must lie somewhere else—in the missional model of ministry, a model that is based upon the embracing of the theology and practice of the call of every single one of its members—laity along with clergy—to specific ministry in the city.

---

[130] I am a Presbyterian Church (USA) minister, and therefore have access to church membership statistics for my denomination. Consequently, I am using them for this comparative study that I am making here. But this case can be made for all denominational churches.

The City is the Birthplace of the Emerging Church

In 1987, I read a study done by the Seventh Day Adventist Church on why some of their urban churches were growing and others were not.[131] That study really intrigued me. The study exposed very distinct trends in the growing urban SDA churches and counter trends in their declining urban churches. The particular value of this study was that the myths normally considered as strategic for church growth (conservative theology, dynamic preaching, prominent edifice) could not be used. Because they were all churches of one theologically uniform denomination, there were no significant differences in theology, church polity, or liturgics to "explain away" the growth or decline. What that study's author, Monte Sahlin, concluded was that growing SDA churches have: "(1) a clear sense of mission which a large percentage of members personally own; (2) the ability to attract educated, younger adults; (3) a solid program of community service in which the members are involved: and (4) the ability to . . . equip new members to witness to the unchurched."[132]

I was very intrigued with their conclusions. And I began to think to myself, "I wonder if these premises hold up in other denominations, in other traditions, and in other mega-cities around the world?" So I began to observe effective, growing churches in the cities in which I was ministering on behalf of World Vision's Urban Advance (1987–1995), and later as president of Partners in Urban Transformation (1996–2009). Over those years, I observed city churches in the USA, the UK, Australia, New Zealand, Latin America, Africa, and Asia.[133] And here is what I discovered.

The first thing I discovered was that there were certainly elements these churches *did not have* in common. Their non-commonality is important because some of these fly in the face of the assumptions many Christians make about church growth.

---

[131] Monte Sahlin, "A Study of Factors Relating to Urban Church Growth in the North American Division of Seventh Day Adventists" (Andrews University, the Institute of Church Ministry, 1986).

[132] Sahlin, *Study*, 26.

[133] I visited and surveyed most of these churches between 1988 and 2009 while working for the Office of Urban Advance of World Vision International or Partners in Urban Transformation. I gathered information on six of the listed churches without making an on-site visit. From this study of these congregations, I determined that 41 of them were particularly effective in urban mission and outreach while successfully building strong and financially secure congregations. I then isolated the characteristics of those congregations which made them effective and which they held in common with other effective churches. I include those characteristics in this chapter. A list of the churches surveyed is found in Appendix V.

Theologically, they were not uniformly conservative. Some of the significantly growing urban churches were theologically progressive; still others were quite radical (particularly politically). Some were Armenian and others Reformed in theology, and still others were charismatic or Pentecostal. Still others were theologically Lutheran or Thomistic.

Second, the pastors were not uniformly dynamic. Some of them were poor preachers, others were theologically naïve, and others highly sophisticated both theologically and sociologically. They were all kinds.

Likewise, the location and nature of the church building seemed incidental. In the churches I visited, I found that some were centrally located; others were on a side street in the worst possible slum. Some of these congregations worshipped in beautiful gothic structures, while the majority were in converted warehouses or rented buildings. One of them simply met in houses.

But all these churches had certain common characteristics that I believe significantly contributed to their effectiveness. Let's look at those characteristics:

First, each effective church operated out of a common focus of mission that was perceived, affirmed, and articulated by most of the congregation. Rather than these churches trying to do all things equally well and trying to be all things to all people, *each effective church I visited concentrated on a single primary mission focus.* More important was that this mission focus could be both articulated and affirmed by most of the congregation.

When I would go to these churches and meet with the pastor, I would expect that pastor to be able to tell me what his/her church was all about. But then I would go to Sabbath worship services, and I would ask the people sitting around me or would talk with people standing in the narthex after worship or gathering together afterward in the coffee hour, "Tell me about your church." And in situation after situation, these lay people would respond with the same articulation of mission—but in their own words. They, themselves, had inculcated and could articulate with affirmation and even conviction the primary mission focus of that church. And I found in many of the places I visited, the reason why they could do this is because they had been involved in determining that mission focus.

Equally important was that the mission focus of each of these congregations was outside itself. Each mission focus dealt with that purpose for which the congregation believed God had called that church into that community. It was striking that none of these mission foci turned inward. None said, "We are going to be a joyous fellowship of believers" or "We will seek to be the family of God." That is not a mission but is, instead, a state of being; it is life and existence as opposed to purpose, direction and activity.

Second, each church was committed to outreach which was assumed by the entire congregation. How outreach was defined and carried out in ministry was influenced by the particular theological perspective of each church. Some churches saw outreach in terms of evangelism, with the understanding that the job of each church member was to witness to his or her faith and to thus win people to Jesus Christ. Other churches understood outreach as working for social justice in their cities and others as providing social services to people. Still other churches defined outreach as seeking the transformation of the city. The church would define for itself what outreach meant. But the point is that, however it defined outreach, *the effective urban churches were those that saw their church as existing, not for itself, but for the world outside itself, and perceived that as its reason for existing.*

But a commitment to outreach was not the only thrust of these churches. The other perspective these congregations held was that *such outreach was to be assumed by the entire congregation.* In none of these churches did they operate out of the assumption that it was the pastor's or the elders' or the Outreach Committee's job to do outreach. All of them saw it as their responsibility for the implementation of the gospel through their congregation. They saw it as every member's responsibility!

Third, each effective urban church had created and implemented a means by which church members were both empowered to discover their ministry and equipped to carry out that ministry together with other church members. It was not simply that the church had a common mission with which everyone agreed. Nor was it simply that every member of the congregation felt that she or he had a responsibility either to proclaim the faith or to work for social righteousness. It was also that each church had devised some structure or strategy by which the church members were empowered to discover and carry out their unique and particular ministry and were able to act out that ministry within the parameters of that congregation. It is this third factor that I believe is most strategic in enabling these congregations to become effective, growing churches in even the worst of urban conditions.

What are the implications of these three common characteristics for the call of God to the Body of Christ in today's urban world and to each individual urban Christian?

The Church Which Empowers Members for Mission

When I talked with the pastors of the effective churches I observed, most suggested essentially the same thing. In one way or another, they said to me that in order to be effective in the city, they discovered that *their church needed to free itself from seeking to preserve itself as an institution*. Instead, it had to concentrate upon becoming a movement.

If a church concentrates on preserving itself as an institution, it will inevitably turn inward. And it will become caught up in maintaining itself. Precisely to the degree that it tries to preserve itself, it will lose itself.

Jesus once said, "Those who want to save their life will lose it, and those who lose their life for my sake will save it." (Luke 9:24). Jesus was stating something very profound not simply about the individual Christian, but about the Body of Christ. If the Church is caught up in trying to preserve its institution, if all of its energy is invested in trying to preserve itself, then preservation and continuance is exactly what is going to slip out of its grasp.

On the other hand, if it forgets about itself and becomes involved in reaching out to the world around it, then the church will discover that its institution is being preserved. In other words, the very act of ignoring your preservation and concentrating upon your institution as a congregation will lead to the strengthening of your congregation—without even trying!

If your objective in addressing the needs of your community is to make your church grow (and thus preserve it), people will see through that very quickly and they will reject your witness. If you are focusing on mission in order to grow, then you are compromising both that mission and the church's growth. If, on the other hand, people feel that you are genuinely concerned for them and the needs of the city, then they will be attracted to your church simply because its witness is genuine. The objective of the church ought to be to give its life away—to proclaim, live out, and practice the gospel in the midst of the city's issues, pains, powerlessness, and greed.

The second thing these pastors said to me was that if it is to be really effective in reaching out to the city, then *the church must be willing to abandon a structure and model of ministry that concentrates upon the operation of programs*. This, in turn, must mean a willingness to forsake a committee structure and process designed to sustain these programs.

None of these churches I studied—though some were several thousand in membership— had a large committee structure. Many of them had no committees at all except a board of elders, deacons, or vestry to assume the formal governance of the church. Nor did these churches have large interior programs to sustain. Many didn't even have a fund drive to raise their annual budget.

This struck a chord in me, because the church I pastored in Detroit had a typical congregational structure when I came to it (a ruling board, a board of trustees, a full spectrum of programming and administrative committees, etc.). It was a congregation of 1,100 members, ten committees, and countless programs. I observed that the running of all these committees and their programming was absorbing all the energy of the people so that they could not concentrate that energy on mission. That is, they were so absorbed in doing church work that they didn't have the time or energy to do the work of the church.

I proposed to the governing board, therefore, that we reduce the ten committees to four. These four groups were the board of elders which would absorb both the work of that church's spiritual guidance and governance and its trustee function, the deacons to assume all congregational care, and two other committees—a committee on outreach/mission and a committee on spiritual formation (worship and education). And that entire church of 1,100 ran quite well on just four programmatic/administrative bodies. Although this was only one of several contributing factors, after we reduced our structure to the minimum we felt we had to have in order to function, the membership of our congregation (which had been in decline for 16 years) stopped declining and began to grow so that the year before I left, my church had the most growth of any church in that regional judicatory of our denomination. Our income in three years doubled, and our mission giving increased five times over. Why? The people's energies were going into something other than the maintenance of the institution.

It is important to understand that I am not suggesting that a church not have structure. What I am suggesting is that church structures need to evolve out of the mission focus and purpose of that church. The primary task is for the church to get clarity on what that church perceives itself called by God to do in the world beyond itself. The structure of that church must then be one that is created in order to enable that mission to be effectively carried out. Thus, the "form" of the church's structure is following the "function" of that church at a particular place in its journey and mission as a congregation. This is an approach to organization profoundly different than one that seeks to maintain a structure that does not change, irrespective of the specific conditions of the congregation at that point in time.

Most of the effective urban churches I have surveyed follow this principle of "form follows function." Their structures are created for a purpose, and once that purpose is adequately served, that structure is dissolved. Such an operational perspective is one that takes a utilitarian, pragmatic approach to structure (what do we need *now* to get the job done) rather than one that seeks to maintain continuing structures irrespective of the needs and capabilities of that congregation. I am therefore not suggesting a structureless process, but rather a process where the structure comes out of the mission of the church, is periodically evaluated, and is readjusted to enable that congregation to fulfill its present mission in the most effective way.

How, then, does the internal work and the mission outreach of the church get done if not through committees? The work gets done by people who feel called by God to assume that ministry—a dynamic that is profoundly different than being appointed to serve on a committee. That brings us to the third insight from these pastors.

The third reality that was confirmed for me in visiting with these pastors is that *the essential task of the church is to empower and equip people to discover and carry out their own ministry.* The primary task of the church is to enable its members to discover and to live into that ministry to which God has called each one of them. The purpose of the church is to enable people to live practically and concretely into both the theology and practice of their vocation.

As I looked at these different churches, they all had different ways of living out a commitment to the world. But their common denominator was that each perceived the task of their church leadership as that of devising and carrying out a process that enabled the church members to minister with other church members in the world. In other words, *the church members do not exist to serve the church. The church exits to equip its members to serve the world!*

Perhaps it was expressed most eloquently by one pastor. "Laity need to believe their ministry calling is important to God, to the church, and to the culture.

They need to know their calling is just as important as the pastor's or the missionary's calling."[134]

The churches I surveyed certainly didn't follow a common pattern of enabling people to follow God's calling on their lives. The strategies of these churches were as diverse as the churches themselves. But all saw the leadership task to be that of empowering and equipping their members to discover and carry out ministry in the world. Thus, all of them had created some structure and strategy to enable the congregation to live into that third principle.

In this book, I have suggested three structures that I found worked in the churches I served—strategic mission planning, mission groups, and broad-based community organizing. But all existed to provide concrete means by which our church members could live out their sense of call.

So It All Comes Back to Our Call

The doctrine of vocation that we have examined in this book can be summarized in one question: "Why do you exist?" Put theologically, the question is "What is your purpose in life?" The biblical answer is "Your purpose in living is to serve God by serving humanity." You have been created, chosen, and called by God to be used by God in a particular way. And all that you have gone through in life, all the experiences you have had, all the problems with which you have coped, every rejection you have ever faced as a human being, every celebration in which you have shared, every victory you have tasted, all has gone into making you into who you are right now. Why? So that God can use you in a special way.

Every human being has been created by God to serve Christ in the world in a particular way. And when we discover the deep gladness of our own lives—our redemption in Jesus Christ—and we allow ourselves to be open to the pain of the world and gravitate toward that issue of the world that hurts us the most, that is where our deep gladness and the world's deep hunger come together. And that is where God calls us to serve him. But that call is not to a solitary mission, but to a Body of Christ that is also called. And your call strengthens its call, and its call strengthens your call. You are called together to be "Christ-ones"—Christians—to the world!

---

[134]Frank Tillapaugh and Richard Hurst, *Calling* (Colorado Springs, CO: Dreamtime Publishing, 1997), 101–102.

The future of the church in the city lies in our capacity to move out of the ways of being "church" that are familiar to us in order to embrace "church" as that community that enables its participants to discover and carry out their call together. But in order to do that, it means that we as the church must be willing to plumb the depths of the doctrine of call. We need to rediscover that doctrine, both for ourselves in order to more clearly understand our own calling, and in order to provide guidance to our brother and sister church members as they seek God's call upon their lives.

Therefore, the crucial question with which each of us needs to face ourselves is, "What is my responsibility to enable my church, not so much to be an institution or to focus itself around programs which serve the church and perpetuate its life, but rather enable my church to give its life away and through that giving away, discover authentic life and ministry for itself in our city?"

And Us!

In the Gospel of Mark, Jesus tells three parables in one pericope, which is immediately followed by Mark's telling of Jesus calming a storm at sea. Is this an interesting but haphazard juxtaposition of stories? I think not! The parables tell of the lighting of a room by putting a lamp, not under a bushel basket but on a stand to give light to the house (4:21–25), a seed planted by a farmer that mysteriously grows but which he harvests and uses when it is ripe (vv. 26–29), and then the way that the smallest of seeds—a mustard seed—becomes the largest of bushes (vv. 30-32). And then these three parables are followed by the story of Jesus sailing with his disciples across the Sea of Galilee and being struck with a fierce storm, which Jesus then calms (vv. 35–41).

There is a common theme running through all these stories that, obviously Mark intended. Each of these parables recognize God's power and mystery, while discerning what it is we are to do and not do. Thus, we do not understand why the wick of a lamp burns and sheds light, but we use it to give light to our house at night. We do not understand how a seed grows into a plant, but nonetheless, we both plant it and harvest it for our food and financial benefit. We do not understand how the smallest of all seeds grows into the largest bush, but we rest in its shade. And, finally, in Jesus's calming of the Sea of Galilee from a fishing boat caught in a storm, we don't understand how Jesus did it. But we take relief in the ensuing calm. And we ask, "Who can this be? Even the wind and the sea obey him!" (v. 41)

In other words, there is God's work and there is our work. And God demonstrates to us his power and sovereignty through his work—while all we can do is wonder and stand in awe! Nonetheless, even in the midst of such awe, we have the work to which God calls us—and it is that work that we are to do. But we do that work, knowing that God is God—and we are not! So we recognize we won't bring in the kingdom of God. But, rather, we are to contribute our specific and small work to that kingdom—recognizing that God calls us to be faithful, not necessarily successful!

Every Thanksgiving Day morning, my father (and after his death, my mother) would take my brother, sister, and me into downtown Philadelphia to watch the annual Thanksgiving Day Parade. Sponsored by Gimbel Brothers Department Store since 1920, the parade would form in North Philadelphia and march south down Broad Street to Penn Plaza, where it arrived under the stern eye of William Penn's statute standing 500 feet above ground level on the Philadelphia City Hall tower. There, Penn—and all at the Plaza watching the parade—would see the parade turn east and continue on down Market Street to Gimbel Brothers. The parade would begin with the mounted police of Philadelphia on their prancing chestnut horses, would be followed by the parade's grand marshal in a classic convertible, and then bands and floats and giant balloons and cowboys and clowns and stunt riders and what-have-you. Finally, the parade would be concluded with Santa Claus riding into the city on a giant float with eight massive reindeer. At its conclusion, the parade would move down Market Street where it would stop in front of Gimbel's Department Store where there would be a large fire-truck ladder against the building. Santa would then climb that ladder to an upper story of the department store, go through an open window and there be in court ready to receive children—thus confirming to all the children that the truly authentic, real live Santa was at Gimbel's while only cheap imitations were at Wanamakers, Lits, and Strawbridge & Clothier! I absolutely loved this parade!

When I was six, however, I shared with my father that, although I loved the parade, it seemed to go on forever! He responded, "Well, then, Robert, we need to change your perspective!" I had no idea what that big word "perspective" meant, but I knew my dad was going to do something exciting!

My father was a lawyer, and his law office was on a top floor of a skyscraper on the southeast corner of Penn Plaza, directly across from Philadelphia's City Hall and at the junction of Broad and Market Streets. That Thanksgiving Day, instead of standing at the curb on Market Street to watch the parade go by, my father took us into that building and to his office. He instructed me to stand by the large window and look up Broad Street.

As all of us stood there looking up Broad Street, we could see the parade forming in the far north of our city and then start marching down Broad Street. We watched it grow ever closer until the mounted police turned the corner at Market and led the parade east on that street. The most exciting moment came for me when I saw the mounted police approaching Gimbel Brothers store while, at the same time, Santa Claus and his giant float were moving into the line of march way up Broad Street at the city line. In that one short moment, I was able to encompass the entire parade in motion—but only because of my changed perspective!

That's what this book has been about. It was written to change your perspective! I wrote it in order to say to every lay person, "You are important to God. You are important enough to God for him to sacrifice his Son so that you might be redeemed. And you are important enough to God that he has created, chosen, and called you to be like his Son, living your life to do God's particular and specific will in the world!" You have been called by God to serve God by serving humanity in a particular way. And your heart will rest in God only when you have discovered that way, and walk in it! So, believe that you are called. And then walk that walk to which you have been called! Amen.

APPENDICES

Appendix I:	Worksheets
Appendix II:	Mission Call Discernment Process
Appendix III:	Mission Groups
Appendix IV:	Organizing Networks
Appendix V:	Surveyed Churches

APPENDIX 1: WORKSHEETS

Worksheet I-1:

Meeting My Deep Gladness

Please move to a quiet location, where you can be alone without being disturbed, turn off your personal electronic communication devices (e.g., cell phone, smart phone, etc.). In silence, allow your thoughts and feelings to center down. Enjoy the beauty and the quiet of the world around you. Relax your mind and soul. Then, when you feel at a restful place inside yourself, slowly and meditatively read the following scripture passage. Allow yourself to reflect upon it.

The scripture is Luke 1:26–56.

Some questions are here suggested to help you live into this scripture. You are invited to work with these questions that seem right to you to reflect upon; write your responses on the back of this paper or in your journal. Spend as much time as you need with each of these questions; do not rush your response to them.

1. What is this passage saying? How would I briefly summarize it in my own words?

2. What was Mary's deep gladness? What did that gladness have to do with God, with herself, with those closest to her, with the world, and particularly the suffering ones in the world?

3. How did Mary get in touch with that gladness within herself? How was it confirmed and nurtured?

4. What has the Almighty done for you (vs. 49)? What most gladdens and delights your heart?

5. What do you most delight in when you think of God? What delights you the most about yourself? What brings you the most joy in other people, especially those close to you?

6. How would you describe the deep gladness in your soul?

Worksheet I-2

Discerning My Call

Enter into silence. Ask for the discernment of the Holy Spirit. Concentrate your attention deep within yourself, and do not begin to write until you sense you are ready.

Work with these questions by journaling them:

1. Imagine yourself doing what you would do, if you could do anything in the world you choose. Write it down.

2. Imagine yourself doing what you would most like to do if you were doing something that benefited humanity or spoke to a particular pain of the world. Write that down.

3. Compare the two answers. What relationships, if any, exist between the two answers?

4. What talents do you think you would need to address that human pain or need effectively? What do you see as even the faintest glimmer of those talents within yourself?

5. Who do you know who seems to feel the same need to address that human pain?

6. What risks would need to be taken by you, if you were to practice a ministry addressing those human needs?

Worksheet I-3

Living Into Community

Enter into silence. Ask for the discernment of the Holy Spirit. Concentrate your attention deep within yourself, and do not begin to write until you sense you are ready.

Work with these questions by journaling on them.

1. What are the small groups (20 or less participants) in your church in which you participate? List them.

2. What are the small groups (20 or less participants) ***outside your church*** in which you participate? List them.

3. How would you compare and contrast the small groups in which you participate within your church and the small groups outside your church?

4. Which do you find most helpful to you, and in what ways?

5. What would you wish for yourself in a small group in your church?

6. Do you have that in any of your church groups? If so, which one?

7. If not, is there one that has the potential of fulfilling your wish? If so, what needs to happen to make that wish come true?

8. How can the small church group you envision best enable and equip you for living out the mission to which you feel called?

Worksheet I-4

Calling Forth My Gifts

You cannot call forth your own gifts. Only your brothers and sisters in Christ can do that. Therefore, this exercise needs to be a group exercise. The group ought to be one which knows you exceedingly well, and hopefully is focused in a single mission that draws them together.

Each member of the group should go off by him/herself and should work slowly and deliberatively with these questions. First, pray for eyes of discernment and for a humble spirit. Then, fill out one worksheet on each member of the group, so that you have as many completed worksheets as you have members in the group. Then everyone should return to share their responses to these questions, and to use those responses as the wellspring for discussions together about each member of the group.

1. Name of the person upon whom you are reflecting:

2. When you consider this person, what do you see as their strongest talents, abilities or skills? Name one instance when you saw that gift used well by this person.

3. What are that person's strongest spiritual gifts (apostolic ministry, prophetic ministry, teaching, exhortation, service, leadership, faith, the ministry of money, healing, miracles, discernment of spirits, speaking in tongues, interpreting tongues)? Name one instance when you saw that gift used well by this person.

4. What are that person's strongest gifts that all Christians hold in common (love, joy, peace, patience, kindness, generosity, faithfulness, gentleness, self-control)? Name one instance when you saw that gift used well by this person.

When you return to the group, select one person and have all the other members of the group read their responses to question #2. The only response that the person being bathed by this sharing is "Thank you!" Then move to question #3 and repeat the process, and then repeat the process once again for question #4. Then select another person and repeat.

APPENDIX II: MISSION CALL DISCERNMENT PROCESS

Church Call Discernment II-1

Generic Agenda

DISCERNMENT WEEKEND

(Church Call Discernment Retreat)

Friday:

6:00	Training of Small Group Leaders
6:30	Dinner for all Participants)
7:00	Welcome to Retreat – Pastor
7:15	Opening Worship – Pastor or Comm.
7:45	Orientation to Retreat – Retreat Leader
8:15	Presentation on Mission – Research Committee
9:00	Adjournment with Prayer

Saturday:

8:00	Breakfast
8:30	Gathering of participants, singing – Worship Team
8:45	Worship – Worship Team
9:00	Plenary Bible Study (John 12:20-27) – Retreat Leader
9:45	Individual Bible Reflection
10:30	Break
10:45	Biblical Reflection on Church's Mission and Call – Small Groups

11:30	Singing — Worship Team
11:35	Plenary Sharing from Small Groups — Retreat Leader
12:30	Lunch and Free Time
1:30	Singing — Worship Team
1:35	Preparation for Mission Focusing — Retreat Leader
2:00	Development of Mission Foci in Small Groups — Small Groups
2:45	Plenary: Construction of Common Mission Focus — Retreat Leader
3:10	Mission Statement Writing Committee Assigned — Retreat Leader (committee writes statement from 3:10 to 5:00)
3:15	Break
3:30	Singing—Worship Team
3:35	Plenary on Mission Implications — Retreat Leader
3:45	Work on Mission Implications — Small Groups
4:30	Report of Small Groups on Mission Implication — Retreat Leader
5:00	Writing Committee Presents Proposed Committee — Retreat Leader Mission Call Statement; Debated, Revised, Approved
5:45	Vespers — Worship Team
6:00	Dinner and/or Adjournment for the Day

Sunday:

9:00	Training of Church Committee Chairs for Retreat Work — Retreat Leader
9:30	Sunday Worship
10:30	Coffee Hour
11:00	Singing — Worship Team
11:05	Plenary Review of Discernment Weekend Work Thus Far — Retreat Leader Review Schedule and Assign Next Steps
11:20	Creation of Mission, Interior Life and Institutional — Church Committees Objectives to Implement Mission Call
1:00	Luncheon
1:45	Singing — Worship Team

1:50 Report of Church Committees on Recommended Mission — Retreat Leader

Interior Life and Institutional Objectives

2:15 Plenary Debate and Action on All Objectives — Retreat Leader

3:15 Closing Celebration/Worship — Worship Team

3:30 Close of Discernment Weekend

REFLECTION ON JOHN 12:20-27

You have rushed to get to this important gathering of your congregation. You have had to give up important engagements or activities to set aside this time. Rather than simply rush into a crowded agenda, allow God to prepare your mind and heart for this day. "Be still and know that the Lord is God" (Ps. 46:10), so that you can hear God's voice whispering to you.

Please take the time allotted to prepare yourself for this day by doing the following:

- **Enter into Silence** and spend a few minutes enjoying the quiet around you and within you. When you feel your soul and body is sufficiently removed from the rush of getting here today, then . . .

- **Read John 12:20-27** reflectively

- **Reflect on John 12:27** specifically. Now consider the following questions, reflect on your answers and write your response to these questions when you are ready:

1. How is my soul troubled over my church?

2. Why has God preserved us as God's people here, maintaining a loving home and a congregation, both for ourselves and for our community? *For what purpose do I believe God has brought us as a church to this hour?*

- Bring your responses before God in prayer. Are you hearing God's voice speaking to you or only your own agenda reflecting itself through your response? Continue to pray and to work with your response until you feel it is the word God would have you give to this gathering today.

John 12:20-27

Now among those who went up to worship at the festival were some Greeks. They came to Philip, who was from Bethsaida in Galilee, and said to him, "Sir, we wish to see Jesus." Philip went and told Andrew, then Andrew and Philip went and told Jesus.

Jesus answered them, "The hour has come for the Son of Man to be glorified. Very truly, I tell you, unless a grain of wheat falls into the earth and dies, it remains just a single grain, but if it dies, it bears much fruit. Those who love their life lose it, and those who hate their life in this world will keep it for eternal life. Whoever serves me must follow me, and where I am, there will my servant be also. Whoever serves me, the Father will honor.

"Now my soul is troubled. And what should I say, 'Father, save me from this hour'? No, it is for this reason that I have come to this hour. Father, glorify your name."

APPENDIX III: MISSION GROUPS

Mission Groups III-1

Job Description of the Moderators Council

The name of the body will be the Moderators Council. The Council will meet quarterly and will also be on call. The Council will be made up of the moderator or moderator's appointee from each mission group, the church staff responsible for the provision of staff support to a given mission group (if any), and the Coordinator of Mission Groups. The Coordinator of Mission Groups will chair all meetings, and will represent the Council before the church's governing board. The Council will be under the authority of the board and accountable to it.

The tasks of the Council will be twofold.

First, it will be responsible for providing opportunity for moderators to share with each other what is happening in their respective mission groups (so that all can stay informed about the work of all), to rejoice together around victories, and to reflect together about identified issues, and problems.

Second, it will plan those common activities and events that the Council perceives as strengthening the work, life, and witness of the mission groups. That can include common shared events (e.g., Alternative Christmas Fair), training events, opportunities to share the work of individual mission groups with the congregation, the production of publicity or published items, or whatever else the Council might determine (once the board has given permission for the same). At present, those common activities consist of the following:

1. Make sure that each mission group completes the annual evaluation and budget request process in October– November for the ensuing year, as required by the board.

2. Provision for each mission group to share its mission annually with the congregation and sound a call to the congregation for new members.

3. Commonly shared events undertaken jointly by the mission groups, such as:
    - Mission Groups Sunday (all ministries celebrated)
        - January
    - Missions Celebration (missions our church supports)
        - June
    - Rally Sunday (the annual start of church programming)
        - September
    - Alternative Christmas Celebration
        - December

Mission Groups III-2

Job Description for the Coordinator of Mission Groups

This is a description of the work to be performed by the person who is either employed by the church or is a volunteer who provides oversight and direction to the church's mission groups. Either as staff or a volunteer, this person is directly accountable to the senior pastor of the church as his/her supervisor and to the governing board for policy purposes.

The responsibility of the Coordinator of Mission Groups is as follows:

1. Commit one's self to the ministry of enablement, both to encourage the unique work of each mission group and to keep them working together.
2. Play a key enabling role (but not the assumption of the group's responsibility) in the formation of a new mission group in whatever ways will allow that group to prosper in the performance of its mission.
3. Sense when and where established groups need help and unobtrusively provide that help, withdrawing immediately afterward (e.g., helping a group that feels overwhelmed by the governing board's evaluation and accountability structure to do an evaluation).
4. Be a pastoral support to mission groups as needed, especially to their moderators, mission, and spiritual directors.
5. Help people and groups who are sensing a call to a mission but haven't yet acted on it, to organize the call in order to discern whether there is sufficient congregational response to justify the formation of a mission group.
6. Work with any mission group in their task of spending quality time in spiritual reflection at each meeting (Bible study, prayer, sharing), either as they request it or as the coordinator perceives it being needed.
7. Call and chair the meetings of the Moderators Council. This includes creating the agenda for each meeting. Those meetings, occurring once each quarter, should concentrate upon two agendas: providing opportunity for moderators to share with each other what is happening in their

respective mission groups (so that all stay informed about the work of all) and planning common activities that foster congregational awareness of the mission groups or undertake shared efforts.

8. Make sure the following common tasks are undertaken jointly by the ministry groups. Present common tasks are:
    - Ministry Groups Sunday (all ministries celebrated)
        - January
    - Missions Celebration (missions our church supports)
        - June
    - Rally Sunday (the start-up of church programming)
        - September
    - Annual Session (evaluation & next year budgeting)
        - October
    - Alternative Christmas Celebration
        - December
9. Make sure that each mission group undertakes the tasks expected of it and to share its mission afresh with the congregation, to sound an annual call to the congregation for new members and to celebrate the commitment and work of those members who elect to leave the group. This work normally entails creating the narthex bulletin board display for that month, sharing with the congregation and sounding its call on a designated Sunday of that month, having a table on the patio for coffee hour interaction with the congregation, and sounding that call at public worship.

The investment of the coordinator's time is extremely uneven (except for dated organizing activities, as listed above); thus, the work, in a week, can vary from between 10 hours to no time invested at all. It is imperative that the coordinator have the interior self-discipline that he or she can set one's own schedule and fulfill the obligations of this work.

Mission Groups III-3

Annual Mission Group Evaluation & Next Year's Suggested Goals and Budget

The questions which each of our church's mission groups are requested to answer and to submit to the church's governing board for annual review, plans, and budget are listed below Each ministry group is requested to complete this form and submit it to the church office by October 15 of this year. Thank you.

1. What were your mission group's mission goals for this year?

2. What was accomplished this year in implementing these goals?

3. What were goal failures experienced?

4. What were your mission group's life together goals for this year?

5. What were your accomplishments in implementing these goals? Failures?

6. How is the implementation of this year's goals contributing toward the achieving of the mission call of this congregation?

7. What are your mission objectives for next year?

8. What are your mission group's life together objectives for next year?

9. What needs to be your operational budget for next year? If you had to reduce that budget by 20%, where would those cuts be? What will be the impact on the carrying out of your mission if these cuts were to take place?

Appendix IV: Organizing Networks

The world of community and broad-based organizing is essentially built around networks of city-based organizations coming together to provide training, resources, and the training, supervision, and accreditation of community organizers. Most of these networks function primarily in the USA, although a few are active internationally, as well. The organizing networks are as follows:

DART (Direct Action and Research Training)

The DART Center

9401 Biscayne Blvd., Suite 215

Miami Shores, FL. 33138

Phone: (305) 576-8020

www.thedartcenter.org

John Aeschbury, Executive Director

Holly Holcomb, Associate Director

Leah Wiley, Training Coordinator

Ben MacConnell, Organizer Recruiter

DART is a network of 20 affiliated grassroots congregation-based community organizations, primarily doing institutional organizing in southern states and in the Midwest of the USA. It tends to organize in midsize cities (e.g., Dayton, Columbus, Louisville, Jacksonville) rather than mega-cities. It has a very strong biblical training component that includes introductory training in how to read and use the Bible to do social analysis and to work for corporate and social reform in cities through community organizing. Its annual Clergy Conference is a continuing means for honing biblical interpretation and organizing skills of its pastors and church leaders.

Gamaliel

Gamaliel Foundation

221 N. LaSalle St., Suite 1320
Chicago, IL. 60601

Phone: (312) 357-2639

www.gamaliel.org

Ana Garcia-Ashley, Executive Director

Jay Schmitt, Chief Operational Officer

Cheryl Liske, International Leadership Assembly Director

Gamaliel is a network of 43 affiliates, concentrating on organizing in the United States and South Africa. It began in 1968 to support the Contract Buyers League, an African American organization protecting homeowners on Chicago's Westside who were being discriminated against by banks and saving and loan associations. In 1986, it was reorganized to provide organizing resources to low income communities. Gamaliel has done some effective theological work, especially through their occasional theology papers and through pastors' conferences.

(IAF) Industrial Areas Foundation

220 West Kinzie Street

Chicago, IL. 60610

Phone: (312) 245-9211

www.industrialareasfoundation.org

Metro IAF office:

1226 Vermont Ave., NW

Washington, DC 20005-3615

(202) 518-0815

West/Southwest IAF office:

1106 Clayton Lane, Suite 120W
Austin, TX 78723
(512) 459-6551

Ernesto Cortes, Jr., National Co-Director (see W/SW Region)
Michael Gecan, National Co-Director, (see Metro IAF Region)

The IAF is the oldest and largest of the organizing networks in the USA, as well as doing organizing in Australia, Canada, Great Britain and Germany. The IAF was founded by Saul Alinsky in 1942 to coordinate his organizing work in the major cities of the US. It still continues the organizing task through two regional organizations working in 78 cities; those cities tend to be the largest of USA cities (e.g., New York, Los Angeles metropolis, Chicago metropolis, Houston, Baltimore, Dallas, etc.). Organizing is broad-based and includes middle-class suburbs as well as inner cities. In its organizing, it has developed several national initiatives. These include the Nehemiah Homes (building affordable housing through organizing the poor in Baltimore, Boston, the Bronx, Brooklyn, Houston, Los Angeles, Philadelphia), the Alliance School Program (which organizes parents to be involved in the decision-making and the schooling of their children's schools) and Project QUEST (job creation, training, and placement).

(PICO) People Improving Communities through Organizing

171 Santa Rosa Avenue
Oakland, CA. 94610
Phone: (510) 655-2801; (866) 550-7426
www.piconetwork.org

Scott Read, Executive Director
Rev. Michael McBride, Director of Urban Strategies
Rev. Michael Ray Mathews, Director of Clergy Organizing
Stephanie Gut, Director of Organizational Development

PICO began as an organizing effort on the west coast ("PICO" used to stand for Pacific Institute for Community Organizing), but is now organizing in US cities as far east as Camden, New Jersey. It is the second largest organizing network in the US. PICO brings people together to strengthen families and improve communities. Since 1972, PICO has created innovative strategies to increase access to health care, improve public schools, make neighborhoods safer, create housing opportunities, redevelop communities and revitalize American democracy. PICO makes a major emphasis upon theological reflection and the building of a relational culture.

Appendix V: Surveyed Churches

The following churches have a reputation for having an impact upon their respective cities. I studied them between 1987 and 2009, during my work with both World Vision International and Partners in Urban Transformation. My objective was to see if there were any common characteristics of a majority of these urban churches, even though they are on separate continents, are of different denominations, theological traditions, and church polity. A limitation of this study was that I was confined in my selection of churches to the limitations of my travel schedule (for example, I did very little interacting with churches in Europe and none in the Near East or the Pacific islands). I present the common characteristics I discovered in Chapter 16 of this book. The churches that I surveyed are as follows:

Africa:

Buru Buru Church of God, Nairobi, Kenya
Mbare Christian Church, Harare, Zimbabwe
Ngong Presbyterian Church, Nairobi, Kenya
Nkolokoti Church, Blantyre, Malawi

Asia, Australia, New Zealand:

Ashburton Baptist Church, Melbourne, Australia
Eagles Evangelism, Singapore
Holy Cross Church (Church of South India), Chennai (Madras), India
Newmarket Baptist Church, Melbourne, Australia
Parish of the Risen Christ (Roman Catholic), Manila, Philippines
Sacred Heart Roman Catholic Church, St. Kilda, Melbourne, Australia

Te Atatu Bible Church, Auckland, New Zealand
Wesley Methodist Church (Church of North India), Mumbai (Bombay), India
Westgate Baptist Church, Melbourne, Australia

Latin America:

Barro Preto Baptist Church, Belo Horizonte, Brazil
Belem Assemblies of God Church, Belem, Brazil
Central Presbyterian Church, Manaus, Brazil
Christian Church of Brasilia, Brasilia, Brazil
Concordia Seventh-Day Adventist Church, Belo Horizonte, Brazil
Eighth Presbyterian Church, Belo Horizonte, Brazil
Goiania Presbyterian Church, Goiania, Brazil
Horeb Baptist Church, Mexico City, Mexico
Manaus Four Square Tabernacle, Manaus, Brazil
Paroquia de la Resurreccion Church (Roman Catholic), Mexico City, Mexico
Shekinah Baptist Church, Belo Horizonte, Brazil
Torre Methodist church, Recife, Brazil

United Kingdom:

Anfield Road Fellowship, Liverpool, England
Holy Trinity Brompton Church (Church of England), London, England
Icthus Christian Fellowship, London, England
Kensington Baptist Church, Bristol, England
Plaistow Christian Fellowship, London, England
Romford Baptist Church, London, England
St. Clement's Church (Church of England), Bradford, England
St. Mungo's Church (Church of Scotland), Glasgow, Scotland
St. Nicholas of Tolentino (Roman Catholic) Church, Bristol, England
St. Paul's Shadwall (Church of England), London, England

United States of America:

Bear Valley Baptist Church, Denver, CO

Church of the Saviour, Washington, DC
Community Church for Christ, Oakland, CA
Edgewater Presbyterian Church, Chicago, IL
Englewood United Methodist Church, Chicago, IL
Faith Lutheran Church (ELCA), Detroit, MI
Faith United Presbyterian Church, Los Angeles, CA
First Christian Church, Pomona, CA
First Presbyterian Church, Pomona, CA
First Presbyterian Church of Hollywood, Los Angeles, CA
Formosan Presbyterian Church, Los Angeles, CA
Fuente de Vida Church, Los Angeles, CA
Grosse Pointe Woods Presbyterian Church, Detroit, MI
Haeram Korean Church, Los Angeles, CA
Immanuel Church, Los Angeles, CA
Keystone Baptist Church, Chicago, IL
LaSalle Street Church, Chicago, IL
LaVerne Heights Presbyterian Church, LaVerne (Los Angeles area), CA
Madison Street Church, Riverside, CA
New Life African Methodist Episcopal Zion Church, Brockton, MA.
New Song Community Church, Baltimore, MD
Rock Evangelical Free Church, Chicago, IL
St. Ambrose Roman Catholic Church, Detroit, MI
St. Luke's United Methodist Church, Oklahoma City, OK
St. Paul's American Methodist Episcopal Church, San Bernardino, CA.
St. Paul Community Baptist Church, New York, NY
St. Stephen's Church of God in Christ, San Diego, CA
South Lawn United Methodist Church, Chicago, IL
Wilshire Presbyterian Church, Los Angeles, CA.

Bibliography

Theology of the City

Augustine of Hippo, St. *City of God, The*. New York: Doubleday, 1958 (original work: 426 AD).

Bakke, Ray. *A Theology As Big As the City*. Downers Grove, IL: InterVarsity Press, 1997

Bruggemann, Walter. *The Prophetic Imagination*. Philadelphia: Fortress Press, 1978

Elliot, Charles. *Praying the Kingdom: Towards a Political Spirituality*. New York: Paulist Press, 1985.

Howard-Brook, Wes. *Becoming Children of God: John's Gospel and Radical Discipleship*. Maryknoll, NY: Orbis Press, 1994.

Kraybill, Donald B. *The Upside-Down Kingdom*. Scottsdale, PA: Herald Press, 1978.

Linthicum, Robert C. *City of God; City of Satan: A Biblical Theology of the Urban Church*. Grand Rapids, MI.: Zondervan/HarperCollins, 1991.

___________________. *Commentary on Deuteronomy: Polis Bible Commentary Series*. Eugene, OR: Urban Loft Publishers, 2017.

Myers, Ched. *Binding the Strong Man: A Political Reading of Mark's Story of Jesus*. Maryknoll, NY: Orbis Press, 1988.

Tonga, Benjamin. *Gospel for the Cities*. Maryknoll, NY: Orbis Press, 1985.

Trocme, Andre. *Jesus and the Nonviolent Revolution*. Eugene, OR: Wipf and Stock, 1998 (original work, 1973).

Wink, Walter. *Engaging the Powers: Discernment and Resistance in a World of Domination*. Minneapolis, MN: Augsburg Fortress, 1992.

____________. *The Powers That Be: Theology for a New Millennium*. New York: Doubleday, 1998.

Vocation – Doctrine and Praxis

Bessenecker, Scott A. (ed.) *Living Mission: The Vision and Voices of New Friars*. Downers Grove, IL.: InterVarsity Press, 2010.

Bolles, Richard N. *What Color Is Your Parachute?* Berkeley, CA: Ten-Speed Press, 2014.

Calvin, John. *Institutes of the Christian Religion, The: Book III*. Grand Rapids, MI.: Eerdmans, 1957 (original work: 1536).

Cosby, N. Gordon. *By Grace Transformed: Christianity for a New Millennium*. NY: Crossroads, 1999.

Dwinell, Michael. *Being Priest to One Another*. Liguori, Missouri: Triumph Books, 1993.

Engdahl, Derek W. *The Great Chasm: How to Stop Our Wealth from Separating Us from the Poor and God*. Pomona, CA: Servant Partners Press, 2015.

Heidelberg Catechism. The Book of Confessions. Louisville, KY: Office of the General Assembly, The Presbyterian Church (USA), 1999 (original date: 1562).

Hillman, James. *The Soul's Code: In Search of Character and Calling.* New York: Warner Books, 1996.

Hollis, James. *Finding Meaning in the Second Half of Life: How to Finally Really Grow Up!* New York: Gotham Books, 2006.

Katie, Byron. *A Thousand Names for Joy: Living in Harmony with the Way Things Are.* New York: Harmony Press, 2007.

Luther, Martin. *Epistle to the Hebrews.* Philadelphia, PA: Westminster Press, 1967 (original work: 1518)

O'Connor, Elizabeth. *Call to Commitment.* NY: Harper and Row, 1963.

__________________. *Cry Pain, Cry Hope: Thresholds to Purpose.* Waco, TX: Word, 1987.

__________________. *New Community, The: A Portrait of Life Together.* New York: Harper and Row, 1976.

Palmer, Parker. *A Hidden Wholeness.* San Francisco: Jossey-Bass, 2004.

Rohr, Richard. *Falling Upwards: A Spirituality for the Two Halves of Life.* San Francisco: Jossey-Bass Publishers, 2011.

Theological Declaration of Barmen. The Book of Confessions. Louisville, KY: Office of the General Assembly, The Presbyterian Church (USA), 1999 (original work: 1934).

Volf, Miroslav. *Work in the Spirit: Toward a Theology of Work* Oxford, England: Oxford University Press, 1991.

Warren, Rick. *The Purpose-Driven Life: What On Earth Am I Here For?* Grand Rapids, MI: Zondervan, 2002

Westminster Confession of Faith, the Shorter Catechism and the Larger Catechism. The Book of Confessions. Louisville, KY: Office of the General Assembly, The Presbyterian Church (USA), 1999 (original work: 1649).

Whyte, David. *The Three Marriages: Reimagining Work, Self and Relationship.* New York: Riverhead Books, 2009.

Urbanism and Urbanization

Dogan, Mattei and John D. Kasarda. *Mega-Cities: the Metropolis Era.* Beverly Hills, CA: Sage Foundation, 1988.

Dogan,Mattei and John D. Kasarda. *A World of Giant Cities.* Beverly Hills, CA: Sage Foundation, 1988.

Fulton, William. *The Reluctant Metropolis: The Politics of Urban Growth in Los Angeles.* Point Arena, CA: Solano Press Books, 1997.

Gibbs, Jewel Taylor. *Young, Black and Male in America: An Endangered Species*. Dover Maine: Auburn House Publishing Co., 1988.

Gitlin, Todd. *The Twilight of Common Dreams: Why America is Wracked by Culture Wars*. NY: Metropolitan Press, 1995.

Greider, William. *Who Will Tell the People? The Betrayal of American Democracy*. NY: Simon and Shuster, 1994.

Handy, Charles. *The Age of Paradox*. Boston, MA: Harvard Business School Press, 1994.

Jacobs, Jane. *Cities and the Wealth of Nations*. NY: Random House, 1984.

Lerner, Michael. *The Left Hand of God: Healing America's Political and Spiritual Crisis*. San Francisco, CA: HarperCollins, 2006

Mumford, Lewis. *The City in History: Its Origins, Its Transformations and Its Prospects*. NY: HBJ, 1961.

Palen, J. John. *The Urban World, 2nd Edition*. NY: McGraw-Hill Book Co., 1981.

Pinker, Steven. *The Better Angels of Our Nature: Why Violence Has Declined*. New York: Penguin Books, 2011.

Sassen, Saskia. *The Global City*. Princeton, NJ: Princeton University Press, 1991.

Siegel, Fred. *The Future Once Happened Here: New York, DC, LA and the Fate of America's Big Cities*. NY: The Free Press, 1997.

Stark, Rodney. *Cities of God: The Real Story of How Christianity Became an Urban Movement and Conquered Rome*. San Francisco, CA: HarperCollins, 2006.

Wallerstein, Immanuel. *Utopistics: Historical Choices of the Twenty-First Century*. New York: The New Press, 1998.

Urban Ministry

Bakke, Ray and Sam Roberts. *The Expanded Mission of City Center Churches*. Chicago, IL: International Urban Associates, 1998.

Conn, Harvie M. *A Clarified Vision for Urban Mission*. Grand Rapids, MI: Zondervan, 1987.

Gornik, Mark R. *To Live in Peace: Biblical Faith and the Changing Inner City*. Grand Rapids, MI.: Eerdmans, 2002.

Grigg, Viv. *Cry of the Urban Poor*. Monrovia: MARC Publications, 1992.

Gunder, Darrell. *The Missional Church*. Grand Rapids, MI: Eerdmans, 1998.

King, Martin Luther Jr. *Why We Can't Wait*. New York: Signet, 1963.

Kunjufu, Jawanza. *Black Economics: Solutions for Economic and Community Empowerment*. NY: African Image, 1991.

Linthicum, Robert C. *Transforming Power: Biblical Strategies for Making a Difference in Your Community*. Downers Grove, IL: InterVarsity Press, 2003.

Newbigin, Lesslie. *The Gospel in a Pluralistic Society*. Grand Rapids, MI: Eerdmans, 1989.

Ortiz, Manuel. *The Hispanic Challenge: Opportunities Confronting the Church.* Downers Grove, IL: InterVarsity Press, 1993.

Regele, Mike. *Death of the Church.* Grand Rapids, MI: Zondervan, 1995.

Rusaw, Rick and Eric Swanson. *The Externally-Focused Church.* Loveland, CO: Group Publishing, 2004.

Sample, Tex. *Lifestyles and Mainline Churches.* Louisville, KY: Westminster Press, 1990).

Schaller, Lyle E. *Center City Churches: The New Urban Frontier.* Nashville, TN: Abingdon, 1993.

Scott-Meyers, Eleanor. *Envisioning the New City: A Reader on Urban Ministry.* Louisville, KY: Westminster, 1992.

Sider, Ronald J. et.al. *Churches That Make A Difference.* Grand Rapids, MI: Baker Books, 2002.

Smith, Donald P. *Congregations Alive: Practical Suggestions for Bringing Your Church to Life Through Partnership in Ministry.* Louisville, KY: Westminster, 1981.

Smith, T. Aaron, *Thriving In the City: A Guide for Sustainable Incarnational Ministry Among the Urban Poor.* Pomona, CA: Servant Partners Publications, 2015.

Tillipaugh, Frank R. and Richard Hurst, *Calling.* Colorado Springs, CO: Dreamtime Publishing, 1997.

Villafane, Eldin. *Seek the Peace of the City: Reflections on Urban Ministry.* Grand Rapids, MI: Eerdmans, 1995.

Yamamori, Tetsunso, Bryant L. Myers and Kenneth L. Luscombe, *Serving With the Urban Poor.* Monrovia, CA: MARC Publications, 1998.

Community, Broad-based and Grassroots Organizing

Alinsky, Saul D. *Reveille for Radicals.* New York: Vintage Books, 1980 (original work, 1945).

______________. *Rules for Radicals.* New York: Random House, 1971.

Chambers, Ed. *Roots for Radicals: Organizing for Power, Action and Justice.* London: Continuum Press, 2003.

Dorrien, Gary J. *Reconstructing the Common Good.* Maryknoll, NY: Orbis Press, 1990.

Freeman, Samuel G. *Upon This Rock: The Miracles of a Black Church.* NY: HarperCollins, 1993.

Friere, Paulo. *Pedagogy of the Oppressed.* London: Continuum, 1984 (original work, 1972).

Gecan, Michael. *Going Public: An Organizer's Guide to Citizen Action.* NY: Anchor Books, Inc., 2002.

Horwitt, Sanford. *Let Them Calll Me Rebel: Saul Alinsky – His Life and Legacy.* NY: Random House, 1989.

Jacobsen, Dennis. *Doing Justice: Congregations and Community Organizing.* Philadelphia: Fortress Press, 2001.

Linthicum, Robert C. *Building A People of Power: Equipping Churches to Transform Their Communities.* Eugene, OR.: Wipf and Stock, 2015 (original work, 2006)

____________________. *Empowering the Poor: Community Organizing Among the City's 'Rag, Tag and Bobtail'.* Monrovia, CA: MARC Publications, 1999 (original work, 1991).

____________________, Mike Miller and Marilyn Stranske, *Building A People of Power: A Video Course on Congregation-based Community Organizing* (14 videos/DVDs, workbook and facilitator's handbook). Colorado Springs, CO: Procla-Media Productions, 2002.

Miller, Mark and Aaron Schutz. *People Power: The Community Organizing Tradition of Saul Alinsky.* Nashville, TN: Vanderbilt University Press, 2015.

Pierce, Gregory F.A. *Activism That Makes Sense: Congregations and Community Organization.* Chicago, IL: ACTA Publications, 1984.

Rogers, Mary Beth. *Cold Anger: A Story of Faith and Power Politics.* Denton, TX: University of North Texas Press, 1990.

Stout, Jeffrey. *Blessed Are the Organized: Grassroots Democracy in America.* Princeton, NJ: Princeton University Press, 2015.

Warren, Mark R. *Dry Bones Rattling: Community Building to Revitalize American Democracy.* Princeton, NJ: Princeton University Press, 2001.

Church of the Saviour, Washington, DC

Cosby, N. Gordon. *By Grace Transformed: Christianity for a New Millennium.* NY: Crossroads, 1999

__________________. *Handbook for Mission Groups.* Waco, TX: Word Books, 1976

Murchison, Joe. *Caution to the Wind.* Kearney, NE: Crosstraining Publ., 2008

Nouwen, Henri J.M. *Life of the Beloved: Spiritual Living in a Secular World.* NY: Crossroads, 1992

O'Connor, Elizabeth. *Call to Commitment: The Story of the Church of the Saviour.* NY: Harper and Row, 1963

__________________. *Journey Inward, Journey Outward.* NY: Harper and Row, 1968

__________________. *New Community, The: A Portrait of Life Together.* NY: Harper and Row, 1976

__________________. *Servant Leaders, Servant Structures.* Washington, DC: Servant Leadership School, 1991

INDEX

D

E

F

G

H

I

J

N

O

P

R

Y

Z

www.ingramcontent.com/pod-product-compliance
Lightning Source LLC
Chambersburg PA
CBHW070016100426
42740CB00013B/2514
9780692873083